The Prodigal Church:
Rescuing Spirituality from Religion

By Joseph Lumpkin

Joseph Lumpkin

The Prodigal Church: Rescuing Spirituality from Religion

The Prodigal Church:
Rescuing Spirituality from Religion

Copyright © 2010 by Joseph Lumpkin
All rights reserved.

Printed in the United States of America. No part of this book may be used or reproduced in any manner whatsoever without written permission except in the case of brief quotations embodied in critical articles and reviews.

Fifth Estate, Post Office Box 116,
Blountsville, AL 35031

First Edition
Cover Designed by An Quigley

Printed on acid-free paper

Library of Congress Control No: 2010920630
ISBN: 9781933580876

Fifth Estate, 2010

Joseph Lumpkin

The Prodigal Church: Rescuing Spirituality from Religion

Table of Contents

Authors Preface	9
To Know Him	12
Introduction and Theology	16
Framework of Christianity	18
The Bible	20
Canon of Scripture	30
Inerrant Scripture	36
From God – Charity of Heart	57
Of Flesh, Law, and Man	60
Transitions of Love	67
A People in Error	70
Keeping it Simple	82
A Common Creed	92
The Trinity	97
The Virgin Birth	106
Sex and the Divided Soul	111
Polygamy	118
Celibacy	127
Transubstantiation	137
Rapture	143
Apocalypse	147
Sabbath vs. Sunday	152
Tithes and Offerings	161
The Problem with Persuasion	179
A Gift of Love	181
Count it all Grace	186
What is Grace	189
Faith	192
Prayer and Faith	196
Desire, Sin, and Evil	211
Original Sin	215
Salvation, Standing, State of Mind	224
The Presence of God	227

Mary	229
Baptism	235
Predestination and Foreknowledge	240
Paradox of the Way	251
Binary Problem – Heaven, Hell, War	258
Christ and the Incarnation	261
Dark Night	264
No Place for Ego	267
To Reach the Mountain	268
Traps and Snares	272
Regret, Guilt, and Shame	277
Condemnation, Conviction, Judging	282
Being Bond together with God	284
God, Worship, and Obedience	289
A Place to Place the Mind	290
Still the Mind	294
Quiet the Mind	296
Mysticism and Recidivism	300
The Danger of Gifts	302
In Remembrance of Him	305
Presenting Christ in us to the World	307
In This Life	310
Seeking the Truth Beyond the Book	315
Conclusion	318
Appendix "A"	323
Appendix "B"	377
Bibliography	383

Joseph Lumpkin

Author's Preface

Before starting research in preparation for the writing of this book, I was happy and comfortable in my theological cave. Like most Christians, I accepted what was being preached and taught without question. After all, questions would take effort to answer and would disturb the status quo. Even in the years of attending a small Baptist college, doctrine was discussed, but never challenged. It was defended and explained in order to make us conformed, not to the will of God, but to the stance of the church.

After a few weeks of research in the labyrinths of historical and scientific resources, examination became more and more painful. It was difficult to set aside my preconceived ideas, since I was very heavily invested in the church's teaching, which I had accepted. Years of study and more than one degree would be nullified if my cherished beliefs were wrong. The fellowship of those good souls in the denomination to which I belonged would be strained under the weight of my heresy. But it was too late to stop the accumulating insight.

Slowly, information mounted and I was forced to ask myself what was real and what really mattered. How could I believe without asking the deeper questions? What does tradition and doctrine have to do with the love of God? Whose rules are we following? How did they evolve to this point? Now, the reader may have to ask the same questions and decide where the line is drawn between church and God.

History could not be discounted. Facts could not be dismissed. However, there must be more than one viewpoint in all of this. There is the control of religion and the freedom and bright light of that which is spiritual.

Most would agree that the modern church has become a disgraceful place, which still houses an eternal truth. Even when faced with this knowledge it is difficult to break away from our traditions. How do we rescue our own spirituality from the church? We shall cut tradition away from truth and let truth stand on its own. Tradition is a prison housing truth and religion is the hangman of spirituality. Both truth and spirit can be rescued with the courage to question and still believe.

We will attempt to use the "double-edged approach" of faith in God and historical - political scrutiny of the church. The errors of religion are placed along side the beauty of the spiritual view of the mystical church. It is hoped that such a dual approach may lend itself to a more balanced view while mimicking the feelings many of us now harbor for the modern church.

We come to the church with fear and disdain of its judgment and greed, all the while seeking God's love and mercy. When the truth is revealed God can still be seen in the rubble of what has become the church. He is beckoning the individual soul. The personal path is made clear in these pages.

Since the fourth or fifth century A.D. the two faces of religion have divided Christianity. Spirituality and legalism cannot coexist. Legalism is compelled to eat its partner whole, or else spirituality must, like a beaten bride, be divorced from religion to survive. Therefore, within this book, history and theology are covered, along with possible spiritual implications and solutions. If we can throw away religion while clinging to Christ we throw open the doors of the spirit and allow the free grace of God to reign once again.

Organized Christianity has probably done more to retard the ideals that were its founder's than any other agency in the world.
- Richard Le Gallienne

The church has failed to follow her appointed pathway of separation, holiness, heavenliness and testimony to an absent but coming Christ; she has turned aside from that purpose to the work of civilizing the world, building magnificent temples, and acquiring earthly power and wealth, and, in this way, has ceased to follow in the footsteps of Him who had not where to lay His head. - C. I. Scofield

Men never do evil so completely and cheerfully as when they do it with religious conviction. -- Blaise Pascal

Of all bad men religious bad men are the worst. --C.S. Lewis

I consider Western Christianity in its practical working a negation of Christ's Christianity." "I like your Christ, I do not like your Christians. Your Christians are so unlike your Christ." "If it weren't for Christians, I'd be a Christian." "If Christians would really live according to the teachings of

Christ, as found in the Bible, all of India would be Christian today.

- Mahatma Gandhi

The world is by no means averse to religion. In fact, it is devoted to it with a passion. It will buy any recipe for salvation as long as that formula leaves the responsibility for cooking up salvation firmly in human hands. The world is drowning in religion. But it is scared out of its wits by any mention of the grace that takes the world home gratis. --Robert Farrer Capon

Religion is the fashionable substitute for belief. - Oscar Wilde

Everyday people are straying away from the church and going back to God. --Lennie Bruce

The self-righteous, relying on the many good works he imagines he has performed, seems to hold salvation in his own hand, and considers Heaven as a just reward of his merits. In the bitterness of his zeal he exclaims against all sinners, and represents the gates of mercy as barred against them, and Heaven as a place to which they have no claim. What need have such self-righteous persons of a Savior? They are already burdened with the load of their own merits. Oh, how long they bear the flattering load, while sinners divested of everything, fly rapidly on the wings of faith and love into their Savior's arms, who freely bestows on them that which he has so freely promised! --Jeanne Guyon

Let your religion be less theory and more of a love affair. --G.K. Chesterton

TO KNOW HIM

It was a simple and elegant plan – God with us, God in us, we in Him. My God, what have we done?

In the beginning the church was a fellowship of men and women centering on the living Christ. Then the church moved to Greece where it became a philosophy. Then it moved to Rome where it became an institution. Next, it moved to Europe, where it became a culture. And, finally, it moved to America where it became an enterprise. -- Richard Halverson

Christianity is no longer a spiritual state. It has become superficial and narcissistic, a diluted religion that has lost its roots of love and forgiveness. Modern Christianity has become so bogged down in doctrine and church laws as to be legalistic and judgmental by nature and impudent in force.

It is possible the demise of contemplative worship in the West is a direct result of an ever-accelerating lifestyle of greed and selfishness. We now live in a world where there are more people living in greater personal isolation.

We have turned away from intimate, face-to-face, conversations and replaced the eloquent, heart-felt letters of the past with sparse abbreviations of instant messaging. We text, twitter, facebook, and email snippets of thoughts, never becoming connected or close. Because it is more difficult to lie and cheat those we know, our society has begun to fall apart because our separation allows for ease of mutual destruction. Sadly, our lifestyle has influenced our worship, giving rise to drive-in churches and an ever-growing detachment from the deeper journey.

We seek entertainment, not connection. Our fast-food religion focuses on one or two exciting hours a week. There are no more voices crying in the wilderness because the wilderness of the heart is left unexplored and there are none who dare venture into the dark regions of the soul where God awaits in the quiet, lonely darkness. Each church has substituted its own group of rules in place of the real journey and awakening. Like a committee following "Robert's Rules of Order," we try to live within the rules, but that does not allow us to meet the author. What shall we do?

The future of Christianity may lie solely in the mystical tradition, which demands a direct and personal relationship with God. Any hope of true salvation and personal growth in Christianity hinges on the depth of our relationship with God himself. The entire Christian faith is based on a direct and unique connection between the individual and God. In this aspect, Christianity is a mystical and dynamic faith. The Christian faith demands union and communion with the creator wherein He teaches us, guides us, and loves us. Through gratitude, meditation, adoration, and prayer we are joined with Him and transformed from within. Such love and transformation engendered by this relationship can reunite Christians with the power, grace, glory, and love meant for all who seek the living God.

With most people, and sadly, with most Christians, a crucial gap remains between God and man. What is needed is not the teaching of doctrine, law, or church tradition, nor is it any social or moral message. We need a heart-to-heart dialogue with God. We need and long for a relationship with our creator in which He loves and teaches us as a father would a child. A child knows he is loved by the kiss on his cheek, the words, the touch, and the embrace. It is in this type of communion we "know" God. He has bid us come, but the modern church has forgotten the path. It is still there, beneath the hedges of religion, rules, and pride. The hedges and briars of laws and church doctrine must be cleared away to find the path.

Jesus said:

Matthew 5:3 Blessed [are] the poor in spirit: for theirs is the kingdom of heaven.

Matthew 5:4 Blessed [are] they that mourn: for they shall be comforted.

Matthew 5:5 Blessed [are] the meek: for they shall inherit the earth.

Matthew 5:6 Blessed [are] they which do hunger and thirst after righteousness: for they shall be filled.

Matthew 5:7 Blessed [are] the merciful: for they shall obtain mercy.

Matthew 5:8 Blessed [are] the pure in heart: for they shall see God.

Matthew 5:9 Blessed [are] the peacemakers: for they shall be called the children of God.

Matthew 5:10 Blessed [are] they which are persecuted for righteousness' sake: for theirs is the kingdom of heaven.

Matthew 5:11 Blessed are ye, when [men] shall revile you, and persecute [you], and shall say all manner of evil against you falsely, for my sake.

Matthew 5:12 Rejoice, and be exceeding glad: for great [is] your reward in heaven: for so persecuted they the prophets which were before you.

How have we gone from meekness and love to this modern mess where everyday church members leave more wounded than when they arrived?

One may think in reading this work it is a treatise against doctrine or opposed to theology. One may think it is purely a work calling us back to some simplistic, emotional, or childish view of faith. This could not be further from the truth. This book is a call for balance, and a summoning of us inward and away from the superficial, outward-looking worship practiced today. The inner path is not simplistic, but it is simple. It is not childish, but it is childlike. It is not emotional but it gives way to a path, which leads to a depth beyond empty knowledge and passing emotion. This path will lead us to the heart of knowing. There we will see faith has been waiting all the while.

The formula of the worship of today is equal parts of emotional gratification, superficial study of scripture, and adherence to rules of denomination. We have neglected the one thing that stands as the banner of Christianity - a relationship with God through Christ our Lord. The Christian faith is the only religion in which God seeks out man. God seeks to engage man in a relationship that is personal, emotional, and unique.

It may be argued the Jewish faith encourages a relationship of this type. However, in Christ we have a God who has shed his heavenly state in order to seek out man. He extends his hand to us so we may see that He understands us. God demonstrates this by living as we live, suffering as we suffer, and experiencing life as only man can in order that He, God, might have compassion (a word meaning to suffer together) on us and empathy (meaning to feel the same thing) with us so that we may know He knows us and we may have a personal relationship with Him. For, if God is omniscient He would have already known what it was like to be man, but we could not have conceived of His knowledge.

In Christ we have the hero-God-king who relinquished everything including His life in order to seek, love, and save His people. There is nothing left emotionally undone in this formula God has given us. It is in the church of today the formula becomes incorrect. Denominationalism has supplanted Scripture and following a set of rules has become more important than love and forgiveness. It is essential to seek and know God if we are to be changed by His love into His image. Only in this marvelous transformation can we hope to come close to doing what He has asked:

Love God with your whole being. Love your fellow man as yourself. It is foolish to think that doctrine and Scripture could keep us on a path. If that were the case Christ would have not needed to come or die. Theology serves to clarify ones' beliefs in order that they may be articulated, but declaring a belief is not that same as living it.

We may become theologians, but to no avail. The study of theology does not serve to edify man. It seems almost arrogant to endeavor to study He who is omnipotent and omniscient. Learning scripture and points of doctrine serves to enhance our knowledge, but not our heart. We may seek to gain insight into God's patterns and personality through study. This is admirable to a point; however, time may be best served by being in His presence. To know Him is always better than to study Him.

To better know Him is the purpose of this meager work. In order to accomplish this, doctrine will be challenged and theology will be pushed aside so we may laugh at our errors, question our ways, and seek a higher path.

Let us try not to take ourselves too seriously. According to Robin Williams, angels have wings because they take themselves lightly. If we can look at the history and reasoning behind our most sacred doctrines with an open mind and a modicum of levity, we may see the humor in the folly of the church, if not the whole of humanity. It serves us well to remember that God is real, but religion is man-made.

INTRODUCTION AND THEOLOGY

Doctrine is like glass. The truth can be seen through it, but through it the truth cannot be touched.

Theology – noun

(1)   - The study of the nature of God.

(2)   - The study of religious beliefs and theory when systematically developed.

Greek, from theos ' god' + -logia (see -logy – denoting a subject of study.)

Theology, in the first definition, may be the most arrogant pursuit of mankind. It is the pinnacle of presumption to think that man could study, understand, or explain God. The study of theologians and their doctrine is far easier to apprehend. The effect of theologians and kings on our present day religious practices cannot be denied. Some can be laughed at and others barely tolerated. Thus, in this book we will focus primarily on the second definition of theology and leave the first to each individual and their personal encounter with God.

To get to the reason and history behind the formation of certain doctrine we must attempt to view Christianity outside the restricted context of church tradition and Bible alone. Historical documents will be used to confirm and supplement the writings and thoughts of the early church fathers.

The extreme to which the church has gone in order to protect and justify its various decisions regarding points of faith is fascinating, but tends to obscure the truth. Revisionist history, coercion, and propaganda were the order of the day when the major items of doctrine were being decided. In fact, many of those truths that we hold so dear in our Christian faith were decided, if not invented, through or because of political means, and not by theological insight. Many doctrines went well beyond what the early church held as truth in an attempt to unite some and cull others so the body could be more easily governed. To look behind the curtain of church history, information should be viewed with a political as well as scientific bias, and compared with other historical documents of the time.

The reader is invited to consider the history and virtue of the doctrines of his church based on this new insight and to make a more educated personal stand.

Most Christians have not taken time to fully examine their own personal beliefs. They have not fully researched the doctrines of their own church. Many people accept what they have been told, indoctrinated in, or raised to believe. The deeper structure of their faith has never been critiqued or challenged.

Although after confronting these issues the reader may end the journey believing exactly as he or she began. If a single question causes discomfort or reexamination, this work will have served its purpose, which is to escape tradition and examine the Christian faith afresh, with newer and wider eyes. If the reader end the journey believing as they did from the start, they will be able to articulate their belief and reasoning on a much deeper level.

1 Corinthians 2 (New King James Version)

1 And I, brethren, when I came to you, did not come with excellence of speech or of wisdom declaring to you the testimony of God. 2 For I determined not to know anything among you except Jesus Christ and Him crucified.

Joseph Lumpkin

FRAMEWORK OF CHRISTIANITY

I am no friend of present-day Christianity, though its Founder was sublime.
Vincent Van Gogh, letter to Theo van Gogh, Oct. 1884

As we look at various major systematic theologies, we are likely to see contradictions. There are contradictions between systems, and even more disturbing, there are contradictions within systems. It is not pleasant, and can even be painful, to come face to face with major errors in logic and practice within our own system of beliefs. We are trained to trust what we are told. We are trained to accept ambiguity. We are programmed to file conflicting statements under the heading of "mystery." But mystery, mistake, and misdirection are difficult to separate at times.

Believing that one system is superior to another is like children attempting to jump to the moon. Coming an inch or two closer makes little difference. However, holding on to one way or another, believing that it is the only way, makes for comfortable feelings of superiority and separation from others of differing views. With enough people practicing the same arrogance, a denomination is born and exclusivity begins. Others assure those within the group of their "rightness" and the delusion deepens. Those on the outside see clearly the idolatry of it all. It is the ability to raise doctrine or Bible verse to the status of god or idol that births denominations. Never should a book or belief take the place of the One being sought through them.

Spiritually immature religious systems pile law upon law and rule upon rule to the point of exaggerated exclusivity, conformity, and control. At times the immaturity is a function of age and development of the religion. Age usually brings grace, compassion, and mercy to individuals as well as religions. Some religions are born in peace, have their adolescence in violence, and mature into compassion and understanding.

It may be an over-simplification, but let us take two major religions as an example and calculate one hundred years in the lifetime of religions as a single year in the life of a person.

The Christian year, 2009 is the Islamic year, 1430. That would make the first person 20 years old and the other person 14 years of age.

Christianity is a young adult, in this scheme, whereas Islam is pubescent. Christianity is only beginning to escape its rebellious, hostile, and selfish behavior. Islam has not. The Christian crusades only ended in the thirteenth century. That is close to the same age as Islam is now. Christians went on to conquer and kill countless people in the name of God for hundreds of years. Islam continues its warlike and egocentric behavior, even now. The main difference is that when Christians were at the height of bloodlust there were swords and spears. The killing season of Islam gives them access to nuclear and biological weapons. Add to that the pathological exclusivity of young religions such as Islam and you have jihad here, jihad there, and everywhere jihad.

What is more difficult to recognize is that personal systems are the same. In Christianity, those denominations that are prone to legalism, exclusive, or regulation are those where members pay more attention to doctrine than communion with God and their fellow man. They are divisive and exclusive and at times hateful and aggressive.

Jesus never questioned anyone about his or her theology or doctrine. He wanted to know if the person was in a relationship with him.

He never told anyone they would be rich or successful. He knew that suffering was the only tool to break our illusion of control and superiority and bring us closer to God.

In short, as we look into the history, doctrines, and views of various denominations, let us keep in mind that many times we seem very sure about things we could not possibly know or prove to be true.

Fundamentalism in any religion brings division, intolerance, and hate. The opposite state of religion is spirituality. Spiritual maturity may be measured, not in exclusivity, or in the rules we keep, or how certain we are in our doctrines, but in our inclusive, loving treatment of others and the openness of our hearts toward God.

Christianity came into existence to lighten the heart, but now it needs to burden the heart to start with so it can lighten it afterwards. Consequently, it will perish.

FRIEDRICH NIETZSCHE, *Human, All Too Human*

He who begins by loving Christianity better than Truth will proceed by loving his own sect of church better than Christianity, and end by loving himself better than all.

SAMUEL TAYLOR COLERIDGE, *Aids to Reflection: Moral and Religious Aphorisms*

THE BIBLE

I want to take the word Christianity back to Christ himself, back to that mighty heart whose pulse seems to throb through the world today, that endless fountain of charity out of which I believe has come all true progress and all civilization that deserves the name. I go back to that great Spirit which contemplated a sacrifice for the whole of humanity. That sacrifice is not one of exclusion, but of an infinite and endless and joyous inclusion. And I thank God for it.

JULIA WARD HOWE, *What is Religion?*

In the ancient religious world, Judaism stood apart in several ways. In the pantheon of gods and the vast number of religions, Judaism had a book on which its followers relied as a record of both history and a codified system of rules. It did not matter that most Jews could not read, what mattered was that there was a touchstone and compass to rely on, and there were those in synagogues who could read the holy words to the worshipers. Later Jews would institute an educational regime that demanded young men be able to read and recite the Torah as a rite of passage to adulthood.

Following in the footsteps of the Jews, the early Christians would also become "people of the book." Modern day Christianity has come to rely so much on the Bible that entire denominations rise and fall based solely on unique interpretations of one or two verses. But is this reliance on the Bible out of perspective or out of balance? There will be many such questions and investigations pursued in this book, but because Christianity has taken its cue from Judaism and its focus on a book, we will begin our quest by challenging what we have been taught regarding the Holy Bible.

The preliminary, if not the primary questions to be addressed before we can continue, are those which will affect all other biblical investigations from this point forward. The framing of these questions are more difficult than they may appear.

The first question is slightly easier than the next, but is bound to elicit an emotional, if not visceral response. The first question to answer is, "Do we really need the Bible?" Is the Bible necessary for our salvation? Is it necessary for one's "walk with Christ?" To put it another way, can we know and commune with God if we have no Bible?

Consider this – For approximately 400 years there was no consensus of what books would make up the volume we call the Bible. Although it is true that the Jewish converts had the Torah to depend on, the pagan converts had nothing, only the words of the apostles describing Jesus, his purpose, his death, and his resurrection. Did the first 400 years of believers go to hell for not following every detail of the not-yet-available book?

For over a thousand years after the Bible canon was established only the rich, powerful, and clergy had access to a Bible. The clergy revealed only a small amount of information to the illiterate working class under their control. It was within this time period that much of the church doctrine was instituted in order to bring the masses under further control by convincing them that the church and its priests stood between them and heaven, or hell. Many of the church's doctrines made the masses spiritual slaves to the clergy as they began to lord over them the rite of baptism to remove original sin or the rite of communion for salvation.

Rates of infant mortality ran very high. Some sources place death rates for mother or child in childbirth at one in four. The instituted belief in original sin placed the newborn child in a position dangling over the pit unless the child was baptized as soon as possible, based on the belief that baptism removes Original Sin. To save the adult from hell, only the priest had the power to transubstantiate the host, or communion wafer, into the body of Christ in order to forgive those pesky personal sins and save the souls of the common man.

The clergy held the power and the Bible, yet, through it all, the common folk held fast to the simple story of Jesus, the Christ, the anointed one of God, and how he was born of a virgin, taught love and forgiveness, died for the sins of the world, and was resurrected by the spirit of God.

Do we need the Bible to be saved? I hope not. There were over 1400 years between the beginning of Christianity and the mass availability of Bibles via the invention of the printing press.

The second question is, "What is the Bible?" The flippant or sophomoric response may come closest to the basic truth. The Bible is a volume containing a collection of books compiled over time by consent of clergy or ruling authority in order to uphold and re-enforce a set of historical or doctrinal viewpoints. This would mean many available books not upholding a predetermined view would be deemed unfit and were not included. It would also mean as the church split or diverged to a significant degree their beliefs and therefore their Bible would change. As proof of this statement, we can compare the major "arms" of the Christian church and their Bibles.

The King James Bible contained 73 books, including the Apocrypha until 1782, when an American printer first removed the Apocrypha and produced an "unauthorized" version of the King James Bible. Most printers did not clear inventories and change to the sixty-six book version we know today until the late 1800's when editions of the "Official King James Version" began to be printed without the Apocrypha in 1885. Thus, most Bibles printed before 1885 still had the Apocrypha, or at least most of the Apocrypha. As it turns out, various religions have differing versions of the Bible, made up of divergent lists of books. The Protestant church has its sixty-six books, the Catholics have kept the Apocrypha. The Eastern Orthodox Church claims three more books than the Catholics, and the Ethiopic Church has a total of eighty-one books in its Bible.

The etymologically of the word "apocrypha" means "things that are hidden," but why they were hidden is not clear. Some have suggested that the books were "hidden" from common use because they contained esoteric knowledge too profound to be communicated to any except the initiated (compare 2 Esd 14.45-46). Others have suggested that such books were hidden due to their spurious or heretical teaching.

According to traditional usage "Apocrypha" has been the designation applied to the fifteen books, or portions of books, listed below. (In many earlier editions of the Apocrypha, the Letter of Jeremiah is incorporated as the final chapter of the Book of Baruch; hence in these editions there are fourteen books.)

Tobit, Judith, The Additions to the Book of Esther (contained in the Greek version of Esther), The Wisdom of Solomon, Ecclesiasticus, The Wisdom of Jesus son of Sirach, Baruch, The Letter of Jeremiah, The Prayer of Azariah, The Song of the Three Jews, "Susanna, Bel, and the Dragon," 1 Maccabees, 2 Maccabees, 1 Esdras, The Prayer of Manasseh, and 2 Esdras.

In addition, the present expanded edition includes the following three texts that are of special interest to Eastern Orthodox readers are 3 Maccabees, 4 Maccabees, and Psalm 151.

None of these books are included in the Hebrew canon of Holy Scripture. All of them, however, with the exception of 2 Esdras, are present in copies of the Greek version of the Old Testament known as the Septuagint. The Old Latin translations of the Old Testament, made from the Septuagint, also include them, along with 2 Esdras. The Eastern Orthodox Churches chose to include 1 Esdras, Psalm 151, the Prayer of Manasseh, 3 Maccabees, and 4 Maccabees, which is placed in an appendix as a historical work.

At the end of the fourth century, Pope Damasus commissioned Jerome to prepare a standard Latin version of the Scriptures called the Latin Vulgate. Jerome wrote a note or preface, designating a separate category for the apocryphal books. However, copyists failed to include Jerome's prefaces. Thus, during the medieval period the Western Church generally regarded these books as part of the Holy Scriptures.

In 1546, the Council of Trent decreed that the canon of the Old Testament included the Apocrypha with the exception of the Prayer of Manasseh and 1 and 2 Esdras. Later, the church completed the decision by writing in its Roman Catholic Catechism, "Deuterocanonical does not mean Apocryphal, but simply later added to the canon."

The position of the Russian Orthodox Church as regards the Apocrypha appears to have changed during the centuries. The Holy Synod, ruling from St. Petersburg was in sympathy with the position of the Reformers and decided to exclude the Apocrypha and since similar influences were emanating from the universities of Kiev, Moscow, Petersburg, and Kazan, the Russian Church became united in its rejection of the Apocrypha.

A full explanation of how the church of today got from the hundreds of books examined for canon to the eighty-one books of Ethiopia and finally to the mere sixty-six books of the Protestant Bible, is a matter of wide ranging discussion and varied opinions, to be taken up at another time. For now, let us simply acknowledge that the Bible many hold to with such passion and steadfastness is not the same book throughout Christendom. Thus, when one declares with pious passion, "I believe in the Bible!" We must immediately ask, "Which one?"

Below, we can see the differences between the canon of the Protestant, Catholic, and Orthodox bibles, including that of the Ethiopic Orthodox church. We have also listed those books used by the Church of Jesus Christ of Latter day Saints (LDS).

Old Testament

(Protestant)

Genesis, Exodus, Leviticus, Numbers, Deuteronomy, Joshua, Judges, Ruth, 1Samuel, 2 Samuel, 1 Kings, 2 Kings, 1 Chronicles, 2 Chronicles, Ezra, Nehemiah, Esther, Job, Psalms, Proverbs, Ecclesiastes, Song of Solomon, Isaiah, Jeremiah, Lamentation, Ezekiel, Daniel, Hosea, Joel, Amos, Obadiah, Jonah, Micah, Nahum, Habakkuk, Zephaniah, Haggai, Zecariah, Malachi.

Old Testament

(Roman Catholic)

Genesis, Exodus, Leviticus, Numbers, Deuteronomy, Joshua, Judges, Ruth, 1 Samuel, 2 Samuel, 1 Kings, 2 Kings, 1 Chronicles, 2 Chronicles, Ezra, Nehemiah, Tobit, Judith, Esther (includes additions to Esther), 1 Maccabees, 2 Maccabees, Job, Psalms, Proverbs, Ecclesiastes, Song of, Songs (Song of Solomon), Wisdom of Solomon, Sirach (Ecclesiasticus), Isaiah, Jeremiah, Lamentations, Baruch (includes Letter of Jeremiah), Ezekiel, Daniel (includes Susanna & Bel and the Dragon), Hosea, Joel, Amos, Obadiah, Jonah, Micah,

Joseph Lumpkin

Nahum, Habakkuk, Zephaniah, Haggai, Zecariah, Malachi

Old Testament

(Ethiopic Narrower Canon)

Genesis, Exodus, Leviticus, Numbers, Deuteronomy, Enoch, Jubilees, Joshua, Judges, Ruth, 1 Samuel, 2 Samuel, 1 Kings, 2 Kings, 1 Chronicles, 2 Chronicles, Ezra, Nehemiah, 3rd Ezra, 4th Ezra, Tobit, Judith, Esther (includes additions to Esther), 1 Macabees, 2 Macabees, 3 Macabees, Job, Psalms (+ Psalm 151), Proverbs (Proverbs 1-24), Täagsas (Proverbs 25-31), Wisdom of Solomon, Ecclesiastes, Song of Solomon, Sirach (Ecclesiasticus), Isaiah, Jeremiah, Baruch (includes Letter of Jeremiah), Lamentations, Ezekiel, Daniel, Hosea, Amos, Micah, Joel, Obadiah, Jonah,, Nahum, Habakkuk, Zephaniah, Haggai, Zecariah, Malachi.

Protestants, Roman Catholics, and Greek Orthodox Christians agree on the same 27 books for the composition of the New Testament; however some smaller groups of Christians do not. The Nestorian, or Syrian Church, recognizes only 22 books, excluding 2 Peter, 2 and 3 John, Jude and Revelation.

But wait, there's more. The narrow canon of the Ethiopic church contains 81 books but the broader canon contains several more books. The Ethiopian Orthodox Church includes the same 27 books in its "narrower" canon but adds 8 books to its "broader" canon: "four sections of church order from a compilation called Sinodos, two sections from the Ethiopic Books of Covenant, Ethiopic Clement, and Ethiopic Didascalia."

In addition to the Protestant Old and New Testaments, the Church of Jesus Christ of Latter-day Saint, (the Mormon or LDS church), uses "The Book of Mormon," "The Doctrine and Covenants," and "The Pearl of Great Price."

Which Bible do you believe in? Why do you think your Bible is the correct one? If you are a member of a typical Protestant church, your Bible is among the smallest of all and its configuration is among the newest. Do you think God had less to say as time went on? Have you ever considered that you may be missing something of significance? With the exception of the Church of Jesus Christ of Latter Day Saints, who have added books to their canon list, in general the Bible seems to be shrinking as one views it from the timeline beginning with the list of books considered for canon at Counsel of Nicaea, those held by the Orthodox Church, those held by the Catholic Church, and finally those books left in the Protestant Bible.

What about the books that are mentioned in the Bible, even quoted in the Bible, but not contained in the Bible? Are they worth looking into? There are several books mentioned in the Bible, which are excluded from it. They are not spiritual canon, either because they were not available at the time the canon was originally adopted, or at the time they were not considered "inspired." In cases where inspiration was questioned, one could argue that any book quoted or mentioned by a prophet or an apostle should be considered as spiritual canon, unfortunately this position would prove too simplistic since certain records such as census are also mentioned.

Books and writings can fall under various categories such as civil records and laws, historical documents, or spiritual writings. A city or state census is not inspired, but it could add insight into certain areas of life. Spiritual writings which are directly quoted in the Bible serve as insights into the beliefs of the writer or what was considered acceptable by society at the time. As with any new discovery, invention, or belief, the new is interpreted based upon the structure of what came before. This was the way it was in the first century Christian church as beliefs were based upon the old Jewish understanding. Although, one should realize pagan beliefs were also added to the church as non-Jewish populations were converted, bringing with them the foundations of their beliefs on which they interpreted Christianity. In the case of Jude, James, Paul, and others, the Jewish past was giving way to the Christian present but their understanding and doctrine were still being influenced by what they had learned and experienced previously. It becomes obvious that to understand the Bible one should endeavor to investigate the books and doctrines that most influenced the writers of the Bible.

The LDS (Mormon) Church also asserts that books mentioned but not found in the Bible are of spiritual value. That is not to say that they are on the same level of inspiration, but only that they carry value in understanding the Bible by forming a more full and detailed picture of history, customs, and beliefs.

The Dead Sea Scrolls found in the caves of Qumran are of great interest in the venture of clarifying the history and doctrine in existence between biblical times and the fixing of canon. The scrolls were penned in the second century B.C. and were in use at least until the destruction of the second temple in 70 A.D. Similar scrolls to those found in the eleven caves of Qumran were also found at the Masada stronghold which fell in 73 A.D. Fragments of every book of the Old Testament except Esther were found in the caves of Qumran, but so were many other books. Some of these books are considered to have been of equal importance and influence to the people of Qumran and to the writers and scholars of the time. Some of those studying these or similar scrolls found in Qumran were the writers of the New Testament.

Knowing this, one might ask which of the dozens of non-canonical books most influenced the writers of the New Testament. It is possible to ascertain the existence of certain influences within the Bible by using the Bible itself. The Bible can direct us to other works in three ways. The work can be mentioned by name, as is the Book of Jasher. The work can be quoted within the Bible text, as is the case with the Book of Enoch. The existence of the work can be alluded to, as in the case of the missing letter from the apostle Paul to the Corinthians.

In the case of those books mentioned in the Bible, one can set a list as the titles are named. The list is lengthier than one might first suspect. Most of these works have not been found. Some have been unearthed but their authenticity is questioned. Others have been found and the link between scripture and scroll is generally accepted. Following is a list of books mentioned in the Holy Bible.

The Book of Jasher: There are two references to the book in the Old Testament:

2 Samuel 1:18 - Behold, it is written in the Book of Jasher. "So the sun stood still, and the moon stopped, until the nations avenged themselves of their enemies."

Joshua 10:13 - Is it not written in the Book of Jasher? And the sun stopped in the middle of the sky and did not hasten to go down for about a whole day.

There are several books, which have come to us entitled, "Book of Jasher." One is an ethical treatise from the Middle Ages. It begins with a section on the Mystery of the Creation of the World: It is clearly unrelated to the Biblical Book of Jasher.

Another was published in 1829 supposedly translated by Flaccus Albinus Alcuinus. It opens with the Chapter 1 Verse 1 reading: "While it was the beginning, darkness overspread the face of nature." It is now considered a fake.

The third and most important Book of Jasher, first translated into English in 1840. It opens with Chapter 1 Verse 1 reading: "And God said, Let us make man in our image, after our likeness, and God created man in his own image." A comparison of Joshua 10:13 with Jasher 88:63-64 and 2Sam. 1:18 with Jasher 56:9 makes it clear that this Book of Jasher at least follows closely enough with the Bible to be the Book of Jasher mentioned in the Bible.

Other books mentioned by name in the Bible are:

1. The Book of Wars of the Lord: "Therefore it is said in the Book of the Wars of the Lord." Num. 21:14

2.   The Annals of Jehu: "Now the rest of the acts of Jehoshaphat, first to last, behold, they are written in the annals of Jehu the son of Hanani, which is recorded in the Book of the Kings of Israel." 2 Chronicles 20:34

3.   The treatise of the Book of the Kings: "As to his sons and the many oracles against him and the rebuilding of the house of God, behold, they are written in the treatise of the Book of the Kings. Then Amaziah his son became king in his place." 2 Chronicles 24:27

4.   The Book of Records, Book of the Chronicles of Ahasuerus: "Now when the plot was investigated and found to be so, they were both hanged on a gallows; and it was written in the Book of the Chronicles in the king's presence." ... "During that night the king could not sleep so he gave an order to bring the book of records, the chronicles, and they were read before the king." Esther 2:23; 6:1

5.   The Acts of Solomon: "Now the rest of the acts of Solomon and whatever he did, and his wisdom, are they not written in the book of the Acts of Solomon?" 1 Kings 11:41

6.   The Sayings of Hozai: "His prayer also and how God was entreated by him, and all his sin, his unfaithfulness, and the sites on which he built high places and erected the Asherim and the carved images, before he humbled himself, behold, they are written in the records of Hozai." 2 Chronicles 33:19

7.   The Chronicles of David: "Joab the son of Zeruiah had begun to count them, but did not finish; and because of this, wrath came upon Israel, and the number was not included in the account of the Chronicles of King David." 1 Chronicles 27:24

8.   The Chronicles of Samuel, Nathan, Gad: "Now the acts of King David, from first to last, are written in the Chronicles of Samuel the seer, in the Chronicles of Nathan the prophet and in the Chronicles of Gad the seer." 1 Chronicles 29:29

9.   Samuel's book: "Then Samuel told the people the ordinances of the kingdom, and wrote them in the book and placed it before the Lord." 1 Samuel 10:25

10.   The Records of Nathan the prophet: "Now the rest of the acts of Solomon, from first to last, are they not written in the Records of Nathan the prophet, and in the prophecy of Ahijah the Shilonite, and in the visions of Iddo the seer concerning Jeroboam the son of Nebat?" 2 Chronicles 9:29

11.   The Prophecy of Ahijah the Shilonite: "Now the rest of the acts of Solomon, from first to last, are they not written in the Records of Nathan the prophet, and in the prophecy of Ahijah the Shilonite, and in the visions of Iddo the seer concerning Jeroboam the son of Nebat?" 2 Chronicles 9:29

12. The Treatise of the Prophet Iddo: "Now the rest of the acts of Abijah, and his ways and his words are written in the treatise of the prophet Iddo." 2 Chronicles 13:22

Joseph Lumpkin

The existence of a book can be inferred as well, this is clearly seen with several missing epistles. Paul's letter to the church at Laodicea: "When this letter is read among you, have it also read in the church of the Laodiceans; and you, for your part read my letter that is coming from Laodicea." Colossians 4:16 (Since three earlier manuscripts do not contain the words "at Ephesus" in Eph 1:1, some have speculated that the letter coming from Laodicea was in fact the letter of Ephesians. Apostolic fathers also debated this possibility.)

In Paul's first letter to Corinth, he predated that letter by saying: "I wrote you in my letter not to associate with immoral people" (1 Corinthians 5:9) (This could be a reference to the present letter of 1 Corinthians, but likely refers to a missing text.)

These writings were important enough to quote or refer to in subsequent writings preserved now as scripture. Matthew 2:23 cites a now fulfilled prophecy from "the prophets" that Christ would be a Nazarene (someone from Nazareth), but this prophecy is not found anywhere in any existing Old Testament canon. Matthew was citing scripture, which is missing now. Another example of missing scripture is the text containing the words of Christ that Paul quotes in Acts 20:35 "remember the words of the Lord Jesus, how he said, 'It is more blessed to give than to receive.'" This saying of Christ appears in none of the Gospels. Here Paul was writing to foreign converts who were not around to hear Christ preach, so how were they to "remember" those words? Paul obviously must have been citing it from a sacred writing that they had, which we are missing.

Without question, the Bible alone shows that there are sacred writings that early Christians and Jews respected as scripture but which we no longer have. I could also add that the many books such as the Shepherd of Hermas, were respected by many early Christians as scripture but are no longer included in modern canons.

According to the theory of continuing revelation or evolving truth, one freely accesses the truth as it is made available to them. Those books quoted or mentioned in the Bible, even if they are found after the Bible canon was established, are considered spiritually valuable and are sought after. Each of us must decide our own stance on this issue. If the missing books of Corinthians or Ephesians were found and verified as authentic, would you add them to your personal Bible? What about books mentioned or quoted in the Bible, such as Enoch, Jubilees, or others? Jude 15 is a direct quote from Enoch chapter 2, which was written almost three hundred years before Jude. (See "The Lost Book of Enoch," published by Fifth Estate.) What if you were to find out that these books were only lost to the Western Christians and the

Eastern Christian Church had included them all along in their Bible as canon? Would you consider the fact that the younger Protestant Church may have missed something important, or would you dig in your heels and proclaim that the sixty-six books were the only truth?

Some of these books are out there now and can be obtained easily in their modern English translation.

(To see a list of available translations go to www.fifthestatepub.com.)

Surely there will be some who would quote Revelation 22: 18 –

Rev. 22:18 I warn everyone who hears the words of the prophecy of this book: If anyone adds anything to them, God will add to him the plagues described in this book. 19 And if anyone takes words away from this book of prophecy, God will take away from him his share in the tree of life and in the holy city, which are described in this book.

To those, I can only point out that this was a common curse of the time and was the only method of copyright available to the masses. A curse of this sort is found in many books written in the same period. Also, let us keep in mind that the Book of Revelation is not the Bible. It was written as a single book. The author never suspected we would place it in a volume and then pronounce the volume to be canon. The curse applies to Revelation only, if one believes in such curses. Protestants, like myself, should all pray the curse is impotent, since we have taken away several entire books to end up with our scant sixty-six-book volume.

THE CANON OF SCRIPTURE

The Question of Canon must come first.

In classical Greek the world "canon" signifies properly, "a straight rod," or "a carpenter's rule." In the early ages of the Christian religion it was used with considerable indefiniteness of meaning, though generally denoting a standard of opinion and practice. Later it came to be used as a testing rule in art, logic, grammar, and ethics. Still later the sacred writings received the name of the "Canon of the Scriptures." When, we use the term, we may mean one of two things, or both:

    1. The Canon of Truth--referring to the restriction of the number of books that compose the sacred volume. As such it was first used in the year A.D. 367.

2. The Rule of Faith and Life--referring to the application of the sacred Scriptures as a rule of our lives. This term is used in Galatians 6:16; Philippians 3:16.

The sense in which we use the word in this chapter is that those books are canonical which Christians have regarded as authentic, genuine, and of divine authority and inspiration. These books are to be found in the Bible.

Why was a Canon of the Bible necessary?

Old Testament canon had already been set. It would form the root that grew the flower of the Christian faith. The Old Testament was honored by Jesus, who read from it in the synagogue, thus it was accepted without question by the first Christians, who were Jews. This would form half of Christian canon. New Testament canon was being developed in the form of writings of the Apostles and their disciples. So long as the living voices of prophets and apostles were heard, there was no pressing need for a canon of Scripture. They were the canon. But as soon as these men were dead it became necessary that their writings be gathered together to know what their messages were to the churches, and to preserve those writings from corruption. These are the Gospels and letters to the churches. But soon there were numerous books being written under the names of the deceased Apostles. Many had questionable authorship. Some actually written by apostles were omitted or lost.

Hence the question arose as to which of these were authentic and really inspired.

Of course, this overlooks the idea that men outside the immediate twelve and their students could be inspired. This was a question that was bound to come up.

Leave it to the irony of fate to accelerate the decision of which books are canon.

Between 302 and 311 A.D. the Emperor Diocletia began his last, largest, and bloodiest official persecution of Christianity. It did not destroy the empire's Christian community; indeed, after 324 Christianity became the empire's preferred religion under its first "Christian" emperor, Constantine. However, Diocletia's bloodlust forced the first real pressure from the outside of the church to define canon.

In A.D. 302 the Emperor Diocletia issued in an edict that all the "sacred" books should be destroyed by fire. The question arose as to which books rightly deserved the name of inspired or sacred. Pagans were left to decide this, but they did so, to some degree, according to which books were held in the highest esteem by the Christian community itself.

The persecutors demanded that the Scriptures should be given up. The Christians refused. The reaction of the believers informed the Emperor's men as to which books were held as inspired among the Christian community. At this time there were many Gospels, Epistles, and apocalyptic books such as Revelation in circulations. Some were even written by real apostles other than Matthew, Mark, Luke, and John, such as Thomas, Barnabas, and others. Even though some of these books were being read and circulated within the community, none made it into canon for reasons we will soon cover. There were also dozens of false and spurious gospels and epistles. People read some of these books as entertainment but counted them as less than inspired. They simply made for a good story.

Canon started with the books accepted as inspired by the majority of Christians. This we will explore in more detail.

For now, let us examine the Gospels.

Why Do We Have Only Four Gospels?

Some temperaments are attracted by the idea of self-discovery and internal spiritual searches, others want to be led and need stability. The early Church could provide for both. Though the Church had the advantage of resting on a basis of the inspiration from the ancient roots of Judaism, its development was not fettered by its past. Jesus proved the Old Testament was true but now completed and accomplished in him. To believers, the Old Testament was passé, to a large extent, having been fulfilled. This single fact allowed the church to be re-founded and re-formed. Now, a New Testament was beginning with new revelation, new writers, and new beliefs.

At this point the church was open and free to move in any direction but was intellectually in a weak position until and unless it could define, articulate, and support specific doctrines. The roots of the church would supply the starting point, since there are no greater authoritative and inspired books than the ancient Jewish Bible. This would continue to be canon and would become the Old Testament. But, although a canonized New Testament was necessary to establish a more defined direction, the need for it was only slowly realized. A community can only invest letters, books, or words with canonical authority if they are seen as having intrinsic merit, popular approval, and are perceived to have a high degree of authority, repute, and inspiration. All of these attributes turn out to be quite subjective. Official canonization cannot create scripture; it can only recognize as inspired, books, which are already thought to be authentic and have the merit of following a selected doctrine. The issue of doctrine may be the most important over time because it allows those in control and making the decisions of what is canon to choose books validating their own doctrine and control. For, as a power structure forms that has the weight and following to choose and enforce canon, so does the goal of the governing body to ensure its continuation.

The formation of an authoritative canon of the New Testament would have been natural. It is the order of things that some books would be discarded and others embraced, simply because some were written better than others, seemed wiser, and were more sensible or applicable. However, the timeline was greatly accelerated owing to the growing prevalence of schools of divergent theology, grouped together under the name of Gnosticism.

It must be stressed again that what is divergent is judged by those in control. One reason that Gnosticism did not gain an upper hand was the number of systems led by various Gnostic leaders differed too greatly and could not agree enough to gain unity. But common to them all is the idea that matter is evil, and therefore the material universe could not have been the creation of the Supreme God. Because of this, it was believed an inferior or lesser god was the creator, but the Supreme God gave us Christ, who came to deliver man both from this world and its lesser gods. Gospels, Acts, and other writings circulated widely, in which Christ was created as a spirit and had no real body of flesh and blood. This means He suffered only in semblance on the cross. Other schools taught that the Christ spirit came down upon the man Jesus at the baptism with the sign of the dove descending on Him, and the Spirit was taken up again to heaven at the Crucifixion but before His death.

A quote signifying this was in the Apocryphal Gospel of Peter claiming that at His death Jesus proclaimed:

"My Power, My Power, why hast thou forsaken Me?"

In order to stop the splintering, religious authorities were forced to draw a line between books, which were "permitted to be read," and were accepted as true doctrine and those not accepted.

Leaders of competing theologies emerged. Marcion came to Rome from Pontus on the Black Sea in A.D. 139, and lived there for about four years, attending the Church in an attempt to persuade them of his doctrine. He was unable to convert the Roman Church to his views, so he proceeded to found a new church. He reasoned that there was so much obvious difference in temperament and tactics between the God of the Old Testament and the God that Jesus preached that they must be two different beings. The Old Testament God he rejected as being punitive and the inferior of the two deities. This inferior God was the Creator of this evil world. The Superior and Good God was the deliverer of mankind and was revealed in Christ. This means the Apostles had misunderstood Christ, His nature, and purpose. Christ's new revelation was therefore repeated to Paul. With this in mind, Marcion created his own Bible to reflect his theology by carefully removing all Jewish-Christian texts in conflict with his own.

Marcion was dedicated and fervent in his beliefs and convictions and within his lifetime he had founded a well-organized church extending throughout the Roman Empire. Its members, in the asceticism of their lives and their readiness for martyrdom, were claimed to excel those of the Catholic Church. But Marcion was overtaken by a growing presence.

The emerging power would come to be known as the Catholic Church. This, however, gives way to misunderstanding since this church was the body united before the great schism, which began in 191 and was completed in 1054 from which the Orthodox Churches broke away. Or one could better say the Catholics broke from the single and unified communion. The most powerful leader of the Roman arm sent a letter of excommunication to the leader of the Eastern arm of the church. Why? Because he refused to come under complete control of the Bishop of Rome. But here I digress.

Many gospels and epistles were circulating in the early church. Dozens were thought to be authentic. By the year A.D. 180 the four gospels had attained general recognition in the major churches of Antioch, Ephesus, and Rome.

Jerome tells us that Theophilus, the bishop of the church at Anitoch around 180 A.D., wrote a commentary on the four Gospels. Theophilus quotes the Fourth Gospel of John as "inspired scripture."

Still, there were many other gospels that could have been considered, so why did we end up with only four? The answer can be explained in three reasons. One was the fact that these four particular gospels fit together, harmonized, and did not contradict each other, as some others would have. Secondly, they upheld the theology of the authorities choosing the books. The third reason seems very arbitrary. There were other gospels that would have harmonized fairly well. Granted, the number would have been small, but we could have easily had five, six, or maybe more gospels in the Bible.

Adversus Haereses, a representative of the official view at Rome and Ephesus in 185 wrote:

It is impossible that the Gospels should be in number either more or fewer than these. For since there are four regions of the world wherein we are, and four principal winds, and the Church is as seed sown in the whole earth, and the Gospel is the Church's pillar and ground, and the breath of life: it is natural that it should have four pillars, from all quarters breathing incorruption, and kindling men into life. Whereby it is evident, that the Artificer of all things, the Word, who sitteth upon the Cherubim, and keepeth all together, when He was made manifest unto men, gave us His Gospel in four forms, kept together by one Spirit... For indeed the Cherubim had four faces, and their faces are images of the dispensation of the Son of God... For the Living Creatures are quadriform, and the Gospel also is quadriform [Ibid. iii. 11. 8.]

The reasoning seems fanciful and contrived, but it is supremely interesting for what it implies. These gospels were accepted and circulated prior to the decision. They were the most popular among the churches. Beyond this, we have four gospels because someone thought it was the right number simply because there are four cardinal directions and a Cherub was described as having four faces.

It should be noted that even after slimming the number to four, there were still many attacks by other sects due to discrepancies between the four gospels. The thought was if the small number of select gospels could not totally agree then there was room for their selected gospels and beliefs also.

Today, most theologians look at the Gospel of Mark as the proto-gospel, which was used by Matthew and Luke as a source to write their own gospels. The Gospel of John was likely written outside the influence of Mark. Thus, the harmony of the gospels can be explained by the common source material of Matthew, Mark, and Luke. The reason for the discrepancies will be touched on later, but for now let us simply say that the Gospels are only what they say they are. They are the good news. They never purport to be history or any such precise writings. They are simply the memoirs of four men telling what they remember about those days when the good news was delivered.

So, with the majority of the Gospels written from the same source, and thus fitting together or harmonizing well, and with the reason to have only four gospels established, (albeit with a superficial and superstitious excuse), the church settled gratefully on Matthew, Mark, Luke, and John as the four cornerstones to build the New Testament.

But wait – these books are not really New Testament books. The new covenant between God and His people could not start until the price of a blood sacrifice was paid and accepted. Remember, the sign of acceptance was to be the resurrection of the perfect sacrifice. The result was to be grace, mercy, forgiveness, and the Holy Spirit as a comforter to His people. This was completed in the book of Acts.

INERRANT SCRIPTURE

From the very beginning of the faith, when letters and books were being copied by hand and passed from one person to the next, there were glaring errors. As letters were collected and compared, it became obvious that there were major problems.

Origen (185 – 254) wrote in his thesis, Contra Celsum, "We must say that an attempt to substantiate almost any story as historical fact, even if it is true, and to produce complete certainty about it, is one of the most difficult tasks and in some cases is impossible."

To Origen, there were obvious discrepancies, such as the difference in chronology and geography concerning the story of Jesus cleansing the temple. Yet, since the Scriptures are inspired by the Spirit they cannot contain errors, and at three different times in his commentaries Origen explicitly states, "inspiration implies freedom from error."

But how can the Scriptures be free from error, even if inspired by the Holy Spirit, when they contain such obvious problems? For Origen, the apparent distortion of historical information is not necessarily the result of some scribal or other literary error, but purposefully put into the text by the Holy Spirit as a reminder that we must not depend on the purely historical reading. Origen writes:

"The differences among manuscripts have become great, either through the negligence of some copyists or through the perverse audacity of others; they either neglect to check over what they have transcribed, or, in the process of checking, they make additions or deletions as they please".

"The divine wisdom has arranged for certain stumbling-blocks and interruptions of the historical sense to be found therein, by inserting in the midst a number of impossibilities and incongruities, in order that the very interruption of the narrative might as it were, present a barrier to the reader and lead him to refuse to proceed along the pathway of the ordinary meaning: and so, by shutting us out and debarring us from that, might recall us to the beginning of another way, and might thereby bring us, through the entrance of a narrow footpath, to a higher and loftier road and lay open the immense breadth of the divine wisdom."

He continued by saying, what may appear as errors to us are intended by the Holy Spirit, to call the reader's attention to "the impossibility of the literal sense", and therefore signal the need for "an examination of the inner meaning."

Origen believed, in his own words, that scripture "...contains three levels of meaning, corresponding to the threefold Pauline (and Platonic) division of a person into body, soul and spirit. The bodily level of Scripture, the bare letter, is normally helpful as it stands to meet the needs of the more simple. The psychic level, corresponding to the soul, is for making progress in perfection.... The spiritual interpretation deals with 'unspeakable mysteries' so as to make humanity a "partaker of all the doctrines of the Spirit's counsel".

Origen actually believed that it was impossible for the scriptures to have errors so the errors found in scripture must have been placed there by God to provoke us to look at some deeper meaning.

A pagan opponent of Origen, named Celsus was not so kind when he wrote, "Some believers, as though from a bout of drinking, go so far as to oppose themselves and change the texts of the gospels three or four or several times over, as to change its character to enable them to deny difficulties in the face of criticism."

There were variations between books, and that was bad enough, but after manuscripts of various books were combined into the codices to make the Bible, the errors or differences between the various Bibles translated from them would become all too apparent. One might assume that the older versions would be less corrupt, but that would not necessarily be true. Look at copies in terms of genetics and lineage. If the original epistle was copied two times in 80 A.D. and the second copy had an error, we have only one copy left that was not a corrupt version. Now assume the flawed copy made it to a library and was preserved but the faithful version is copied and the copies were copied through ten generations of copies. If one of these copies of the faithful version lands in a church in 600 A.D. it would have a much longer lineage. It would be natural to assume the 80 A.D. version was less corrupt, but in fact if the 600 A.D. version did not pick up errors along the way it would be the one that is true to the original text.

Now assume that through time we collect fragments here and there and at times we are fortunate enough to find the occasional complete books. We can compare versions and maybe even track the lineage or "text family" of the fragments and books. If we compare fragments or books which have various "text families" we may see that books from pedigree "A, B, and C" say one thing but "D" says something different. If they started out with different copyists we can assume that one made a mistake. It becomes especially obvious if the word is one that looks or sounds like the rest but does not make as much sense.

These explanations are, to say the least, simplistic but they give a glimpse into the issues at hand, and those are; which manuscripts are the least corrupt and

Joseph Lumpkin

which ones should be used to translate into some other tongue, such as English, in order to produce a Bible? It is not like we do not have several manuscripts to choose from. We have hundreds of fragments. Men have been searching through churches, archives, libraries, sand dunes, caves, and hardened soil for a thousand years to find traces of ancient Christian books.

To prove a point, here is a list of the first 20 out of over 100 as they are categorized.

The list contains:

Papyrus numbers and collection, dates, contents, text family,

owner or place.

P1 -P.Oxy. 2 - 3rd cent. - Matt 1- Alexandrian

Philadelphia, Pennsylvania- Univ. of Penn. Museum

P2 - 6th cent.- John 12 - Mixed

Florence, Italy -Museo Archeologico

P3 -6th-7th cent. -Luke 7, 10 - Alexandrian

Vienna, Austria – Österreichische Nationalbibliothek

P4 -3rd cent. - Luke 1-6 - Alexandrian

Paris, France - Bibliothèque Nationale

P5 -P.Oxy. 208 - 3rd cent. - John 1, 16, 20

Western London, England - British Museum

Pap. 782 + Pap. 2484

P6 -4th cent. - John 10-11 agrees with B & Q

Strasbourg, France - Bibliothèque de la Université

Pap. copt. 351r, 335v, 379, 381, 383, 384

P7 - 5th cent. - Luke 4 (This item has been LOST. It was formerly in Kiev, Ukraine: Library of the Ukranian Academy of Sciences)
Petrov 553

P8 - 4th cent.- Acts 4-6 - mixed: Alexandrian & Western
(Item LOST, formerly in Berlin, Germany: Staatliche Museen_
P. 8683

P9 - P.Oxy. 402 - 3rd cent. - I John 4
Cambridge, Massachusetts -Harvard Semitic Mus.

P10 - P.Oxy. 209 - 4th cent. - Rom 1 - Alexandrian
Cambridge, Massachusetts - Harvard Semitic Mus.

P11 - 7th cent. -I Cor 1-7 - Alexandrian
Leningrad, Russia - State Public Library

P12 - P.Amh. 3b – late 3rd cent. - Heb 1
New York, New York - Pierpont Morgan Library

P13 - P.Oxy. 657 - 3rd–4th cent. - Heb 2-5, 10-12 - Alexandrian
London, England - British Museum

P14 - 5th cent.? - I Cor 1-3 – Alexandrian
Mt. Sinai -St. Catherine's Monastery Library

P15- P.Oxy. 1008 - 3rd cent.- I Cor 7-8 - Alexandrian
Cairo, Egypt - Egyptian Museum

Joseph Lumpkin

P16 - P.Oxy.1009 - 3rd–4th cent. - Phil3-4 -Alexandrian
Cairo, Egypt – Museum of Antiquities

P17 - P.Oxy.1078 - 4th cent. - Heb9 - mixed
Cambridge, England – University Library

P18 - P.Oxy.1079 - 3rd–4th cent. -Rev1 – agrees with: A, B, and C
London,England –British Museum

P19 - P.Oxy.1170 -4th–5th cent. - Matt10-11 - mixed
Oxford, England – Bodleian Library

P20 - P.Oxy.1171 - 3rd cent. - Jas2-3 - Alexandrian
Princeton, New Jersey – University Library

(These are but a few. There are over a hundred more.)

This brings us to the next pertinent problem, which is that of translation. We should question the source text or codices used. Some sources are better and more faithful than others. For example, if we know that the Vulgate was corrupted we should not use that source. We should go back to a Greek source. The source of the Latin Vulgate was the codex Vaticanus, named for the fact it was housed in the Vatican library. But some Greek sources have errors also. An example within the Vaticanus codex is found in Hebrew 1:3. In his book, Misquoting Jesus, Bart Ehrman describes how scribes battle over words within this chapter and verse, as with the entire Bible. According to most manuscripts the word Pheron is used and the verse is translated, "Christ bears all things through the word of His power." But in the Vaticanus the word Phaneron is used and the verse is rendered, "Christ manifests all things through the word of His power." Then a second scribe read it and decided that "manifests" is an uncommon word so he changes it back to "bears." A century later a third scribe notices the alteration done by the second scribe and assumes the second scribe had exercised too much freedom, presuming to alter the original text. He changed the word back to "manifests" and added a note of indignation to the margin that read, "Fool and knave, leave the old reading. Don't change it." Sermons and entire theologies turn on a single word. In some manuscripts the word may not even be there.

Experts compare texts and render a version they believe is as close to the original uncorrupt text as possible. Out of this practice a manuscript is built that will be used to render an English translation. Some manuscripts will be better than others. Some will have the latest discoveries incorporated into the manuscripts. Thus, first we must question the sources used. Since we had been hand-copying manuscripts for fifteen hundred years, errors that occurred early, or errors occurring in manuscripts that were being copied and passed around more than others become entrenched. In fact, they become an accepted part of our bible.

One such example is the story of Jesus and the woman caught in adultery. This is a wonderful story. It shows the grace and kindness of Jesus. It is also absent certain details like, where was the man who was also caught? Was he also forgiven? Was the law of punishment simply forgotten by the priests as the story was told in the town? As it turns out, we do not have to speculate. The story is missing from the older manuscripts. A scribe, who had an apparent mind toward drama more than truth, added it.

The above example is used every Sunday to teach the mercy and forgiveness of Christ, but it is not likely that denominations were founded upon its existence. Not so with the next example.

In the closing verses on Mark, the story is building rapidly to a crescendo. Jesus has been resurrected. Mary has discovered his body is missing. She runs to tell the disciples. Jesus is on his way to them. They do not believe Mary, but then, there he is! Jesus appears! Then the disciples are told to go out into all the world, preach, make converts, and if you are a true believer there are signs that will follow you. You will be able to pick up snakes, drink poison, heal the sick, drive out demons, and speak in tongues.

The following section of Mark does not appear in the older or more reliable manuscripts.

Mark 16

9 When Jesus rose early on the first day of the week, he appeared first to Mary Magdalene, out of whom he had driven seven demons. 10 She went and told those who had been with him and who were mourning and weeping. 11 When they heard that Jesus was alive and that she had seen him, they did not believe it. 12 Afterward Jesus appeared in a different form to two of them while they were walking in the country. 13 These returned and reported it to the rest; but they did not believe them either. 14 Later Jesus appeared to the Eleven as they were eating; he rebuked them for their lack of faith and their stubborn refusal to believe those who had seen him after he had risen. 15 He said to them, "Go into all the world and preach the good news to all creation. 16 Whoever believes and is baptized will be saved, but whoever does not believe will be condemned. 17 And these signs will accompany those who believe: In my name they will drive out demons; they will speak in new tongues; 18 they will pick up snakes with their hands; and when they drink deadly poison, it will not hurt them at all; they will place their hands on sick people, and they will get well." 19 After the Lord Jesus had spoken to them, he was taken up into heaven and he sat at the right hand of God. 20 Then the disciples went out and preached everywhere, and the Lord worked with them and confirmed his word by the signs that accompanied it.

Now, we have a problem, because entire denominations are based on the existence of this text.

At times the error is compounded.

Matthew 17:21 is a duplicate of Mark 9:29. It was apparently added by a copyist in order to harmonize the gospels, however, Mark 9:29 was not in the oldest manuscripts either.

At times there are even variations within the additions. In Mark 9:29 Jesus comments that a certain type of indwelling demon can only be exorcised through "prayer and fasting" (KJV). This is also found in the Rheims New Testament. But the word "fasting" did not appear in the oldest manuscripts. New English translations have dropped the word.

Slight alterations can have ripple effects that produce entire doctrines.

Luke 3:22 is a passage that describes Jesus' baptism by John the Baptist. According to Justin Martyr, the original version has God proclaiming, "You are my son, today have I begotten thee." Clement of Alexandria, Augustine, and other ancient Christian authorities agree on this version. The implication is that Jesus was first recognized by God as his son at the time of baptism. This would agree with certain Gnostic teachings. To distance the passage from the Gnostic viewpoint the words were altered to read, "You are my son, whom I love." This would come to be one of the passages on which the doctrine of the Trinity was based. Christian belief became set that Jesus was the son of God at his birth, (as described in Luke and Matthew) or before the beginning of creation (as in John), and not at his baptism.

Some additions are for theatrical effect and matter little to the overall message.

In John 5:3-4 "a great multitude" of disabled people waited by the water for an angel to come and "trouble the water," at which time it had healing properties for the first person who stepped in. A blind man was there. But the blind man could not see the water or the angel and those that were crippled stood little chance of being first. The passage seems out of place and makes little sense. Part of Verse 3 and all of Verse 4 are missing from the oldest manuscripts of John.

Scribes get carried away and begin writing instead of copying.

In John 21 the apostles are fishing and catching nothing. Jesus appears and tells them to throw the net on the other side of the boat. By doing so they haul in as many fish as the boat can hold. Jesus eats with them and then begins the famous dialogue with Peter about loving Jesus and feeding His sheep. There is general agreement among liberal and mainline Biblical scholars that the original version of the Gospel of John ended at the end of John 20. Scholars do not agree if John 21 was an afterthought or an addition, although most hold with the latter view.

Then, there are errors that reflect values and prejudices of the time.

1 Corinthians 14:34-35 appears to prohibit all talking by women during services. But it contradicts verse 11:5, in which St. Paul states that women can actively pray and prophesy during services. The question has been, "was this opinion for that one church or was this behavior to be held by all churches?" It is obvious to some theologians that verses 14:33b to 36 are a later addition. Bible scholar, Hans Conzelmann, comments on these three and a half verses: "Moreover, there are peculiarities of linguistic usage, and of thought. [within them]." If they are removed, then Verse 33a merges well with Verse 37 in a seamless transition. If he is correct, many churches will have to re-think their sexist views.

In Revelation 1:11, the phrase "Saying, I am Alpha and Omega, the first and the last..." (KJV) which is found in the King James Version was not in the original Greek texts. It is also found in the New King James Version (NKJV) and in the 21st Century King James Version (KJ21) The latter are basically re-writes of the original KJV. The Alpha Omega phrase is not found in virtually any ancient texts, nor is it mentioned, even as a footnote, in any modern translation or in Bruce Metzger's definitive 'A Textual Commentary' on the Greek New Testament, Second Edition.

Many sources, including United Bible Societies and Ontario Consultants on Religious Tolerance were used for the previous section and speak well to this issue.

Before we accept the version of the Bible we are reading we must be sure of its source. We must know if it was the most reliable source available. We must know how the manuscript was translated.

There are several ways to translate. The large number of translations are usually grouped into three main categories. A literal translation attempts to translate word for word and is a type of interlinear approach. They are usually the most accurate but also the most difficult to read. This is because English differs from Greek in the order of subject, verb, and predicate. The sentence structure becomes tangled and confusing. Then, there is that looming problem when words do not have an exact match and a phrase is used to render a word or two.

A dynamic translation attempts to keep the literal approach but restructures the sentences and grammar to make the Bible more readable. This opens the translation up to some degree of subjectivity and error.

Contemporary English translations are the easiest to read because they attempt to capture the meaning of the text and place the thought into modern English. The result is easy to read, but the text is highly subjective and should be approached with great care.

One should always question the purpose of a new translation. Was the translation commissioned for the purpose of expanding a particular denomination? In such cases it is quite possible that the wording and flavor of the text was bent to conform to the beliefs of the church body underwriting the translation. It would seem to be pure foolishness for a church to bend the scriptures to their will instead of re-examining and reforming their doctrine, but the former is done far too often.

One such obvious tact used in a modern church was that of the "New World Bible." The denomination using this version is adamantly opposed to the doctrine of the trinity. By altering their Bible by a single word, nay - a single letter, they manage to negate the existence of the trinity. They simply inserted the letter "a."

New World Translation of the Holy Scriptures

John 1:1 In [the] beginning the Word was, and the Word was with God, and the Word was a god.

Compare to the NIV, which echoes most other Bibles.

John 1:1 (New International Version)

1In the beginning was the Word, and the Word was with God, and the Word was God.

With such translations freely circulating, how can one claim the Bible is inerrant?

Most translations have the general error induced by starting with their own personal beliefs, and thus the subconscious prejudice of how the verse should be rendered.

Having covered the three main approaches to translations, it needs to be restated that every translation requires interpretation. At times this can be rather subjective. Why? Because languages do not translate word for word. Not every word has a unique word to match it in the other language. There are idioms, expressions, and metaphors that become meaningless in other tongues. Some languages even have different verb tenses and there is no direct single verb that fits the translation. Greek has verbs that indicate an action happening in the past with continuing effects back in time. There are also verbs that indicate an event in the present with consequences continuing far into the future. English has no such equal. Some languages are richer in expression than English (such as Greek) or smaller in vocabulary (such as Hebrew). A translator must interpret the original meaning and find an equivalent wording. This is why at times a phrase will end up replacing a word or two. It is also why this makes the result subject to the biases of the translator. The translator must also attempt to put aside his personal beliefs so as not to bend a translation to mean something more or less than what it actually says.

This is a human process of choices and biases. Interpretations will differ and errors will occur.

To complicate things, all ancient manuscripts do not support a number of verses. Some verses only occur in latter versions, sometimes within only a set text family. Translators have to decide which verses to leave out of the text. Most translators will mark any verse left out of the majority of manuscripts with a note in the margin or a footnote with the omitted verse.

It is extremely ironic that one of the most well known and foundational sections of the Bible demonstrates both of the above points of translation and omission. It is the Lord's Prayer.

First, let us examine the The King James' version of The Lord's Prayer from Matthew 6:9-13: "After this manner therefore pray ye: 'Our Father which art in heaven, Hallowed be thy name. Thy kingdom come. Thy will be done in earth, as it is in heaven. Give us this day our daily bread. And forgive us our debts, as we forgive our debtors. And lead us not into temptation, but deliver us from evil: For thine is the kingdom, and the power, and the glory, for ever. Amen.'"

Now let us read the Lord's prayer in the NIV.

Prayer from Matthew 6:9-13: "This, then, is how you should pray: 'Our Father in heaven, hallowed be your name, your kingdom come, your will be done on earth as it is in heaven. Give us today our daily bread. Forgive us our debts, as we also have forgiven our debtors. And lead us not into temptation, but deliver us from the evil one.'

Ignoring the difference between the Elizabethan English and modern English, there are two glaring differences in the last verse between the King James' Lord's prayer.

The KJV asks for deliverance from "evil" while the NIV asks to deliver us from "the evil one." There is a huge theological difference between the two. The Greek text actually uses an adjective with an article, making "the evil one" the only correct translation. We pray to be delivered from the evil one, not from any danger, disaster, or from the general ugliness of the world.

Look at the last line. "For thine is the kingdom, and the power, and the glory, for ever, Amen." This verse does not occur in older manuscripts. It only occurs as an addition to manuscripts of a certain "lineage" past a certain date. The doxology of the prayer is not contained in Luke's version. It is also missing from the earliest manuscripts of Matthew, representative of the Alexandrian text. It is present, however, in the manuscripts representative of the Byzantine text. To help date these two periods one should know that the Byzantine Empire began around 1557, and the Codex Alexandrinus is a 5th century Greek Bible, so we are talking about a period of almost one-thousand years.

Therefore the differences between the various English translations, such as the KJV and the NIV can come down to choices in interpretations as well as a choice of which ancient manuscripts to use as a source. Sometimes errors occur.

When errors do happen from the copyists' standpoint they can usually be attributed to a hand full of reasons. Errors in translations come from several directions. There are errors of the eye, where the copyist or scribe may read the text incorrectly, and transposing letters to make a new word and then write or interpret accordingly.

Errors of speech occur when a reader is dictating to a copyist and the scribe hears the word but confuses it with another word, which is pronounced in a similar manner but is incorrect.

Errors of the mind occur when the scribe reads a line and simply forgets the exact wording, producing an inexact copy, such as a substitute of the word "out" for "from" or the word "karpos (fruit) instead of "karphos" (speck). Other tricks the mind can play are to include explanatory notes found in the margins of many manuscripts within the main body of the text.

Intentional changes occur when a well-meaning scribe attempts to correct what he assumes to be an error in linguistics, which is not an error at all. Other intentional errors occur when attempting to align the Bible with biblical history, as it is understood at the time of copying.

A very obvious and specific error occurs when the scribe attempts to "harmonize" various passages in the Bible in order to make them less divergent or contradictory.

There are errors that can be introduced due to doctrine. These occur when one group decides to alter the manuscript to more closely reflect their own biases. Several of these may be found in the 16th century and include certain changes of an anti-Semitic view.

There are subtle changes that may occur in what is called "liturgical errors." These tend to be minor changes in word or flow to make the liturgy flow easier or make it easier to remember or follow.

In the more recent past, the errors of eye and mind were compounded when the printing press was invented. Errors usually assigned to one or two books could now be propagated through hundreds of Bibles at once.

King Charles I ordered 1,000 Bibles from an English printer named Robert Barker in 1631. It was an edition of the King James Bible. Only after the Bibles were delivered did anyone notice a serious mistake. In one of the Ten Commandments [Exodus 20:14], a very small word was forgotten by the printers. The word "not" was left out. This changed the 7th commandment to say "Thou shalt commit adultery!" Most of the copies were recalled immediately and destroyed on the orders of Charles I. But there are 11 copies still remaining. They are known as the "Wicked Bible." (The Bible museum in Branson - Missouri has one on display.) The printer was fined the equivalent of $400, a lifetime's wages at the time. It should be observed that the Ten Commandments of this Bible were easier to follow.

The word "not" was also left out in the 1653 edition. In 1 Corinthians 6 verse 9 it was printed: "Know ye not that the unrighteous shall inherit the kingdom of God" - instead of ""Know ye not that the unrighteous shall not inherit the kingdom of God." Again it was recalled immediately. It is known as the "Unrighteous Bible."

The Murderer's Bible - printed in 1801 - declared: "these are murderers" (instead of murmurers) and continued - "let the children first be killed" (instead of "filled.")

Perhaps the error in Psalm 119 verse 161 in a 1702 version summed it all up: instead of "princes" it read - "<u>printers</u> have persecuted me." It is known as the Printer's Bible.

These are but a few of the more noteworthy mistakes, but these mistakes must bring into question the doctrine of the inerrancy of the Bible. Most fundamental denominations hold to the fact that the Bible is complete and without error. It may be neither.

The history of the English Bible is a fascinating story. It serves to prove a point or two about how the church intentionally changed the Bible and then protected the alterations on penalty of death. Our starting point in this history is the production of Wycliff's hand-written English Bible, which was the result of the "Morning Star Reformation" led by John Wycliffe.

The first hand-written English language Bible manuscripts were produced in the 1380's A.D. by John Wycliffe, an Oxford professor. Wycliffe was a well-known theologian in Europe who stood in opposition to the teaching of the organized Church, which he believed to be contrary to the Bible. He enlisted his followers, called the Lollards, and his assistant Purvey, along with others to act as scribes to produce dozens of English manuscripts. They were translated out of the Latin Vulgate, which was known to be somewhat corrupt, but was the only source text available to Wycliffe. The Pope was so infuriated by his rebellion, his actions, his teachings and his translation of the Bible into English, that 44 years after Wycliffe had died, the Pope ordered the bones of Wycliffe to be dug-up, crushed, and the dust of his bones were thrown in the wind to be carried out over the river.

John Hus was one of Wycliffe's followers. Hus actively campaigned for Wycliffe's work and ideas. Both men firmly believed that people should be permitted to read the Bible. They believed Bibles should be available in native tongues and all men should have the right to read it in their own language. Hus and Wycliffe openly opposed the tyranny of the Roman church. The edicts issued from the Pope threatened anyone possessing a non-Latin Bible with execution. The edict was carried out when Hus was burned at the stake in 1415, with Wycliffe's manuscript Bibles used as kindling for the fire. The last words of John Hus were that, "in 100 years, God will raise up a man whose calls for reform cannot be suppressed." Almost exactly 100 years later, in 1517, Martin Luther nailed his famous 95 Theses of Contention (a list of 95 issues of heretical theology and crimes of the Roman Catholic Church) to the church door at Wittenberg. The prophecy of Hus had come true.

Sometime in the 1450's Johann Gutenberg invented the movable type printing press. The result was amazing and immediate. Copies of books could now be mass-produced in a short time. Distribution for illegal books happened in an underground network. The first book to ever be printed was a Latin language Bible, printed in Mainz, Germany. This was essential to the success of the Reformation.

Thomas Linacre was a self-styled Greek scholar active in the 1490's. He was an Oxford professor, and the personal physician to King Henry the 7th and 8th. Thomas Linacre, a very bright man, decided to learn Greek in order to read the Bible for himself. After reading the Gospels and comparing the same texts to those in the Latin Vulgate, he wrote in his diary, "Either this is not the Gospel... or we are not Christians." The Latin had become so corrupt that it misrepresented and mangled the message of the Gospel. The church knew this but worked to keep a strangle hold on power instead of putting forth the effort to correct the Vulgate. Throughout all of this the Church threatened to kill anyone who read the scripture in any language other than Latin from any other source but the Vulgate. This was because many of the Vulgate's corruptions were intentionally placed to support church doctrine. Instead of building doctrine around the Bible, the church bent the Bible to support doctrine. This was not that difficult since Latin was not an original language of the scriptures and the conversion between Greek and Latin could be worded as the church wished.

John Colet, another Oxford professor was the son of the Mayor of London. In 1496 he began reading the New Testament in Greek. Soon after he decided to translate it into English for his students at Oxford. Later he provided texts for the public at Saint Paul's Cathedral in London. The people were so excited to actually read and understand the Bible, that within six months it was reported that each Sunday there were 20,000 people attempting to get into the church and an equal number surrounding the church to listen and possibly obtain a document. Fortunately for Colet, his political connections spared him from execution.

Erasmus was considered one of the greatest biblical scholars of all time. In 1516 he picked up the challenge of Linacre and Colet to correct the corrupt Latin Vulgate. He did this with the help of a printer named John Froben. Together, they published a Greek-Latin Parallel New Testament. He used the Greek, which he had managed to collate from a half-dozen partial old Greek New Testament manuscripts he had acquired. This produced the first non-Latin (Vulgate) text of the scripture to be produced in a millennium. The Greek-Latin Parallel New Testament focused attention on just how corrupt and inaccurate the Latin Vulgate used by the church was. Now people began to see how important it was to go back and use the original Greek and Hebrew texts. To translate the Bible into any native tongue more faithfully one must begin with the most accurate texts. Translations rendered from corrupt translations simply compounded error. The driving force keeping the act of translating illegal became obvious when Pope Leo X himself declared, "The fable of Christ has been quite profitable to me." The Pope feared loss of control and loss of revenue.

William Tyndale (1494-1536) holds the distinction of being the first man to ever print the New Testament in the English language. Tyndale was a true scholar and a genius. He was fluent in eight languages to the point that it was said one would think any one of them to be his native tongue. He is frequently referred to as the "Architect of the English Language", (even more so than William Shakespeare) as so many of the phrases Tyndale coined are still in our language today.

Tyndale was a Biblical translator and martyr; born most probably at North Nibley, about 15 miles south-west of Gloucester, England, in 1494. He died at Vilvoorden, about 6 miles north-east of Brussels, Belgium, Oct. 6, 1536.

Tyndale was descended from an ancient Northumbrian family. He went to school at Oxford, and afterward to Magdalen Hall and Cambridge.

Tyndale translated the Bible into an early form of Modern English. He was the first person to take advantage of Gutenberg's movable-type press for the purpose of printing the scriptures in the English language. Tyndale held and published views considered heretical by the Catholic Church, and the Church of England established by Henry VIII. His Bible translation also included notes and commentary promoting these views. In the house of Walsh he disputed with Roman Catholic dignitaries, exciting much opposition, which led to his removal to London around Oct., 1523. A clergyman of the Roman Catholic Church once infuriated Tyndale by proudly proclaiming, "We are better to be without God's laws than the Pope's". Tyndale was enraged by what he viewed as the unreasonable and ungodly Roman Catholic heresies, to which he replied, "I defy the Pope and all his laws. If God spare my life ere many years, I will cause the boy that drives the plow to know more of the scriptures than you!"

Tyndale's translation was banned by the authorities, and

His death would occur a few years thereafter.

Foxe's Book of Martyrs records that in that same year, 1517, seven people were burned at the stake by the Roman Catholic Church for the crime of teaching their children to say the Lord's Prayer in English rather than Latin.

In 1517 Martin Luther declared his intolerance for the Roman Church's corruption on Halloween in 1517, by nailing his 95 Theses of Contention to the Wittenberg Church door.

Luther, who would be exiled in the months following the Diet of Worms Council in 1521 that was designed to martyr him, would translate the New Testament into German for the first time from the 1516 Greek-Latin New Testament of Erasmus, and publish it in September of 1522. Luther also published a German Pentateuch in 1523, and another edition of the German New Testament in 1529. In the 1530's he would go on to publish the entire Bible in German.

William Tyndale had wanted to use the same 1516 Erasmus text as a source to translate and print the New Testament in English for the first time in history. Tyndale showed up on Luther's doorstep in Germany in 1525, and by year's end had translated the New Testament into English. Tyndale had been forced to flee England, because of the wide-spread rumor of his project. Inquisitors and bounty hunters were constantly hounding Tyndale to arrest and kill him.

The authorities failed and Tyndale published his Bibles. They were burned as soon as the Bishop could confiscate them, but copies trickled through and actually ended up in the bedroom of King Henry VIII. The public fascination continued to grow as well as the panic within the Roman Catholic Church. They attempted to counter the outcry by declaring the new translation contained thousands of errors. This became the excuse for burning hundreds of New Testaments. The fact was that they could find no errors in the texts. The church continued to enforce its edicts and anyone caught with a Tyndale Bible risked death by burning.

Having God's Word available to the public in the language of the common man, spelled disaster to the church. The church could not continue doing things that were so completely contrary to the Bible, such as selling indulgences (the forgiveness of sins one was planning to commit) or selling the release of loved ones from Purgatory.

Salvation through faith, not works or donations, was becoming the cry to battle. These were just a few things to come out of the Luther – Tyndale crusade.

Tyndale was betrayed by a fellow Englishman who was supposedly his friend. Tyndale was imprisoned for about 500 days before he was strangled and then burned at the stake in 1536. His last words were, "Oh Lord, open the King of England's eyes". This prayer would be answered in 1539, when King Henry VIII commanded the printing of an English Bible known as the "Great Bible."

Myles Coverdale and John Rogers were disciples of Tyndale. They continued the English Bible project after his death. Coverdale finished translating the Old Testament, and in 1535 he printed the first complete Bible in English. He made use of Luther's German text and the Latin as his sources. The first complete English Bible was printed on October 4, 1535, and is known as the Coverdale Bible.

John Rogers went on to print the second complete English Bible in 1537. It was, however, the first English Bible translated from the original Biblical languages of Hebrew & Greek. He printed it under the pseudonym "Thomas Matthew", a pen-name actually used by Tyndale at one time. He could have done this to honor the fact that a considerable part of this Bible was the translation of Tyndale before his murder at the hands of the church. The Bible was a composite made up of Tyndale's Pentateuch, his New Testament 1534-1535 edition, Coverdale's Bible, and some of Roger's own translation of the text. It remains known as the Matthew-Tyndale Bible. A second-edition printing was done in 1549.

In 1539, Thomas Cranmer, the Archbishop of Canterbury, hired Myles Coverdale at the command of King Henry VIII. His task was to publish the "Great Bible". It became the first English Bible authorized for public use. The Bible was distributed to Anglican Churches. One was chained to the pulpit, and a person to read the Bible was provided so that even the illiterate could hear the Word of God in plain English. William Tyndale's prayer had been granted three years after his martyrdom. Cranmer's Bible, published by Coverdale, was known as the Great Bible due to its great size: a large pulpit folio measuring over 14 inches tall. Seven editions of this version were printed between April of 1539 and December of 1541.

King Henry VIII had not actually changed his mind regarding publishing the Bible in English for the masses. He did it because he was angry with the Pope for refusing to grant his divorce. King Henry responded by marrying his mistress anyway, and having two of his many wives executed. Henry was the second son in the family and was destined to be a priest. Henry VIII had three siblings, two girls and one boy. His brother was called Arthur. Arthur was Prince of Wales. When Henry VII, his father, was still alive, Arthur died. Which made Henry VIII heir to the throne. Henry knew the church inside and out. In his anger he renounced Roman Catholicism, and removed England from Rome's religious control. Henry declared himself the new head of the Church. To this day the Kings of England are sworn to be "Defender of the Faith." His first act was to strike Rome in the heart of the church by funding the printing of the scriptures in English. This gave way to the first legal English Bible.

After King Henry VIII and then King Edward VI died, the reign of Queen "Bloody" Mary began. From 1540's through the 1550's she was possessed in her obsession to return England to the Roman Church. In 1555, she had John "Thomas Matthew" Rogers and Thomas Cranmer burned at the stake. Mary went on to burn hundreds for the "crime" of being a Protestant. This era was known as the Marian Exile. Religious refugees fled from England, but there was no truly safe place anywhere near except for Switzerland.

The Church at Geneva, Switzerland, was sympathetic to religious refugees and was one of only a few safe havens. Myles Coverdale and John Foxe, publisher of "Foxe's Book of Martyrs," along with Thomas Sampson and William Whittingham met there in the 1550's, with the protection of the great theologian John Calvin and John Knox, the reformer of the Scottish Church. They undertook to produce a Bible that would educate their families while they continued in exile. The New Testament was completed in 1557, and the complete Bible was first published in 1560. It became known as the Geneva Bible. Due to the use of the word "Breeches," which is an antiquated form of "Britches" (pants), some people referred to the Geneva Bible as the Breeches Bible. The Geneva Bible was the first Bible to add numbered verses to the chapters, so that referencing specific passages would be easier. Every chapter was also accompanied by extensive marginal notes and references so thorough and complete that the Geneva Bible is also considered the first English "Study Bible". William Shakespeare quotes hundreds of times in his plays from the Geneva translation of the Bible. The Geneva Bible became the

Bible of choice for over 100 years of English speaking Christians. Between 1560 and 1644 at least 144 editions of this Bible were published.

Examination of the 1611 King James Bible shows clearly that its translators were influenced much more by the Geneva Bible, than by any other source. The Geneva Bible itself retains over 90% of William Tyndale's original English translation. The Geneva in fact, remained more popular than the King James Version until decades after its original release in 1611. The Geneva holds the honor of being the first Bible taken to America, and the Bible of the Puritans and Pilgrims. It is truly the "Bible of the Protestant Reformation." The famous Geneva Bible has been out-of-print since 1644, so the only way to obtain one is to either purchase an original printing of the Geneva Bible, or a less costly facsimile reproduction of the original 1560 Geneva Bible.

In 1568, a revision of the Great Bible known as the Bishop's Bible was introduced. Despite 19 editions being printed between 1568 and 1606, this Bible, referred to as the "rough draft of the King James Version", never gained much of a foothold of popularity among the people. The Geneva may have simply been too much to compete with.

By the 1580's, the Roman Catholic Church saw that it had lost the battle to suppress the Bible and repress the people. In 1582, they ceased their fight for "Latin only" and began an official Roman Catholic English translation. In an attempt to continue control through the corrupt translation of the Latin Vulgate, it was decided that the English translation should use Vulgate as the only source text. Because it was translated at the Roman Catholic College in the city of Rheims, it was known as the Rheims New Testament. The Douay Old Testament was translated by the Church of Rome in 1609 at the College in the city of Douay. The combined product is commonly referred to as the "Doway/Rheims" or "Douay/Rheims" Version.

In 1589, Dr. William Fulke of Cambridge published the "Fulke's Refutation". Fulke printed in parallel columns the Bishops Version along side the Rheims Version, in an attempt to show the error and distortion of the Douay/Rheims.

With the death of Bloody Mary and then Queen Elizabeth I, Prince James VI of Scotland became King James I of England. The Protestant clergy, feeling less religious tyranny, approached the new King in 1604 with the desire for an updated and less confrontational Bible. The new translation was to replace the Bishop's Bible first printed in 1568. They wished to keep the scholarship and accuracy but do away with the rather acrid marginal notes proclaiming the Pope an Anti-Christ, and such. This suited the king, who many regarded as a closet Catholic. The leaders of the church desired a Bible with word clarification and cross-references, available to the masses.

In 1611 the first of the 16-inch tall pulpit addition was printed. It is known as "The 1611 King James Bible". A typographical error in Ruth 3:15 rendered a pronoun "He" instead of "She" in that verse in some printings. This caused some of the 1611 First Editions to be known by collectors as "He" Bibles, and others as "She" Bibles. Yes, I regret to say that even the sacred KJV had errors.

One year after the pulpit-size King James Bibles were printed and chained to every church pulpit in England, personal copies of the Bible became available.

One of the great ironies of history is that many Protestant Christian churches today declare the King James Bible as the only legitimate English language translation but it is not even a Protestant translation. Remember, the King of England is the "Defender of the Faith" for the Anglican Church, which is considered by most not to be a Protestant faith, but a Catholic sect.

After England broke from Roman Catholicism in the 1500's, the Church of England, also called "The Anglican Church," continued to persecute Protestants throughout the 1600's. One famous example of this is John Bunyan, who while in prison for the crime of preaching the Gospel, wrote one of Christian history's greatest books, Pilgrim's Progress. Throughout the 1600's, as the Puritans and the Pilgrims fled the religious persecution of England to cross the Atlantic and start a new free nation in America, they took with them their precious Geneva Bible, and rejected the King's Bible. America was founded upon the Geneva Bible, not the King James Bible. However, as time went on and the newer edition of the K.J.V. gained in popularity in America it eclipsed the Geneva Bible.

Until the appearance of the English Revised Version of 1881-1885 the King James Version was the Bible of choice for most. It is a little-known fact that for the past 200 years, all King James Bibles published in America are actually the 1769 Baskerville spelling and wording revision of the 1611. The original "1611" preface is deceivingly included by the publishers, and no mention of the fact that it is really the 1769 version is to be found, because that might hurt sales. The only way to obtain a true, unaltered, 1611 version is to either purchase an original pre-1769 printing of the King James Bible, or a less costly facsimile reproduction of the original 1611 King James Bible.

The differences between the two versions are easy to spot since there are no less than 24,000 differences in words, grammar, and punctuation between the four major revisions of the 1611 KJV between the 1613 and 1769 versions. (Here I must ask my Independent Baptist Brothers who defend the KJV as the only true Bible; "Which of these versions is the perfect word of God?")

In 1663 John Eliot published the first Bible printed in America. It was a translation in the native Algonquin Indian Language. The first English language Bible to be printed in America by Robert Aitken in 1782 was a King James Version. Robert Aitken's 1782 Bible was the only Bible ever authorized by the United States Congress. President George Washington commended him for providing Americans with Bibles during the embargo of imported English goods due to the Revolutionary War.

In the 1880's England planned a replacement for their King James Bible, known as the English Revised Version (E.R.V.). It would become the first English language Bible to gain popular acceptance after the King James Version. The widespread popularity of this modern-English translation was the first bible to eliminate the 14 Apocryphal books. Up until the late 1800's every Protestant Bible, as well as the Catholic Bibles had 80 books, not 66. The exception was the little known "Robert Aitken's Bible" of 1782. It was the King James Bible published without the apocrypha.

The inter-testament books written hundreds of years before Christ called "The Apocrypha" were part of virtually every printing of the Tyndale-Matthews Bible, the Great Bible, the Bishops Bible, the Protestant Geneva Bible, and the King James Bible until their removal from the K.J.V. around 1885. The original 1611 King James contained the Apocrypha, and King James threatened anyone who dared to print the Bible without the Apocrypha with heavy fines and a year in jail. Only for the last 120 years has the Protestant Church rejected these books, and removed them from their Bibles. This has left most modern-day Christians believing the popular myth that there is something "Roman Catholic" about the Apocrypha. That was not true, and no consistent reason for the removal of the Apocrypha in the 1880's has ever been officially issued by mainline Protestant denominations. It is thought that since the Apocrypha had fallen into disuse and was thought of as a historical reference but not on the same spiritual level as the Old or New Testament, the removal made little spiritual difference and saved a little money.

Knowing all of the above... knowing how corrupt the Vulgate and all translations issuing from it are, I ask again, "Is the Bible inerrant?"

The Bible is a wonderful gift from God. It is a great road map to live by, but it is not God. The Bible has been passed through the hands of men. Scribes, copyists, translators, collectors, and printers have all made their marks. Men make mistakes. Nothing mankind has touched is without error. When we raise the Bible to the Status of God and begin worshipping the book instead of the Spirit who inspired it, we fall into legalism. Legalism breeds judgment, divisions, and hate. It is at this point that Christians begin hurting those of differing beliefs, including other Christians who may have another point of view. We fall into the same category as the extremists we so despise. Christian extremists have damaged more Christians than Islamists Most of them were hurt within the only place they thought was safe – the church.

What does all of this information have to do with rescuing spirituality from religion? Our church is truly a prodigal church. It has produced a Bible befitting itself. But the Bible should never take the place of God. Time spent in silence is worth more than time spent researching and studying those things we already know we should do. As much as possible, be at peace with all men. Be still and know He is God. Wait upon the Lord. Be childlike. Find joy. Be happy. Give to others. Seek God. Most of all, find the love within you.

To add a spot of humor and irony to your life, it should be pointed out with a smile that even though it has been stated that the Bible may not be without error, we will still be quoting from it regularly since we continue to speak about the Christian faith and the Bible is the only external common link we share between most denominations. The Holy Bible may have errors in it. It may be incomplete. In some churches and denominations the Bible may have been raised to a status as high, if not higher than God. The arrogance of certainty by some regarding the meanings of texts within the Bible has caused war and bloodshed. Yet, it is the book that guides a faith. Even though it is Christ who should guide Christianity, and even though the Holy Spirit offers a direct connection to Him, we rely on the Bible as a roadmap to reach Him when we cannot or will not find that connection. God, protect our path.

Sources: University of Texas at Dallas - on line library

williamtyndale.com

Regent University - on line library

American Bible Society

FROM GOD, CHARITY OF HEART

There are two states in a man's life – to love, and a call to be loved. We seek unconditional love because only through this God-like love we rest assured of being accepted with all sins and shortcomings that haunt us every waking hour and in our nightmares. It seems right that we would seek to deliver this kind of love to those closest to us such as our children, spouse, and friends. This kind of love flows from the heart of God. It flows through us to others.

Meaning of Agape': a·ga·pe NOUN: 1. Christian Love as revealed in Jesus, seen as spiritual and selfless and a model for humanity. 2. Love that is spiritual, not sexual, in its nature. 3. Christianity in the early Christian Church, the love feast accompanied by Eucharistic celebration.

Agape' is God's pure unconditional Love and it's always used as such in the Bible. *Nancy Missler*

Agape' (noun) and *agapao* (verb) -- This is the word of Godly love. This special significance really comes in the New Testament period. *Agape'* is not found in secular literature, at least to any great extent, during the biblical period. The writers of the Septuagint use the noun some twenty times, but use the verb form over 250 times. In general terms, the Septuagint translators "invented" a new meaning for *agape'* by using it to replace the Hebrew *hesed*, a word meaning loving-kindness. Jude Ministries

Look closely at the difference in translations when it comes to the word agape'.

1CO 13:13 And now abideth faith, hope, charity (agape'), these three; but the greatest of these is charity. 14:1 Follow after charity (agape'), and desire spiritual gifts, but rather that ye may prophesy

1CO 13:13 And now abide faith, hope, love (agape'), these three; but the greatest of these is love (agape')

1CO 8:1 ... Knowledge puffeth up, but charity (agape') edifieth. 2 And if any man think that he knoweth any thing, he knoweth nothing yet as he ought to know. 3 But if any man love God, the same is known of him.

1CO 13:1 Though I speak with the tongues of men and of angels, and have not charity, (agape') I am become as sounding brass, or a tinkling cymbal. 2 And though I have the gift of prophecy, and understand all mysteries, and all knowledge; and though I have all faith, so that I could remove mountains, and have not charity (agape'), I am nothing. 3 And though I bestow all my goods to feed the poor, and though I give my body to be burned, and have not charity (agape'), it profiteth me nothing. 4 Charity (agape') suffereth long, and is kind; charity (agape') envieth not; charity (agape') vaunteth not itself, is not puffed up, 5 Doth not behave itself unseemly, seeketh not her own, is not easily provoked, thinketh no evil; 6 Rejoiceth not in iniquity, but rejoiceth in the truth; 7 Beareth all things, believeth all things, hopeth all things, endureth all things. 8 Charity (agape') never faileth:...

So many things flow from the love of God in us. Actions reach out to others in compassion and giving that arise from the impulse of love planted so deeply in our hearts we cannot resist. By these acts, and by this love we shall know we are saved.

1PE 1:22 Seeing ye have purified your souls in obeying the truth through the Spirit unto unfeigned love of the brethren, see that ye love one another with a pure heart fervently: 23 Being born again, not of corruptible seed, but of incorruptible, by the word of God, which liveth and abideth for ever.

1JO 3:14 We know that we have passed from death unto life, because we love the brethren...

JAM 2:14 What doth it profit, my brethren, though a man say he hath faith, and have not works? can faith save him? 15 If a brother or sister be naked, and destitute of daily food, 16 And one of you say unto them, Depart in peace, be ye warmed and filled; notwithstanding ye give them not those things which are needful to the body; what doth it profit? 17 Even so faith, if it hath not works, is dead, being alone. 18 Yea, a man may say, Thou hast faith, and I have works: shew me thy faith without thy works, and I will shew thee my faith by my works. 19 Thou believest that there is one God; thou doest well: the devils also believe, and tremble. 20 But wilt thou know, O vain man, that faith without works is dead?

True faith in Christ, which is salvation, cannot be kept within. It will spring forth in action because it engenders love. One could go around the world doing good works and not be saved. One must look at the reason and origin of the acts. The works may seem good to us but they do not arise from a heart of love and are not of God. A saved man, who would have the love of God in him, could not live without loving. God in us brings forth love and love will bring forth action and works of love, compassion, mercy, and charity.

MAT 7:18 A good tree cannot bring forth evil fruit, neither can a corrupt tree bring forth good fruit. 19 Every tree that bringeth not forth good fruit is hewn down, and cast into the fire. 20 Wherefore by their fruits ye shall know them.

EPH 5:9 (For the fruit of the Spirit is in all goodness and righteousness and truth;) 10 Proving what is acceptable unto the Lord.

GAL 5:22 But the fruit of the Spirit is love, joy, peace, longsuffering, gentleness, goodness, faith, 23 Meekness, temperance: against such there is no law. 24 And they that are Christ's have crucified the flesh with the affections and lusts. 25 If we live in the Spirit, let us also walk in the Spirit.

OF FLESH, LAW, AND MAN

If those who had set themselves to explain the various theories of Christianity had set themselves instead to do the will of the Master, how different the world would be now! --George MacDonald

Christianity is a direct connection between God and man, and thus must be viewed in this context continually. Man was made for God by God and as such, the fleshly clothing of the body cannot be in enmity with God. For how could Christ offer up to God anything corrupt? He could not. So if Christ, having been born in the flesh, offered up to God his body as a sacrifice, it becomes obvious the nature of flesh is not corrupt. Unlike the Gnostic and Eastern religions, Christianity does not seek to be free of the fleshy clothing of the body in order to be glorified; instead we seek to be clothed thrice, first in this body, then with the glory of God as He would allow His spirit to reside with us in this earthly tent, and finally with a heavenly garment given us by Christ as we are changed to be like Him when we shall see Him.

1JO 3:2 Beloved, now are we the sons of God, and it doth not yet appear what we shall be: but we know that, when he shall appear, we shall be like him; for we shall see him as he is.

The body is not a prison to be endured but a vehicle by which God may be worshiped and praised. Indeed, the flesh, being the same in kind as that of Christ himself, is the temple of the Holy Spirit and is the way through which God now chooses to announce His plan of salvation as it is written:

ROM 10:13 For whosoever shall call upon the name of the Lord shall be saved. How then shall they call on him in whom they have not believed? and how shall they believe in him of whom they have not heard? and how shall they hear without a preacher? 15 And how shall they preach, except they be sent? as it is written, How beautiful are the feet of them that preach the gospel of peace, and bring glad tidings of good things!

It is therefore not the flesh, which wars against God, but the law of carnality that the flesh obeys. As it has been from his creation, man has obeyed this carnal law and has, through his mortal weakness, turned away from the higher law, which is a spiritual law.

ROM 7:22 For I delight in the law of God after the inward man: 23 But I see another law in my members, warring against the law of my mind, and bringing me into captivity to the law of sin which is in my members.

Still, man was commanded to follow God's laws and could not do so. Even as we agreed that the law was good, even as we could hear God's will speaking to us through the law, even as we adopted the law as our mandate, we failed to keep the law. Not one man in thousands of years and millions of lifetimes, or for that matter in the whole of humanity, could fulfill the law. How then could God be called a good and faithful judge when it was not possible to keep His commandments? What wise judge would give a man an impossible task and then demand his life when it could not be done? But one man has kept the law and by doing so both condemned us and saved us. Condemnation did not come from Him but in the fact the law was kept and fulfilled by Him. Man was shown it was possible to keep the law and was thus condemned by the law having no excuses left. Yet, in the complete and perfect fulfillment of the law, Christ was blameless and in this state He died to impart to us His perfection, having laid down His life for this purpose, to pay for our sins with His perfect life, trading sin for death as it is written, "The wages of sin is death".

When we were deceived by sin to think the fulfillment of our desires would bring us life, or at least a richer life, we became the slave of sin, led away by our own greed as surely as any sailor was seduced and shanghaied into slavery. Unable to see the fruits of our decision, we stumble forward as children, blind to the consequences of our actions. As mutual trust of friends or spouses is broken by a single lie, so sin enters in by a single act, neither path having been conceived by the liar or sinner until consequences destroy him. Sadly, we all know this but all lie and sin. Thus, in trying to bring about a better life, we bring forth death which is the payment meted out by our master to us. In spite of our actions and consequences, following Christ fulfilled the law for us. We who are incapable of doing so would be saved by the law itself through an act of grace, in which an innocent life was offered up freely for those who were not innocent. Even though our bodies still war against us to obey the laws of carnality our spirit lives in Christ and through Christ because of His righteousness.

MAT 5:17 Think not that I am come to destroy the law, or the prophets: I am not come to destroy, but to fulfil. 18 For verily I say unto you, Till heaven and earth pass, one jot or one tittle shall in no wise pass from the law, till all be fulfilled.

The lowest carnality, which is pride and is the primal sin, is seen in the desire to "be good" as the law gives zeal to the unenlightened man.

PRO 13:10 *Only by pride cometh contention: but with the well advised is wisdom.*

PRO 16:18 *Pride goeth before destruction, and an haughty spirit before a fall.*

1JO 2:16 *For all that is in the world, the lust of the flesh, and the lust of the eyes, and the pride of life, is not of the Father, but is of the world.*

PHI 3:4 *Though I might also have confidence in the flesh. If any other man thinketh that he hath whereof he might trust in the flesh, I more: 5 Circumcised the eighth day, of the stock of Israel, of the tribe of Benjamin, an Hebrew of the Hebrews; as touching the law, a Pharisee; 6 Concerning zeal, persecuting the church; touching the righteousness which is in the law, blameless. 7 But what things were gain to me, those I counted loss for Christ. 8 Yea doubtless, and I count all things but loss for the excellency of the knowledge of Christ Jesus my Lord: for whom I have suffered the loss of all things, and do count them but dung, that I may win Christ, 9 And be found in him, not having mine own righteousness, which is of the law, but that which is through the faith of Christ, the righteousness which is of God by faith:*

In pursuit of the letter of the law the foundation and reason of the law is lost beneath man's self-righteousness. The foundation and reason of the law was always love. Love of God and love of one's fellow man is the whole of all law, as stated by Christ. It is also the only thing we cannot "do", since these are internal and attitudinal things springing from one's nature and not one's actions. How could our nature be changed? Man was given the law by God to force this question to be asked. God becomes the only answer due to man's inadequacies to change his own nature.

Instead of embracing this knowledge and admitting dependence on God, man turns a blind and prideful eye to the only law that matters and focuses on those items of action he can hope to obey. We tithe, go to church, pray before meals, work in the church, and dress according to church standards. We know all of the answers in Sunday school, exhibit a never fading smile, and can defend and explain our theology, but we do not have love in our hearts and the Spirit of the living God is not resident in us. This is form without substance; answers without understanding. It is modern Phariseeism.

1CO 13:3 And though I bestow all my goods to feed the poor, and though I give my body to be burned, and have not charity, it profiteth me nothing.

Spiritual pride is the most common form of sin in the church. It is all-pervasive and is a direct indication of the flesh rearing its ugly head as we insist action and law count more than grace and love. Men may be blind, but God is not. The spirit of the law, which is faith, humility, and love, will be judged as righteousness. So flesh, in an attempt to "do" and "act" zealously toward the keeping of the law, plunges man headlong into condemnation thinking, in his pride, man could keep that which is perfect. Man convinces himself of this but ignoring those areas he cannot control, such as his own heart, he focuses instead on an outward show of law and duty. But the law was made to show man his shortcomings and thus draw him back to Him who is perfect, the maker and keeper of the law.

LUK 18:11 The Pharisee stood and prayed thus with himself, God, I thank thee, that I am not as other men are, extortioners, unjust, adulterers, or even as this publican. 12 I fast twice in the week, I give tithes of all that I possess. 13 And the publican, standing afar off, would not lift up so much as his eyes unto heaven, but smote upon his breast, saying, God be merciful to me a sinner. 14 I tell you, this man went down to his house justified rather than the other: for every one that exalteth himself shall be abased; and he that humbleth himself shall be exalted.

It was pride in the angelic host that was the cause and root of sin. It was pride that was propagated into man and caused the downfall. It is pride that controls and blinds us.

ISA 14:11 Thy pomp is brought down to the grave, and the noise of thy viols: the worm is spread under thee, and the worms cover thee.12 How art thou fallen from heaven, O Lucifer, son of the morning! how art thou cut down to the ground, which didst weaken the nations!

GEN 2:25 And they were both naked, the man and his wife, and were not ashamed.3:1 Now the serpent was more subtle than any beast of the field which the LORD God had made. And he said unto the woman, Yea, hath God said, Ye shall not eat of every tree of the garden? 2 And the woman said unto the serpent, We may eat of the fruit of the trees of the garden: 3 But of the fruit of the tree which is in the midst of the garden, God hath said, Ye shall not eat of it, neither shall ye touch it, lest ye die. 4 And the serpent said unto the woman, Ye shall not surely die: 5 For God doth know that in the day ye eat thereof, then your eyes shall be opened, and ye shall be as gods, knowing good and evil. 6 And when the woman saw that the tree was good for food, and that it was pleasant to the eyes, and a tree to be desired to make one wise, she took of the fruit thereof, and did eat, and gave also unto her husband with her; and he did eat.

It continues to be pride that keeps us from seeing the truth of our own nature and existence. Pride and arrogance are grouped together with evil, although we may think evil is on a different and lower level, closer to Satan himself. These four, pride, arrogance, insolence, and evil arise from the same root and are manifestations of the same, all too common, human condition.

Pride causes hate, as we judge others to be somehow less or inferior. They same psychological rules of war follow us into our daily lives and then into our churches. We first dehumanize others. Then we demonize. Then we can justify hating them, and even killing them, all in the name of God.

"It should be made clear that in order to live a Christian life, any Christian must be able to discriminate and hate, because that's what the bible says."

Bernhard Kuiper

PRO 8:13 The fear of the LORD is to hate evil: pride, and arrogancy, and the evil way, and the froward mouth, do I hate.

The root and cause of all four arise from a self-centered viewpoint that takes no one else into consideration. They come from tunnel vision so narrow as to include only the person and his desires. This calls into question the nature of evil. Does evil have a reasoned intent to hurt, kill, and destroy or is there an egomaniacal innocence to evil? Could it be that complete evil is actually a blind selfishness? It is not that the evil man does not make evil plans, he does, but he seldom if ever takes his consequences or the feelings of others into consideration. Only his feelings matter to him. His thoughts and actions are based on fulfilling his own desires at the expense of all others. Feelings and welfare of others do not come into play, nor do they cross his mind. The nature of evil is a twisted, childish, innocent, self-centeredness. How strange and paradoxical; how appropriate Satan should take what was so much a part of him and then assist man in finding it in himself.

ISA 14:12 How art thou fallen from heaven, O Lucifer, son of the morning! how art thou cut down to the ground, which didst weaken the nations! 13 For thou hast said in thine heart, I will ascend into heaven, I will exalt my throne above the stars of God: I will sit also upon the mount of the congregation, in the sides of the north: 14 I will ascend above the heights of the clouds; I will be like the most High.

Truth, love, and mercy are found on the path to God. Putting others before oneself, feeling with and for others, seeking the will of God over our own, this is the path to God and to truth. Compassion and love give way to mercy and mercy is the essence of grace.

PSA 100:3 Know ye that the LORD he is God: it is he that hath made us, and not we ourselves; we are his people, and the sheep of his pasture. 4 Enter into his gates with thanksgiving, and into his courts with praise: be thankful unto him, and bless his name. 5 For the LORD is good; his mercy is everlasting; and his truth endureth to all generations.

PSA 25:10 All the paths of the LORD are mercy and truth unto such as keep his covenant and his testimonies. 11 For thy name's sake, O LORD, pardon mine iniquity; for it is great. 12 What man is he that feareth the LORD? him shall he teach in the way that he shall choose. 13 His soul shall dwell at ease; and his seed shall inherit the earth.

PSA 26:3 For thy loving kindness is before mine eyes: and I have walked in thy truth. 4 I have not sat with vain persons, neither will I go in with dissemblers. 5 I have hated the congregation of evildoers; and will not sit with the wicked.

PSA 31:5 Into thine hand I commit my spirit: thou hast redeemed me, O LORD God of truth.

PSA 85:10 Mercy and truth are met together; righteousness and peace have kissed each other. 11 Truth shall spring out of the earth; and righteousness shall look down from heaven.

PSA 100:5 For the LORD is good; his mercy is everlasting; and his truth endureth to all generations. 101:1 I will sing of mercy and judgment: unto thee, O LORD, will I sing.

What is the truth? Jesus Christ is truth.

JOH 1:14 And the Word was made flesh, and dwelt among us, (and we beheld his glory, the glory as of the only begotten of the Father,) full of grace and truth.

"People who want to share their religious views with you almost never want you to share yours with them." Dave Barry

So, what can we say about sin and pride? The most prideful people pray the loudest and announce their good deeds to the world. Those who read and quote their Bible the most are the same that judge and condemn. Those who taut their faith are the same ones proclaiming they can heal and deliver you – but their promises go unfulfilled. It must take more than mouthing words and memorizing passages to free the soul.

TRANSITIONS OF LOVE

"If I could just see him", I said, "I know I could have faith." "If I could only look into His eyes, I know I would love Him with all my heart." "If I could hear His sweet voice I would be His forever." So weak is the heart that we play these games of excuses with ourselves, explaining why we waiver in our faith or feeling. But, these excuses are worthless.

Three years they were together. Peter had seen Jesus almost every day for three years. He had seen Him walk on water. He had seen Him die and now Jesus sat in front of Peter talking to Him. The conversation was simple, but the Lord's words were carefully chosen. They cut to the point in one question. Before we explore the conversation we must hearken back to the meaning of the word "Agape'". Remember it is an unconditional love full of grace and completeness.

Agape' is the word for Godly love. It is charity, selfless love, giving without expectation. To love with one's whole heart unselfishly.

This is quite different from the other word for love used between them.

"Philo" is a brotherly love. It is fondness, friendship, and family type of love.

Let us look closely at the conversation between Peter and Jesus. Notice the root words of Philo and Agape' within the words chosen by each, Jesus and Peter.

JOH 21:14 This is now the third time that Jesus shewed himself to his disciples, after that he was risen from the dead. 15 So when they had dined, Jesus saith to Simon Peter, Simon, son of Jonas, lovest (agapas) thou me more than these? He saith unto him, Yea, Lord; thou knowest that I love (philo) thee. He saith unto him, Feed my lambs. 16 He saith to him again the second time, Simon, son of Jonas, lovest (agapas) thou me? He saith unto him, Yea, Lord; thou knowest that I love (philo) thee. He saith unto him, Feed my sheep. 17 He saith unto him the third time, Simon, son of Jonas, lovest (philis) thou me? Peter was grieved because he said unto him the third time, Lovest (philo) thou me? And he said unto him, Lord, thou knowest all things; thou knowest that I love (philo) thee. Jesus saith unto him, Feed my sheep.

Concentrating on the questions and answers only, the conversation takes on a startling contrast. Peter was attempting to answer the question to Jesus' satisfaction without lying, but his heart betrayed him.

Simon Peter, do you love me with all your heart?

Lord, you know I love you like a brother.

Simon, son of Jonas, do you love me with all your heart?

Lord, you know I love you like a brother.

Simon Peter, son of Jonas, do you love me like a brother?

Yes, Lord, you know I love you like a brother.

Peter, having lived with God, seen Him die for his sins, and now looking into the face of the resurrected Lord, can only admit fondness. What fools we are to think we could do better. But there is hope! The comforter, the Holy Spirit descended at Pentecost and the church was born, but so were the hearts of man. Now able to live and move and have our being with the Spirit of the living God within us, our hearts are converted.

1PE 1:7 That the trial of your faith, being much more precious than of gold that perisheth, though it be tried with fire, might be found unto praise and honour and glory at the appearing of Jesus Christ: 8 Whom having not seen, ye love (agapate'); in whom, though now ye see him not, yet believing, ye rejoice with joy unspeakable and full of glory: 9 Receiving the end of your faith, even the salvation of your souls.

1PE 4:8 And above all things have fervent charity (agapin) among yourselves: for charity (agapin) shall cover the multitude of sins.

Peter, being changed through the power of the spirit of God living within him, was brought to a state of love so deep and profound that at the time of his death he requested to be crucified upside-down, not being worthy to even die as Jesus died. Such a glorious change will happen to us also, not being contingent upon seeing Him except in spirit. The change is forged by His spirit in us.

Is this true? Really? It was for Peter, but not for most of us. Why? It seems obvious that the "Baptism in the Holy Spirit" preached by "Pentecostal" churches such as the Church of God, Assembles of God, Holiness, and Full Gospel churches has little to no affect on believers. There are no appreciable differences in rates of divorce, domestic violence, and other such crimes. The experience does not seem to curb our selfish responses at all. The "event" impartes no power or special ability to resist sin or heal the sick. Why then did Peter show such a marked change?

The modern church's idea of the "Baptism of the Holy Spirit" is incorrect. It is not formulaic. A person cannot walk down an aisle, pronounce a certain prayer, and have hands laid on them by others equally misinformed people in order to receive from God a specific gift in planned spontaneity. One cannot stand and demand from God some action or gift. God is likely not intimidated or coerced easily. The church is playing a dangerous game in an attempt to fool its members into believing they are receiving some gift or power through that church's doctrine and teaching. Pastors lead members into thinking the church and its members are special and receive special treatment from God.

It is not that this gift does not exist. It is simply that "this ain't it."

Peter did not have a Bible, at least not a New Testament. He had time with Jesus, and time to examine his own lapses, and he was spurred on to do the latter since he was looking into the resurrected face of the one he betrayed. This does not mean we can cure or clean ourselves. It points more to the fact that we have no idea how desperately bad and broken we are. Thus, we hold tightly to the idea that we are good enough to receive some gift, making pure grace null and void. Spiritual pride allows the delusion to continue. Everyone wants to be special and accepted. No one readily admits they were carried away by emotion and not by a spiritual experience.

If one wants to be reborn, they have only to die. If one wants to be remade, they have only to be broken. But most cannot die to self and few will endure the crushing weight of true spiritual prostration. Yet, in all of this and in spite of it, some do change, and in some there are gifts. Grace does abound beyond our foolish attempts to pretend to be holy.

Christians have always tended to transform the Christian Revelation into a Christian religion. Christianity is said to be a religion like any other or, conversely, some Christians try to show that it is a better religion than the others. People attempt to take possession of God. Theology claims to explain everything, including the being of God. People tend to transform Christianity into a religion because the Christian faith obviously places people in an extremely uncomfortable position - that of freedom guided only by love and all in the context of God's radical demand that we be holy. --Jacques Ellul

A PEOPLE IN ERROR

Why are you proud, dust and ashes?
The Tree of Life by St. Bonaventure

Fundamentalism isn't about religion. It's about power.
SALMAN RUSHDIE

Christianity as a specific doctrine was slain with Jesus, suddenly and utterly. He was hardly cold in his grave, or high in his heaven (as you please), before the apostles dragged the tradition of him down to the level of the thing it has remained ever since.
GEORGE BERNARD SHAW, preface to *Androcles and the Lion*

Any relationship based on an exchange of tangibles is only as stable as the desire for or supply of the tangibles. This includes salvation, heaven, and glory. It is in this simple statement the failure of "mundane" Christianity rests.

Devotion based on threat becomes servitude. The devotee, situated as an ox between the carrot of heaven and the goad of hell, is bound to fail, just as the ox will tire and fall. But, devotion springing from a heart of love is not indenturement but service, not blackmail but charity. It is not in seeking the rewards of Christ but in seeking the heart of Christ we find the answer. We must love without motive, and not let this aim itself become a motive. Love must spring from a pure heart. Even seeking a pure heart is a motive, which defeats the purpose of God flowing through us unimpeded by us. To approach the heart of God is to have God bring us to Him. Thus, we do nothing but become beggars, waiting for an act of grace. Rules, doctrine, heaven, and hell do not matter. Church law and opinion become dung. Our hearts cry out for the beloved. Only He matters. It is only Him we seek.

Each year the church loses thousands of souls. Men and women give up, become discouraged and turn their backs on the church. They become apostate all because of false expectations and teachings. Many understand the true path at the time of conversion. They experience the heart of God and are joyous in it, but soon they are drawn away from God and are made to listen to doctrine and church laws which have nothing to do with what they are experiencing. The flame dies as the heart dies when one lives too long away from the beloved. They desire to return to the beloved but the church can no longer show them the way, but only continue to preach moral lessons and church doctrine, which are as devoid of the life of God as the dried bones of a man's corpse.

This thing called Christianity is a heart condition. It is a relationship. It is a love affair. It is a mystical and circular relationship of "bringing forth". These are the three comings of Christ: His incarnation at the crowning of creation, the second coming when we invite Him into our hearts, and the third coming is when He comes in glory at the end of the age. God created man and then became man. Man submits to God and through God's salvation man brings forth the spirit of God into this world where it is shared with others. In time, those with whom we share will also welcome into themselves the Spirit of God where there will be love and communion and birth of the spirit of Christ on earth through them. What could be more intimate than to be made by God and have God birthed in you? What could be more personal than the same vows of marriage to love, honor, and obey said to a Holy and sacred spouse? He is a spouse who knows us because He made us. He knows us because we live in Him. He knows us because He lives within us.

We cannot know God through doctrine, although doctrine attempts in someway to describe, qualify, and quantify God's laws. This approach is much like using the laws in our legal system to describe our lifestyle of personal freedom here in the United States. The confusion arises from the use of the word "know". There are different levels or ways to "know". One can know about something or someone by reading a book. This is knowledge without application. One can know something or someone by experiencing it or them. In the experiencing of the thing there is a depth and understanding which comes with being in relationship with the person or thing.

Scripture gives us information and knowledge about God. It does not give us the experience of God, nor does Scripture give us a relationship with God. If it did then anyone who read the Bible would be enlightened. Doctrines are rules and laws derived from the interpretation of Scripture or assigned as a rule by a body governing a denomination. Doctrine comes about for two main reasons; to defend against a heresy, and to describe a difference between theological ideas. In the early days of the church, doctrine was used primarily to defend against ideas the founding fathers saw as antithetical to

Christianity. Some of the New Testament letters were written in part to correct errors in doctrine such as the idea that Jesus did not have a body of flesh. (See the Second Book of John, written around 95 A.D.) These are necessary to those who do not understand the idea of Christianity, thinking it is a religion and set of beliefs, or a group of people to be led. Christ himself reduced all doctrine to two phrases.

MAT 22:36 Master, which is the great commandment in the law? 37 Jesus said unto him, Thou shalt love the Lord thy God with all thy heart, and with all thy soul, and with all thy mind. 38 This is the first and great commandment. 39 And the second is like unto it, Thou shalt love thy neighbour as thyself. 40 On these two commandments hang all the law and the prophets. "

The meaning and implications are obvious. If we have the proper relationship with God and our fellow man we would not sin, assuming the we are consistent. Therein lies the problem.

This is, on the surface, too much to ask of our sinful nature. It does, however, show us the exact place doctrine plays, or should play, in our Christian lives. Even in knowing what is right and wrong, we choose to do what relieves our desires. Knowing the rules, laws, or doctrine does no good since it is beyond our power to consistently do what is right. We are doomed to fail, and knowing this He came to pay the debt for our failure. If we were capable of following the laws of God, Christ would not have had to come. But, Christ is the crown of humanity and would have come anyway so that He might glorify mankind, which was chosen by God.

Doctrine, in the first century, was used almost exclusively, to define relationships. The doctrine of the Apostles centered almost entirely on clarifying the proper relationship between God and Christ, Christ and believers, believers and non-believers, Christian and the state, as well as relationships between members. Christianity, as established by the founder, is a mystical and social Gospel.

The other use of doctrine today is to establish a framework of beliefs, which are used to distinguish one denomination from another. Most of us do not even know what our own denominations proclaim as doctrine. In the church which I attend, we have a wonderful Sunday school class and lively discussions ensue. Many of us were talking about the "priesthood of the believer". This is a concept that holds there is no difference between the ability of a priest or a layperson who is a Christian to approach God, pray, anoint, give communion, or lay on hands since the full price of sacrifice had been paid for all believers.

All agreed that anyone who belonged to Christ was a child of God and could ask the Father for any of these things. "Why is it then that the Book of Discipline tells us the only one who can bless the host is an ordained minister of this denomination?" After a moment of stunned silence I was asked to "show them in the book". I did so and the response was, "Well, no one believes everything that their denomination believes." That much is true. Denominations spring up as a result of the narrow-minded and tunnel vision tendencies of humankind. An idea or theological point is seized upon, usually to the exclusion of other balancing points. As it was with the views of predestination and foreknowledge, both of which have points and counterpoints in scripture, the full truth will not be known and cannot be comprehended until such time as our finite minds are made infinitely perfect.

Yet, these are but two of the divisive views over which stubborn people fight and part fellowship, all in the name of knowing God better. If we were to do away with such trivial notions and rest in His perfect mind we would find how much we cannot know and how little difference it makes to the final destination of loving Him. For Christians, not the religious, not the churchgoers, but for those who actively seek His heart and not their rules; doctrine, church tradition and laws serve little purpose at all. Many times it is a limitation and hindrance to the journey of reaching toward Him. Do we love God? Do we love the brethren? Let us go on from here.

Doctrine is like glass, you can see the truth through it but it separates you from the truth. Scripture is not God. Church tradition is not God. Doctrine serves as measuring rods by which we may see our shortcomings and inadequacies based on a system of beliefs held to be a standard. But the yardstick is likely to be held up as a measurement between members.

2TI 3:15 And that from a child thou hast known the holy scriptures, which are able to make thee wise unto salvation through faith which is in Christ Jesus. 16 All scripture is given by inspiration of God, and is profitable for doctrine, for reproof, for correction, for instruction in righteousness: 17 That the man of God may be perfect, throughly furnished unto all good works.

We may learn of Him through doctrine but that is not the same as knowing Him.

Only in a living, growing relationship can we EXPERIENCE God. This is the only way to KNOW Him. We must now go beyond doctrine into His heart so that we may form a relationship with Him. Doctrine and law become of no consequence when we are obedient to the one who is the source of righteousness. How can we go against God's law when we are obedient to and guided by the Spirit of God? Yet, should we say we would not sin? Our imperfect and unstable gaze would betray us. But the work of God in us will be seen as we revisit our sins less and less often over longer and longer intervals as He remakes us into His image. The use of doctrine should be limited to assuring we do not stray from this path.

It is because of man's unsteady and skewed gaze that the curse of denominations arose. The very idea that we could see God's entire picture at once, clearly, and in balance speaks to the egotism of man. Denomination can be defined as a focus or obsession on an idea or set of ideas to the point of the imbalance of the whole. Whether it is baptism by water, the faithfulness of God in the face of our faithlessness, the power of the clergy over the members, divorce, works verses grace, predestination verses foreknowledge, who can give communion, or the number of days the baptismal water should be kept, a church may split and denominations may arise over the dispute. Within the church, all denominations arose out of disputation over points of political control, doctrine, or interpretation of scripture, most of which are vain and meaningless. None of which would have happened if the love of God had overcome the love of selfish pride and the search for power.

To keep this kind of conflict from happening in our own hearts, let us put Christ first. Our theology will become simple and God centered as we turn away from the wisdom and opinions of man. Let us do as Paul said,

"For I determined not to know any thing among you, save Jesus Christ, and him crucified. And I was with you in weakness, and in fear, and in much trembling. And my speech and my preaching was not with enticing words of man's wisdom, but in demonstration of the Spirit and of power: That your faith should not stand in the wisdom of men, but in the power of God." 1CO 2:2 -5

HEB 5:13 For every one that useth milk is unskillful in the word of righteousness: for he is a babe. 14 But strong meat belongeth to them that are of full age, even those who by reason of use have their senses exercised to discern both good and evil. 6:1 Therefore leaving the principles of the doctrine of Christ, let us go on unto perfection; not laying again the foundation of repentance from dead works, and of faith toward God, 2 Of the doctrine of baptisms, and of laying on of hands, and of resurrection of the dead, and of eternal judgment. 3 And this will we do, if God permit.

This "perfection" (maturing) we seek is beyond the basic principles we have studied all of our lives. What we seek does not abide in words but in the act of loving Him. We must now put learning into action.

1JO 3:13 *Marvel not, my brethren, if the world hate you. 14 We know that we have passed from death unto life, because we love the brethren. He that loveth not his brother abideth in death. ...16 Hereby perceive we the love of God, because he laid down his life for us: and we ought to lay down our lives for the brethren....18 My little children, let us not love in word, neither in tongue; but in deed and in truth.*

ACTS 17:27 *That they should seek the Lord, if haply they might feel after him, and find him, though he be not far from every one of us: 28 For in him we live, and move, and have our being; as certain also of your own poets have said, For we are also his offspring.*

JOH 17:19 *And for their sakes I sanctify myself, that they also might be sanctified through the truth. 20 Neither pray I for these alone, but for them also which shall believe on me through their word; 21 That they all may be one; as thou, Father, art in me, and I in thee, that they also may be one in us: that the world may believe that thou hast sent me. 22 And the glory which thou gavest me I have given them; that they may be one, even as we are one: 23 I in them, and thou in me, that they may be made perfect in one; and that the world may know that thou hast sent me, and hast loved them, as thou hast loved me.*

ROM 8:9 *But ye are not in the flesh, but in the Spirit, if so be that the Spirit of God dwell in you. Now if any man have not the Spirit of Christ, he is none of his. 10 And if Christ be in you, the body is dead because of sin; but the Spirit is life because of righteousness. 11 But if the Spirit of him that raised up Jesus from the dead dwell in you, he that raised up Christ from the dead shall also quicken your mortal bodies by his Spirit that dwelleth in you.*

We have become justified by our faith in Jesus Christ, yet we still measure ourselves against the law. Salvation is not quid pro quo. We can never live up to the law. Why do we still strive to keep the law? If we keep the law because we believe it assures our salvation we are wrong. For all have sinned and fallen short, all have failed to keep the law, and all were doomed to die in sin. Then grace came to us all.

Christians seek to do the law. Most Christians still live as if they were under the law. Most struggle daily to do what God has said is impossible to do.

They become fatigued, defeated, or self-righteous in their struggle. Some become proud of their accomplishments in keeping the law. They convince themselves they have somehow come up to God's standards and are justified by their actions. These have not plumbed the depths of their lying and deceiving hearts. None are good but God. Most people realize the impossibility of fulfilling the law. They become beaten down by their own sin.

Yet, we are released from our sin through faith. Many lean to their memories of what they have accomplished for God. Preachers, pastors, and Sunday school teachers point to time and effort spent in ministry as if there were some payment with which to recompense God. It is like trading rags for gold. God will not allow us to settle on our lees. (In the making of wine the winemaker would pour the wine though cloth in order to strain it of the lees or sediment. The sediment or lees that was left would settle to the bottom of the jar. He would then pour off the clarified wine into another vessel and repeat the process again until the wine was pure. If the lees were to settle and the wine not be purified it would spoil and become rancid.) This is not to better our standing before God, but to better our state of being.

The error in understanding comes from the confusion between our "STATE" and our "STANDING". Our standing before God is one of righteousness. Our state is that of a wretched man. We stand blameless before God because Christ Jesus has fulfilled the law for us and died for us as the breaking of the law required from us. He released us from the law and any debt we have owed and would owe the law. Our state as human beings has not changed. We are still wretched sinners. It is our flesh and sinful nature, warring against the spirit, which causes our state to be different from our standing. These two, state and standing, cannot be confused. Jesus gives us our standing before God once and for all through His death on the cross. Our state is changed slowly as we are conformed into His image as the Spirit lives within us. We may work to better our state so that God may be more easily seen in us and that He may be glorified in the eyes of others.

MAT 5:16 Let your light so shine before men, that they may see your good works, and glorify your Father which is in heaven.

Do not think for one moment you can add a single atom to the work done by Christ to establish our standing before God. We have no need for law. Christ was the end of the law for us. If God is in us and we are in Him then the law has turned to love. We can be free to love and do what we will if the spirit of God guides us. Yet, being unstable creatures with deceptive hearts, we need the Holy Scriptures in order to check ourselves and avoid straying into error. We should not seek to be free of the law, nor should we seek to be bound by the law. We should go beyond this trap of law and seek only God and His will.

Our State is bound in Christ's death and God's forgiveness.

JOB 14:16 For now thou numberest my steps: dost thou not watch over my sin? 17 My transgression is sealed up in a bag, and thou sewest up mine iniquity.

EPH 1:10 That in the dispensation of the fullness of times he might gather together in one all things in Christ, both which are in heaven, and which are on earth; even in him: 11 In whom also we have obtained an inheritance, being predestinated according to the purpose of him who worketh all things after the counsel of his own will: 12 That we should be to the praise of his glory, who first trusted in Christ. 13 In whom ye also trusted, after that ye heard the word of truth, the gospel of your salvation: in whom also after that ye believed, ye were sealed with that Holy Spirit of promise, 14 Which is the earnest of our inheritance until the redemption of the purchased possession, unto the praise of his glory.

1JO 2:1 My little children, these things write I unto you, that ye sin not. And if any man sin, we have an advocate with the Father, Jesus Christ the righteous: 2 And he is the propitiation for our sins: and not for ours only, but also for the sins of the whole world.

In this dual existence of standing and state, man is kept safe from himself and his sinful nature, which he cannot control. Jesus keeps us as His own, having bought us with His life. We are His. The price for breaking God's spiritual law was paid. The fine was collected and the punishment meted out. Jesus paid it all and took the punishment for us. Our standing with God, our judge, is good once again and we are counted as righteous. Yet, the state of man at the point of salvation has not changed. He is the same in the natural or carnal sense as he was the moment before. From this point on the state of man will be altered by the spirit working in him and by his obedience to the spirit. It may happen in leaps of epiphany as he sees his errors and sinful ways or it may happen in long periods of maturing as God works to mold us into His image. This is not to say instantaneous healing does not occur. It certainly does, but it does not happen all the time and is in God's hands. Like epiphanies that remain, healings are not the rule, but through acts of grace, God sheds His love on us as He wills and as we allow.

Like a sculptor working in stone, the image God wishes to reveal in us is manifest by removing those pieces He does not want in us: pride, arrogance, lust, greed, and all of the other unwanted parts of sinful man. Our state, in time, should become more and more like our standing and like that of Adam before the fall wherein there is more obedience and friendship to God and less rebelliousness and sin. It may be argued that we have some say so in our state in that we can choose to do God's will or not. We may choose to follow the spirit's leadings or not. In this narrow and inadequate way we are culpable. The culpability only serves to enforce our need for a savior each time we choose to give in to our desires instead of His will.

1CO 6:12 All things are lawful unto me, but all things are not expedient: all things are lawful for me, but I will not be brought under the power of any. 13 Meats for the belly, and the belly for meats: but God shall destroy both it and them. Now the body is not for fornication, but for the Lord; and the Lord for the body. 14 And God hath both raised up the Lord, and will also raise up us by his own power. 15 Know ye not that your bodies are the members of Christ? shall I then take the members of Christ, and make them the members of a harlot? God forbid. 16 What? know ye not that he which is joined to a harlot is one body? for two, saith he, shall be one flesh. 17 But he that is joined unto the Lord is one spirit.

I am not preaching freedom from God, only freedom from the law. I am not espousing freedom to sin, but freedom from sin. If we believe Jesus saved us and wishes to husband our spirit, why then do we seek to lord over our own actions and thoughts? We cannot be holy. We cannot keep ourselves from sin. He must move in us to do these things. Thus, our energies should be spent in listening to Him and being guided by Him, not in seeking to keep ourselves under some private spiritual law. In our yielding to Him, we become servant and spouse to Him.

JOH 1:17 For the law was given by Moses, but grace and truth came by Jesus Christ.

ROM 2:11 For there is no respect of persons with God. 12 For as many as have sinned without law shall also perish without law: and as many as have sinned in the law shall be judged by the law; 13 For not the hearers of the law are just before God, but the doers of the law shall be justified. 14 For when the Gentiles, which have not the law, do by nature the things contained in the law, these, having not the law, are a law unto themselves:15 Which shew the work of the law written in their hearts, their conscience also bearing witness, and their thoughts the meanwhile accusing or else excusing one another; 16 In the day when God shall judge the secrets of men by Jesus Christ according to my gospel.

Righteousness is not the absence of unrighteousness. Just as a good man is not a man who simply does not steal or kill. The absence of evil does not make one good. It leaves one in a state of common conformity and lukewarm social acceptability. There must be an action or actions to bring someone from that which is not bad to that which is good. Man cannot change his state of unrighteousness since only one action can be performed which will bring him into a state of righteousness. This change of state is called justification. The act of justification is possible because of the act of redemption. To redeem something is to buy it. Christ paid our debt to God and thus bought our freedom from sin and its "fines". Christ bought us as one would buy a slave.

ROM 6:14 For sin shall not have dominion over you: for ye are not under the law, but under grace. 15 What then? shall we sin, because we are not under the law, but under grace? God forbid. 16 Know ye not, that to whom ye yield yourselves servants to obey, his servants ye are to whom ye obey; whether of sin unto death, or of obedience unto righteousness? 17 But God be thanked, that ye were the servants of sin, but ye have obeyed from the heart that form of doctrine which was delivered you. 18 Being then made free from sin, ye became the servants of righteousness.

So, we are bought when we accept His payment, His life for our sins. This act of paying for us is redemption. It is acquired through faith in the fact that Christ came in the flesh and died for this purpose. Following on the heels of redemption is justification. Christ is sinless and we, upon being redeemed by faith are also justified by faith being in Christ and therefore justified in Him for He is just and perfect. We are made righteous by being clothed in righteousness because we are clothed in Him. We are justified through faith in Christ, not by man's own righteousness, for there is no deed or deeds man could perform that would make him righteous in the sight of God.

Since sin and unrighteousness are the flowers that spring from the root of man's nature it seems obvious man would not have the power to love God and neighbor with any more consistence than his sinful nature could endure. Certainly, man could not love either more than himself. Knowing man cannot fulfill the inner law of love, God has created a path through which man can be redeemed by the love of another who has perfect love. It is Christ. He is our atonement, our redeemer, our justifier, our reconciler, our Lord, our King, our God. Man is reconciled to God once again and for the final time.

ROM 3:20 Therefore by the deeds of the law there shall no flesh be justified in his sight: for by the law is the knowledge of sin. 21 But now the righteousness of God without the law is manifested, being witnessed by the law and the prophets; 22 Even the righteousness of God which is by faith of Jesus Christ unto all and upon all them that believe: for there is no difference: 23 For all have sinned, and come short of the glory of God; 24 Being justified freely by his grace through the redemption that is in Christ Jesus:

ROM 3:28 Therefore we conclude that a man is justified by faith without the deeds of the law.

ROM 6:14 For sin shall not have dominion over you: for ye are not under the law, but under grace. 15 What then? shall we sin, because we are not under the law, but under grace? God forbid. 16 Know ye not, that to whom ye yield yourselves servants to obey, his servants ye are to whom ye obey; whether of sin unto death, or of obedience unto righteousness? 17 But God be thanked, that ye were the servants of sin, but ye have obeyed from the heart that form of doctrine which was delivered you. Being then made free from sin, ye became the servants of righteousness.

ROM 10:4 For Christ is the end of the law for righteousness to every one that believeth.

ROM 13:10 Love worketh no ill to his neighbour: therefore love is the fulfilling of the law.

1CO 15:55 O death, where is thy sting? O grave, where is thy victory? 56 The sting of death is sin; and the strength of sin is the law. 57 But thanks be to God, which giveth us the victory through our Lord Jesus Christ.

GAL 2:16 Knowing that a man is not justified by the works of the law, but by the faith of Jesus Christ, even we have believed in Jesus Christ, that we might be justified by the faith of Christ, and not by the works of the law: for by the works of the law shall no flesh be justified.

GAL 5:2 Behold, I Paul say unto you, that if ye be circumcised, Christ shall profit you nothing. 3 For I testify again to every man that is circumcised, that he is a debtor to do the whole law. 4 Christ is become of no effect unto you, whosoever of you are justified by the law; ye are fallen from grace. 5 For we through the Spirit wait for the hope of righteousness by faith. 6 For in Jesus Christ neither circumcision availeth any thing, nor uncircumcision; but faith which worketh by love.

ROM 3:23 For all have sinned, and come short of the glory of God; 24 Being justified freely by his grace through the redemption that is in Christ Jesus: 25 Whom God hath set forth to be a propitiation through faith in his blood, to declare his righteousness for the remission of sins that are past, through the forbearance of God; 26 To declare, I say, at this time his righteousness: that he might be just, and the justifier of him which believeth in Jesus. 27 Where is boasting then? It is excluded. By what law? of works? Nay: but by the law of faith. 28 Therefore we conclude that a man is justified by faith without the deeds of the law.

We all have roadmaps. They are usually torn or misfolded.

KEEPING IT SIMPLE

"An individual Christian may see fit to give up all sorts of things for special reasons - marriage, or meat, or beer, or cinema; but the moment he starts saying the things are bad in themselves, or looking down his nose at other people who do use them, he has taken the wrong turning."
C.S. Lewis

"Christianity supplies a Hell for the people who disagree with you and a Heaven for your friends"
Elbert Hubbard

As we strive for the balance between faith and knowledge, we tend to focus on knowledge or doctrine and what we believe within the world of our faith. It is important to know what we believe as Christians and it is important to be able to articulate and explain it. The point must not be lost, however, that all beliefs, and the doctrine that springs from them, come down to points of faith since even the Bible, its contents, and its inerrancy. If one believes these things, must be taken on faith. Since in the end all points of Christianity rest on faith, it seems reasonable to keep our points of doctrine simple and seek instead Him who sustains our faith. Not to sound too trite about this, but we should not sweat the small stuff, and most points of doctrine beyond the essentials are small or fine points. All points, even the larger ones, are only opinions of men based on scripture, which may or may not be translated or interpreted well.

What are the points of concern? What points should we sweat? To find out what the early church fathers, thought we could examine various Christian creeds. These are lists of basic and fundamental beliefs. Each creed was made up of statements of belief. These statements were considered points on which there must be agreement before someone could be accepted into the early church as a Christian. Departure from the basic points of faith was considered a heresy. Although the word "heresy" has taken on a tone we do not like to use today in our permissive society we should consider well the lines we should draw within our own lives beyond which beliefs or actions become unacceptable, lest we also slip into heresy.

The Nicene Creed

When the Council of Nicaea (A.D. 325) rejected the teaching of Arius, it expressed its position by adopting one of the current Eastern symbols and inserting into it some anti-Arian phrases, resulting in this creed. At the Council of Constantinople (A.D. 381) some minor changes were made, and it was reaffirmed at the Council of Chalcedon (A.D. 451). It is an essential part of the doctrine and liturgy of the Lutheran churches. Historically it has been used especially at Holy Communion on Sundays and major feasts (except when the Apostles' Creed is used as the Baptismal Creed).

We believe in one God,
the Father, the Almighty,
maker of heaven and earth,
of all that is, seen and unseen.
We believe in one Lord, Jesus Christ,
the only Son of God,
eternally begotten of the Father,
God from God, Light from Light,
true God from true God,
begotten, not made,
of one Being with the Father.
Through Him all things were made.
For us and for our salvation
He came down from heaven;
by the power of the Holy Spirit
He became incarnate from the Virgin Mary, and was made man.
For our sake He was crucified under Pontius Pilate;
He suffered death and was buried.
On the third day He rose again
in accordance with the Scriptures;
He ascended into heaven
and is seated at the right hand of the Father.
He will come again in glory to judge the living and the dead,

and His kingdom will have no end.
We believe in the Holy Spirit, the Lord, the giver of life,
who proceeds from the Father and the Son.
With the Father and the Son He is worshiped and glorified.
He has spoken through the Prophets.
We believe in one holy catholic and apostolic Church.
We acknowledge one baptism for the forgiveness of sins.
We look for the resurrection of the dead,
and the life of the world to come. Amen.

The Old Roman Creed

AS QUOTED BY TERTULLIAN (c. 200)

De Virginibus Velandis	Tertullian	De Praescriptione
Believing in one God Almighty, maker of the world,	We believe one only God	I believe in one God, maker of the world,
and His Son, Jesus Christ,	and the son of God Jesus Christ,	the Word, called His Son, Jesus Christ,
born of the Virgin Mary,	born of the Virgin,	by the Spirit and power of God the Father made flesh in Mary's womb, and born of her
crucified under Pontius Pilate,	Him suffered died, and buried,	fastened to a cross.
on the third day brought to life from the dead,	Brought back to life,	He rose the third day,
received in heaven,	taken again into heaven,	was caught up into heaven,
sitting now at the right hand of the Father,	sits at the right hand of the Father,	set at the right hand of the Father,

will come to judge the living and the dead	will come to judge the living and the dead	will come with glory to take the good into life eternal, and condemn the wicked to perpetual fire,
	who has sent from the Father the Holy Ghost.	sent the vicarious power of His Holy Spirit,
		to govern believers (In this passage articles 9 and 10 precede 8)
through resurrection of the flesh.		restoration of the flesh.

This table serves to show how incomplete the evidence provided is by mere quotations of the Creed, and how cautiously it must be dealt with. Had we possessed only the "De Virginibus Velandis", we might have said that the article concerning the Holy Ghost did not form part of Tertullian's Creed. Had the "De Virginibus Velandis" been destroyed, we should have declared that Tertullian knew nothing of the clause "suffered under Pontius Pilate". And so forth. While no explicit statement of this composition by the Apostles is forthcoming before the close of the fourth century, earlier Fathers such as Tertullian and St. Irenaeus insist that the "rule of faith" is part of the apostolic tradition. Tertullian in particular in his "De Praescriptione" insists that the rule was instituted by Christ and delivered to us by the apostles.

II. The Old Roman Creed

The Catechism of the Council of Trent apparently assumes the apostolic origin of our existing creed. Pointing to the old Roman form as a template, however that if the old Roman form had been held to be the inspired utterance of the Apostles, it would not have been modified too easily at pleasure of the local churches. In particular, it would never have been entirely supplanted by today's form. Printing them side-by-side best reveals the difference between the two:

Roman	Today
(1) I believe in God the Father Almighty;	(1) I believe in God the Father Almighty *Creator of Heaven and earth*
(2) And in Jesus Christ, His only Son, our Lord;	(2) And in Jesus Christ, His only Son, our Lord;
(3) Who was born of (de) the Holy Ghost and of (ex) the Virgin Mary;	(3) Who was *conceived* by the Holy Ghost, born of the Virgin Mary,
(4) Crucified under Pontius Pilate and buried;	(4) *Suffered* under Pontius Pilate, was crucified, *dead*, and buried;
(5) The third day He rose again from the dead,	(5) *He descended into hell*; the third day He rose again from the dead;
(6) He ascended into Heaven,	(6) He ascended into Heaven, sitteth at the right hand of God the Father *Almighty*;
(7) Sitteth at the right hand of the Father,	(7) From thence He shall come to judge the living and the dead.
(8) Whence He shall come to judge the living and the dead.	(8) *I believe* in the Holy Ghost,
(9) And in the Holy Ghost,	(9) The Holy *Catholic* Church, *the communion of saints*
(10) The Holy Church,	(10) The forgiveness of sins,
(11) The forgiveness of sins,	(11) The resurrection of the body, and
(12) The resurrection of the body.	(12) *life everlasting.*

Please note that the Roman form does not contain the clauses "Creator of heaven and earth", "descended into hell", "the communion of saints", "life everlasting", nor the words "conceived", "suffered", "died", and "Catholic". Many of these additions, but not quite all, were probably known to St. Jerome in Palestine (c. 380.--See Morin in Revue Benedictine, January, 1904) Further additions appear in the creeds of southern Gaul at the beginning of the next century, but Tertullian probably assumed its final shape in Rome itself some time before A.D. 700 (Burn, Introduction, 239; and Journal of Theology Studies, July, 1902). We are not certain as to the reasons leading to the changes, but it could be speculated that they were written as implicit defenses of heresies that were popular throughout the time of the alterations.

The Apostles' Creed

The Apostles' Creed, as we have it now, dates from the eighth century. However, it is a revision of the so-called Old Roman Creed, which was used in the West by the third century. Behind the Old Roman Creed, in turn, were variations, which had roots in the New Testament itself. While this creed does not come from the apostles, its roots are apostolic. It serves as a Baptismal symbol in that it describes the faith into which we are baptized and is used in the rites of Baptism and Affirmation of Baptism.

I believe in God, the Father almighty,
creator of heaven and earth.
I believe in Jesus Christ, His only Son, our Lord.
He was conceived by the power of the Holy Spirit
and born of the Virgin Mary.
He suffered under Pontius Pilate,
was crucified, died, and was buried.
He descended into hell.*
On the third day he rose again.
He ascended into heaven,
and is seated at the right hand of the Father.
He will come again to judge the living and the dead.
I believe in the Holy Spirit,
the holy catholic Church,
the communion of saints,
the forgiveness of sins,

the resurrection of the body,
and the life everlasting. Amen.

*or "He descended to the dead."

Text prepared by the International Consultation on English Texts (ICET) and the English Language Liturgical Consultation (ELLC). Reproduced by permission.

This exposition of the creed was made at the request of Laurentius, a Bishop whose see is unknown, but is conjectured by Fontanini, in his life of Rufinus, to have been Concordia, Rufinus' birthplace. Here is the English translation of the creed, which Rufinus was asked to make commentary on. The date of the writing was about 307 A.D.

I believe in God the Father Almighty, invisible and impassible. And in Jesus Christ, His only Son, our Lord; Who was born from the Holy Ghost, of the Virgin Mary; Was crucified under Pontius Pilate, and buried; He descended to hell; on the third day He rose again from the dead. He ascended to the heavens; He sitteth at the right hand of the Father; Thence He is to come to judge the quick and the dead. And in the Holy Ghost; The Holy Church. The remission of sins. The resurrection of this flesh.

The Chalcedonian Creed

The Chalcedonian Creed was adopted in the fifth century, at the Council of Chalcedon in 451, which is one of the seven Ecumenical councils accepted by Eastern Orthodox, Catholic, and many Protestant Christian churches.

We, then, following the holy Fathers, all with one consent, teach men to confess one and the same Son, our Lord Jesus Christ, the same perfect in Godhead and also perfect in manhood; truly God and truly man, of a reasonable [rational] soul and body; consubstantial [co-essential] with the Father according to the Godhead, and consubstantial with us according to the Manhood; in all things like unto us, without sin; begotten before all ages of the Father according to the Godhead, and in these latter days, for us and for our salvation, born of the Virgin Mary, the Mother of God, according to the Manhood; one and the same Christ, Son, Lord, only begotten, to be acknowledged in two natures, unconfusedly, unchangeably, indivisibly, inseparably; the distinction of natures being by no means taken away by the union, but rather the property of each nature being preserved, and concurring in one Person and one

Subsistence, not parted or divided into two persons, but one and the same Son, and only begotten, God the Word, the Lord Jesus Christ; as the prophets from the beginning [have declared] concerning Him, and the Lord Jesus Christ Himself has taught us, and the Creed of the holy Fathers has handed down to us.

The Athanasian Creed

This creed is of uncertain origin. It was supposedly prepared in the time of Athanasius, the great theologian of the fourth century, although it seems more likely that it dates from the fifth or sixth centuries and is Western in character. It assists the Church in combating two errors that undermined Bible teaching: the denial that God's Son and the Holy Spirit are of one being with the Father; the other a denial that Jesus Christ is true God and true man in one person. It declares that whoever rejects the doctrine of the Trinity and the doctrine of Christ is without the saving faith. Traditionally it is considered the "Trinitarian Creed" and read aloud in corporate worship on Trinity Sunday.

Whoever wants to be saved should above all cling to the catholic faith.
Whoever does not guard it whole and inviolable will doubtless perish eternally.
Now this is the catholic faith: We worship one God in Trinity and the Trinity in unity, neither confusing the persons nor dividing the divine being.
For the Father is one person, the Son is another, and the Spirit is still another.
But the deity of the Father, Son, and Holy Spirit is one, equal in glory, coeternal in majesty.

What the Father is, the Son is, and so is the Holy Spirit.
Uncreated is the Father; uncreated is the Son; uncreated is the Spirit.
The Father is infinite; the Son is infinite; the Holy Spirit is infinite.
Eternal is the Father; eternal is the Son; eternal is the Spirit:
And yet there are not three eternal beings, but one who is eternal;
as there are not three uncreated and unlimited beings, but one who is uncreated and unlimited.

Almighty is the Father; almighty is the Son; almighty is the Spirit:
And yet there are not three almighty beings, but one who is almighty.
Thus the Father is God; the Son is God; the Holy Spirit is God:
And yet there are not three gods, but one God.

Thus the Father is Lord; the Son is Lord; the Holy Spirit is Lord:
And yet there are not three lords, but one Lord.
As Christian truth compels us to acknowledge each distinct person as God and Lord, so catholic religion forbids us to say that there are three gods or lords.
The Father was neither made nor created nor begotten;
the Son was neither made nor created, but was alone begotten of the Father;
the Spirit was neither made nor created, but is proceeding from the Father and the Son.

Thus there is one Father, not three fathers; one Son, not three sons; one Holy Spirit, not three spirits.

And in this Trinity, no one is before or after, greater or less than the other;
but all three persons are in themselves, coeternal and coequal; and so we must worship the Trinity in unity and the one God in three persons.
Whoever wants to be saved should think thus about the Trinity.
It is necessary for eternal salvation that one also faithfully believes that our Lord Jesus Christ became flesh.

For this is the true faith that we believe and confess: That our Lord Jesus Christ, God's Son, is both God and man.

He is God, begotten before all worlds from the being of the Father, and He is man, born in the world from the being of his mother -- existing fully as God, and fully as man with a rational soul and a human body; equal to the Father in divinity, subordinate to the Father in humanity.

Although He is God and man, He is not divided, but is one Christ.
He is united because God has taken humanity into himself; He does not transform deity into humanity. He is completely one in the unity of his person, without confusing his natures. For as the rational soul and body are one person, so the one Christ is God and man.

He suffered death for our salvation.
He descended into hell and rose again from the dead.
He ascended into heaven and is seated at the right hand of the Father.
He will come again to judge the living and the dead.
At his coming all people shall rise bodily to give an account of their own deeds.

Those who have done good will enter eternal life,
those who have done evil will enter eternal fire.
This is the catholic faith.

One cannot be saved without believing this firmly and faithfully.

Text prepared by the International Consultation on English Texts (ICET) and the English Language Liturgical Consultation (ELLC). Reproduced by permission.

As seen in the examination of these creeds or statements of faith, there is a tendency to expand and change creeds to defend against and virtually close the doors to heresies that rear their heads throughout the existence of the creeds. Thus, just as doctrines spring into existence as an argument and defense against errors in the faith, so creeds change for the same purpose. This sprawl tends to be destructive for several reasons, not the least of which is expanding creeds take expanded time to understand and defend each area of belief. Man's ability to corrupt is endless and man's heresies are endless, thus, in time a creed could expand to become longer than the scripture itself. Expanding creeds take away from the other areas such as worship and prayer in our spiritual lives.

The simple answer to this is to understand if the Holy Spirit were guiding all of us we would be in one accord as a team under the same harness and reins. To worry about others and our defense against their errors is to weaken our own faith by spending less time with Him who guides us away from error. We cannot stop others from proceeding into error. We should never be too sure we are not the ones in error. We can only attempt to avoid error by fully understanding the few fast and hard beliefs held firm by Jesus and use them as guidelines to ensure ourselves a clear view and understanding of the Christian faith. Remember, the first and most basic doctrine define relationships between God, Christ, believers, non-believers, and government.

When it comes to doctrine, to those that believe, no explanation is necessary, but for those who do not believe, no explanation will suffice.

A COMMON CREED EXPLAINED

I believe in God, the Father almighty, creator of heaven and earth.

GEN 1:1 *In the beginning God created the heaven and the earth.*

GEN 2:4 *These are the generations of the heavens and of the earth when they were created, in the day that the LORD God made the earth and the heavens,*

I believe in Jesus Christ, his only Son, our Lord.

MAR 1:1 *The beginning of the gospel of Jesus Christ, the Son of God;*

LUK 2:11 *For unto you is born this day in the city of David a Saviour, which is Christ the Lord.*

He was conceived by the power of the Holy Spirit

MAT 1:18 *Now the birth of Jesus Christ was on this wise: When as his mother Mary was espoused to Joseph, before they came together, she was found with child of the Holy Ghost.*

And born of the Virgin Mary.

MAT 1:18 *Now the birth of Jesus Christ was on this wise: When as his mother Mary was espoused to Joseph, before they came together, she was found with child of the Holy Ghost.*

LUK 1:26 *And in the sixth month the angel Gabriel was sent from God unto a city of Galilee, named Nazareth, 27 To a virgin espoused to a man whose name was Joseph, of the house of David; and the virgin's name was Mary. 28 And the angel came in unto her, and said, Hail, thou that art highly favoured, the Lord is with thee: blessed art thou among women. 29 And when she saw him, she was troubled at his saying, and cast in her mind what manner of salutation this should be. 30 And the angel said unto her, Fear not, Mary: for thou hast found favour with God. 31 And, behold, thou shalt conceive in thy womb, and bring forth a son, and shalt call his name JESUS. 32 He shall be great, and shall be called the Son of the Highest: and the Lord God shall give unto him the throne of his father David:...*

He suffered under Pontius Pilate

MAT 27:1 *When the morning was come, all the chief priests and elders of the people took counsel against Jesus to put him to death: 2 And when they had bound him, they led him away, and delivered him to Pontius Pilate the governor.*

Was crucified, died, and was buried.

MAT 27:35 *And they crucified him, and parted his garments, casting lots: that it might be fulfilled which was spoken by the prophet, They parted my garments among them, and upon my vesture did they cast lots.*

MAT 27:50 *Jesus, when he had cried again with a loud voice, yielded up the ghost.*

MAT 27:57 *When the even was come, there came a rich man of Arimathaea, named Joseph, who also himself was Jesus' disciple: 58 He went to Pilate, and begged the body of Jesus. Then Pilate commanded the body to be delivered. 59 And when Joseph had taken the body, he wrapped it in a clean linen cloth, 60 And laid it in his own new tomb, which he had hewn out in the rock: and he rolled a great stone to the door of the sepulcher, and departed.*

He descended into hell.*   *or "He descended to the dead."

1PE 3:18 *For Christ also hath once suffered for sins, the just for the unjust, that he might bring us to God, being put to death in the flesh, but quickened by the Spirit: 19 By which also he went and preached unto the spirits in prison; 20 Which sometime were disobedient, when once the longsuffering of God waited in the days of Noah, while the ark was a preparing, wherein few, that is, eight souls were saved by water. 21 The like figure whereunto even baptism doth also now save us (not the putting away of the filth of the flesh, but the answer of a good conscience toward God,) by the resurrection of Jesus Christ:*

On the third day He rose again

LUK 24:6 *He is not here, but is risen: remember how he spake unto you when he was yet in Galilee, 7 Saying, The Son of man must be delivered into the hands of sinful men, and be crucified, and the third day rise again. 8 And they remembered his* words, 9 And returned from the sepulcher, and told all these things unto the eleven, and to all the rest.

He ascended into heaven

EPH 4:7 *But unto every one of us is given grace according to the measure of the gift of Christ. 8 Wherefore he saith, When he ascended up on high, he led captivity captive, and gave gifts unto men. 9 Now that he ascended, what is it but that he also descended first into the lower parts of the earth? 10 He that descended is the same also that ascended up far above all heavens, that he might fill all things.*

And is seated at the right hand of the Father

1 PE 3:22 *Who is gone into heaven, and is on the right hand of God; angels and authorities and powers being made subject unto him.*

He will come again to judge the living and the dead

ACT 17:30 *And the times of this ignorance God winked at; but now commandeth all men every where to repent: 31 Because he hath appointed a day, in the which he will judge the world in righteousness by that man whom he hath ordained; whereof he hath given assurance unto all men, in that he hath raised him from the dead.*

ROM 2:16 *In the day when God shall judge the secrets of men by Jesus Christ according to my gospel.*

ROM 14:10 *But why dost thou judge thy brother? Or why dost thou set at naught thy brother? for we shall all stand before the judgment seat of Christ. 11 For it is written, As I live, saith the Lord, every knee shall bow to me, and every tongue shall confess to God. 12 So then every one of us shall give account of himself to God.*

2TI 4:1 *I charge thee therefore before God, and the Lord Jesus Christ, who shall judge the quick and the dead at his appearing and his kingdom; 2 Preach the word; be instant in season, out of season; reprove, rebuke, exhort with all longsuffering and doctrine.*

I believe in the Holy Spirit

LUK 11:13 If ye then, being evil, know how to give good gifts unto your children: how much more shall your heavenly Father give the Holy Spirit to them that ask him?

The holy catholic (universal) Church

MAT 16:18 And I say also unto thee, That thou art Peter, and upon this rock I will build my church; and the gates of hell shall not prevail against it.

ACT 11:26 And when he had found him, he brought him unto Antioch. And it came to pass, that a whole year they assembled themselves with the church, and taught much people. And the disciples were called Christians first in Antioch.

1CO 1:2 Unto the church of God which is at Corinth, to them that are sanctified in Christ Jesus, called to be saints, with all that in every place call upon the name of Jesus Christ our Lord, both theirs and ours: 3 Grace be unto you, and peace, from God our Father, and from the Lord Jesus Christ.

The communion of saints

HEB 10:23 Let us hold fast the profession of our faith without wavering; for he is faithful that promised; 24 And let us consider one another to provoke unto love and to good works: 25 Not forsaking the assembling of ourselves together, as the manner of some is; but exhorting one another: and so much the more, as ye see the day approaching.

ACT 14:27 And when they were come, and had gathered the church together, they rehearsed all that God had done with them, and how he had opened the door of faith unto the Gentiles.

1CO 10:16 The cup of blessing which we bless, is it not the communion of the blood of Christ? The bread which we break, is it not the communion of the body of Christ? 17 For we being many are one bread, and one body: for we are all partakers of that one bread.

The forgiveness of sins

ACT 13:38 Be it known unto you therefore, men and brethren, that through this man is preached unto you the forgiveness of sins:

ACT 26:18 To open their eyes, and to turn them from darkness to light, and from the power of Satan unto God, that they may receive forgiveness of sins, and inheritance among them which are sanctified by faith that is in me.

EPH 1:7 In whom we have redemption through his blood, the forgiveness of sins, according to the riches of his grace;

The resurrection of the body

PHI 3:10 That I may know him, and the power of his resurrection, and the fellowship of his sufferings, being made conformable unto his death; 11 If by any means I might attain unto the resurrection of the dead.

1PE 1:3 Blessed be the God and Father of our Lord Jesus Christ, which according to his abundant mercy hath begotten us again unto a lively hope by the resurrection of Jesus Christ from the dead, 4 To an inheritance incorruptible, and undefiled, and that fadeth not away, reserved in heaven for you, 5 Who are kept by the power of God through faith unto salvation ready to be revealed in the last time.

And the life everlasting. Amen.

JOH 3:16 For God so loved the world, that he gave his only begotten Son, that whosoever believeth in him should not perish, but have everlasting life.

Do we need a creed to know God? No. Most new Christians do not know a creed but have hearts open to God. That is the secret of joy. Not a creed, but a heart of gratitude, open and joyous in God.

THE TRINITY

The Trinity, the doctrine that many hold so dear, is never mentioned in the Bible, and was not discussed nor considered by the early church. The doctrine was crafted in a political effort to unite the church in order that it might be more easily ruled and controlled.

Adolf von Harnack (May 7, 1851–June 10, 1930), a German theologian and prominent church historian affirms that the early church view of Jesus was as Messiah, and after his resurrection he was 'raised to the right hand of God' but not considered as God. (See Mark 16:19). This was the baseline view by the church in the first century. From this point of view, an evolution of infiltration began that would culminate in the doctrine of the trinity.

Bernard Lonergan, a Roman Catholic priest and Bible scholar, explains that the educated Christians of the early centuries believed in a single, supreme God. This was the same basic view as held by the Jewish believers of the time.

As for the Holy Spirit, McGiffert tells us that early Christians considered the Holy Spirit "not as a separate entity, but simply as the divine power, working in the world and particularly in the church". It is the power or will of God working in the world.

Durant articulated the evolution of early Christianity when he said: "In Christ and Peter, Christianity was Jewish; in Paul it became half Greek; in Catholicism it became half Roman" (Caesar 579).

The Christian church has always been in turmoil. In the days of the Apostles the church was far from unified. Throughout his book "Orthodoxy and Heresy in Earliest Christianity", the German New Testament scholar, and early Church historian, Walter Bauer, explores the fact that Gnosticism influenced many early Christians forming heresies here and there throughout the budding Christendom. In his work 'The Greek Fathers", James Marshall Campbell, a Greek professor, explains that the fear of Gnosticism was prevalent in the early church. Sects of Gnosticism varied in their Greek influence but the seeds were primarily of Greek origin and carried within it the mythos and theosophy of Plato and the Greeks that divided the universe into opposing realms of matter and spirit. In this world-view the body was a prison for the captive spirit like that of the "iron maiden" torture device of years to come.

The late Professor Arthur Cushman McGiffert interprets some of the early Christian fathers as believing Gnosticism to be "identical to" in all intents and purposes with Greek polytheism. Gnosticism had a mixed influence on the early Christian writers, sending them in various directions in their Christology. That these philosophies of the Greek, Romans, and Gnostics affected Christianity is a historical fact.

What did these philosophers teach about God? In Plato's Timeus, 'The Supreme Reality appears in the trinitarian form of the Good, the Intelligence, and the World-Soul'. Laing attributes elaborate trinitarian theories to the Neoplatonists, and considers Neoplatonic ideas as 'one of the operative factors in the development of Christian theology'. One of the questions posed in the book is simply, " What is real in Christianity." What would Christianity be if we were to find and eliminate most outside influences?

Durant ties in philosophy with Christianity when he states that the second century Alexandrian Church, from which both Clement and Origen came, 'wedded Christianity to Greek philosophy'; and finally, Durant writes of the famed pagan philosopher, Plotinus, that 'Christianity accepted nearly every line of him...'

As the apostles died, various writers undertook the task of defending Christianity against the persecutions of the pagans. The problem was that they were so tainted due to education and environment that some of the defenders did more harm than good.

The most famous of these Apologists was Justin Martyr (c.107-166). He was born a pagan, became a pagan philosopher, then a Christian. He believed that Christianity and Greek philosophy were related. As for the Trinity, McGiffert asserts, "Justin insisted that Christ came from God; he did not identify him with God". Justin's God was "a transcendent being, who could not possibly come into contact with the world of men and things". The Church was divided by Gnosticism, enticed by philosophy, and corrupted by paganism, but there were geographic divisions also, with East and West differing greatly.

As a reminder, sects of Gnosticism were differing combinations of Christianity and the Greek teachings, most centering around those of Plato. To the Gnostic Christians the material world and the spiritual world were very much at odds and could not coexist. Due to the increasing influence of Platoism and Gnosticism, the relationship between spirit and flesh as viewed by the church was shifting quickly. The body, once viewed as the vehicle and temple of the spirit and inseparable from it, was now viewed as a flesh prison for the spirit and opposed in nature to it. These views would turn the dancing and joyous Jewish celebration of life into repression and sorrow.

Changes would echo through time in various forms, ending in the stoicism of the sexual abstinence of priests and finally the self-flagellation of some monks. (Self-flagellation seems to have taken root in the dark ages during the plague when monks thought it would appease God if they punished themselves by beating themselves with whips.) In the early church the changes would be seen in the struggle to articulate the relationship between the various forms of the newly emerging Godhead. The Father was a spirit. The Holy Ghost was obviously a spirit, since it was the will of God who was pure spirit. It was the existence of Jesus and His position and state within the spiritual and material worlds that gives pause within the various sects of the early church.

The Eastern Church, centered in Alexandria, Egypt, and the Western Church, centered in Rome, Italy, grew in divergence. The Eastern Church was inquisitive and had an environment of free thought as a reflection of the surrounding Greek culture. The theological development of the East is best represented in Clement and Origen.

Clement of Alexandria (c.150-220) was trained in the "Catechetical School of Alexandria," a place of training for Christian theologians and priests. Even though Clement was trained here, his views were influenced by Gnosticism. If one were to wish for a single focused statement explaining the Greek influence on the Christian Church, it would likely be the following by McGiffert; "Clement insists that philosophy came from God and was given to the Greeks as a schoolmaster to bring them to Christ as the law was a schoolmaster for the Hebrews". McGiffert further states that Clement considered "God the Father revealed in the Old Testament" separate and distinct from the "Son of God incarnate in Christ," with whom he identified the Logos.

Campbell continues this line of explanation when he says; "[with Clement the] philosophic spirit enters frankly into the service of Christian doctrine, and with it begins... the theological science of the future". However, it was his student, Origen, who "achieved the union of Greek philosophy and Christianity".

To sum up this bit of church history; Clement believed that just as the law was given to the Jews as a schoolmaster to bring them into the understanding that they needed a savior, philosophy was given to the Greeks to enable them to bring reason and a scientific approach to Christianity to establish its theology.

Campbell considered Origen (c.185-253) to be the founder of theology", the greatest scholar of the early church and the greatest theologian of the East. Durant adds that "with [Origen] Christianity ceased to be only a comforting faith; it became a full-fledged philosophy, buttressed with scripture but proudly resting on reason". However, the reason it rested on was directed and disciplined by the Greek style and content of thought. This is why in Origen the church experiences a changing view of God.

According to Pelikan"s Historical Theology, Origen was the "teacher of such orthodox stalwarts as the Cappadocian Father's, (Cappadocian was an area stretching from Mount Taurus to the Black Sea), but also the "teacher of Arius' and the "originator of many heresies"." Centuries after his death, he was condemned by councils at least five times; however, both Athanasius and Eusebius had great respect for him.

Origen turned his attention to the trinity, beginning with what he called the "incomprehensible God." He applied Stoic and Platonic philosophies in true Greek style. Origen believed the Father and Son were separate "in respect of hypostasis" (substance), but "one by harmony and concord and identity of will". If we stop at this point and poll members of most major denominations we are likely to find this to be the understanding of the majority, for how can a God who is pure spirit be of the same substance as Jesus, who is flesh and blood? Origen then went on to claim the Son was the image of God, probably drawing on the scripture where Christ proclaimed, "If you have seen me you have seen the father." In this he seems to contradict himself, anthropomorphizing to the point of endowing God with the limits of a human body made of a substance differing from that of which Jesus was made.

Keeping in mind that Gnosticism, as well as certain Greek philosophies, tend to divide the universe into realms of the spiritual and material, Origen, seeing those realms in opposition, maintained that there was a difference between "the God" and "God." He attempted to explained that "the God" [God himself] was a unity to himself and not associated with the world but, "Whatever else, other than him who is called is also God, is deified by participation, by sharing in his divinity, and is more properly to be called not "the God" but simply "God"" (Quotes are mine for clarification.) With such theological hair-splitting we enter into confusion and error.

As Origen and others introduced more and more Greek influences into the Eastern Church, it became more mystical, philosophical, and at times obtuse. This line of thought brought us from the Jewish proclamation of, Deuteronomy 6:4 "Hear, O Israel: The LORD our God, the LORD is one" and placed us into the first stage of the trinity by dividing God in twain. The simple and direct teaching of Christ to love God and treat others with dignity gave way to the complex, sophisticated, and often convoluted arguments as men found their self-importance in their ability to divide, and persuade.

It was Tertullian (c.160-230) who first coined the term trinitas from which we derive our English word "trinity". Tertullian writes, "...the unity makes a trinity, placing the three in order not of quality but of sequence, different not in substance but in aspect, not in power but in manifestation". Tertullian did not consider the Father and Son co-eternal. He considered God the creator of all. God must, therefore, pre-date everything that exists, even the first creative impulse, which would have created the pre-incarnate Christ. To clarify his belief Tertullian wrote, "There was a time when there was neither sin to make God a judge, nor a son to make God a Father". Tertullian also rejected the idea of God and Christ being co-equal. He reasoned that God was and contains everything, thus the Son cannot contain everything. He explains, "For the Father is the whole substance, whereas the Son is something derived from it". Another way to see his point is to say that all things are contained in or are part of God, thus Christ is in or part of God. The fullness of God could not be physically contained in Christ. (This statement flew in the face of Col. 2:9, which states that the fullness of the deity lives in Christ.) The idea of Trinitas is the beginning of the Trinitarian discussion in earnest, but it will take time to grow and develop into the full doctrine of the Trinity established under the political pressure of Constantine.

The world around the early Church was changing. The Roman Empire began to crumble and Constantine came to power. He wished to unify the Empire, and although he was a pagan, living in a society of polytheists, he chose Christianity, as a vehicle to work his will. What better way to unite a nation than through the growing monotheistic faith? But Christianity was far from unified; so to unify the empire the king had to unify the faith.

In 318 A.D., controversy over the matter of the Trinity had blown up again between Arius, a deacon, and Alexander, the bishop of the church in Alexandria, Egypt. Bishop Alexander of Alexandria and his deacon, Athanasius, believed there were three persons in one god.

This time Emperor Constantine involved himself. The emperor began to send letters encouraging them to put aside what the emperor called their "trivial" disputes regarding the nature of God and the "number" of God. As a polytheist, the emperor saw the argument over the semantics of whether one worshipped a single god, three gods or "three gods in one" as trivial and inconsequential. Arius, Presbyter in Alexandria, and Eusebius, Bishop of Nicomedia believed in only one indivisible god. According to the concept of homo-ousion, Christ the Son was consubstantial, that is to say the Son shares the same substance with the Father. Arius and Eusebius disagreed. Arius thought the Father, Son, and Holy Spirit were materially separate and different. He believed that the Father created the Son. Arius and his followers, the Arians, believed if the Son were equal to the Father, there would be more than one God. If one were to sum up the heart of the matter within the debate, it would be over the status of the Son as compared to the Father.

To exemplify the points of contention, an essay by Wright regarding Arius reports; "Arius was a senior presbyter in charge of Baucalis, one of the twelve "parishes" of Alexandria. He was a persuasive preacher, with a following of clergy and ascetics, and even circulated his teaching in popular verse and songs. Around 318 A.D., he clashed with Bishop Alexander. Arius claimed that Father alone was really God; the Son was essentially different from his father. He did not possess by nature or right any of the divine qualities of immortality, sovereignty, perfect wisdom, goodness, and purity. He did not exist before he was begotten by the father. The father produced him as a creature. Yet as the creator of the rest of creation, the son existed "apart from time before all things". Nevertheless, he did not share in the being of God the Father and did not know him perfectly. Wright concludes that before the 3rd century the "three were separate in Christian belief and each had his or it's own status."

The dispute became louder and more strident until it spilled over once again into the Christian community, causing division and controversy within the church body. The emperor's plan to unify the faith in order to unify the nation was being placed in jeopardy. In 325 A.D. the church faced two serious points of strife. The date of observance of the Passover on Easter Sunday had become an issue, and the concept of the Trinity was in full debate. Serious questions were being raised as to whether the church would remain intact. Letters from Constantine failed to settle the dispute, so the emperor called the "Council of Nicea."

Constantine chose leaders, which would represent each major division within the church and invited these bishops to join him in the seaside village of Nicea. There they formed a council, which Constantine hoped could unify the church. McGiffert tells us about the council. There were three main groups represented at this council: Eusebius of Nicomedia, who represented the Arian view of the Trinity, Alexander of Alexandria presenting the Athanasian version, and a very large party led by Eusebius of Cesarea. The Cesarea contingent was made up of those who wanted unity and peace. Their theological stance was not one so immovable and intractable that it would interfere with their desire for peace. It should be noted that Alexander of Alexandria was the bishop who was involved in the "discussion" with Arius, which began the final fray. He was so self-assured that he would not move on his idea of the Trinity. It is amazing that any man could be so self-assured about his knowledge of the mind and substance of God. It is presumption.

There is a general rule of negotiations. If you are sitting at the table with your enemies, the one who moves first loses. The moment a line is drawn or a position is articulated, it sets a limit on the discussion. If the 'negotiation is about price, the price stated would serve only as a limit from which to work. It was the mistake of Eusebius of Nicomedia to submit the Arian creed first. This served only to set a stage from which the other groups could spring. Their creed was summarily rejected. Then the more amicable of Eusebius of Cesarea submitted their creed, known as the Cesarean baptismal creed. Now the Alexandrian group knew where both parties stood. They would use this information to institute a brilliant political maneuver. Instead of submitting a creed of their own, the Alexandrian group modified the creed from Eusebius. The changes were not substantial enough to change the deeper intent of the creed. Eusebius was compelled to sign the creed. Now two of the three parties were united and the Arians were out of the negotiations. The majority of Eastern bishops sided with Arius in that they believed Christ was the Son of God 'neither consubstantial nor co-eternal' with his Father, but it no longer mattered.

Constantine saw well over two-thirds of the church in one accord, at least on paper. He now began to pressure all bishops to sign. Arians refusing to sign were exiled. Constantine exiled the excommunicated Arius to Illyria. Constantine's friend Eusebius, who eventually withdrew his objection, but still wouldn't sign the statement of faith, and a neighboring bishop, Theognis, were also exiled to Gaul. Constantine would reverse his opinion about the Arian heresy, and have both exiled bishops reinstated three years later, in 328 A.D. At the same time, Arius would also be recalled from exile; but for now, it was political blackmail.

The pressure from the emperor was so great and his reactions so feared that attendees justified their signatures thusly; Apuleius, wrote "I pass over in silence… those sublime and Platonic doctrines understood by very few of the pious, and absolutely unknown to every one of the profane." "the soul is nothing worse for a little ink."

Abu Al-Hassan Al-Nadwi reported that out of the 2030 attendees, only 318 readily accepted this creed ("Al-Seerah Al-Nabawiyya", p. 306). Only after returning home did other attendees such as Eusebius of Nicomedia, Maris of Chaledon and Theognis of Nicaea summon the courage to express to Constantine in writing how much they regretted having put their signatures to the Nicene formula, "We committed an impious act, O Prince," wrote Eusebius of Nicomedia, "by subscribing to a blasphemy from fear of you."

Thus Constantine had his unified Church, which was not very unified. McGiffert asserts that Eusebius of Cesarea was not altogether satisfied with the creed because it was too close to Sabellianism (Father, Son, and Holy Spirit are three aspects of one God). Lonergan shows just how much of the creed Eusebius took exception to as the words were explained. "Out of the Father's substance" was now interpreted to show that the Son is "out of the Father", but "not part of the Father's substance." "Born not made" because "made" refers to all other creatures "which come into being through the Son", and "consubstantial" really means that the Son comes out of the Father and is like him.

Lonergan goes on to explain that the language of debate on the consubstantiality of the Father and the Son has made many people think that the "Church at Nicea had abandoned the genuine Christian doctrine, which was religious through and through, in order to embrace some sort of hellenistic ontology". Nicene dogma marked the "transition from the prophetic Oracle of Yahweh... to Catholic dogma".

The evolution of the Trinity can be seen in the words of the Apostles' Creed, Nicene Creed, and the Athanasian Creed. As each of the creeds became more wordy and convoluted, the simple, pure faith of the Apostolic church became lost in a haze. Even more interesting is the fact that as the creeds became more specific (and less scriptural) the adherence to them became stricter, and the penalty for disbelief harsher.

In stark contrast, is the simple oneness of the Hebrew God. After the Council of Chalcedon in 451, debate was no longer tolerated and those opposing the Trinity were considered to commit blasphemy. Sentences ranged from mutilation to death. Christians now turned on Christians, maiming and slaughtering thousands because of this difference of belief.

The reign of Constantine marks the time of the transformation of Christianity from a religion into a political system; and though, in one sense, that system was degraded, in another it had risen above the old Greek mythology. The maxim holds true in the social as well as in the mechanical world, that, when two bodies strike, the form of both is changed. Paganism was modified by Christianity; Christianity by Paganism. In the Trinitarian controversy, the chief point in discussion was to define the position of "the Son."

After the divisions regarding the Trinity had subsided, the church continued to narrow its tolerance and tighten its grip.

Creeds and, to a degree religions, are based on exclusivity. They seek to exclude all who do not conform to a certain set of beliefs. All others are excluded and usually punished, shunned, condemned, or killed. As people in power are inclined to do, the fist of control tightens over time. In following this pattern, creeds tend to get longer, more specific, and thus more exclusive. Points of little concern in one creed become of greater importance in the next creed, as we tend to increasingly choke on gnats.

What are the points of concern? What points should we sweat? To find out what the early church fathers thought, we could examine various Christian creeds. These are lists of basic and fundamental beliefs. Each creed was made up of statements of belief. These statements were considered points on which there must be agreement before someone could be accepted into the early church as a Christian. Departure from the basic points of faith was considered a heresy. Although the word "heresy" has taken on a tone we do not like to use today in our permissive society we should consider well the lines we should draw within our own lives beyond which beliefs or actions become unacceptable, lest we also slip into heresy.

As seen in the examination of these creeds or statements of faith, there is a tendency to expand and change creeds to defend against and virtually close the doors to all things viewed as heresies that rear their heads throughout the existence of the creeds. Thus, just as doctrines spring into existence as an argument and defense against errors in the faith, so creeds change for the same purpose. This sprawl tends to be destructive for several reasons, not the least of which is expanding creeds take expanded time to understand and defend each area of belief. Man's ability to corrupt is endless and man's heresies are endless, man's ability to tolerate individual thought is miniscule. We are charged to work out our own salvation with fear and trembling. Our ability to do this is dependant on the church to allow free thought. The heresy of free thought is seldom allowed.

When it comes to doctrine, to those that believe, no explanation is necessary, but for those who do not believe, no explanation will suffice.

To keep our eyes on the ball, the major questions need to be asked again. For what purpose was the Bible written? How should we interpret the Bible? Should the Bible be read as the literal word of God? Is the Bible inerrant, or is it a group of books written by men. How should we approach the Bible in order to glean insight and not overreach the original intent of the writers?

Virgin Birth

HUMAN PATHENOGENESIS

Christians celebrate the birth of a human baby to his mother, a young virgin named Mary. Is this scientifically possible? We know that wasps, fish, birds, and lizards can produce healthy offspring asexually, but what about people? Are virgin births possible without medical intervention?

Yes, but the chances are over a billion to one. I would call that a miracle.

Spontaneous asexual reproduction, which can occur to a human virgin, is called parthenogenesis. In cases of parthenogenesis (virgin birth), an ovum, or egg, starts to divide by itself without fertilization, producing an embryo.

Because there is no source of paternal chromosomes, duplication of maternal ones would be the only way to fill the needed number of chromosomes for the embryo. This asexual reproductive method is common among invertebrates but as we go up the evolutionary scale this ability declines. It becomes very rare among warm-blooded vertebrates. Certain conditions such as illness, pathogens, and external stimuli can produce pathological parthenogenesis, which has been observed in higher animals, such as the frog, fowl, and certain mammals, but this type of parthenogenesis usually gives rise to female offspring or sometimes an abnormal male.

In 1900 Jacques Loeb accomplished the first clear case of artificial parthenogenesis when he pricked unfertilized frog eggs with a needle and found that in some cases normal embryonic development ensued. In 1936 Gregory Pincus induced parthenogenesis in a rabbit's ovum by changing temperature and adding chemical agents. Artificial parthenogenesis has been achieved by mechanical, chemical, and electrical means. Several types of animal eggs have been used in experiments but the experiments usually result in incomplete and abnormal development.

The first cloned human embryo was produced in October 2001. Eggs had their own genetic material removed and were injected with the nucleus of a donor cell. This is not the same as parthenogenesis, which uses the intact nucleus and genetic materials. Attempts at artificial parthenogenesis in humans have not yet been successful. In one experiment human eggs were incubated under special conditions to prompt them to divide and grow. One embryo grew to six cells before it stopped dividing. In fact several types of experiments were devised but efforts met with only limited success. In spite of the failed experiments, there is still some evidence that parthenogenesis does occasionally occur in humans without outside intervention.

There are many instances in which impregnation has allegedly taken place in women without there being any possibility of the semen entering the female genital passage. In some cases it was found either in the course of pregnancy or at the time of childbirth that the female passages were obstructed. However, it must be stated here that some of these women were having sexual intercourse but studies at that time indicated that the path between vagina and ovaries were missing or occluded. In 1956 the medical journal Lancet published a report concerning 19 alleged cases of virgin birth among women in England, who were studied by members of the British Medical Association. The six-month study convinced the investigators that human parthenogenesis was physiologically possible and had actually occurred in some of the women studied. Dealing with known methods, tests, and instrumentation of the 1950s may add a seed of doubt to the science and the conclusions of the experiments, but scientists of the time believed virgin birth was possible.

It is possible that some cases of human parthenogenesis involve self-fertilization rather than true virgin birth, as there are cases of sperm being produced in women by vestigial male reproductive glands. These are unused, and at times undiscovered glands, which are left over from embryonic development, that can achieve some low level of function under certain conditions, usually in cases of arousal or excitement.

Could a virgin conceive and give birth? Yes, but a number of rare events would have to occur in close succession, and the chances of these all happening in real life are virtually zero.

In normal fertilization the function of the sperm is two-fold. Its chemical makeup causes the egg to begin to divide. The genetic material of the sperm supplies half of the chromosomes needed to make the complete blueprint of the offspring. Fertilization and hereditary transmission are distinct operations and functions.

If the fertilizing enzyme (occytase) is isolated from the sperm and added to the egg, the egg would start to divide, but there would be no parental genetic material. If the egg could continue to segment and produce an offspring it would carry only maternal chromosomes. This experiment was attempted on sea-urchin eggs and caused them to develop. This enzyme (occytase) seems to be present in mammalian blood, since the addition of ox's blood to unfertilized eggs produced the same effects. This proved that chemical substances could replace one of the functions of the sperm – to trigger the segmentation of the ovum - while the other function of conveying genetic material can be dispensed with, in which case the offspring have purely maternal characteristics.

Eggs can show at least a beginning of segmentation under normal conditions, but sperm, which are highly alkaline, appear to accelerate the process by compensating for the excessive acidity of the medium surrounding the egg rather than a chemical deficiency in the egg itself. An acid condition of the blood prevents the parthenogenetic development of ova in the ovaries, while increased alkalinity appears to favor parthenogenetic development.

For a virgin to get pregnant, one of her eggs would have to produce, on its own, the biochemical changes indicative of fertilization. An egg will only start dividing when a spike in cellular calcium occurs. This normally occurs as a result of a sperm's entry during fertilization. But if the egg happens to experience a spontaneous calcium spike, it will start reacting as if it's been fertilized.

These events occur in the eggs or egg precursor cells of one out of every few thousand women. But what about the problem of the missing chromosomes? The egg would then have to divide abnormally to compensate for the lack of sperm DNA.

If an egg completes the final stage of a cell division known as meiosis II, it loses half of its genetic material to make room for the sperm's DNA. But if there's no sperm, each half of the divided egg cell will end up short, and both will die. In order for our virgin birth to proceed, the egg must, therefore, not complete meiosis.

Assuming both the calcium spike and the error in mitosis occur, the egg cell may then begin the process of parthenogenesis. When this happens to an egg-precursor cell, it can give rise to a tumor made up of many different types of tissue — liver, teeth, eye, and hair, for example, this is because unfertilized eggs lack specific instructions about gene expression from the sperm. Because of this, parthenogenesis in humans never produces viable embryos.

Fertilized eggs are working with two sets of genes, one set from the mother and one from the father. Some genes use only one copy, while the other remains dormant. Some of the signals for which copies should be turned off come from the sperm cell. So, if there's no sperm, certain genes will be over-expressed, and the "embryo" will die when it is only about five days old.

By eliminating a pair of maternal genes this problem can be avoided. A Japanese team was able to create, via parthenogenesis, a viable baby mouse that was seemingly unaffected by its lack of paternal imprinting. Although the scientists engineered these changes in the lab, there's at least a theoretical possibility that this could happen spontaneously via random gene deletions.

So, while it's possible for a human baby to be born of a virgin mother, it's very, very unlikely: These two genetic deletions might each have a one in one-billion chance of occurring, and that's not counting the calcium spike and division problem required to initiate parthenogenesis in the first place.

Is it possible for a virgin to have a child? Yes – but it would be a miracle, and would likely take an outside source of manipulation to begin the process and re-order the chromosome count.

Luke 1 (New International Version)

26In the sixth month, God sent the angel Gabriel to Nazareth, a town in Galilee, 27to a virgin pledged to be married to a man named Joseph, a descendant of David. The virgin's name was Mary. 28The angel went to her and said, "Greetings, you who are highly favored! The Lord is with you."

29Mary was greatly troubled at his words and wondered what kind of greeting this might be. 30But the angel said to her, "Do not be afraid, Mary, you have found favor with God. 31You will be with child and give birth to a son, and you are to give him the name Jesus. 32He will be great and will be called the Son of the Most High. The Lord God will give him the throne of his father David, 33and he will reign over the house of Jacob forever; his kingdom will never end."

34"How will this be," Mary asked the angel, "since I am a virgin?"

35The angel answered, "The Holy Spirit will come upon you, and the power of the Most High will overshadow you. So the holy one to be born will be called the Son of God.

References

J.B. Cibelli, R.P. Lanza and M.D. West, with C. Ezzell, 'The first human cloned embryo', Scientific American, Jan. 2002, http://sciam.com/explorations/2001/112401ezzell/index.html.

Raymond Bernard, The Mysteries of Human Reproduction, Mokelumne Hill, CA: Health Research, n.d., pp. 47-50, 56-63.

Ibid., pp. 3-10.

Ibid., pp. 11-28, 89-93.

Ibid., pp. 51-5, 117; F.H. Buzzacott and M.I. Wymore, Bi-sexual Man or Evolution of the Sexes, Health Research, 1966 (1912), pp. 32-4; Hilton Hotema,

Secret of Regeneration, Health Research, 1963, ch. 204-205, 211.

Secret of Regeneration, ch. 208-210, 234; Gray's Anatomy, http://www.bartleby.com/107.

Peter Tompkins and Christopher Bird, The Secret Life of Plants, New York: Harper & Row, 1973, pp. 54-5, 197-9; R. VanWijk, 'Bio-photons and bio-communication', Journal of Scientific Exploration, vol. 15, pp. 183-97, 2001.

The Mysteries of Human Reproduction, pp. 42, 109.

Ibid., pp. 118-9.

SEX AND THE DIVIDED SOUL

Everywhere and always, since its very inception, Christianity has turned the earth into a vale of tears; always it has made of life a weak, diseased thing, always it has instilled fear in man, turning him into a dual being, whose life energies are spent in the struggle between body and soul. In decrying the body as something evil, the flesh as the tempter to everything that is sinful, man has mutilated his being in the vain attempt to keep his soul pure, while his body rotted away from the injuries and tortures inflicted upon it.

EMMA GOLDMAN, *Mother Earth*, April 1913

And God created . . . every living creature that moveth . . . and God saw that it was good. And God blessed them, saying, Be fruitful and multiply. . . . God said, Let us make man in Our image, after Our likeness. . . . And the Lord God said, It is not good that the man should be alone; I will make him an help meet for him. . . . [So] in the image of God created He him; male and female created He them. And God blessed them, and God said unto them, Be fruitful and multiply, and replenish the earth, and subdue it. . . . And God saw everything that He had made, and, behold, it was very good (Genesis 1:21-26 ; 2:18 ; 1:27-31).

"Be fruitful and multiply!" "Reproduce!" was one of the first things God commanded the creatures of His glorious creation. And then again, after the great deluge, God reminded Noah and all that survived with him that they had an important job to do. Reproduce!

Bring forth with thee every living thing that is with thee, of all flesh, both of fowl, and of cattle, and of every creeping thing that creepeth upon the earth; that they may breed abundantly in the earth, and be fruitful, and multiply upon the earth. And God blessed Noah and his sons, and said unto them, Be fruitful, and multiply, and replenish the earth (Genesis 8:17 ; 9:1).

Throughout history, God put His stamp of approval on human sexuality and reproduction. To Abraham and later to Jacob (Israel) He basically said, "I am God and I want you to reproduce!"

I am God Almighty: be fruitful and multiply; a nation and a company of nations shall be of thee, and kings shall come out of thy loins (Genesis 35:11 ; see also Genesis 12:1,2,7).

And the Lord said to Hosea [God's prophet], Go, take unto thee a wife of whoredoms and children of whoredoms. . . . So he [Hosea] went and took Gomer the daughter of Diblaim; which conceived, and bare him a son (Hosea 1:2,3).

In the post-apostolic period Christian writers began expressing much more restrictive views of the role of sex in human life. . . . Church leaders needed to deal with the problems that sexual relations raised within the Christian community. There was a broad agreement that marital sex was acceptable, although a number of important writers sought to discourage sex among the devout. A few aberrant Christian groups taught that Christians were not subject to sexual restrictions and might have relations with anyone whom they pleased. Other doctrinal deviants wished to ban all sexual relations, even in marriage (Brundage, 1987: 74, 75).

What the modern world still understands by "sin" stems not from the teaching of Jesus of Nazareth, or from the tablets handed down from Sinai, but from the early sexual vicissitudes of a handful of men who lived in the twilight days of imperial Rome (Tannahill, 1992: 138).

Marriage is honourable, and the bed undefiled (Saint Paul, Hebrews 13:4).

In the first three hundred years of its existence, the Church placed few restrictions upon its clergy in regard to marriage. Celibacy was, as Paul indicated, a matter of choice (Thomas, 1986: 8).

Robert T. Francoeur, a Catholic priest and a fellow of the Society for the Scientific Study of Sex, is Professor of Human Embryology and Sexuality at Fairleigh Dickenson University and has written no less than twenty books on human sexuality. This very respected author and academic, in his essay *The Religious Suppression of Eros*, gives us the following summary of the sexual derailment of Christianity:

To understand the evolution from the early sex-affirming Hebraic culture to Christianity's persistent discomfort with sex and pleasure, we have to look at three interwoven threads: the dualistic cosmology of Plato [i.e. the soul and mind are at war with the body], the Stoic philosophy of early Greco-Roman culture [i.e., nothing should be done for the sake of pleasure], and the Persian Gnostic tradition [i.e., that demons created the world, sex and your body-in which your soul is trapped, and the key to salvation is to free the spirit from the bondage of the body by denying the flesh]. Within three centuries after Jesus, these influences combined to seduce Christian thinkers into a rampant rejection of human sexuality and sexual pleasure.

Many people forget that the pleasure-loving Greek society contained anti-sexual ascetic extremes as well. Even Epicurus, who loved good food, condemned sex, saying, "Sexual intercourse never benefited any man" (Davies, 1984: 176). Diogenes, a famous Greek cynic, lived in a washtub to shun the temptations of the flesh, and the Greek Stoics only permitted sex for procreation purposes. It was these and other ascetic forces, not the sensual expressions of Greek culture that came to most affect Christianity.

Plato, though personally favorably inclined toward prostitutes, homosexuals and pedophilia, none-the-less taught in *The Laws* that the world would be a better place if all sex were "starved." Socrates and Plato both taught that all sexual activity was harmful to the health of the soul. Plato's teachings were revised in the third century, and Plotinus, the chief protagonist of this neo-Platonism, went far beyond Plato in denigrating sex, teaching that mystical ecstasies could be had through denying the body.

MARRIAGE, MISOGAMY AND SAINT AUGUSTINE

Saint Augustine, the leading theologian of the fourth century, embraced the faith on April 25, 387 along with his "illegitimate" son, leaving behind his wife and his second mistress. He had already split up from his first concubine, the mother of his son, after 17 years of living together. He turned his home in Hippo into a monastery, and as Bishop of Hippo, proceeded to make many literary contributions to Christianity. Unfortunately, his sexual views were sadly affected by the monastic temperament of the times, perhaps an over-compensation for the sexuality of his liberal youth.

It was Saint Augustine who, according to Nigel Davies in *The Rampant God*, "set the final seal on the anti-sexual bias of the Church" (Davies, 1984: 180). Before becoming a Christian, Saint Augustine had studied the works of Plotinus, and for eleven years was a member of the Manichaean sect, whose founder taught that Adam and Eve resulted from the Devil's children having sex, and procreation was just another evil part of the Prince of Darkness' creation.

Saint Augustine did, however, consider sex a necessary evil, though certainly not something to be enjoyed. He even thought it was permissible to take a second wife if the first was barren, and grudgingly admitted that Adam and Eve may have had sex in the Garden before their Fall, but theorized that it was a very cold dutiful mechanical act without passion. After daring to suggest that even if they did have sex in the Garden, he assures his readers that they certainly would not have enjoyed it.

Perish the thought, that there should have been any unregulated excitement, or any [excitement so great that they would ever] need to resist desire! (Augustine c. duas epist, Pelag. I 34, 17).

Methodius thought sex was "unseemly," and Ambrose, a "defilement." Saint John Chrysostom, the "golden-mouthed" orator of the fourth century, had little golden to say about the fair sex in general: "Among all savage beasts, none is found as harmful as woman."

As the Church became part of the mainstream of Roman life, it borrowed increasingly from the pagan world, from which it had formerly been almost totally estranged. In the process, both Christian institutions and thought were irrevocably altered. These developments also signaled the beginning of radical changes in the ways the authorities of both Church and government dealt with sexual matters (Brundage, 1987: 76).

By the eighth century an enormously strict system of sexual rules and penalties was firmly in place, covering every imaginable thought and action related to sex. Jesus, as the Merciful Intercessor, the joyful Messenger of God's love and forgiveness of all sins, as well as His free gift of Salvation through faith, were trodden underfoot by an emerging supposed sex-hating ascetic god who demanded complete sacrifice and much suffering from humanity. The message of damnation soon replaced the Good News that even the vilest of sinners could be forgiven and saved through Jesus. In fact, "it came to be held that only one person in a million could hope to reach Heaven" (Taylor, 1970: 69).

In *A Handbook of Church History* by Samuel G. Greene, we learn that:

False notions of Christian purity led in many instances to the voluntary separation of husband and wife. . . . Justinian was the first in the Eastern Empire to forbid married persons to be elected bishops. [Subdeacons could still have wives.] In the West, endeavours to enforce celibacy on all the clergy were made with indifferent success, until the days of Hildebrand (Gregory VII), in the Eleventh Century, by whom the law was made absolute. The East, on the contrary, while eventually (after the Synod of Trulla, A.D. 692) requiring celibacy in the bishop, not only permits, but encourages the marriage of the rest of the clergy (Greene, 1907: 229).

The real "sin" of sex, however, was not so much the procreative act, loathsome as it was perceived to be. It was the experience of sexual pleasure that was the prime source of sin. Many took steps to make sure that even marital sex was limited to procreation purposes and was made as unenjoyable as possible; some even rigged up animal skin barriers with a hole cut in the rough hide that caused the maximum discomfort and allowed the minimum of body contact between a copulating couple. This device and others presumably reduced the amount of sin involved by reducing the amount of pleasure (Taylor, 1970: 51). Saint Paul was never so unkind. He insisted that men and women should not "defraud" each other of their sexual rights, seeing their bodies were needed by and belonged to each other (1 Corinthians 7:4,5).

A few Christian churches today still teach that sex is solely for the purpose of procreation and not for pleasure. Would they be so zealous, we wonder, if they realized that it's not the Bible they have to thank for this harsh approach to sexual joys, but heathen teachers and non-Christian philosophers like Seneca the Younger and Musonius Rufus, Stoic contemporaries of Jesus, and others- And it was the Greek Stoic Artemidorous, not "missionary" Christians, who first taught that the only morally acceptable position for intercourse was male-superior face-to-face (Francoeur: *The Religious Suppression of Eros*).

In modern times, several passages in the Bible are used as justification for condemning "fornication." However, "porneia," the word used in the Greek Bible, actually had many meanings such as whoremongering and excessive, illicit sex, and not simply casual sex between couples, as is pointed out by

Brundage:

Several passages in the Gospels condemn porneia. This word carried a number of different meanings. At times porneia means prostitution, at other times it refers to non-marital sex in general.[17] It is difficult to be certain, for example, whether the term applied to premarital intercourse between persons betrothed to one another or, indeed, to any type of non-commercial, heterosexual relations of the kind conventionally labeled fornication. Since neither the Torah nor rabbinical teachers contemporary with Jesus prohibited intercourse between unmarried partners as a moral offense, perhaps porneia referred primarily to sex with prostitutes, adultery, and other promiscuous relationships [18] (Brundage 1987: 58).

Regarding sexual liberties which were taken by the early Church, we know that they did have some trouble with "wild fire" in certain quarters, as indicated by Saint Paul's rebuke to the Corinthians, where reports of fornication and incest were quite common:

It is reported commonly that there is fornication among you, and such fornication as is not so much named among the Gentiles, that one should have his father's wife (1 Corinthians 5:1).

Saint Paul subscribed marriage as a solution to such excesses:

Nevertheless, to avoid fornication, let every man have his own wife, and let every woman have her own husband (1 Corinthians 7:2).

Much of Paul's conservatism may be attributed not only to his strict Pharisaic background, but also to the fact that most of his Greek and Asian converts had come out of cultures in which male and female temple prostitution were noble professions. And, sexual excesses and orgies were a way of life amongst the pagans of the Near East. This is why many scholars interpret a number of New Testament references to "fornicators" to be specifically talking about "[male] temple prostitutes," not inclusive of all those who engage in sex with a partner to whom they are not married.

Paul's pronouncements regarding sex, as applied by sexually conservative Christians, come in direct conflict with the central theme of the Epistles. We believe that Jesus has delivered us from the old Mosaic laws and purity requirements, regarding sex between consenting adult men and women. For "Christ hath redeemed us from the curse of the [Mosaic] Law" (Galatians 3:13), "blotting out the handwriting of ordinances that was against us [the old Law], which was contrary to us, and took it out of the way, nailing it to His cross" (Colossians 2:14).

According to Aquinas, masturbation was a greater sin than fornication. The death of Judah's son, Onan, who "spilled his seed" (i.e., performed *coitus interruptus*) rather than willingly impregnate his widowed sister-in-law as custom required, is often mistakenly pointed out as the example of how displeasing to God masturbation must be.

And Judah said unto Onan, Go in unto thy brother's wife, and marry her, and raise up seed to thy [deceased] brother. And Onan knew that the seed should not be his; and it came to pass, when he went in unto his brother's wife, that he spilled it on the ground, lest that he should give seed to his brother. And the thing which he did displeased the Lord: wherefore He slew him (Genesis 38:8-10).

Read in context, however, one quickly sees that what provoked God to slay Onan was his selfishness, greed and sexual withholding and refusing to sexually accommodate Tamar, his brother's widow, not wanting her to have any children to inherit part of the family property. In slaying Onan, God was insisting Tamar receive justice, but He also had another reason to be concerned about her success in sex; she was chosen to be an ancestor of Jesus. As a spicy epilogue, Tamar assisted God's purpose by posing as a prostitute, thereby luring Judah to fulfill his Godly duty (Genesis 38:13-26).

Peter Abelard (1079-1142), one of the leading medieval theologians and the famous lover of Heloise, openly opposed this anti-sexual value system. Abelard wrote:

No natural pleasure of the flesh may be declared as sin, nor may one impute guilt when someone is delighted by pleasure where he must necessarily feel it. . . . From the first day of our creation when man lived without sin in paradise, sexual intercourse and good tasting foods were naturally bound up with pleasure. God himself had established nature in this way (cited by Robert T. Francoeur in his essay, *The Religious Suppression of Eros*).

Abelard's liberal views were not well received by at least one powerful priest. When Abelard's secret love affair was discovered with Heloise (a student he was tutoring, who was the niece of the Canon of the Cathedral of Notre Dame), Heloise's outraged clerical uncle, Fulbert, had him castrated.

The Janus Report on Sexual Behavior, published in the US in 1993, was described as "the first broad-scale scientific national survey since Kinsey." The report revealed that forty-four percent of "very religious" people and fifty percent of "religious" people, and fifty-nine percent of "slightly religious" people admitted they had sex before marriage. "Very religious" people slightly outscored "religious" people fifty-seven percent to fifty-six percent in their personal agreement with the statement, "Sensually, I feel that sex is deliciously sensuous" (Janus, 1993: 252, 255). Another surprising discovery made by these scientists was in response to the question "I've had extramarital affairs." Thirty-one percent of people in the "very religious" category indicated they had at least one affair, whereas only twenty-six percent of those people who thought of themselves as simply "religious" said they had been involved in extra-marital sex. Forty-four percent of the "non-religious" responders admitted to extramarital sex (op. cit., 249).

Breaching the ego boundary brings two into one and is a precursor to our union with God.

POLYGAMY

One of the most difficult distinctions to make is the one between social and religious pressures. This became quiet apparent during a trip to Argentina. The plan was to go in with a team and build a church for a certain Pentecostal denomination. I had listened to church teaching and dogma for a couple of years. Some things seemed reasonable. Many did not, but at least the rules were applied across the board with equal rigidity to all. At least that is what I assumed before the aircraft landed.

After driving to the outskirts of Buenos Aires and into the countryside we arrived at the church. Services were being held in a large tent. There we met the church leaders.

In the U.S. version of the church, we were taught that no divorced person could hold a high church office. Certainly no remarried person could ascent to the throne of the pulpit. Now we were building a church so that a large congregation and several pastors could hold services in a brick building. Upon getting to know the pastors it became obvious that they were working under a different set of rules from their North American counterparts. Most of the congregation and all of the pastors were married but none were living with their wives. All were living with a mistress. Most had been with a paramour many years and had children within the second relationship.

For more than a half century Argentina had been under control of very conservative Catholic leaders. Many rules of the church had become law. Divorce was illegal in Argentina at that time. Social pressures had compelled the people to marry young and have children. If the couples separated they had no recourse but to continue their lives alone or in adultery.

Under these circumstances the church would have few people to man and expand the denomination in that country. So, does the church stand firm on its convictions or look the other way? In the end, denominations are organizations built on money and numbers. If you are in the U.S. and are a divorced person who is being discriminated against by a church, you should know that if you were the same person in the same denomination in another country you would be treated differently. The view is driven by social conventions.

The other side of the coin is equally amusing. During a trip to Trinidad - Tobago I was teaching a class in religious studies. Afterward a student approached to ask a few questions. He enquired into my church membership and education. When I mentioned the word "Baptist" he recoiled as if being shot.

Later I spoke to our host about the reaction. What I was told made me chuckle, but also heightened my concern about interactions between churches and cultures.

The Spiritual Baptist faith is based in Trinidad and Tobago. It has African influences but Spiritual Baptists consider themselves to be Christians. The Baptist faith was brought to Trinidad by the Merikins, former American slaves who were recruited by the British to fight for them during the Revolutionary War of 1812. Ex-slaves were settled in remote areas of Trinidad.

Whereas Voodoo is in Haiti and is a mixture of Catholicism and African pagan religions, in Trinidad and Tobago, the Spiritual Baptist faith is a mixture of Christian Protestantism and African Paganism and, even though they consider themselves to be Christian, they are related to Voodoo.

What does this have to do with polygamy? Hopefully, these little anecdotes will help us remember that when it comes to what is considered normal, we are dealing with two influences, which can be difficult to separate. The rules of society and those of religion collide and combine. If we wish to have a theological or religious debate we must seek to rightly divide the entangled cords of religion and culture.

While visiting India, missionaries met a man who had two wives. He had married a woman whom he loved and cared for. She was from a family of four and had a younger sister. Her parents died, leaving her younger sister to live on the streets. The young woman would have been reduced to being a prostitute in order to survive. The older sister approached her husband, asking him if he would love and care for her younger sister, marry her, and save her from the nightmare awaiting her on the streets of Deli. The husband agreed and took the younger sister as his second wife. The two sisters live in harmony and safety for years, until the missionaries arrived.

After they managed to convert the husband the missionaries informed him it would be necessary to divorce one of his wives or go to hell for adultery. Thus, the Christian preachers assigned a helpless, loving, and innocent young woman to a life of hell as a street prostitute. She was found dead, having been raped, beaten, and stabbed.

The story is true and illustrates the damage and pain unlearned and narrow religious minds can produce. What sense could it possibly make to demand the divorce and destruction of a loving family in exchange for a particular brand of Christianity? Polygamy is not a theological problem. It is a cultural one. Some Eastern cultures permit this state of marriage today. Most Western cultures do not openly embrace polygamy, however, there are several churches practicing it and many groups or subcultures live in households where polygamy is practiced between consenting adults. Church members

Joseph Lumpkin

protect themselves from prosecution by taking one wife as a legal spouse and the other women as spiritual wives, joined by a pastor but not in a civil union.

In mainstream America, we have our own issues. Many churches, such as the Church of Christ and other denominations will not allow any person to hold office if they have been remarried. However, in my little area of the conservative South, the majority of members have lived with someone before marring another. The vast majority had intercourse at least once before getting married to some other person.

The wake-up call is that in Bible times there was no certain or distinct ceremony that marked the official beginning of a marriage. Pagans had various rites, and Jews had theirs, but the actual marriage was marked with sexual intercourse. If you slept with someone, you were married. (But then C.O.C. people should know this since they claim their church is not a religion or a denomination because it has supposedly been the same since the beginning. Right – I think that church was founded in 1923.) Even today marriages may be annulled if intercourse has not taken place. Further, in the Catholic faith there are times when a marriage may be annulled if children are not born and certainly may be annulled if consummation has not taken place.

The point is that we overlook mountains of cultural norms, which violate biblical norms, and then exclude and embarrass good people who have done little if anything wrong. So we allow the man who had sex with a dozen women, but did not marry until he was fifty, to lead the church because he has been married only once by cultural standards, but we rip a pastor out of the pulpit because his wife left him and he chooses not to die alone. Brilliant!

Judaism and Christianity are Eastern religions. Both were born in the Middle East. We in the west have managed to paint Jesus as a blue-eyed, brown-haired, thin man, when it is far more likely Jesus was a short, stocky, black-haired, brown-eyed individual. We placed our cultural imprint on how Jesus looked. We have done the same with marriage, stripping away what the Bible says and replacing it with our own societal norms. This is not the greater sin. The real error is to read and interpret the scriptures in this prejudiced light and then to force the error on all others under our authority.

That God Himself has more than one wife, in a symbol or type, comes as a shock to most Bible believing western Christians.

In Ezekiel 23 the Lord speaks of the divided kingdom of Israel as two wives who had committed adultery.

Ezekiel 23 (NIV)

Two Adulterous Sisters

1 The word of the LORD came to me: 2 "Son of man, there were two women, daughters of the same mother. 3 They became prostitutes in Egypt, engaging in prostitution from their youth. In that land their breasts were fondled and their virgin bosoms caressed. 4 The older was named Oholah, and her sister was Oholibah. They were mine and gave birth to sons and daughters. Oholah is Samaria, and Oholibah is Jerusalem.

5 "Oholah engaged in prostitution while she was still mine; and she lusted after her lovers, the Assyrians-warriors 6 clothed in blue, governors and commanders, all of them handsome young men, and mounted horsemen. 7 She gave herself as a prostitute to all the elite of the Assyrians and defiled herself with all the idols of everyone she lusted after. 8 She did not give up the prostitution she began in Egypt, when during her youth men slept with her, caressed her virgin bosom and poured out their lust upon her."

9 "Therefore I handed her over to her lovers, the Assyrians, for whom she lusted. 10 They stripped her naked, took away her sons and daughters and killed her with the sword. She became a byword among women, and punishment was inflicted on her.

11 "Her sister Oholibah saw this, yet in her lust and prostitution she was more depraved than her sister. 12 She too lusted after the Assyrians – governors and commanders, warriors in full dress, mounted horsemen, all handsome young men. 13 I saw that she too defiled herself; both of them went the same way." 14 "But she carried her prostitution still further. She saw men portrayed on a wall, figures of Chaldeans portrayed in red, 15 with belts around their waists and flowing turbans on their heads; all of them looked like Babylonian chariot officers, natives of Chaldea. 16 As soon as she saw them, she lusted after them and sent messengers to them in Chaldea. 17 Then the Babylonians came to her, to the bed of love, and in their lust they defiled her. After she had been defiled by them, she turned away from them in disgust. 18 When she carried on her prostitution openly and exposed her nakedness, I turned away from her in disgust, just as I had turned away from her sister. 19 Yet she became more and more promiscuous as she recalled the days of her youth, when she was a prostitute in Egypt. 20 There she lusted after her lovers, whose genitals were like those of donkeys and whose emission was like that of horses. 21 So you longed for the lewdness of your youth, when in Egypt your bosom was caressed and your young breasts fondled. 22 "Therefore, Oholibah, this is what the Sovereign LORD says: I will stir up your lovers against you, those you turned away from in disgust, and I will bring them against you from every side- 23 the Babylonians and all the Chaldeans, the men of Pekod and Shoa and Koa, and all the Assyrians with them, handsome young men, all of them governors and commanders, chariot officers and men of high rank, all mounted on horses. 24 They will come against you with weapons, chariots and wagons and with a throng of people; they will take up positions against you on every side with large and small shields and with helmets. I will turn you over to them for punishment, and they will punish you according to their standards. 25 I will direct my jealous anger against you, and they will deal with you in fury. They will cut off your noses and your ears, and those of you who are left will fall by the sword. They will take away your sons and daughters, and those of you who are left will be consumed by fire. 26 They will also strip you of your clothes and take your fine jewelry. 27 So I will put a stop to the lewdness and prostitution you began in Egypt. You will not look on these things with longing or remember Egypt anymore.

28 "For this is what the Sovereign LORD says: I am about to hand you over to those you hate, to those you turned away from in disgust. 29 They will deal with you in hatred and take away everything you have worked for. They will leave you naked and bare, and the shame of your prostitution will be exposed. Your lewdness and promiscuity 30 have brought this upon you, because you lusted after the nations and defiled yourself with their idols. 31 You have gone the way of your sister; so I will put her cup into your hand. 32 "This is what the Sovereign LORD says: "You will drink your sister's cup, a cup large and deep; it will bring scorn and derision, for it holds so much. 33 You will be filled with drunkenness and sorrow, the cup of ruin and desolation, the cup of your sister Samaria.

34 You will drink it and drain it dry; you will dash it to pieces and tear your breasts. I have spoken, declares the Sovereign LORD. 35 "Therefore this is what the Sovereign LORD says: Since you have forgotten me and thrust me behind your back, you must bear the consequences of your lewdness and prostitution." 36 The LORD said to me: "Son of man, will you judge Oholah and Oholibah? Then confront them with their detestable practices, 37 for they have committed adultery and blood is on their hands. They committed adultery with their idols; they even sacrificed their children, whom they bore to me, as food for them. 38 They have also done this to me: At that same time they defiled my sanctuary and desecrated my Sabbaths. 39 On the very day they sacrificed their children to their idols, they entered my sanctuary and desecrated it. That is what they did in my house. 40 "They even sent messengers for men who came from far away, and when they arrived you bathed yourself for them, painted your eyes and put on your jewelry. 41 You sat on an elegant couch, with a table spread before it on which you had placed the incense and oil that belonged to me. 42 "The noise of a carefree crowd was around her; Sabeans were brought from the desert along with men from the rabble, and they put bracelets on the arms of the woman and her sister and beautiful crowns on their heads. 43 Then I said about the one worn out by adultery, 'Now let them use her as a prostitute, for that is all she is.' 44 And they slept with her. As men sleep with a prostitute, so they slept with those lewd women, Oholah and Oholibah. 45 But righteous men will sentence them to the punishment of women who commit adultery and shed blood, because they are adulterous and blood is on their hands. 46 "This is what the Sovereign LORD says: Bring a mob against them and give them over to terror and plunder. 47 The mob will stone them and cut them down with their swords; they will kill their sons and daughters and burn down their houses. 48 "So I will put an end to lewdness in the land, that all women may take warning and not imitate you. 49 You will suffer the

penalty for your lewdness and bear the consequences of your sins of idolatry. Then you will know that I am the Sovereign LORD."

Jeremiah 2

Israel Forsakes God

1 The word of the LORD came to me: 2 "Go and proclaim in the hearing of Jerusalem: " 'I remember the devotion of your youth, how as a bride you loved me and followed me through the desert, through a land not sown.

3 Israel was holy to the LORD, the firstfruits of his harvest; all who devoured her were held guilty, and disaster overtook them,' declares the LORD.

4 Hear the word of the LORD, O house of Jacob, all you clans of the house of Israel. 5 This is what the LORD says: "What fault did your fathers find in me, that they strayed so far from me? They followed worthless idols and became worthless themselves. "

Jeremiah 3

1 "If a man divorces his wife and she leaves him and marries another man, should he return to her again? Would not the land be completely defiled? But you have lived as a prostitute with many lovers — would you now return to me?" declares the LORD. 6 During the reign of King Josiah, the LORD said to me, "Have you seen what faithless Israel has done? She has gone up on every high hill and under every spreading tree and has committed adultery there. 7 I thought that after she had done all this she would return to me but she did not, and her unfaithful sister Judah saw it. 8 I gave faithless Israel her certificate of divorce and sent her away because of all her adulteries. Yet I saw that her unfaithful sister Judah had no fear; she also went out and committed adultery. 9 Because Israel's immorality mattered so little to her, she defiled the land and committed adultery with stone and wood. 10 In spite of all this, her unfaithful sister Judah did not return to me with all her heart, but only in pretense," declares the LORD. 11 The LORD said to me, "Faithless Israel is more righteous than unfaithful Judah. 12 Go, proclaim this message toward the north: " 'Return, faithless Israel,' declares the LORD, 'I will frown on you no longer, for I am merciful,' declares the LORD, 'I will not be angry forever. 13 Only acknowledge your guilt — you have rebelled against the LORD your God, you have scattered your favors to foreign gods under every spreading tree, and have not obeyed me,' " declares the LORD. 14 "Return, faithless people," declares the LORD, "for I am your husband. I will choose you — one from a town and two from a clan — and bring you to Zion. 15 Then I will give you shepherds after my own heart, who will lead you with knowledge and understanding. 16 In those days, when your numbers have increased greatly in the land," declares the LORD, "men will no longer say, 'The ark of the covenant of the LORD.' It will never enter their minds or be remembered; it will not be missed, nor will another one be made. 17 At that time they will call Jerusalem The Throne of the LORD, and all nations will gather in Jerusalem to honor the name of the LORD. No longer will they follow the stubbornness of their evil hearts. 18 In those days the house of Judah will join the house of Israel, and together they will come from a northern land to the land I gave your forefathers as an inheritance.

Jer 31: 31 "The time is coming," declares the LORD, "when I will make a new covenant with the house of Israel and with the house of Judah. 32 It will not be like the covenant I made with their forefathers when I took them by the hand to lead them out of Egypt, because they broke my covenant, though I was a husband to them," declares the LORD.

Do we really believe God actually married these two whoring sisters? The two nations were His spiritual wives in type and shadow and in the metaphor of religious language. The metaphor was chosen because people of the time could relate to it easily. No one will dispute that in Old Testament times most leaders, kings, and men who could financially afford it had more than one wife.

According to the Torah or Old Testament, the law compelled Polygamy among God's people. It is interesting that in scripture there is a compulsion to have more than one wife. The command was not a specific command to have plural wives but polygamy had to occur as a consequence of obedience to another command, that a man was to raise up an heir for a dead relative. Keep in mind that this is God's command, through his prophet Moses, the proper name for the Law being "the Law of God, given to Moses." (Ezra 7:6, Nehemiah 10:29 & 2nd Chronicles 34:14) The law is described in Deuteronomy 25:5 (NASB) and says, when brothers live together and one of them dies and has no son, the wife of the deceased shall not be married outside the family to a strange man. Her husband's brother shall go in to her and take her to himself as wife and perform the duty of a husband's brother to her. It shall be that the firstborn whom she bears shall assume the name of his dead brother, so that his name will not be blotted out from Israel.

Deuteronomy 25:7 - 10 "But if the man does not desire to take his brother's wife, then his brother's wife shall go up to the gate to the elders and say, 'My husband's brother refuses to establish a name for his brother in Israel; he is not willing to perform the duty of a husband's brother to me.' Then the elders of his city shall summon him and speak to him. And if he persists and says, 'I do not desire to take her'."

1 Samuel 25:39 Then David sent word to Abigail, asking her to become his wife. 40 His servants went to Carmel and said to Abigail, "David has sent us to you to take you to become his wife." 41 She bowed down with her face to the ground and said, "Here is your maidservant, ready to serve you and wash the feet of my master's servants." 42 Abigail quickly got on a donkey and, attended by her five maids, went with David's messengers and became his wife. 43 David had also married Ahinoam of Jezreel, and they both were his wives. 44 But Saul had given his daughter Michal, David's wife, to Paltiel son of Laish, who was from Gallim.

1 Chronicles 4:5 Ashhur the father of Tekoa had two wives, Helah and Naarah.

2 Chronicles 11:22 Rehoboam appointed Abijah son of Maacah to be the chief prince among his brothers, in order to make him king. 23 He acted wisely, dispersing some of his sons throughout the districts of Judah and Benjamin, and to all the fortified cities. He gave them abundant provisions and took many wives for them.

Here we will resist going further, for to list all of the times multiple wives were recorded in the Old Testament would take up too much of this book.

Now we know that the Old Testament permitted polygamy and under certain circumstances, compels a man to take his brother's wife, if he should die, in order to continue his inheritance. Where most casual Bible readers balk is in connecting polygamy to the New Testament. This is actually very simple and direct. Look at the NIV translation of the following verses.

1 Timothy 3

1Here is a trustworthy saying: If anyone sets his heart on being an overseer, he desires a noble task. 2Now the overseer must be above reproach, the husband of but one wife, temperate, self-controlled, respectable, hospitable, able to teach, 3not given to drunkenness, not violent but gentle, not quarrelsome, not a lover of money. 4He must manage his own family well and see that his children obey him with proper respect. 5(If anyone does not know how to manage his own family, how can he take care of God's church?) 6He must not be a recent convert, or he may become conceited and fall under the same judgment as the devil. 7He must also have a good reputation with outsiders, so that he will not fall into disgrace and into the devil's trap. 8Deacons, likewise, are to be men worthy of respect, sincere, not indulging in much wine, and not pursuing dishonest gain. 9They must keep hold of the deep truths of the faith with a clear conscience. 10They must first be tested; and then if there is nothing against them, let them serve as deacons. 11In the same way, their wives are to be women worthy of respect, not malicious talkers but temperate and trustworthy in everything.

12A deacon must be the husband of but one wife and must manage his children and his household well. 13Those who have served well gain an excellent standing and great assurance in their faith in Christ Jesus.

For centuries, through the vague wording of the KJV Bible, this passage was used by some denominations to exclude all divorced men and every woman from the clergy. It is true that the phrase can be interpreted, "A bishop must be a one-woman man." Some view the verse as a test for fidelity, pointing out that polygamy was not the norm in the Greco-Roman world. This is true but there was a great mixing of cultures and increasing pagan and foreign influences being transmitted from various sources. The Greco-Roman world was not the universe. There were other cultures to consider. Those in the Middle East, where Christ was born and was crucified, had their own customs.

First Timothy was written after the apostle Paul had been imprisoned in Rome for the first time. After he was released, he wrote this letter to Timothy, who by this time had served as a son in the gospel with the apostle for several years. He was probably in his late twenties or early thirties, and the apostle had sent him to Ephesus, the great commercial and pleasure resort on the shores of the Mediterranean in Asia Minor. In this great crossroad and cultural melting pot all cultures would be encountered and addressed.

Paul, being well educated and well traveled, would have known the farther East one traveled the more polygamy would be encountered. Many Bedouins, Arab tribes, and nomadic people practice polygamy still today. The meaning is made clear in the NIV Bible. In the verses above we see the admonition to limit one's household to a single wife if you wish to serve the church. It is not that having more than one wife was a sin. Nowhere are we told that polygamy is now wrong. We are only told that having more than one wife is not the optimum condition if one is to serve the church. The reason seems axiomatic. One cannot take the time and energy needed to keep up more than one household well and also serve the widows and orphans along with the church community. Jesus, living in a society permitting polygamy, never addressed it as a problem. Why do we? It is not because of our religion, but how we chose to interpret it through the blinders of our society.

CELIBACY

Christianity has enriched the erotic meal with the appetizer of curiosity and spoiled it with the dessert of remorse.
KARL KRAUS, *Half-Truths and One-and-a-Half Truths*

1 Timothy 4 (New International Version)

1 The Spirit clearly says that in later times some will abandon the faith and follow deceiving spirits and things taught by demons. 2 Such teachings come through hypocritical liars, whose consciences have been seared as with a hot iron. 3 They forbid people to marry and order them to abstain from certain foods, which God created to be received with thanksgiving by those who believe and who know the truth. 4 For everything God created is good, and nothing is to be rejected if it is received with thanksgiving, 5 because it is consecrated by the word of God and prayer.

Matthew 8 (New International Version)

14 When Jesus came into Peter's house, he saw Peter's mother-in-law lying in bed with a fever. 15 He touched her hand and the fever left her, and she got up and began to wait on him.

So, if the Catholic Church is correct and Jesus did tap Peter for the job of running the church or carrying forth the faith after He was killed, then Jesus designated Peter, a married man, to be the first pope. We will forego the discussion of who was actually running the show after the death of Jesus. It was, by the way, James who was the heir apparent, and not Peter. But we will leave that for another day.

Priests had married in Judaism. The priesthood itself was usually a hereditary profession, and it would seem that Christ accepted this part of the tradition in his choice of Peter.

To be fair, in that day and time, Paul believed that due to the need of travel and the likelihood of martyrdom it was best if those spreading the Gospel didn't have a family. Paul did go on to mandate that bishops, elders and deacons be only "the husband of one wife." This was because polygamy among all ranks of the clergy persisted. Supporting a large family did not leave time or energy for the ministry. By the third century bishops were required to be monogamous.

There were certain pressures within the early church. Some were political and driven out of greed. Some were religious in nature.

Of the religious pressures were the teachings of the Gnostic Christians, which caused great focus on the evils of the flesh. Spirit and the material world were at odds in their theology. Thus, the idea was that what starved the flesh of its natural desires must also feed the spirit. Neoplatonism was alive and well, and a major influence in the life and beliefs of Augustine.

Neoplatonism was the dominant philosophy of the ancient pagan world from the time of Plotinus in the mid-third century A.D., to the closing of the schools of philosophy at Athens by the Christian emperor Justinian in A.D. 529. It incorporated the best of Aristotle, Pythagoras, Plato, and the Stoics, so as to make a synthesis of the collected wisdom of the ancient world. Neoplatonism was not only a philosophy; it also met a religious need by showing how the individual soul might reach God. Thus it presented with traditional Greek rationalism a scheme of salvation comparable with those schemes offered by Christianity and the Mystery religions. It also began to influence Christian thinkers, notably Augustine.

Before receiving the final push from Augustine, the change in the church's views on marriage began with the Council of Elvira in Spain in about 306 A.D., which prohibited bishops, deacons and priests from marrying.

Already in 305 A.D., before the Church's liberation under Constantine, the Council of Elvira in Spain passed the following decree: "That bishops, priests and deacons, and in general all the clergy, who are specially employed in the service of the altar, abstain from conjugal intercourse. Let those who persist be degraded from the ranks of the clergy" (Can. 33). And by the end of the fourth century, the Second Council of Carthage in Africa declared, "What the apostles taught in the early Church preserved, let us too observe." Celibacy, I insist, is not a post factum afterthought of the Church. It is an anti factum, reality, practiced by the Church and wanted by those who wanted to be Christ's priests."

But this was influenced only partially by pagan philosophies. A political storm of greed was building.

Shortly after The Council of Elvira, the early church fathers began to stigmatize sex as sinful in their writings. St. Ambrose (340-397 A.D.) wrote, "The ministerial office must be kept pure and unspoiled and must not be defiled by coitus," and the former libertine, and some would argue – former sex addict, St. Augustine (354-430 A.D.) even went so far as to consider an erect penis a sign of man's insubordination.

Let us remember, Augustine was fighting his own demons in this arena. Certainly there will be times, if one is an addict, that total abstinence is easier than moderation, but for those who have normal drives, the suppression of normal human drives usually gives way to corruption and re-direction of those drives. It may be from this simple statement that pedophilia and homosexuality within the priesthood arises.

Augustine thought, "spontaneous sexual desire is…the clearest evidence of the effects of original sin."

Augustine concluded that human government, (and this certainly included the church,) were an indispensable defense against the forces of sin. This, we assume, was because government of any sort sets limitations, rules, and punishments for actions it deems unsuitable. But this is nothing more than replacing the Old Testament law with man's law. The latter will work no better than the first. It is a change of heart that is needed, not a change of taskmasters.

In every instance Augustine talks about sex, he implies that it was wrong or at least the reasons for having sex were wrong. However, it seems that he takes this belief a little too far. Maybe this stemmed from his studying with the Manichees and their belief that the body was the cause of evil. Maybe it stemmed from his interpretation of Catholicism and the Bible. Truly, Augustine is the first writer to show a change from a liberal view of sex to an extremely conservative view of sex and to argue the benefits that he believed it brought him. Even though his book is clearly Catholic propaganda, he shows himself as a lost sheep found, a reformed sinner; and that is a powerful message for many people. Like any good fundamental preacher of any faith, he knew that if something were good for his addictive personality it must be good for and forced upon all people. In short, Augustine believed the devil was not in the details, but lived in his pants. The equation of sin with sex is evident throughout Augustine's writing.

"I intend to remind myself of my past foulnesses and carnal corruptions, not because I love them but so that I may love you, my God" (Augustine, 24).

From his birth in a North African town, Augustine knew the religious differences overwhelming the Roman Empire: his father was a pagan who honored the old Punic gods; his mother was a zealous Christian. But the adolescent Augustine was consumed with sex and high living, and not with God.

At age 17, Augustine set off to school in Carthage in North Africa. There the underachiever became enraptured with his studies and started to make a name for himself. He immersed himself in the writings of Cicero and Manichaean philosophers and rejected his mother's religion.

His studies completed, Augustine returned to his home town of Thagaste to teach rhetoric Manichaeism. The philosophy was based on the teachings of the Persian, Mani, and was a dualist corruption of Christianity. It taught that the world of light and the world of darkness constantly war with each other, catching most of humanity in the struggle. Along with the religion of Zoroastrianism, these two religions influenced the dualistic outlook of Christianity the most. Augustine tried to hide his views from his mother, Monica, but when she found out, she threw him out of the house.

Augustine moved to Rome and there he began attending the cathedral to hear preaching of Ambrose the bishop. He kept attending because of Ambrose's preaching. He soon dropped his Manichaeism in favor of Neoplatonism, the philosophy of both Roman pagans and Milanese Christians.

His mother finally caught up with him and decided to find her son a proper wife. Augustine had a concubine he deeply loved, who had given him a son, but he would not marry her because it would have ruined him socially and politically.

Some believe that the conjunction of the emotional strain of grief in abandoning his lover along with the shift in philosophies left Augustine in a mode of self-loathing, which centered on his sexuality, which he saw as the blame for his pain. He attempted to renounce sex. For years he had sought to overcome his fleshly passions and nothing seemed to help. Becoming hypersensitive regarding the least of transgressions, he would reflect even on prepubescent tricks. Writing about the pear stealing of his youth, he reflected, "Our real pleasure consisted in doing something that was forbidden. The evil in me was foul, but I loved it." The self-loathing reformed sex addict overcompensated and became unstable, yet, the writings of Augustine would shape the church in time to come.

With the advent of the Dark Ages around 500, the upheavals in society saw a decline in clerical discipline and with it, a return to marriage and even the keeping of concubines by priests. During this time, the wealth of the church was also increasing, a development not lost on Rome. Many priests were leaving church lands to their heirs, and others handed down land of their own through primogeniture.

Now, this may not have been such a big deal if it weren't for the fact that priests were becoming wealthy. A priest or bishop would inform someone with land and means that they might burn in hell for their actions (or inactions). But perhaps they could be absolved if they left their lands to the Church. The duke or earl or baron would sign over a portion of his land or funds to the cleric in return for Salvation.

The bishops were leaving these acquisitions to their heirs. So the families of the bishops were becoming wealthy and powerful, the heads of State were losing revenues from taxes and the church was losing an opportunity to become the richest nation on Earth.

In 1018 A.D., Pope Benedict began to get serious about the matter when he decreed that descendants of priests could not inherit property.

The Second Lateran Council finally made celibacy a law of the Church in 1139 A.D. Pope Gregory VII, who had assumed vast power by declaring himself the supreme authority over all souls, went even further by forbidding married priests from saying mass; he also forbade parishioners from attending masses said by them. Scholars believe that the first written law forbidding the clergy to marry was finally handed down at the Second Lateran Council in 1139 A.D.

The matter was brought up again in the 16th century, when dissenters tried to return to original Church doctrine, but the Council of Trent finalized the doctrine of celibacy in 1563 and the law finally became official doctrine at the Council of Trent in 1563.

In spite of all evidence showing the suppression of normal drives causes corruption and re-direction of such drives, Rome's position on the issue has remained unchanged.

Money and land trump pedophilia and sexual abuse every time.

Just as a matter of curiosity, would it not be interesting to know if the popes that were so "motivated" to make celibacy for clergy mandatory actually followed their own orders? After all, if this command really was a holy order from on high the pope should also obey. But if it were a grab for power and riches then usually the head thief is above the law.

According to Wikipedia and other sources, there have been 265 popes. Many of them were sexually active within their papacy. Some were gay. There are various classifications for those who were sexually active at some time during their life. Periods in parentheses refer to the years of their papacies.

Married before receiving Holy Orders -

It was within canon law, and still is, for priests to have once been married before receiving Holy Orders. In the Eastern Rite branches of the Catholic Church, it is within canon law to be a priest and married (but one may not marry after ordination).

Their example of this is Saint Peter (Simon Peter), whose mother-in-law is mentioned in the Bible as having been miraculously healed (Matthew 8:14-15, Luke 4:38, Mark 1:29-31). According to Clement of Alexandria (Stromata, III, vi, ed. Dindorf, II, 276), Peter was married and had children and his wife

Joseph Lumpkin

suffered martyrdom. In some legends dating from at least the 6th century, Peter's daughter is called Petronilla.

Pope Clement I wrote, "For Peter and Philip begat children; [..] When the blessed Peter saw his own wife led out to die, he rejoiced because of her summons and her return home, and called to her very encouragingly and comfortingly, addressing her by name, and saying, 'Remember the Lord.' Such was the marriage of the blessed, and their perfect disposition toward those dearest to them."

Pope St. Hormisdas (514-523) was married and widowed before ordination. He was the father of Pope St. Silverius.

Pope Adrian II (867-872) was married, before taking orders, and had a daughter.

Pope John XVII (1003) was married before his election to the papacy and had three sons, who all became priests.

Pope Clement IV (1265-1268) was married, before taking Holy Orders, and had two daughters.

Pope Honorius IV (1285-1287) was married before he took the Holy Orders and had at least two sons. He entered the clergy after his wife died, the last pope to have been married.

Sexually active only before receiving Holy Orders -

Pope Pius II (1458-1464) had at least two illegitimate children (one in Strasbourg and another one in Scotland), born before he entered the clergy.

Pope Innocent VIII (1484-1492) (got to love that name) had at least two illegitimate children, born before he entered the clergy. According to the 1911 Encyclopaedia Britannica, he "openly practised nepotism in favour of his children." Girolamo Savonarola chastised him for his worldly ambitions.

Pope Clement VII (1523-1534) had one illegitimate son before he took holy orders. Some sources identify him with Alessandro de' Medici, Duke of Florence but this identification has not been confirmed.

Pope Gregory XIII (1572-1585) had an illegitimate son before he took holy orders.

Sexually active after receiving Holy Orders -

Pope Julius II (1503-1513) had at least one illegitimate daughter, Felice della Rovere (born in 1483, twenty years before his election). Some sources indicate that he had two additional illegitimate daughters, who died in their childhood.[16] Besides, some contemporary (possibly libellous) reports accused him of sodomy. According to the schismatic Council of Pisa in 1511, he was a "sodomite covered with shameful ulcers."

Pope Paul III (1534-1549) held off ordination in order to continue his promiscuous lifestyle, fathering four illegitimate children (three sons and one daughter) by his mistress Silvia Ruffini. He broke his relations with her ca. 1513. There is no evidence of sexual activity during his papacy. He made his illegitimate son Pier Luigi Farnese the first Duke of Parma.

Pope Pius IV (1559-1565) had three illegitimate children before his election to the papacy.

Sexually active during their pontificate -

Along with other complaints, the activities of the popes between 1458 and 1565, helped encourage the Protestant Revolt.

Pope Sergius III (904-911) was supposedly the father of Pope John XI by Marozia, according to Liutprand of Cremona in his Antapodosis, as well as the Liber Pontificalis.However it must be noted that this is disputed by another early source, the annalist Flodoard (c. 894-966), John XI was brother of Alberic II, the latter being the offspring of Marozia and her husband Alberic I. Hence, John too may have been the son of Marozia and Alberic I. Bertrand Fauvarque underlines that the contemporary sources backing up this parenthood are dubious, Liutprand being "prone to exaggeration" while

Joseph Lumpkin

other mentions of this fatherhood appear in satires written by supporters of the late Pope Formosus.

Pope John X (914-928) had romantic affairs with both Theodora and her daughter Marozia, according to Liutprand of Cremona in his Antapodosis: "The first of the popes to be created by a woman and now destroyed by her daughter". (See also pornocracy)

Pope John XII (955-963) (deposed by Conclave) was said to have turned the Basilica di San Giovanni in Laterano into a brothel and was accused of adultery, fornication, and incest (Source: Patrologia Latina). The monk chronicler Benedict of Soracte noted in his volume XXXVII that he "liked to have a collection of women." According to Liutprand of Cremona in his Antapodosis, "they testified about his adultery, which they did not see with their own eyes, but nonetheless knew with certainty; he had fornicated with the widow of Rainier, with Stephana his father's concubine, with the widow Anna, and with his own niece, and he made the sacred palace into a whorehouse." According to The Oxford Dictionary of Popes, John XII was "a Christian Caligula whose crimes were rendered particularly horrific by the office he held". He was killed by a jealous husband while in the act of committing adultery with the man's wife. (See also pornocracy)

Pope Benedict IX (1032-1044, again in 1045 and finally 1047-1048) was said to have conducted a very dissolute life during his papacy. He was accused by Bishop Benno of Placenta of "many vile adulteries and murders."

Pope Victor III referred in his third book of Dialogues to "his rapes, murders and other unspeakable acts. His life as a Pope so vile, so foul, so execrable, that I shudder to think of it." It prompted St. Peter Damian to write an extended treatise against sex in general, and homosexuality in particular. In his Liber Gomorrhianus, St. Peter Damian recorded that Benedict "feasted on immorality" and that he was "a demon from hell in the disguise of a priest", accusing Benedict IX of routine sodomy and bestiality and was said to have sponsored orgies. In May 1045, Benedict IX resigned his office to pursue marriage, selling his office for 1,500 pounds of gold to his godfather, the pious priest John Gratian, who named himself Gregory VI.

Pope Alexander VI (1492-1503) had a notably long affair with Vannozza dei Cattanei before his papacy, by whom he had his famous illegitimate children

Cesare and Lucrezia. A later mistress, Giulia Farnese, was the sister of Alessandro Farnese, who later became Pope Paul III. He fathered a total of at least seven, and possibly as many as ten illegitimate children.[40] (See also Banquet of Chestnuts)

Suspected to have been sexually active with male lovers -

Pope Paul II (1464–1471) was alleged to have died of a heart attack while in a sexual act with a page boy.

Pope Sixtus IV (1471-1484) was alleged to have awarded gifts and benefices to court favorites in return for sexual favors. Giovanni Sclafenato was created a cardinal by Sixtus IV for "ingenuousness, loyalty,...and his other gifts of soul and body", according to the papal epitaph on his tomb. According to Stefano Infessura, in his Diarium urbis Romae, he had a predilection for young boys.

Pope Leo X (1513-1521) was alleged to have had a particular infatuation for Marc-Antonio Flaminio.

Pope Julius III (1550-1555) was alleged to have had a long affair with Innocenzo Ciocchi del Monte. The Venetian ambassador at that time reported that Innocenzo shared the pope's bedroom and bed. According to the The Oxford Dictionary of Popes, he was "naturally indolent, he devoted himself to pleasurable pursuits with occasional bouts of more serious activity."

Continuing with our fun facts, according to "futurechurch.org" here is a list of popes who were the sons of the supposedly asexual clergy.

Popes who were the sons of other popes or other clergy -

Name of Pope	Papacy	Son of
St. Damascus I	366-348	St. Lorenzo, priest
St. Innocent I	401-417	Anastasius I
Boniface	418-422	son of a priest
St. Felix	483-492	son of a priest
Anastasius II	496-498	son of a priest

Joseph Lumpkin

St. Agapitus I	535-536	Gordiaous, priest
St. Silverus	536-537	St. Homidas, pope
Deusdedit	882-884	son of a priest
Boniface VI	896-896	Hadrian, bishop
John XI	931-935	Pope Sergius III
John XV	989-996	Leo, priest

The same source supplied the following list of popes who had children out of wedlock AFTER the celibacy decree was in force.

Popes who had illegitimate children after 1139

Innocent VIII	1484-1492	several children
Alexander VI	1492-1503	several children
Julius	1503-1513	3 daughters
Paul III	1534-1549	3 sons, 1 daughter
Pius IV	1559-1565	3 sons
Gregory XIII	1572-1585	1 son

History sources: Oxford Dictionary of Popes; H.C. Lea

History of Sacerdotal Celibacy in the Christian Church 1957; E. Schillebeeckx

The Church with a Human Face 1985; J. McSorley

Outline History of the Church by Centuries 1957; F.A.Foy (Ed.) 1990

Catholic Almanac 1989; D.L. Carmody

The Double Cross - Ordination, Abortion and Catholic Feminism 1986; P.K. Jewtt

The Ordination of Women 1980; A.F. Ide

God's Girls - Ordination of Women in the Early Christian & Gnostic Churches 1986; E. Schüssler Fiorenza

In Memory of Her 1984; P. DeRosa Vicars of Christ 1988.

TRANSUBSTANTIATION

Transubstantiation comes from the Latin word, "Tansubsubstaniato", meaning "change of substance". This term was not incorporated into a creed until the Forth Lateran Council in A.D. 1215.

According to Catholic authorities, the word was first used by Hildebert of Tours (about 1079). His example was soon followed by Stephen of Autun (1139), Gaufred (1188), and Peter of Blois (about 1200). Several ecumenical councils also adopted the term, such as the Fourth Lateran Council in A.D. 1215, and the Council of Lyons (1274).

The Roman Catholic Church defined and explained Transubstantiation in the Council of Trent (1564) as follows, "By the consecration of the bread and wine, a conversion is made of the whole substance of the bread into the substance of the body of Christ our Lord, and of the whole substance of the wine into the substance of His blood; which conversion is, by the holy Catholic Church, suitably and properly called Transubstantiation."

"In this sacrament are contained not only the true body of Christ, and all the constituents of a true body, such as bones and sinews, but also Christ whole and entire."

"Christ whole and entire, is contained, not only under either species, but also in each particle of the same species." (Species here refers to bread and wine.)

The above information indicates that the Church of Rome teaches that when the priest blesses the bread, it becomes Jesus Christ himself and similarly the wine is Jesus Christ himself, but where did this doctrine come from and when did it start?

If we look at the scriptures and compare the actions of the early fathers we may see what they believed the bread and wine to be.

Acts 2:42 They devoted themselves to the apostles' teaching and to the fellowship, to the breaking of bread and to prayer.

1 Corinthians 10:14 Therefore, my dear friends, flee from idolatry. 15 I speak to sensible people; judge for yourselves what I say. 16 Is not the cup of thanksgiving for which we give thanks a participation in the blood of Christ? And is not the bread that we break a participation in the body of Christ? 17 Because there is one loaf, we, who are many, are one body, for we all partake of the one loaf.

What we know as communion today was called in scripture, "breaking of bread."

The term the "Lord's Supper" was found in notes taken from the Council of Carthage in A.D. 418.

Irenaeus used the term Oblation to agree with the description in 1 Corinthians 11:20 When you come together, it is not the Lord's Supper you eat, 21 for as you eat, each of you goes ahead without waiting for anybody else. One remains hungry, another gets drunk. 22 Don't you have homes to eat and drink in? Or do you despise the church of God and humiliate those who have nothing? What shall I say to you? Shall I praise you for this? Certainly not!

23 For I received from the Lord what I also passed on to you: The Lord Jesus, on the night He was betrayed, took bread, 24 and when He had given thanks, He broke it and said, "This is My body, which is for you; do this in remembrance of Me." 25 In the same way, after supper He took the cup, saying, "This cup is the new covenant in My blood; do this, whenever you drink it, in remembrance of Me." 26 For whenever you eat this bread and drink this cup, you proclaim the Lord's death until He comes.

Eucharist, meaning a thanksgiving, was used by Ignatius, Irenaeus, Origen and others. Justin Martyr, Origen, Eusebius and Chrysostom also call the communion "Memorial" because in it we remember the death of the Lord.

"Mass" was used by Eusebius as a term for the church service. It was not until Ambrose (374-397), that the term Mass was used to denote communion.

Up to this point the term Transubstantiation was never used, and there was no mention of any assumption of bread or wine being anything but symbols.

Documents written by the early church fathers indicates that the Didache, or Teaching of the Twelve Apostles (a document with a questionable dating of 50 A.D. - 200 A.D.) and Justin Martyr (died c. 165 A.D.) never assert the doctrine of the Real Presence of Christ in the sacrament.

Ignatius (died about 107 A.D.) comes the closest to hinting at Transubstantiation of anyone at the time when he rails against Gnostic antagonists when he says, "They do not admit that the Eucharist is the flesh of our Savior Jesus Christ, the flesh which suffered for our sins and which the Father, in His graciousness, raised from the dead." However, this does not mean he is protesting their disbelief in Transubstantiation. Many Gnostics of the time denied Jesus ever came in the flesh, believing him to be only a phantasm. His body, they claimed, was an illusion produced by His spirit.

However, by 200 A.D., we begin to find statements that the bread and wine are strictly Christ's body and blood. One statement occurs in an argument against the Docetists about the reality of Christ's earthly body. One wonders if this was an over-reaction to the Gnostic heresy. Tertullian (c. 160-220 A.D.) and Cyprian (c. 258 A.D.) indicate they believed in the symbolic aspect of the bread and wine representing the body and blood. The men accepted the representation of the elements as the body and blood. Tertullian stated "Christ, having taken the bread and given it to His disciples, made it His body by saying, "This is my body, that is, the figure of my body." Even Orgien, acknowledges "that they (bread and wine) are figures which are written in the sacred volumes; therefore as spiritual not as carnal, examine and understand what is said. For if as carnal you receive them, they hurt, not nourish you."

Serapion (c. 211 A.D.) refers to the elements as "a likeness." Eusebius of Caesarea (c. 339 A.D.) states, "We are continually fed with the Savior's body, we continually participate in the lamb's blood," but follows it up, "with the symbols of his body and saving blood." He states that Jesus instructed his disciples to make "the image of his own body," and employ bread as its symbol.

Both Cyril of Jerusalem (315 – 386 A.D.) and Eusebius of Caesarea denied Transubstantiation. Cyril stated, "Under the type of bread, His body given unto thee, and under the type of wine, His blood given unto thee." Eusebius qualifies communion as "Christ Himself gave the symbols of the Divine ceremony to His own disciples that the image of His own body should be made. He appointed to use bread as a symbol of His own body."

The Apostolical Constitutions (c. 380 A.D.) use words such as "antitypes" and "symbols" to describe the elements, though they speak of communion as the body of Christ and the blood of Christ.

The first move toward Transubstantiation seems to have been introduced by a friar named Anastatius, around A.D. 637. The friar decided to interpret the Lord's Supper in a very literal sense as no one had done before. This introduced the doctrine called, "Real Presence."

John Damascene (676 A.D. – 787 A.D.) is most famous as one who defended and favored the veneration of sacred images, holy pictures, statues and icons. His writings in the Eastern Church are what the Summa of St. Thomas Aquinas are to the West.

In A.D. 754, at the Council of Constantinople, John Damascene states, "The bread and wine are supernaturally changed by the invocation and coming of the Holy Ghost into the body and blood of Jesus Christ, and are not two, but one and the same... The bread and wine are not the type or the figure of the body and blood of Jesus Christ - ah, God forbid! - but the body itself of our Lord deified."

Opposition from within the Roman Catholic Church came in part from Pashus Radbert, who wrote "that there are many that in these mystical things are of another opinion." Others were also against this doctrine within the Roman Catholic Church. Aefric, Abbot of Malmesbury (A.D.905) and Berengarius (A. D. 1029), and St. Bede in the 8th Century joined in the chorus of dissenters over the years.

The Abbot of Corbie advanced the doctrine in A.D. 818 when he wrote a treatise stating, "What was received in the Sacrament is the same flesh as that which was born of the Virgin Mary, and which suffered death for us; and though the figure of bread and wine doth remain, yet you must absolutely believe that, after consecration, it is nothing but the flesh and blood of Jesus Christ." This doctrine was further developed and finally made a dogma by Pope Innocent III (1161-1216).

Now, we are over one-thousand years out from the earliest church leaders. We can see the doctrine of Transubstantiation has taken root, grown, and is now being written into church law. However, the Apostles never addressed this or even thought about this doctrine. They never acknowledged any change in the elements or believed in any corporal presence.

Later, as the epistles were being read and discussed some took to reading the words and interpreting their meaning as purely literal. At that time, most of those in leadership positions warned about this approach.

Even men who were supporters of the Roman Church and the papacy suggested that "there was nothing in the Gospels that may enforce us to understand Christ's words properly, yea, nothing in the text ('This is My body') hinders but those words may as well be taken in a metaphysical sense, as the words of the Apostle, 'the Rock was Christ'... That part, which the Gospel hath not expressed, viz., the conversion of the bread in the body and blood of Christ, we have received expressly from the Church." Bellarmine, (1542 - 1621A.D.) another Roman scholar admitted "there is no express place of Scripture to prove Transubstantiation without the declaration of the Church."

The scholars proclaimed, "Therefore, as we have been given a sound mind and are instructed to search the scriptures to see what is true and then to hold fast to what is true, we find the doctrine of Transubstantiation illogical! The Lord Jesus at the Last Supper handed the broken bread to the apostles and stated, "This is my body." However He was in his earthly body, 100 percent human. Yet this doctrine would destroy human nature by having the ability to be in multiple places at one time. Rome teaches that Christ is corporally on the altar but without any "accidents." Yet again, we are to deny all logic and sensibility to believe that Christ is present upon the altar! (Accidents, in this case means that it has no affect on any senses and cannot be discerned.)

How time and constant political pressure changes things. From the denials of the doctrine by church leaders in the first and second centuries, the pendulum swings slowly, over a thousand years, to the other side. St. Alphonsus de Liguori (1698 – 1787) was the author of the book, "The Glories of Mary." He was a Catholic Priest and theologian. Liguori wrote in his book, The Dignity and Duties of the Priest or Selva; "But our wonder should be far greater when we find that in obedience to the words of his priests - HOC EST CORPUS MEUM (This Is My Body) - God himself descends on the altar, that he comes wherever they call him and as often as they call him, and places himself in their hands, even though they should be his enemies. "

From these words, HOC EST CORPUS MEUM comes our words Hocus Pocus, said by those who thought the doctrine of transubstantiation was simply too much to believe. Pagans and non-papists alike not only condemned the doctrine, but ridiculed it as well. So wide spread was the disbelief that it made its way into our modern vernacular and came to mean anything seemingly magical but fraudulent, as expressed in the phrase, "That is just so much hocus pocus."

These alleged changes of the bread and wine into God Himself are not evident in any outward physical change. Scientific tests have been performed to seek for any amount of blood in the Eucharist during and after the priest's blessing but none were ever found.

Protestants are very proud of their stance on Transubstantiation, but most have not escaped the cloying Catholic doctrine at all. It may be true that most Protestants do not believe the bread or wine becomes the body of Christ, but some churches insist on the bread and wine being blessed only by their own ordained ministers before being passed to the church members. The Methodist Church is one of these, according to their manual called, "The Book of Discipline."

Why do we need a priest to bless the bread and wine? Is the priest representing Christ to us? Are we not equal in the sight of God, or do we believe a four year degree at a religious college brings one some extra especial spiritual power? It is difficult to shake our roots. From Catholic to Episcopal to Methodist, traditions cling and cloud the truth. What is the truth? We are all the same in the eyes of God. Every believer is a priest. The bread is just bread. The wine is just wine… or if you are Baptist or Pentecostal, it is grape juice because we cannot drink like Jesus did.

Grape juice kept in animal skins and urns in the Israeli heat that did not become fermented… now that would be hocus-pocus.

RAPTURE

The word "Rapture" is not found in the English Bible. The word comes from the Latin verb *rapere,* which means "to carry off, abduct, seize or take forcefully." To see the flavor of the word, compare the words "rape" or "raptor", which is a type of bird of prey such as a hawk. The word *rapere* was used in the Latin Vulgate of 405 A.D. to translate the phrase from Thessalonians 4:17, which is the primary biblical reference. The word, "*rapiemur*" "we shall be caught up" translating the Greek word harpagÄ, which *is the* passive mood, future tense of harpazÅ.

Although the doctrine of the resurrection of the dead was taught by Jesus in the Gospels and was an accepted belief common to all Christians, there was no thought, nor discussion in the area of eschatology about the 'Rapture' until the Reformation. Although Christians from the very beginning accepted, as scriptures clearly state, that, at some point the faithful would be "caught up" with Christ, it was always assumed this was a resurrection message. In modern eschatology the same scriptures are interpreted as the doctrine of the 'Rapture'. The Christian denominations that actually put eschatological emphasis on it are mostly those that appeared after the Reformation.

The first known occurrence of a "rapture-like" theology or reference, which could be construed as a rapture doctrine, was that of Ephraem of Nisibis, in 373 A.D., who preached a sermon saying; "For all the saints and Elect of God are gathered, prior to the tribulation that is to come, and are taken to the Lord lest they see the confusion that is to overwhelm the world because of our sins."

The sermon was met with a thousand years of silence and the idea was rejected and ignored. The doctrine did not catch on enough to be repeated or even referenced as a consideration until it was re-visited in the Protestant Reformation and the rise of Dispensationalism.

Then in 1788 a precursor to the doctrine of the rapture appeared as an allusion. The story was written in a book penned in 1788 by a Catholic priest named Emmanuel Lacunza and published in Spain in 1812. The book spread, as did the intrigue of its storyline.

By combining verses and ideas from several books of the Bible, John Darby, a Brethren preacher, developed and taught the Rapture doctrine in 1827. Yes, the idea of the rapture, as set forth in most Protestant churches, has only been around since the early 1800's. This should give pause. It should cause us to ask if this is some new insight and revelation from God, or simply an idea derived from a combination of unrelated texts from various books of the

Bible.

When relating texts from different books of the Bible we must always remember that we are reading separate books written at different times to various churches in differing areas for divergent purposes.

The evangelist, William Blackstone worked the idea into his book and popularized Rapture doctrine in his best seller, "Jesus is Coming." This was the "Left Behind" novel of its day. The idea of the rapture is a great read and makes for a heart stopping storyline. Popularity drove the idea from the novel into the pulpit.

In theological terms, the teaching of the rapture is a new doctrine. Its inception can be traced to an event in 1831 when Margaret McDonald, who claimed that God had shown it to her, first taught it, in Scotland. Chances are, she read it in the 1793 Blackstone novel, who probably heard of Derby's doctrine, who likely encountered the idea from Lacunza's audience.

The idea of the Rapture was slow to gain acceptance until it was promoted by John Nelson Darby, the founder of the Christian (Plymouth) Brethren movement. With the development of Fundamentalist Christianity around the turn of the 20th century, it was Cyrus Ignatius Scofield who became the champion of this new Rapture doctrine. The Rapture doctrine entered mainstream Christianity with its inclusion in the Scofield Reference Bible. There is no real history to the Rapture doctrine until the 1800's.

Since Christianity began, the texts used to justify the rapture theology were always regarded as 'resurrection' texts. Thus the earliest Creeds stated that Christ's return was the time when the Resurrection and Judgment Day would occur. The Nicene Creed reads; "He is seated at the right hand of God from whence He shall come to judge the quick and the dead".

The understanding of these texts is especially the case for 1Thessalonians 4:17 where the context is concern for the fate of those Christians who have already died. The text assures its readers that "the dead in Christ shall rise first" (1Thess. 4:16). "Rising" refers to rising from the dead and thus "resurrection" and not "rapture.

Other texts are as tenuous and weak at best especially when examined in the light of their context. For example, the expression "one shall be taken" in the Olivet Discourse of Matthew 24:40 references a flood first, signifying a disaster had occurred, and thus pointing to another disaster killing many people. For this reason as well as the historical timing of the verse, it has long been regarded by scholars as referring to the first century Roman catapult barrage of Jerusalem during the 42 month siege from A.D. 66 to A.D. 70 in which many people were randomly killed. This occurred after the time frame that Jesus would have given the speech, but during the time Matthew would have written the Gospel.

The verses used to define the rapture are vague in their timing and sequence, especially when added to those of the Book of Revelation. The indeterminate timeframe gave way to four distinct viewpoints. These are called, "pre-tribulation," mid-tribulation," "post-tribulation," and pre-wrath." (Also called pre-trib, mid-trib, post-trib.) Most would equate the category of mid-trib with that of pre-wrath, simply because the common belief is that the Anti-Christ will achieve world dominance and reveal himself only after he is half way into his seven year reign. It is in the latter half of this period that world chaos breaks out.

Here are some of the main scriptures used to form the rapture teaching.

Matthew 24:37-42

37 But as the days of Noe [were], so shall also the coming of the Son of man be. 38 For as in the days that were before the flood they were eating and drinking, marrying and giving in marriage, until the day that Noe entered into the ark, 39 And knew not until the flood came, and took them all away; so shall also the coming of the Son of man be. 40 Then shall two be in the field; the one shall be taken, and the other left. 41 Two [women shall be] grinding at the mill; the one shall be taken, and the other left. 42 Watch therefore: for ye know not what hour your Lord doth come.

I Thessalonians 4:13-18 But we do not want you to be uninformed, brethren, about those who are asleep, so that you will not grieve as do the rest who have no hope. For if we believe that Jesus died and rose again, even so God will bring with him those who have fallen asleep in Jesus. For this we say to you by the word of the Lord, that we who are alive and remain until the coming of the Lord, will not precede those who have fallen asleep. For the Lord himself will descend from heaven with a shout, with the voice of the archangel and with the trumpet of God, and the dead in Christ will rise first. Then we who are alive and remain will be caught up together with them in the clouds to meet the Lord in the air, and so we shall always be with the Lord. Therefore comfort one another with these words.

2 Peter 3:9-12

9 The Lord is not slow in keeping his promise, as some understand slowness. He is patient with you, not wanting anyone to perish, but everyone to come to repentance. 10 But the day of the Lord will come like a thief. The heavens will disappear with a roar; the elements will be destroyed by fire, and the earth and everything in it will be laid bare. 11 Since everything will be destroyed in this way, what kind of people ought you to be? You ought to live holy and godly lives.12 as you look forward to the day of God and speed its coming. That day will bring about the destruction of the heavens by fire, and the elements will melt in the heat.

Joseph Lumpkin

1 Corinthians 15:52

"In a moment, in the twinkling of an eye, at the last trump: for the trumpet shall sound, and the dead shall be raised incorruptible, and we shall be changed."

Phillipians 3:21 "(Christ) shall change our vile body, that it may be fashioned like unto his glorious body, according to the working whereby he is able even to subdue all things unto himself."

Matthew 24:27-31

27 For as the lightning cometh out of the east, and shineth even unto the west; so shall also the coming of the Son of man be. 28 For wheresoever the carcass is, there will the eagles be gathered together. 29 Immediately after the tribulation of those days shall the sun be darkened, and the moon shall not give her light, and the stars shall fall from heaven, and the powers of the heavens shall be shaken: 30 And then shall appear the sign of the Son of man in heaven: and then shall all the tribes of the earth mourn, and they shall see the Son of man coming in the clouds of heaven with power and great glory. 31 And he shall send his angels with a great sound of a trumpet, and they shall gather together his elect from the four winds, from one end of heaven to the other.

Looking at these verses through the eyes of Christians from 33 A.D. to 1800 A.D. one can easily see how all of the verses were assumed to refer to the Resurrection of the Dead. Men, bishops, scholars, and theologians, including those who knew the apostles or their disciples or the students of the disciples, as well as all of Christianity making up the first 1800 years never thought these verses were anything but resurrection texts. Then, a book of fiction was written and a new doctrine emerged. But is it really Biblical or is it myth pressed into the populace by a good book?

The answer may come into a clearer light if one keeps in mind that scriptures quoted are from at least four separate books, written to different people or groups for various reasons and were not meant to be chained into the story of a rapture.

Eighteen hundred years after Jesus, someone writes a good book and a preacher decides to use the idea to fire up his crowd. A man puts a reference to the new idea in his bible notes. People read it and swallow the idea whole without question. The rapture makes for a great story and wonderful drama. It can bring a congregation to its feet or to the altar, but is it real, or are we just that stupid?

APOCALYPSE
End of Days

The doctrine of the rapture was not needed to fire the imagination and produce predictions of the end of time. Apocalyptic proclamations are not directly related to the rapture. Indeed, the teachers of the rapture simply incorporated the doctrine of the rapture into a general apocalyptic view.

Even today there are differing views as to when the rapture will occur within the time of the apocalypse. These differences are called, "pre-trib," mid-trib," and "post-trib," and signify the three main schools of thought regarding the timing of the rapture to the apocalypse. The question is, "Will the church be taken to heaven before, during, or after the chaos, war, death, and destruction foretold in the Bible?"

However, the idea of the Apocalypse itself is based on a literal reading of the Book of Revelation and the assumption that all things written in the book point toward future events.

The Book of Revelation was written sometime around 96 A.D. in Asia Minor. The author was a Christian from Ephesus known as "John the Elder," or "John the Revelator." According to the Book, John was on the island of Patmos, which is not far from the coast of Asia Minor. The reason for his exile was, "because of the word of God and the testimony of Jesus" (Rev. 1.10).

Ephesus was both the capital of the Roman province of Asia and one of the earliest centers of Christianity. The book mentions seven Christian churches in the seven leading cities of Asia Minor -- Ephesus (2.1-7, Smyrna (2.9-11), Pergamon (2.12-17), Thyatira (2.18-29). Sardis (3.1-6), Philadelphia (3.7-13). and Laodicea (3.14-22). These were the centers of the Christian faith in the region at the time. Romans were persecuting Christians and this was what the author was dealing with personally also. The Roman administration was viewed as agents of the devil. Thus, we have the perfect mixture for the writing of apocalyptic literature.

The Book of Revelation uses intricate and unusual symbolic language, allusions, and metaphor. It is difficult for modern readers to follow since many of the symbolic references are now lost. This would not have been the case for people in the ancient world. Not only were they more accustomed to complex apocalyptic literature; they were living within the symbols used within the book. Thus, it could be said that apocalyptic literature was good reading for "insiders." That is to say, it was written for people who already knew the situation and the meanings of the symbols that were used to portray it.

There were several reasons to write in this fashion. The primary one was to save your head from the chopping block. When writing about the emperor it is best to hide the meaning so the audience understands but the meaning could still be denied or ignored if needed.

Another problem for the modern reader is the time-line within the book. It is not linear. For example, events in chapter 12 do not follow in time after the events in chapter 11. Events in chapters 12-13 are meant to explain how those circumstances in chapters 5-11 came about. So the time-line of the story moves in circles, bringing the reader back to the "present situation" as it stood for the ancient readers of Revelation. But what was the situation?

It is now thought that a situation arose in Ephesus after the year 89 A.D. when Domitian instituted a new imperial cult sanctuary dedicated to his family, the Flavian dynasty. It had included his father, Vespasian, who as Roman general led the war against the Jews from 66-69 A.D. When the Emperor Nero was killed, Vespasian was summoned from Judea to Rome to become the new Emperor. Vespasian then appointed his elder son, Titus, as the commander of the legions in Judea. It was Titus who led the siege and destruction of Jerusalem in 70 A.D. When Vespasian died in 79 A.D., Titus became the next Emperor. Titus, however, died just two years later in 81 A.D., and this left the empire to Vespasian's younger son, Domitian. Domitian was known as a strong-willed emperor who tolerated no disagreement with his policies.

Since we are not able to take the time and hundreds of pages needed to discuss in depth the Book of Revelation and its symbols, we will simply give a couple of examples.

Look at the "beast from the sea" in Rev. 17. We can see it is the Emperor himself. This is made clear in a passage, where the symbolism of the seven heads is spelled out.

Rev. 17:9 "This calls for a mind that has wisdom: the seven heads are seven mountains on which the woman is seated; also, they are seven kings, 10 of whom five have fallen, one is living, and the other has not yet come; and when he comes, he must remain only a little while. 11 As for the beast that was and is not, it is an eighth but it belongs to the seven, and it goes to destruction. 12 And the ten horns that you saw are ten kings who have not yet received a kingdom, but they are to receive authority as kings for one hour, together with the beast. 13 These are united in yielding their power and authority to the beast; 14 they will make war on the Lamb, and the Lamb will conquer them...

The "five fallen" refer to the five emperors who have died: Augustus (29 BC -

14 A.D.), Tiberius (14-37 A.D.), Gaius (37-41 A.D.), Claudius (41-54 A.D.) and Nero (54-68 A.D.). "One has a wound" refers to the emperor Nero, who died in 68 A.D. Nero was so horribly evil that contemporary legend had it that he would return from the dead to continue persecuting the Christians.

The angst and trauma Nero left in the Christian world is noted in an unusual bit of symbolism – the number 666.

An ancient type of numerology, called Gematria, was used to "encode" names into numbers.

In Hebrew Gematria, every letter has a corresponding number. Summing these numbers gives a numeric value to a word or name. In Hebrew, "Nero Caesar" is spelled "□□□□ □□□", pronounced "Neron Qe[i]sar". Adding the corresponding values yields 666, as shown:

Resh	Samekh	Qoph	Nun	Vav	Resh	Nun
200	60	100	50	6	200	50

Resh = 200

Samekh = 60

Qoph = 100

Nun = 50

Vav = 6

Resh = 200

Nun = 50

Total = 666

But the really suggestive hint is that the oldest manuscripts don't agree on the number and some have 616 instead. It's much harder to concoct an explanation that fits both numbers, and only one of the proposed interpretations of the Number of the Beast accounts for both, and that is Nero. Remember it was NeRON QeiSaR in Hebrew. But the final N of NeRON is optional. Removing the terminal □ (written as □) makes the name "Nero" rather than "Neron". Subtracting the letter N [Nun] and its value of 50 makes the numeric value 616, which may explain that particular variation found in some older manuscripts.

The hypothesis that 666 is a code for a Roman emperor seems to have historical support. The emperors were noted for their oppression of both Jews and Christians. Both communities were known to use numerology or gematria, as well as codes and symbols when living under Roman rule to avoid persecution.

The German Protestant theologian Ethelbert Stauffer, argued that gematria had been the most popular form of numerology among Jews but also in the rest of the Graeco-Roman world.

By portraying the Emperor and his provincial authorities as "beasts" and henchmen of the dragon, Satan, the author of Revelation was calling on Christians to refuse to take part in the imperial cult, even at the risk of martyrdom.

Based on an enormous amount of data, it seems clear that The Book of Revelation is not some oracle into the future, but a scathing indictment of the Roman Empire in that period and a call to arms for Christians of the time.

However, this does not stop those who read the Bible with an apocalyptic eye from applying the symbolism in some personal formula to predict the end of days. Indeed, man has been seeing the end of time coming almost from the beginning of time. Every year there are those predicting the end of days. There is a list of doomsday and Rapture prophecies, which begin in 2800 B.C. and end in 2012 A.D. in Appendix "A". The list was harvested from several web sites and books. The number of false prophets and prophecies was so overwhelming that the list had to be trimmed down and limited to a stop date of 2012 A.D. The list clearly demonstrates the amazing amount of arrogance contained in certain churches, sects, and denominations as their leaders predict and predict and predict and fail. One must ask, "If a leader is so far off of the spiritual mark so many times in this area, should he or she be trusted in any spiritual area at all?"

However, let us not leave the discussion quite yet. There is still one more major view to examine.

Mankind is notorious for repeating errors. In fact, social, political, and economic errors tend to cycle. If we get passed the insanity of attempting to place dates on the end of time and we focus on the lessons within the book of Revelation, or any other books in the Bible, we will gain immense insight and preparedness for things to come. From the Roman oppression of the church, to the Chinese oppression at Tiananmen Square, to the revitalization of the emperor worship cult in North Korea, the evils of man never fail to repeat.

The call to the spirit within the Book of Revelation to be strong, to endure, and to resist bowing the knee to the evil forces in the world hold true from 70 A.D. to the end of time. We may not know when that will be, but we do know what it will take to endure to the end.

Revelation 3:12 (King James Version)

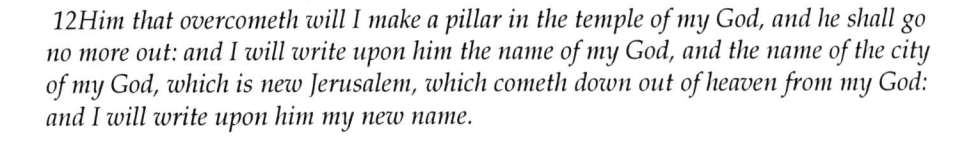

12Him that overcometh will I make a pillar in the temple of my God, and he shall go no more out: and I will write upon him the name of my God, and the name of the city of my God, which is new Jerusalem, which cometh down out of heaven from my God: and I will write upon him my new name.

Be sure to check out Appendix "A" for a good laugh.

SABBATH VERSES SUNDAY

The conversion of worship from Saturday (Sabbath) to Sunday was a slow process, taking several hundred years and the convergence of ideas from both governing and religious authorities.

It is interesting to note that the division of time into a seven day week is not a constant or global rule, nor has it always been that the world enjoyed this common measurement of time. The standard explanation is that the seven-day week was established as imperial calendar in the late Roman Empire, but it existed long before. The seven-day week was perpetuated by the Christian church for historical reasons. The British Empire used the seven-day week and spread it worldwide.

The first pages of the Bible explain how God created the world in six days and rested on the seventh. This seventh day became the Jewish day of rest, the Sabbath, Saturday.

Historians tell us that the birthplace of the 7-day week was likely in the area of Babylon or Persia. The week was brought eastward and became known in Rome before the advent of Christianity.

Days of the week were once named after the seven planets known at the time. These were Saturn, Jupiter, Mars, the Sun, Venus, Mercury, and the Moon. Each had an hour of the day assigned to them, and the planet ruling or visibly brightest during the first hour of any day of the week gave its name to that day.

During the first century, the week of seven days was introduced into Rome from Egypt, and the Roman names of the planets were given to each successive day. Sunday was the first day of the week according to the Jews. Jewish tradition and religious law dictated that they worship on the Sabbath, or seventh day of the week. Since the Jewish people had come out of that area of the world that gave birth to the seven-day week, they simply aligned their worship to the new calendar with new names for days and worshiped on Saturday. But, knowing that Jesus and the apostles worshiped Saturday, how did the church begin to abandon the Sabbath for Sunday worship?

Historical records show that the weekly cycle has remained unchanged from Christ's time so that the Saturday and Sunday of those early centuries are still the Saturday and Sunday of today. This means that the simple explanation of a switched week or calendar is incorrect. The change from Saturday to Sunday was no mistake.

Let us trace the day of worship, beginning with Christ's time. According to Luke 4:16, it was Christ's "custom" to go to the synagogue on the Sabbath day.

We are also told that the women who had followed Him from Galilee "rested the Sabbath day according to the commandment" (Luke 23:56). The book of Luke was written around 60 A.D. There were obviously no significant changes to the day of worship until then since Luke tells the story without any explanation about which day was the Sabbath.

Acts 13:14 tells us that Paul and the Apostles worshipped on the Sabbath. Acts also explains that this was the practice in all major cities, as Paul and the others traveled and preached in the synagogues on the Sabbath. Since the Book of Acts was written around 64 A.D., we can attest that there was no change in worship at that point in time.

The first mention of Sunday observance by Christians comes in the second century from both the cities of Alexandria and Rome. About A.D. 130 Barnabas of Alexandria refers to the seventh-day Sabbath as representing the seventh millennium of earth's history. He goes on to say that the present Sabbaths were unacceptable to God, who would make a beginning of another world (the eighth millennium). Therefore we are to keep the eighth day with joyfulness, the day on which Jesus rose again from the dead.

The above reference seems very odd and convoluted. Yet, it shows that the church of the time was working to lessen the importance of the Sabbath.

Justin Martyr in Rome provides a clear reference to Sunday observance around A.D. 150 stating, "And on the day called Sunday, all who live in cities or in the country gather together to one place, and the memoirs of the apostles (this is what he called the Gospels) or the writings of the prophets are read, as long as time permits; then, when the reader has ceased, the president verbally instructs, and exhorts all to the imitation of these good things." (At this time the church met on both Sabbath and Sunday.)

The church historian of the fifth century A.D., Socrates Scholasticus, wrote, "For although almost all churches throughout the world celebrate the sacred mysteries [the Lord's Supper] on the Sabbath of every week, yet the Christians of Alexandria and at Rome, on account of some ancient tradition, have ceased to do this." And Sozomen, a contemporary of Socrates, wrote, "The people of Constantinople, and almost everywhere, assemble together on the Sabbath, as well as on the first day of the week, which custom is never observed at Rome or at Alexandria." This means that from the time of Justin Martyr in 150 A.D., until the fifth century the church was going through a gradual change. First, the church worshipped on Saturday. Then they began to worship on both Saturday and Sunday.

The fourth century document, The Apostolic Constitutions, says to, "Keep the Sabbath, and the Lord's day festival; because the former is the memorial of the creation, and the latter of the resurrection." "Let the slaves work five days; but on the Sabbath-day and the Lord's day let them have leisure to go to church for instruction in piety."

It appears that Emperor Constantine, wishing to establish a single national holy day, was the author of the final decree that caused Christianity to eventually abandon the Sabbath.

In the early fourth century, Constantine, by his civil legislation, made Sunday a rest day. His "Sunday law" of March 7, 321 A.D., reads: "On the venerable Day of the Sun let the magistrates and people residing in cities rest, and let all workshops be closed. In the country, however, persons engaged in agriculture may freely and lawfully continue their pursuits; because it often happens that another day is not so suitable for grain-sowing or for vine-planting; lest by neglecting the proper moment for such operations the bounty of heaven should be lost."

This began the laws regulating Sunday observance, which we continue in our society under the name, "Blue Laws." It is obvious that this first Sunday law was not particularly Christian in orientation since the Emperor called the day the "venerable Day of the Sun". Constantine sought to merge pagan and Christian holy days to more easily govern the kingdom. He saw the path of least resistance in the change of Christian worship since at that time the church was meeting on the Sabbath to worship and on Sunday to celebrate the resurrection.

A friend of the Emperor and noted theologian, Eusebius, wrote in his commentary on Psalm 92, that Christians would fulfill on the Lord's day all that in this psalm was prescribed for the Sabbath, including worship of God early in the morning. Through the new covenant the Sabbath celebration was transferred to the first day of light (Sunday). By throwing his weight behind the Emperor's decree he assured special treatment for himself and Sunday as the day of worship for Christians.

But Christianity did not lose out completely. We got a few things from the forced amalgam with the sun worshipers. The iconology of the halo was brought into our paintings of Jesus and the saints.

The word "halo" originated from a Greek word that simply meant the sun, or the sun's disk. The pre-Christian Romans named their sun-god Helios and eventually began using the halo in their art, including portraits of their "divine" emperors. When the Romans created emperor worship, they borrowed the image of the halo as a symbol of power and divinity of the emperor. When Constantine brought Christianity into companionship within his state, Christians were exposed to halos from all quarters. The halo was carried into Christian imagery and used to symbolize purity or divinity.

But none of this makes it right. Now we know that the church was led into Sunday worship by a pagan ruler in his attempt to unite his people under certain customs. This meant taking the worship day of the Sun and combining it with the day to worship the Son. So what now? Let's see what bible scholar Jim Lindsey has to say.

The Sabbath
By James Lindsey

Introduction

The Sabbath is a term like any other that at first you think, yeah I know what that is, but then when pressed to define it for someone it seems unclear. Is the Sabbath a day, a shadow, is it ceremonial or moral, when did it begin and who was it for?

There are many today, if asked, "do you observe the Sabbath?" would say yes every Sunday or every Saturday. There would still be others who simply dismiss it as religious bantering with a "who really cares anyway" attitude.

The purpose of this chapter is to answer some of these questions surrounding the Sabbath from the perspective of a man who was reared believing if you don't observe the Sabbath, you are going to burn-up in hell with all those who worship the Sun on Sunday.

So what is the Sabbath?

I believe the answer depends on when you are asking the question. Do you mean during the Old Testament or New Testament period? The first use of the word in a traditional protestant bible is found in Exodus 16:23 relating to the Manna miracle in the wilderness. A careful reading of this verse in context shows that the Sabbath was a part of the commandments (vs.28) of the LORD. The Sabbath was a test. You can see this in Deuteronomy 8:3. So what do we know so far?

- There is no mention of the Sabbath day until Exodus 16:23.
- The Sabbath was a part of the Lord's commandments.
- It was a test of faith.

Please note that some belief systems would argue against the first bullet point. I will address this shortly.

Joseph Lumpkin

The next major reference to the Sabbath is found in the Ten Commandments in Exodus 20: 8-11 (KJV).

(Exo 20:8) Remember the sabbath day, to keep it holy. (Exo 20:9) Six days shalt thou labour, and do all thy work: (Exo 20:10) But the seventh day is the sabbath of the LORD thy God: in it thou shalt not do any work, thou, nor thy son, nor thy daughter, thy manservant, nor thy maidservant, nor thy cattle, nor thy stranger that is within thy gates: (Exo 20:11) For in six days the LORD made heaven and earth, the sea, and all that in them is, and rested the seventh day: wherefore the LORD blessed the sabbath day, and hallowed it.

There are instructions to: Remember – Keep it Holy – Labor six days – Seventh day is the Sabbath of the Lord thy God – Not do any work – Lord blessed the Sabbath day and hallowed it.

But to whom were these commandments given? I was reared by a sweet mother to believe that they were given to me. Yet when I look back a few verses to verse 2 it reads, "I am the LORD thy God, which have brought thee out of the land of Egypt..." Like most of you I have never visited Egypt and I was never brought out by the LORD from Egypt. So, to whom were these commandments given? Well to the slave nation of Israel, of course, whom the LORD took out of Egypt, through the Red Sea, and into the wilderness.

At this point I want to talk to people who believe that these 10 were a restatement of God commandments to their fore-fathers and therefore have always been. PLEASE look at Deuteronomy 5: 2-4 for proof positive that this covenant was made with the nation of Israel exclusively at Horeb!

Deu 5:2 The LORD our God made a covenant with us in Horeb. Deu 5:3 The LORD made not this covenant with our fathers, but with us, even us, who are all of us here alive this day. Deu 5:4 The LORD talked with you face to face in the mount out of the midst of the fire... (Bolding is mine for emphasis).

Can any reasonably intelligent human being really believe that God somehow forgot that he had made this same covenant with Abraham, Isaac and Jacob in the past? It is mind boggling to me, but there are some for doctrinal and false prophet protection will argue against this crystal clear statement!

So recapping as not to forget and to emphasize what we have seen so far from the scriptures:

- There is no mention of the Sabbath day until Exodus 16:23.
- The Sabbath was a part of Lord's commandments.

- It was a test of faith.
- It was a part of the Ten Commandments given exclusively to Israel upon deliverance from Egypt.

Yet some will ask, saying I agree with everything written above, but aren't these moral laws? And if moral laws, aren't we to abide by them even today? To you I say, no. Before you get flustered and angry and begin spouting proof texts to support your belief, let me explain. Just because something has value to a society, doesn't necessarily make it a moral law that must be followed as law. Resting is a great benefit to humankind. Fatigue related depressions are a plaque in modernized societies. Workaholism is separating families and leading to illnesses. Yet rest rejuvenates the mind, body, and spirit. So rest is good and has value to society. On another line of thought there is value to separating diseased people from healthy. It is called quarantining. It is used to protect both the ill and healthy from one another. Yet how many would support the lonely and humiliating practice of "leprosy" colonies today and requiring that people cry out "unclean." to prevent against unknown contact. To use the principles of resting and disease control is both wise and gracious. Yet to enforce old convenant laws today is unnecessary and ungracious.

So what does the Lord Jesus have to say about the Old Covenant that He Himself instituted with the people of Israel. After all it doesn't matter what I say, it's what Jesus teaches and requires that matters, right?

Galatians 4:21-31 is another crystal clear set of instructions for Christians today.

(Gal 4:21) Tell me, you who desire to be under the law, do you not listen to the law? (Gal 4:22) For it is written that Abraham had two sons, one by a slave woman and one by a free woman. (Gal 4:23) But the son of the slave was born according to the flesh, while the son of the free woman was born through promise. (Gal 4:24) Now this may be interpreted allegorically: these women are two covenants. One is from Mount Sinai, bearing children for slavery; she is Hagar. (Gal 4:25) Now Hagar is Mount Sinai in Arabia; she corresponds to the present Jerusalem, for she is in slavery with her children. (Gal 4:26) But the Jerusalem above is free, and she is our mother. (ESV)

Now that you have died to self and been rejuvenated by the Holy Spirit of Jesus Christ, why would you want to be under the bond woman of the law? It is simply crazy to be holding on to that which was sent away. So for every New Covenant Christian reading this book, most of you know this, however many do not. Christ died for everyone... yes everyone! And with his blood he instituted a new covenant. He died and we symbolically die with him too. At death we are freed from our covenant commitments, such as marriage. If you have died in Christ then you are a part of the New and better Covenant. You are the bride of Christ now. So let me ask you this, why are you holding on to the Old and the New together? It is like having an affair against your true husband or wife. So remember to be children of the correct parent.

(Gal 4:28) Now you, brothers, like Isaac, are children of promise. (Gal 4:29) But just as at that time he who was born according to the flesh persecuted him who was born according to the Spirit, so also it is now. (Gal 4:30) But what does the Scripture say? "Cast out the slave woman and her son, for the son of the slave woman shall not inherit with the son of the free woman." (Gal 4:31) So, brothers, we are not children of the slave but of the free woman. (ESV)

Let's pause again for a summary of what we have learned up to now:

- There is no mention of the Sabbath day until Exodus 16:23.
- The Sabbath was a part of Lord's commandments.
- It was a test of faith.
- It was a part of the Ten Commandments given exclusively to Israel upon deliverance from Egypt.
- The New Covenant equates Sinai with Hagar the bond woman of the flesh and better covenant with those who are free and true sons of God.

What has become known as the Jerusalem Council decision adds further insights. I recommend reading the entire account as I will pick out salient parts for my writing. Acts 15:5 tells us the point of discussion. The new believers in Christ at times were confused and didn't yet understand, in my humble opinion, exactly what the crucifixion provided. Praise God that he knew this would be the case and put leaders in place. In Acts 15: 5 we see

"But some of the believers from the party of the Pharisees stood up and said, "It is necessary to circumcise them and to command them to keep the law of Moses! " (HCSB)

Why was cutting the skin from a penis so important to these people. My guess is what it signified. Circumcision was the sign of the Old Covenant. If men still had to be circumcised then they still had to obey the Old Covenant commandments and laws in flesh. A lot was riding on this decision. Must Christians obey the Old Covenant and the entrance sign or is this simply unnecessary?

Act 15:19 Therefore, in my judgment, we should not cause difficulties for those who turn to God from among the Gentiles, Act 15:20 but instead we should write to them to abstain from things polluted by idols, from sexual immorality, from eating anything that has been strangled, and from blood. (HCSB)

I'm very gratified by the decision made at the Jerusalem Council all those many years ago. It seems to me that if the Ten Commandments were so important, the edict would have been; keep them and not just a few social expectable actions. For those who say that Christians today must obey the Old Covenant I simply say, no way! If that were the standard, we'd all be in hell and the Kingdom of God would be a deserted place when it came to human occupants.

I can also remember the argument as a young man, that the Ten Commandments were eternal and not a part of the Old Covenant because God spoke them and wrote them on a table of stone. This sounded pretty good on the surface, but then I realized years later that God spoke all the Old Covenant. Some parts were spoken directly to the people of Israel and as requested by the terrified people, some to Moses. But again what does the bible tell us on this matter? Lets look at Deuteronomy 4:12-14.

Deu 4:12 Then the LORD spoke to you from the fire. You kept hearing the sound of the words, but didn't see a form; there was only a voice. Deu 4:13 He declared His covenant to you. He commanded you to follow the Ten Commandments, which He wrote on two stone tablets.

Deu 4:14 At that time the LORD commanded me to teach you statutes and ordinances for you to follow in the land you are about to cross into and possess (HCSB).

Once again I ask, could it be said any simpler that the Ten Commandments are a part of the Old Covenant?

The scope of this writing is not large enough to go into all the Old Covenant aspect. I would encourage the reader to study the book of Leviticus and observe all the symbolic imaginary and shadows. The Sabbath Rest being Christ, the sacrifices all fulfilled in Christ, the Sanctuary on earth that was a poor representation of the one in heaven (read the book of Hebrews too) etcetera. Why is this reading important? It will help you to know without doubt how wonderfully our Lord and Savior Jesus Christ fulfilled the law and prophets completely and that to look back is to grasp at shadows. The shadow leads you only to the solid image and that is Jesus Christ. So Be Well and Live Saved!

This ends the contribution by Jim Lindsey.

To end this discussion, I would like to represent Romans 14 (KJV) in its entirety, for the sake of context.

Romans 14:1 Him that is weak in the faith receive ye, but not to doubtful disputations. 2 For one believeth that he may eat all things: another, who is weak, eateth herbs. 3 Let not him that eateth despise him that eateth not; and let not him which eateth not judge him that eateth: for God hath received him. 4 Who art thou that judgest another man's servant? to his own master he standeth or falleth. Yea, he shall be holden up: for God is able to make him stand. 5 One man esteemeth one day above another: another esteemeth every day alike. Let every man be fully persuaded in his own mind. 6 He that regardeth the day, regardeth it unto the Lord; and he that regardeth not the day, to the Lord he doth not regard it. He that eateth, eateth to the Lord, for he giveth God thanks; and he that eateth not, to the Lord he eateth not, and giveth God thanks. 7 For none of us liveth to himself, and no man dieth to himself. 8 For whether we live, we live unto the Lord; and whether we die, we die unto the Lord: whether we live therefore, or die, we are the Lord's. 9 For to this end Christ both died, and rose, and revived, that he might be Lord both of the dead and living. 10 But why dost thou judge thy brother? or why dost thou set at nought thy brother? for we shall all stand before the judgment seat of Christ. 11 For it is written, As I live, saith the Lord, every knee shall bow to me, and every tongue shall confess to God. 12 So then every one of us shall give account of himself to God. 13 Let us not therefore judge one another any more: but judge this rather, that no man put a stumblingblock or an occasion to fall in his brother's way.

14 I know, and am persuaded by the Lord Jesus, that there is nothing unclean of itself: but to him that esteemeth any thing to be unclean, to him it is unclean. 15But if thy brother be grieved with thy meat, now walkest thou not charitably. Destroy not him with thy meat, for whom Christ died. 16 Let not then your good be evil spoken of:

17 For the kingdom of God is not meat and drink; but righteousness, and peace, and joy in the Holy Ghost. 18 For he that in these things serveth Christ is acceptable to God, and approved of men.

19 Let us therefore follow after the things which make for peace, and things wherewith one may edify another. 20 For meat destroy not the work of God. All things indeed are pure; but it is evil for that man who eateth with offence. 21 It is good neither to eat flesh, nor to drink wine, nor any thing whereby thy brother stumbleth, or is offended, or is made weak. 22 Hast thou faith? have it to thyself before God. Happy is he that condemneth not himself in that thing which he alloweth. 23 And he that doubteth is damned if he eat, because he eateth not of faith: for whatsoever is not of faith is sin.

This being said, the question remains, shouldn't we seek to do the better thing? The Sabbath was never abolished. Knowing all of this, what will you do now?

TITHES AND OFFERINGS

In the 1970's I sat in front of my black and white TV watching the great Reverend Ike. He was a raucous black TV evangelist with a bright white suit and teeth to match. Ike would stir his audience by alternately showing his wealth and chastising his viewers for being poor. "If you believe money is the root of all evil, send me your evil." "Money is not the root of all evil. Lack of money is the root of all evil."

Reverend Ike had worked out all the angles. You could send in a donation and he would pray that you would receive money. If you felt like God had blessed you, he would take your praise offering. If you felt like your money was somehow impeding your spiritual growth, Ike was there to lessen your burden by taking your evil money or selling you lessons in how to create and handle wealth.

Reverend Ike, whose real name was Frederick Eikerenkoetter, once told his followers "the best thing you can do for the poor is not to be one of them." (Ike died as this book was being published in 2009.)

According to Tvparty.com, a website about vintage TV shows, a newspaper ad from the 70's touting Reverend Ike is quoted:

"If you want 'pie-in-the-sky when you die' then Rev. Ike is not your man. If you want your pie now, with ice cream on top, then see and hear Rev. Ike on TV."

Millions of mostly poor people tuned in each week to hear sermons from the flamboyant Reverend Ike, who drove flashy Cadillacs and stood at the pulpit dripping in gold chains and diamond rings. When criticized for his lifestyle, Ike would defend himself by saying, "There is nothing wrong with a prosperous man of God;" referring back to his catch phrase, "The LACK of money is the root of all evil."

No, this wasn't a sitcom, farce, or satire. Ike's show was a Sunday morning religious must-see for countless poor people wishing and hoping for a way out of poverty and despair.

Ike was not the only televangelist, but he was one of the first to preach a prosperity message, the aim of which was to enable the preacher to prosper. By flaunting his riches and promising viewers they too can be rich, countless prosperity teachers turned the table on the poor, making them poorer. Throughout the early Seventies and even until today, it is the poor, desperate, and hopeless who keep the televangelists in their opulent lifestyle.

Reverend Ike was one of the first television evangelists who shamelessly pandered for cash and was openly proud of what he spent it on – gold, diamonds, new cars and beautiful women. Now the women are kept behind the scenes but little more has changed. Sleazy preachers with wives dressed like Bo Peep wearing a pink Dolly Parton wig wafts across our TVs with little or no complaints from us. We snicker at the antics of preachers who hire hookers and then, sounding like our ex-presidents, claim they never had sex with that woman.

After other preachers saw what could be done to fleece the flocks through TV and radio, televangelists came out in droves to test their skills. Swaggart, Bakker, Crouch, Copeland, Capps, Bishop Eddie Long, and many more built empires on the backs of the poor. Begging for money, crying on cue, and promising God would bless the giver and curse those who did not obey. If the listener was not blessed the preacher would simply claim the giver did not have enough faith, did not give enough money, or had some unnamed sin in his or her life.

Our donations put thousand dollar suits on the backs of these charlatans. Our money put hookers in their beds, bought painfully horrid wigs and non-waterproof makeup for their wives, so that we could see their tears run like mud, down their cheeks as they pleaded for one more dollar. One would think this must truly be the Dark Age of Christianity, but it just gets worse.

Evangelist Oral Roberts attempted and accomplished the emotional blackmail of his followers by threatening to die on cue. He proclaimed; "God will take me home" unless the public donates $8 million over the next two months. If he truly believed that heaven was a better place; one must ask why he did not keep his mouth shut and take the ride.

Bishop Bernard Jordan claims he is a "Master" Prophet. We assume all that came before him must have been regular prophets? But, if Jesus or Samuel had enough money, they too could become a prophet, but only a regular prophet. Not a master prophet. That would cost extra. According to his web site, you too could become a prophet for a gift of $3000. Jordan will gladly teach you the tricks of the trade.

This is a far cry from 1Tim6:8-10,20.

6But godliness with contentment is great gain. 7For we brought nothing into the world, and we can take nothing out of it. 8But if we have food and clothing, we will be content with that. 9People who want to get rich fall into temptation and a trap and into many foolish and harmful desires that plunge men into ruin and destruction. 10For the love of money is a root of all kinds of evil. Some people, eager for money, have wandered from the faith and pierced themselves with many griefs.

20Timothy, guard what has been entrusted to your care. Turn away from godless chatter and the opposing ideas of what is falsely called knowledge, 21which some have professed and in so doing have wandered from the faith.

Grace be with you.

Is this really how tithing is supposed to work? Are we really supposed to give out of our lack to men who are rich, in hope that God will reward our faith? If we give away our child's milk money is it God's responsibility to reward us?

What are tithes and offerings? Are we still supposed to tithe?

The dictionary defines the tithe as : one tenth of annual produce or earnings, formerly taken as a tax for the support of the church and clergy.

- (in certain religious denominations) a tenth of an individual's income pledged to the church.
- [in sing.] (archaic) a tenth of a specified thing : he hadn't said a tithe of the prayers he knew.

verb [trans.] pay or give as a tithe : he tithes 10 percent of his income to the church.

In a brief historical search, one immediately finds that the idea and practice of the tithe is not a new one, nor is it confined to Judeo-Christian peoples. It was common among most warrior nations, of which ancient Israel was one.

"Tithes, a form of taxation, secular and ecclesiastical, usually, as the name implies, consisting of one-tenth of a man's property or produce. The tax probably originated in a tribute levied by a conqueror or ruler upon his subjects, and perhaps the custom of dedicating a tenth of the spoils of war to the gods led to the religious extension of the term, the original offerings to deity being "firstfruits."

"Through the spoils of war, Edward was able to refill the bankrupt treasury. Heavily ransomed prisoners, brought fortunes in gold coin to their noble captors--who, in turn, paid a handsome tithe to the King." (Edward III: King of Illusions)

"It was traditional to give the Byzantine Government a set percentage of the spoils of war." (Chapter III: Eastern Expansion, emphasis added)

The Greeks and Romans practiced tithing.

"In the same manner the Greeks too, the Carthaginians, and the Romans devoted a tenth portion of the spoils of war to their deities." (On the

Acquisition of Territory and Property by Right of Conquest)

"The Greek League against Persia, founded in 481 vows a tenth of the spoils of war to the shrine, and this happens, after Salamis and Plataea." (Herodotus on Greek Religion)

"During the twelfth century, evidence points to the growing significance of warfare between cities in Portugal, Leon, Castile and Aragon. Precise indications are demonstrated in the increasing concern of the makers of the municipal charters in three areas closely related to booty. The first is the royal demand to collect the one-fifth tax on the spoils of war, a tax the Christian rulers inherited from the Muslim practice of laying aside a portion of the gains of the jihad for Allah." (Spoils and Compensations) This practice continues today as the Taliban demands payment from the poppy growers and sellers of opium in Afghanistan to pay for their war against Christian nations.

"For his courageous role in helping to conquer the Volscian town of Corioli, Caius Marcius was offered a tithe. For declining to accept one-tenth of the spoils, he was named Coriolanus" (after the city he conquered.) (Roman Expansion to 133 BC)

"In the days of Abu Bakr much wealth came to the state on account of the spoils of war. The movable property won as booty on the battlefield was known as "Ghanimah." Four-fifths of the spoils of war were immediately distributed among the soldiers who had taken part in the battle. The remaining one-fifth went to the State. The State's one-fifth share was further divided into three parts. One part went to the family of the Holy Prophet, one part went to the Caliph, and one part was spent for welfare purposes." (Political, Social, Economic and Military Organization)

The tithe served a purpose. It could make a government rich, and allow them to wage war. Of these, the Catholic Church did both, and the Vatican became the wealthiest nation on Earth. A tithe to the church was a tax paid to the Vatican.

But, if we strip away the desire for wealth and war, and examine the tithe in a purely religious light, before the formation of the Vatican city-state, we may be able to see what it is and what it means in the New Testament age of grace.

The earliest Christian assemblies patterned themselves after the Jewish synagogues, which were led by rabbis who, like Paul, refused to profit from teaching God's Word. These men all had occupations. Paul, for example, was a tent maker. None took money from the church.

The Jewish rabbis had a saying: "Whoever does not teach his son a trade is as if he brought him up to be a robber." Accordingly, when Paul was on his second missionary journey and came to Corinth, the first thing he did was seek work to sustain his needs. Paul made tents during the week, or perhaps at night, but on the Sabbath he went to the Jewish synagogue to preach about Jesus to the Jews.

From Christ's death until Christianity became a legally recognized religion almost 300 years later, the majority of great church leaders took Jesus' words to the rich young ruler in Luke 18:22 literally "sell all that you have, give it to the poor, and follow me." Historians agree that for the first 200 years of Christianity, leaders and preachers took vows of poverty and worked for a living so that they were self-supporting.

1 Peter 5 (Holman Christian Standard Bible)

1 Therefore, as a fellow elder and witness to the sufferings of the Messiah, and also a participant in the glory about to be revealed, I exhort the elders among you: 2 shepherd God's flock among you, not overseeing out of compulsion but freely, according to God's [will]; not for the money but eagerly; 3 not lording it over those entrusted to you, but being examples to the flock. 4 And when the chief Shepherd appears, you will receive the unfading crown of glory.

There were times when one church supported missions to poorer churches. They donated funds to assist missionary trips to other Christians.

"*I robbed other churches, taking wages of them that I might minister unto you; and when I was present with you and was in want, I was not a burden on any man; for the brethren, when they came from Macedonia, supplied the measure of my want . . .*" (2 Cor. 11:8-9).

1 Thessalonians 2 (Holman Christian Standard Bible)

5 For we never used flattering speech, as you know, or had greedy motives – God is our witness – 6 and we didn't seek glory from people, either from you or from others. 7 Although we could have been a burden as Christ's apostles, instead we were gentle among you, as a nursing mother nurtures her own children. 8 We cared so much for you that we were pleased to share with you not only the gospel of God but also our own lives, because you had become dear to us. 9 For you remember our labor and hardship, brothers. Working night and day so that we would not burden any of you, we preached God's gospel to you. 10 You are witnesses, and so is God, of how devoutly, righteously, and blamelessly we conducted ourselves with you believers. 11 As you know, like a father with his own children, 12 we encouraged, comforted, and implored each one of you to walk worthy of God, who calls you into His own kingdom and glory.

Having seen what greed and preaching for money had done to the Gospel,

Paul sent a letter to Timothy warning him to keep watch for those who wished to make money off of the death of the Lord.

1 Timothy 6 (The Message)

2-5These are the things I want you to teach and preach. If you have leaders there who teach otherwise, who refuse the solid words of our Master Jesus and this godly instruction, tag them for what they are: ignorant windbags who infect the air with germs of envy, controversy, bad-mouthing, suspicious rumors. Eventually there's an epidemic of backstabbing, and truth is but a distant memory. They think religion is a way to make a fast buck.

In an attempt to keep in line with the apostles, early church fathers opposed tithing, but supported the free will donations of believers.

Clement of Rome (c95), Justin Martyr (c150), Irenaeus (c150-200) and Tertullian (c150-220) all opposed tithing as a strictly Jewish tradition. The Didache, a book of conduct and rules that was said to have come from the Apostles but was written around 150-200 A.D., condemns traveling preachers who stay longer than three days and ask for money. And travelers who decided to remain with the established leaders or churches were required to learn a trade.

Two hundred and fifty years after the death of Jesus and the establishment of Christianity there was no tithe. What happened to change all of this? It is quite simple. The church morphed from a spiritual seat of power into a political power base. Like any political structure bent on its own growth and survival, it needed money.

Cyprian (200-258) was a great teacher and orator in Carthage. He was raised a pagan. Cyprian tried unsuccessfully to impose tithing on a governmental level in Carthage, North Africa, around A. D. 250. However at his conversion to Christianity, Cyprian gave away great personal wealth to the poor and lived under a vow of poverty. His idea of tithing included equal re-distribution to the poor. His ideas were not adopted.

Still, at that time there were those fighting to keep spirituality in the church. Many of the greatest spiritual leaders took vows of poverty and preferred to live in monasteries, but their numbers were too few.

Slowly, the need for money grew as the church grew. Most church historians agree that tithing did not become an accepted doctrine in the church for over 700 years after the death of Jesus. According to the best sources, in the year 585, the local church Council of Macon in France, tried unsuccessfully to enforce tithing on its members. This is the last known descent. The church was becoming much too strong. Soon it would have its way.

By the time Christianity became legal in the fourth century the church had acquired a solid structure and hierarchy. It was reborn as a political force whose organization needed money to pay its administrators and overseers. Its purpose turned from the spreading of the Gospel to self-perpetuation and the accumulation of wealth and power.

It is very important to understand the changing structure of the church and its growing demand for funds. Until the establishment of a centralized power, the church was a horizontally structured, grassroots movement. Believers "seeded" the word in others and small groups grew that gathered in homes throughout the area. Pastors or Bishops were overseers for groups in cities, which were spread out like clumps of grass in a desert. Letters were sent between them to keep in touch and encourage each other to persevere and conduct themselves correctly. Donations were kept within the area to supply the needs of the widows, orphans, and infirmed. If needed, a wealthier church might send money to a less prosperous group. No money went to the church at Rome.

When a power base coalesced the structure was turned on its side. Now the Bishop of Rome gained control of Christendom. He appointed men to run the church, do his bidding, and report to him. This is the hierarchy of the modern church and almost every denomination. To sustain his office he needed money. To expand his empire he needed lots of money. The Bishop of Rome, now known as the pope, a word meaning "father", appointed Cardinals, to rule regions, and bishops to rule cities and areas, and priests to rule the people. Now, we have a vertical political structure, whose job is to gather money and send it up the chain to the top. The Vatican became a city-state, ruling the world, waging wars, and through its wealth it changed the face of the world. The pope persuaded King Charlemagne and in the year 777 the king legally allowed the church to collect tithes. This was tantamount to taxation by the church. (See "The history of tithing", found in the Encyclopedia Britannica, Encyclopedia Americana and the Roman Catholic Encyclopedia.")

This was never the purpose of the tithe.

This is the secular history, but what does the Bible say?

The first mention of tithing was in Genesis 14:20 where Abraham 'gave tithes of all' to Melchizedek. Notice how Abraham did this freely. It was not a commandment from God. Abraham was a pagan and he gave the spoils of his conquests and wars freely. Then the next mention of tithing is in Leviticus 27.

Leviticus 27 (New International Version)

1 The LORD said to Moses, 2 "Speak to the Israelites and say to them: 'If anyone makes a special vow to dedicate persons to the LORD by giving equivalent values, 3 set the value of a male between the ages of twenty and sixty at fifty shekels of silver, according to the sanctuary shekel; 4 and if it is a female, set her value at thirty shekels. 5 If it is a person between the ages of five and twenty, set the value of a male at twenty shekels and of a female at ten shekels. 6 If it is a person between one month and five years, set the value of a male at five shekels of silver and that of a female at three shekels of silver. 7 If it is a person sixty years old or more, set the value of a male at fifteen shekels and of a female at ten shekels. 8 If anyone making the vow is too poor to pay the specified amount, he is to present the person to the priest, who will set the value for him according to what the man making the vow can afford.

9 " 'If what he vowed is an animal that is acceptable as an offering to the LORD, such an animal given to the LORD becomes holy. 10 He must not exchange it or substitute a good one for a bad one, or a bad one for a good one; if he should substitute one animal for another, both it and the substitute become holy. 11 If what he vowed is a ceremonially unclean animal – one that is not acceptable as an offering to the LORD -the animal must be presented to the priest, 12 who will judge its quality as good or bad. Whatever value the priest then sets, that is what it will be. 13 If the owner wishes to redeem the animal, he must add a fifth to its value.

14 " 'If a man dedicates his house as something holy to the LORD, the priest will judge its quality as good or bad. Whatever value the priest then sets, so it will remain. 15 If the man who dedicates his house redeems it, he must add a fifth to its value, and the house will again become his.

16 " 'If a man dedicates to the LORD part of his family land, its value is to be set according to the amount of seed required for it – fifty shekels of silver to a homer [i] of barley seed. 17 If he dedicates his field during the Year of Jubilee, the value that has been set remains. 18 But if he dedicates his field after the Jubilee, the priest will determine the value according to the number of years that remain until the next Year of Jubilee, and its set value will be reduced. 19 If the man who dedicates the field wishes to redeem it, he must add a fifth to its value, and the field will again become his. 20 If, however, he does not redeem the field, or if he has sold it to someone else, it can never be redeemed. 21 When the field is released in the Jubilee, it will become holy, like a field devoted to the LORD; it will become the property of the priests. [j]

22 " 'If a man dedicates to the LORD a field he has bought, which is not part of his family land, 23 the priest will determine its value up to the Year of Jubilee, and the man must pay its value on that day as something holy to the LORD. 24 In the Year of Jubilee the field will revert to the person from whom he bought it, the one whose land it was. 25 Every value is to be set according to the sanctuary shekel, twenty gerahs to the shekel.

26 " 'No one, however, may dedicate the firstborn of an animal, since the firstborn already belongs to the LORD; whether an ox [k] or a sheep, it is the LORD's. 27 If it is one of the unclean animals, he may buy it back at its set value, adding a fifth of the value to it. If he does not redeem it, it is to be sold at its set value.

28 " 'But nothing that a man owns and devotes [l] to the LORD -whether man or

animal or family land – may be sold or redeemed; everything so devoted is most holy to the LORD.

29 " 'No person devoted to destruction [m] may be ransomed; he must be put to death.

30 " 'A tithe of everything from the land, whether grain from the soil or fruit from the trees, belongs to the LORD; it is holy to the LORD. 31 If a man redeems any of his tithe, he must add a fifth of the value to it. 32 The entire tithe of the herd and flock – every tenth animal that passes under the shepherd's rod – will be holy to the LORD. 33 He must not pick out the good from the bad or make any substitution. If he does make a substitution, both the animal and its substitute become holy and cannot be redeemed.' "

34 These are the commands the LORD gave Moses on Mount Sinai for the Israelites.

Footnotes:

    Leviticus 27:3 That is, about 1 1/4 pounds (about 0.6 kilogram also in verse 16

    Leviticus 27:3 That is, about 2/5 ounce (about 11.5 grams also in verse 25

    Leviticus 27:4 That is, about 12 ounces (about 0.3 kilogram)

    Leviticus 27:5 That is, about 8 ounces (about 0.2 kilogram)

    Leviticus 27:5 That is, about 4 ounces (about 110 grams also in verse

    Leviticus 27:6 That is, about 2 ounces (about 55 grams)

    Leviticus 27:6 That is, about 1 1/4 ounces (about 35 grams)

    Leviticus 27:7 That is, about 6 ounces (about 170 grams)

    Leviticus 27:16 That is, probably about 6 bushels (about 220 liters)

    Leviticus 27:21 Or priest

    Leviticus 27:26 The Hebrew word can include both male and female.

    Leviticus 27:28 The Hebrew term refers to the irrevocable giving over of things or persons to the LORD.

Leviticus 27:29 The Hebrew term refers to the irrevocable giving over of things or persons to the LORD, often by totally destroying them.

(Quoted from biblegateway.com)

The "first tithe" described in the Torah actually goes not to the poor, but to the tribe of the Levites.

Torah presents the tribe of Levi as a class of itinerant scholars who collect taxes from free citizens. They do this because Levites do not own land and have no place to grow their food. Instead, they are fed by the people through a tax of one tenth of the food.

"Don't abandon the Levite in your gates, for he has no portion and inheritance among you"

(Deuteronomy 14:27).

More precisely, their inheritance is spiritual, not material: *"Therefore, Levi has no portion and inheritance with his brothers; the Lord is his inheritance, as the Lord your God spoke to him" (Deuteronomy 10:9).*

The first tithe, which is given to the tribe of Levi, is meant to compensate them for devotion to God's work:

"And to the children of Levi I have given the tithe in Israel as a portion, in return for the service they serve, the service of the Tent of Meeting" (Numbers 18:21).

The second tithe also was not devoted solely to the poor. The agricultural cycle in the land of Israel is seven years in duration. In the seventh, or Sabbatical year, all produce is freely available to all. In the third and sixth years, there is a second tithe given to the poor. In the remaining four years, the farmer himself takes the second tithe, or its value, and consumes it in Jerusalem together with his family, taking due care to share it also with the less fortunate.

"And the Levite, who has no portion and inheritance with you, will come; and the stranger, and the orphan and the widow in your gates; and they will eat and be satisfied, so that the Lord your God will bless you in everything you do" (Deuteronomy 14:29).

Some think food was used because money was not available. This does not seem to be the case. Money was an essential everyday item. For example Abraham was very rich in silver and gold (Gen 13:2); money in the form of silver shekels paid for slaves (Gen 17:12); Abimelech gave Abraham 1000 pieces of silver (Gen 20:16); Abraham paid 400 pieces of silver for land (Gen 23:9-16); Joseph was sold for silver pieces (Gen 37:28); slaves bought freedom (Ex 23:11); court fines (Ex 21 all; 22 all); sanctuary dues (Ex 30:12); vows (Lev 27:3-7); poll taxes (Num 3:47+), alcoholic drinks (Deu 14:26) and marriage dowries

(Deu 22:29). Joseph gave Benjamin 300 pieces of silver (Gen 45:22). According to Genesis 47:15-17, food was used for barter only after money had been spent. Banking and usury laws exist in Leviticus even before tithing. Yet the tithe contents from Leviticus to Matthew never include money from non-food products and trades.

The Biblical tithing obligation applies only to agricultural produce in the land of Israel. But for hundreds of years it has been customary to donate a portion of our income to charity, and the most accepted amount is one tenth of after-tax income. The Shulchan Aruch (authoritative Code of Jewish law) states that the average person should give one-tenth of his income to charity. However, this is only a custom. This custom retains the spirit of the original agricultural tithe. The personal element is maintained, as this tithe is distributed according to individual discretion.

Although money existed before tithing, the source of God's "tithe" over 1500 years was never money. It was the "tithe of food." Old Testament biblical tithes were always only food from the farms and herds of only Israelites who only lived inside God's Holy Land, the national boundary of Israel. No tithes were accepted from defiled pagan lands. The "increase" was gathered from what God miraculously produced and not from man's craft or ability.

There are 16 verses from 11 chapters and 8 books from Leviticus 27 to Luke 11 which describe the contents of the tithe. And the contents never (again), never included money, silver, gold or anything other than food from inside Israel! (See Lev. 27:30, 32; Num. 18:27-28; Deut. 12:17; 14:22-23; 26:12; 2 Chron. 31:5-6; Neh. 10:37; 13:5; Mal. 3:10-11; Matt. 23:23; Luke 11: 42).

Only those Israelites who earned a livelihood from farming and herding inside Israel were required to tithe under the Mosaic Law. Their increase came from God's hand. Those whose increase came from their own crafts and skills were not required to tithe products and money. The poor and needy did not tithe but received from the tithe freewill offerings.

The "whole" tithe, the first tithe, did not go to the priests at all. It was not even the "best" tenth (Lev 27:30-34). According to Numbers 18:21-24 and Nehemiah 10:37b, it went to the servants of the priests, the Levites. And according to Numbers 18:25-28 and Nehemiah 10:38, the Levites gave the "best tenth of this tithe" (1%) which they received to the priests who ministered the sin sacrifices and served inside the holy places. Priests did not tithe.

Revelation 1:6 (King James Version)

6And hath made us kings and priests unto God and his Father; to him be glory and dominion for ever and ever. Amen.

First-fruits and first-born offerings went directly to the Temple and were required to be totally consumed by ministering priests only inside the Temple (Neh. 10:35-37a; Ex. 23:19; 34:26; Deut. 18:4). The first-fruit was small enough to fit into a hand-held basket (Deut. 26:1-10; Lev. 23:17; Num. 18:13-17; Neh. 12:44; 2 Chron 31:5a). (Note: Levitical cities were not owned by the Levites. They were simply set apart for them, as the cities of sanctuary were set apart.)

The whole Levitical tithe went first to the Levitical cities and portions went to the Temple to feed both Levites and priests who were ministering there in rotation (Neh. 10:37b-39; 12:27-29, 44-47; Num. 18:21-28; 2 Chron 31:5b). While the Levites ate only the tithe, the priests could also eat from the first-fruits, first-born offerings and other offerings.

Jesus was a carpenter; Paul was a tentmaker and Peter was a fisherman. None of these occupations qualified as tithe-payers because they did not farm or herd animals for a living. It is, therefore, incorrect to teach that everybody paid a required minimum of a tithe and, therefore, that New Covenant Christians should be required to at least begin at the same minimum as Old Covenant Israelites. This common false assumption is very often repeated and completely ignores the very plain definition of tithe as food gathered from farm increase or herd increase.

The widow's mite is an example of free-will giving and is not an example of tithing. According to Edersheim none of the Temple's chests were for tithes. The poor received money from those chests before leaving the temple.

It is also wrong to teach that the poor in Israel were required to pay tithes. In fact, they actually received tithes! Much of the second festival tithe and all of a special third-year tithe went to the poor! Many laws protected the poor from abuse and expensive sacrifices which they could not afford (Lev. 14:21; 25:6, 25-28, 35, 36; 27:8; Deu. 12:1-19; 14:23, 28, 29; 15:7, 8, 11; 24:12, 14, 15, 19, 20; 26:11-13; Mal. 3:5; Matt. 12:1, 2; Mark 2:23, 24; Luke 2:22-24; 6:1, 2; 2 Cor. 8:12-14; 1 Tim. 5:8; Jas. 1:27).

In the Hebrew economy, the tithe was used in a totally different manner than it is preached and applied today. Once again, those Levites who received the whole tithe were not ministers or priests -- they were only servants to the priests. Numbers chapter 3 describes the Levites as carpenters, metal workers, leather-craftsmen and artists who maintained the small sanctuary. And, according to First Chronicles, chapters 23-26, during the time of King David and King Solomon the Levites were still skilled craftsmen who inspected and approved all work in the Temple: 24, 000 worked in the Temple as builders and supervisors; 6,000 were officials and judges; 4,000 were guards and 4,000 were musicians. As political representatives of the king, Levites used their tithe income to serve as officials, judges, tax collectors, treasurers, temple guards, musicians, bakers, singers and professional soldiers (1 Chron. 12:23, 26; 23:2-5; 26:29-32; 27:5). It is obvious why these examples of using biblical tithe-income are never used as examples in the church today.

We see that the original tithing obligation of the Torah, and its modern-day equivalent, are far more than a simple "poor tax"; they served as a social security or food bank system. No priest ever got rich off of the tithe.

So what about the New Testament? Is tithing mentioned? We can see Jesus apparently endorsing tithes in Matthew 23:23 and Luke 11:42.

Woe to you, scribes and Pharisees, hypocrites! For you pay tithe of mint and anise and cummin, and have neglected the weightier matters of the law: justice and mercy and faith. These you ought to have done, without leaving the others undone. (Matthew 23:23)

These scriptures are the ones that people use as proof that Jesus commanded that we tithe today, but while Jesus was alive he was still operating under the Old Testament laws and the New Testament had not fully been ratified.

Hebrews 9:15-17 makes it clear that a new testament can only come in place after the death of the testator.

15 And for this reason He is the Mediator of the new covenant, by means of death, for the redemption of the transgressions under the first covenant, that those who are called may receive the promise of the eternal inheritance.

16 For where there is a testament, there must also of necessity be the death of the testator. 17 For a testament is in force after men are dead, since it has no power at all while the testator lives.

New Testament tithing is a gift or donation, not a tithe. This is defined clearly in Second Corinthians, which gives us the principles for giving today.

"So let each one give as he purposes in his heart, not grudgingly or of necessity; for God loves a cheerful giver." (2 Cor 9:7)

2 Cor 8:11 but now you also must complete the doing of it; that as there was a readiness to desire it, so there also may be a completion out of what you have. 12 For if there is first a willing mind, it is accepted according to what one has, and not according to what he does not have. 13 For I do not mean that others should be eased and you burdened; 14 but by an equality, that now at this time your abundance may supply their lack, that their abundance also may supply your lack – that there may be equality. (2 Cor 8:11-14)

(Yes, Christians can be socialists.)

Joseph Lumpkin

An Essay by Russell Earl Kelly, Ph. D. entitled, "TITHING IS NOT A CHRISTIAN DOCTRINE," sums it up this way:

"Christians are commanded to give freely, sacrificially, generously, regularly, joyfully and with the motivation of love for God and man. The following New Covenant free-will principles are found in Second Corinthians, chapters 8 and 9: (1) Giving is a "grace." These chapters use the Greek word for "grace" eight times in reference to helping poor saints.

(2) Give yourself to God first (8:5).

(3) Give yourself to knowing God's will (8:5).

(4) Give in response to Christ's gift (8:9; 9:15).

(5) Give out of a sincere desire (8:8, 10, 12; 9:7).

(6) Do not give because of any commandment (8:8, 10; 9:7).

(7) Give beyond your ability (8:3, 11-12).

(8) Give to produce equality. This means that those who have more should give more in order to make up for the inability of those who cannot afford to give as much (8:12-14).

(9) Give joyfully (8:2).

(10) Give because you are growing spiritually (8:3-4, 7).

(11) Give because you want to continue growing spiritually (9:8, 10-11).

(12) Give because you are hearing the gospel preached (9:13)."

Preachers want us to think that all tithes were formerly taken to the Temple and should now be taken to the "church storehouse" building. Early Christians had no church. If they met in a recognized group they were killed.

Nehemiah 10:37b and Second Chronicles 31:15-19 make it clear that the people were to bring the tithes to the Levitical cities where 98% of the Levites and priests needed them for food (also Num 18:21-24). And Nehemiah 10:38 makes it clear that normally only Levites and priests had the task of bringing tithes into the Temple (also Num 18:24-28).

The "whole" tithe never went to the Temple. According to Numbers 35, Joshua 20, 21 and First Chronicles 6, Levites and priests lived on borrowed land where they farmed and raised (tithed) animals. (Also 2nd Chron. 11:13-14; Neh. 12:27-29; 13:10; Mal. 1:14.)

Malachi 3 may be one of the most abused text in the Bible. The "whole" tithe never was supposed to go to the Temple. In Malachi 3:10-11 tithes are still only food 1000 years after Leviticus 27.

Malachi's audience had willingly reaffirmed the Old Covenant (Neh.10:28-29). The blessings and curses of tithing are identical to and inseparable from those of the entire Mosaic Law. The rain in Deuteronomy 28:12, 23-24 and Leviticus 26:1-4 is only obtained by obedience to all 613 commandments in the Old Testament or Torah. Galatians 3:10 (quoting Deut. 27:26) "For as many as are of the works of the law are under the curse: for it is written, Cursed is every one that continues not in all things which are written in the book of the law to do them." Trying to earn God's blessings through tithing only brings curses for failure to keep all of the law. See also Galatians 3:19.

Beginning in 1:6 "you" in Malachi always refers to the dishonest priests and not the people (also 2:1-10; 2:13 to 3:1-5): "Even this whole nation of you -- priests" (3:9). In 1:13-14 the priests had stolen tithed animals vowed to God.

Malachi 1

1 An oracle: The word of the LORD to Israel through Malachi.

2 "I have loved you," says the LORD.

"But you ask, 'How have you loved us?'

"Was not Esau Jacob's brother?" the LORD says. "Yet I have loved Jacob, 3 but Esau I have hated, and I have turned his mountains into a wasteland and left his inheritance to the desert jackals."

4 Edom may say, "Though we have been crushed, we will rebuild the ruins." But this is what the LORD Almighty says: "They may build, but I will demolish. They will be called the Wicked Land, a people always under the wrath of the LORD. 5 You will see it with your own eyes and say, 'Great is the LORD -even beyond the borders of Israel!' 6 "A son honors his father, and a servant his master. If I am a father, where is the honor due me? If I am a master, where is the respect due me?" says the LORD Almighty. "It is you, O priests, who show contempt for my name. "But you ask, 'How have we shown contempt for your name?' 7 "You place defiled food on my altar. "But you ask, 'How have we defiled you?' "By saying that the LORD's table is contemptible. 8 When you bring blind animals for sacrifice, is that not wrong? When you sacrifice crippled or diseased animals, is that not wrong? Try offering them to your governor! Would he be pleased with you? Would he accept you?" says the LORD Almighty. 9 "Now implore God to be gracious to us. With such offerings from your hands, will he accept you?"-says the LORD Almighty.

10 "Oh, that one of you would shut the temple doors, so that you would not light useless fires on my altar! I am not pleased with you," says the LORD Almighty, "and I will accept no offering from your hands. 11 My name will be great among the nations, from the rising to the setting of the sun. In every place incense and pure offerings will be brought to my name, because my name will be great among the nations," says the LORD Almighty. 12 "But you profane it by saying of the Lord's table, 'It is defiled,' and of its food, 'It is contemptible.' 13 And you say, 'What a burden!' and you sniff at it contemptuously," says the LORD Almighty. "When you bring injured, crippled or diseased animals and offer them as sacrifices, should I accept them from your hands?" says the LORD. 14 "Cursed is the cheat who has an acceptable male in his flock and vows to give it, but then sacrifices a blemished animal to the Lord. For I am a great king," says the LORD Almighty, "and my name is to be feared among the nations."

In Nehemiah 13:5-10 priests had stolen the Levites' portion of the tithe. God's curses on the priests are in 1:14; 2:2 and 3:2-4.

Nehemiah 10:37-39 is the key to understanding Malachi 3:10, The people were commanded to bring their tithes, not to the temple, but to the nearby Levitical cities. Verse 38 says that the priests were with the Levites in the Levitical cities when they received the tithes.

According to Nehemiah 13:5, 9 the "storehouse" in the Temple was only several rooms. The real "storehouses" were in the Levitical cites per Nehemiah 10:37b. Only the Levites and priests normally brought tithes to the Temple (10:38). Two rooms in the Temple were far too small to contain the tithe from the entire nation and most of the Levites and priests lived too far away to eat from them.

Therefore, Malachi 3:10's "Bring ye all the tithes into the storehouse" only makes contextual sense if it is only commanding dishonest priests to replace the tithes they had removed from it or had failed to bring to it.

For several centuries after Calvary, Christians did not even have their own buildings (to call storehouses) because Christianity was an outlaw religion.

Although Jesus taught tithing, the New Covenant did not begin at the birth of Jesus, but at his death.

The only texts in the New Testament about tithing are set against the backdrop of Christians who were still going to the temple to tithe and keeping the law. Acts 2:42-47 and 4:32-35 are not examples of tithing to support church leaders. According to 2:46 the Jewish Christians continued to worship in the Temple. And according to 2:44 and 4:33, 34 church leaders shared what they received equally with all church members.

Finally, Acts 21:20-25 proves that Jewish Christians were still zealously observing all of the Mosaic Law 30 years later, and that must include tithing, otherwise they would not have been allowed inside the Temple to worship. Therefore, any tithes collected by the early Jewish Christians were given to the Temple system and not to support the church.

Like other ordinances of the Law, tithing was only a temporary shadow until Christ comes. (Eph. 2:14-16; Col. 2:13-17; Heb. 7:18; 10:1). The function and purpose of Old Covenant priests was replaced by the priesthood of every believer. No longer are there appointed taskmasters to judge our keeping of the law. Now, each man and woman is a priest, equal in status, responsible to the Lord. This is part of the New Covenant. (1 Pet. 2:9-10; Rev. 1:6; 5:10). Every ordinance which had previously applied to the old priesthood was blotted out at the cross. Jesus is now the only High Priest we have, but Jesus was not from the tribe of Levi, even He was disqualified. Thus the original temporary purpose of tithing no longer exists (Heb. 7:12-19; Gal. 3:19, 24-25; 2 Cor. 3:10-18).

What then is the conclusion of this? How do we give?

The simple truth is this: We must realize that the money we give to our local church or preferred television preacher is not a tithe. It is a sum of money given to insure the continuation of the program we choose to attend or watch. It is a donation. Like a movie ticket, it pays the bills and allows profit, sometimes huge profits, to be realized by the preacher. Very little, if any of that money will go to the poor, widows, orphans, or infirmed. It does not go toward the Kingdom of God. It goes toward growing the kingdom of the preacher. If the church uses some of it for social programs that is wonderful, but it is not the same as feeding the hungry, clothing the destitute, or helping the sick. God enables those he calls by moving the hearts of believers to donate money to their cause. Just because someone's ego drives him or her to spend millions of dollars to get his or her face on TV does not mean I need to support that ego. If my pastor buys an expensive car or house, I am not obligated to support his vanity. The New Testament tells me that I am to see to the widow, orphans, sick, and those in prison. It also hints at the fact that I should not let my preacher starve by "muzzling the mouth of the ox that treads the wheat." Judging by the physique of most pastors in my area, many could use more muzzles and less wheat. Paul's template indicates that pastors should work to support themselves. Nevertheless, we should make sure the pastors have all they need and not all they want.

The closest pattern to the true tithe is the food pantries of some churches and community shelters, where the poor come to be fed. Do not waste your money on the mega-churches and televangelists of today. Let them work in a trade, as Paul did. Instead, give directly to the poor or to those who supply the poor. That way the poor will actually get your dollar's worth and not two cents out of every dollar, as some churches and institutions actually provide after taking their cut.

Give only from the heart. The tithe is no longer an obligation. Give when the spirit moves you to give. A million people could be fed with the money it takes to support some ministries. In my little county there are several large churches. Preachers drive Mercedes and get their hair permed once a month. Their wives have plastic surgeries and wear expensive clothes. They run their churches with an iron fist, demanding their cut from all who enter. Yet, the poor walk the streets, mumbling to themselves, hungry and hopeless.

On a personal note I will say: Our hands are all He has to touch others. Our feet are all He has to find them. Our food can feed them, but at times our money can enable them to continue to drink and do drugs. Feed, clothe, and shelter those in need. Do not enable the situations that have put some in need.

Send your money to a televangelist in hopes of being blessed? Tithe and expect God, who already loves you unconditionally and gave His son as a sacrifice for you, to give you a little extra something?

THE PROBLEM WITH PERSUASION

Of all the systems of religion that ever were invented, there is none more derogatory to the Almighty, more unedifying to man, more repugnant to reason, and more contradictory in itself, than this thing called Christianity ... it produces only atheists and fanatics.

THOMAS PAINE, *The Age of Reason*

JOH 6:44 No man can come to me, except the Father which hath sent me draw him: and I will raise him up at the last day. 45 It is written in the prophets, And they shall be all taught of God. Every man therefore that hath heard, and hath learned of the Father, cometh unto me. 46 Not that any man hath seen the Father, save he which is of God, he hath seen the Father. 47 Verily, verily, I say unto you, He that believeth on me hath everlasting life.

It is a business and numbers count. A preacher without notches on his Bible for each soul "he has saved" is no evangelist at all. There is a critical impediment to persuasive preaching. It is indisputably not real.

Through music and rhetoric, emotions are whipped to a boil. The senses are excited. The mind is persuaded. The spirit remains unchanged. Tens of thousands come to the altar every year. They run, crawl, weep, cry, and finally they leave lost. After the emotional release they feel better but soon they fall back into their old ways and are lost for good, having now lost all hope and faith in the promises made by the preacher. Why? Because a man tried to draw them by persuasion while the Spirit of God must draw them by conviction. There is a problem with persuasive preaching. It destroys faith.

It is God who draws us and God who saves us. It is God's hand that leads us home. It is God who meets us and changes us. It is God who heals us. It is God who embraces us in our times of need. It is God who convicts us but does not condemn us. It is God who forgives and cleanses us. It is not a man, a church, or a denomination. It is the Holy Spirit of the Most High God. There is a problem with persuasive preaching. It places the preacher between the sinner and God.

Joseph Lumpkin

It is our time to be saved only when He opens our eyes to our need of Him. It is only by His grace that we are brought to see our need, our emptiness, our hopeless state. The preacher's words will fade away. The excitement dies down. The music is silent. The preacher has sold us Jesus and persuasion brings buyer's remorse. There is no need for fanfare. Jesus needs only an introducing. His word and His spirit will do the rest. It is not that we should not present our faith to others, but we should never manipulate. There is a problem with persuasive preaching. It confuses the preacher's work for God's grace.

Here is a rule and template that works and makes sense. Until they ask the question they are not ready for the answer – or they simply do not care. Make fewer enemies by respecting the boundaries of others. Shut up and trust God.

This mystical journey is one between man and God. It has nothing to do with anyone else. No preacher can help you, although they may actually hinder you. No church or denomination is your highway or bridge. The timing is the Lord's. The journey is yours. The destination is the heart of God.

A GIFT OF LOVE

Whoever shall introduce into public affairs the principles of primitive Christianity will change the face of the world. --Benjamin Franklin

Interior experiences, those that are spiritual or mystical, lack common language. There are no tangible points of reference neither in item or place that we may compare and establish mutual terms. It is because of this lack of spiritual language that the mystical experience cannot be easily explained. It is alluded to, pointed at, and explained by allegory and metaphor at best. In this context, it is marriage and love, both physical and emotional, which come closest to the mystical experience. On these experiences we shall rely in order to discuss the indescribable.

Mysticism – The doctrine that communion with God and a knowledge of the divine essence may be attained independent of the senses or processes of reason through intuition and insight; hence, the ecstasy of those who claim they have had insight or vision bringing them into spiritual union with the eternal and giving them knowledge of the supernatural.
Webster's New School & Office Dictionary

Doctrine – That which is taught: The principles, belief, or dogma of any church, sect, or party. Webster's New School & Office Dictionary

Communion – Intercourse; fellowship; common possession; a religious body; partaking of the Eucharist. Webster's New School & Office Dictionary

What a terrible blessing and frightening gift has been given man that he should possess such great capacity to love and such vast ignorance of how to love. What divine urgings drive us to seek out in others that part of Him we so dimly recognize and that our hearts would respond so joyously to His reflection we glimpse in the face of our lover. Oh, feral heart who would settle for the corporeal image but refuse the spiritual source when both are offered so openly. So saddening is the need to touch and feel and taste the beloved that it goads us like animals down the wrong path, settling only for someone to hold and shunning the higher and more pure love of Him who created the very object of our mortal love.

This is a short and barren path, on which we seek love with our whole being and settle for the echo of His voice heard distorted in the mundane love of this world. Why do we turn our hearts away from the clarion call of God beckoning us home? Possibly it is because we have no insight into what we are missing. The plan of family is set in heaven to teach us in types and symbols the relationship of Christ to man and man to Christ. It is a sacred lesson learned on earth. Husbands are told to love their wives as Christ loved the church. Wives are told to be obedient to their husbands. Children are protected, nurtured, and loved. Marriage is the deepest exercise of spiritual application in secular life… if we get it right.

EPH 5:22 Wives, submit yourselves unto your own husbands, as unto the Lord. 23 For the husband is the head of the wife, even as Christ is the head of the church: and he is the Savior of the body. 24 Therefore as the church is subject unto Christ, so let the wives be to their own husbands in every thing. 25 Husbands, love your wives, even as Christ also loved the church, and gave himself for it; 26 That he might sanctify and cleanse it with the washing of water by the word, 27 That he might present it to himself a glorious church, not having spot, or wrinkle, or any such thing; but that it should be holy and without blemish. 28 So ought men to love their wives as their own bodies. He that loveth his wife loveth himself.

MAR 10:13 And they brought young children to him, that he should touch them: and his disciples rebuked those that brought them.14 But when Jesus saw it, he

was much displeased, and said unto them, Suffer the little children to come unto me, and forbid them not: for of such is the kingdom of God.15 Verily I say unto you, Whosoever shall not receive the kingdom of God as a little child, he shall not enter therein.16 And he took them up in his arms, put his hands upon them, and blessed them.

We love and cherish one another. We bind our hearts together as lover and beloved. We seek and find a spiritual nature in the relationships of lover, spouse, and family. It is what God intended us to have. Yet, God intended more for us. There is still an emptiness and void unfilled. We love and are unsure of being loved. We are loved but fall short of loving. We wait for that time we may feel possessed and protected by love. We look to the world, but our hearts wait for God. It is not loving or being loved that is needed. We wait on love itself to come. We wait, but He is already here.

PSA 139:7 Whither shall I go from thy spirit? or whither shall I flee from thy presence? 8 If I ascend up into heaven, thou art there: if I make my bed in hell, behold, thou art there. 9 If I take the wings of the morning, and dwell in the uttermost parts of the sea; 10 Even there shall thy hand lead me, and thy right hand shall hold me.

Somehow, our hearts know Him but we cannot see Him. His presence is felt, His spirit is heard, but our eyes are blind, our ears are deaf to the soft rustle of His steps. In the search for love, our hearts frantically scan the faces of those around us. Are you He for whom I search? Are you the Lord? We look into the eyes of everyone passing, testing each one, until we can say, "I look at your face and I see God." When our hearts recognize the face of God in another, we call it love and there we abide. The love of our spouse, at the highest level, is a reflection of the spiritual love we seek in God. The bonding we seek from our spouse is a shadow of a higher need, to bond with God. We love but still, we are not filled. How can the darkened light of our souls illuminate the corners of another's heart? It is a relationship with God that we seek. We await Him who is love. Our relationships with others are divinely inspired by the template of God calling us to a communion with Him. Marriage is sacred. It is based on a divine plan of shadows and types from God showing us how we should love Him and be loved by Him.

SOL 1:15 Behold, thou art fair, my love; behold, thou art fair; thou hast doves' eyes. 16 Behold, thou art fair, my beloved, yea, pleasant: also our bed is green. 17 The beams of our house are cedar, and our rafters of fir. 2:1 I am the rose of Sharon, and the lily of the valleys. 2 As the lily among thorns, so is my love among the daughters. 3 As the apple tree among the trees of the wood, so is my beloved among the sons. I sat down under his shadow with great delight, and his fruit was sweet to my taste. 4 He brought me to the banqueting house, and his banner over me was love.

SON 2:10 My beloved spake, and said unto me, Rise up, my love, my fair one, and come away. 11 For, lo, the winter is past, the rain is over and gone;12 The flowers appear on the earth; the time of the singing of birds is come, and the voice of the turtle is heard in our land; 13 The fig tree putteth forth her green figs, and the vines with the tender grape give a good smell. Arise, my love, my fair one, and come away. 14 O my dove, that art in the clefts of the rock, in the secret places of the stairs, let me see thy countenance, let me hear thy voice; for sweet is thy voice, and thy countenance is comely.

SON 5:2 I sleep, but my heart waketh: it is the voice of my beloved that knocketh, saying, Open to me, my sister, my love, my dove, my undefiled: for my head is filled with dew, and my locks with the drops of the night.

We seek a deep and abiding communion with another because the desire is placed in us. Relationships of husband and wife are driven to a spiritual depth by the same yearning of togetherness set in us by God for Himself. The pattern of true friendship and holy marriage are the worldly symbols of the heavenly marriage between the believer and Christ. Sex becomes spiritual in this context…the ultimate attempt to commune, share, love, and be one in heart and soul. Yet, in our hearts we are being called home to a place we have never been. We pine for a friend and lover we have barely met. Only He can fill our hearts and souls completely. Only in Him can we rest. Only then will our spirits be at peace.

It is not that we do not love friends or family, but there is a higher love and a deeper calling making us know we are not yet fulfilled, not yet at peace, not yet at rest, not yet free of the emptiness that so graciously plagues our souls.

What devastating mercy and vicious grace has been given man that he would receive by some charity of the Spirit of God this disease of sorrow that only God can cure. Only in this relationship called Christianity does God place a hook in our hearts and draw us homeward. Only here do we have the fisher of men. The great physician and loving Father listens for our call. "Lord, what must I do to be saved?" It is the question that starts the journey of a lifetime as God answers in lessons of love for the rest of our lives.

ACTS 16:29 Then he called for a light, and sprang in, and came trembling, and fell down before Paul and Silas, 30 And brought them out, and said, Sirs, what must I do to be saved? 31 And they said, Believe on the Lord Jesus Christ, and thou shalt be saved, and thy house. 32 And they spake unto him the word of the Lord, and to all that were in his house. 33 And he took them the same hour of the night, and washed their stripes; and was baptized, he and all his, straightway.

This relationship is a marriage mystical and eternal. Christ has assumed his rightful place as both redeemer and husband. He is the spiritual head and high priest of the family of God. He is the bridegroom of the believers. He is the beloved.

REV 21:2 And I John saw the holy city, new Jerusalem, coming down from God out of heaven, prepared as a bride adorned for her husband. 3 And I heard a great voice out of heaven saying, Behold, the tabernacle of God is with men, and he will dwell with them, and they shall be his people, and God himself shall be with them, and be their God.

REV 22:17 And the Spirit and the bride say, Come. And let him that heareth say, Come. And let him that is athirst come. And whosoever will, let him take the water of life freely.

Brethren; I am homesick for a place that I have never been but I know a man who knows the way. W.R. Lumpkin

COUNT IT ALL GRACE

When starting the mystical journey it may seem appropriate to bring all of your sins of the past up once again before God and confess all you have confessed before. It may seem good to remember yourself in light of how you were as a sinner. While it is true we are low, unworthy wretches, even this state and all sins are couched in grace. All trials and all sins are not only covered under His grace but are part of His grace. This does not diminish our sins in any way. It does not elevate us spiritually one inch, yet it does show us His magnificent and loving heart. For every step and misstep, all pain and tribulation brought us here to His feet and without any of them we would not be here for such a time as this. Only distress, physical or emotional, forces us to consider our path and only pain of this sort detours us to try other ways. We learn from our mistakes but should not be kept down by them. We repent and must leave the sorrow of our past deeds behind us.

Don't be troubled when you meditate on the greatness of your former sins, but rather know that God's grace is so much greater in magnitude that it justifies the sinner and absolves the wicked. Quotations from Cyril of Alexandria (Commentary on the Gospel of St. Luke)

Such a sweet and wonderful balance is maintained between remembering our wretched state and seeking to forget even ourselves in our search for God.

...if any man or woman should think to come to contemplation without many sweet meditations... on their own wretched state, on the passion, the kindness and the great goodness and the worthiness of God, they will certainly be deceived and fail in their purpose. At the same time, those men and women who are long practiced in these meditations must leave them aside, put them down and hold them far under the cloud of forgetting, if they are ever to pierce the cloud of unknowing between them and their God. From The Cloud of Unknowing

I count it all grace that He knew the path of my sinful steps even before He saved me and still, He saved me. I count it all grace that He somehow wove my freewill into His plan, knowing how low and undeserving I am for His love. I count it all grace, my sins, my strengths, my weaknesses, and all of my limitations are counted as a terrible and undeniable gift designed by God to work in conjunction with the path I walk to lead me homeward to Him.

Known by God from before the beginning, knitted together in the womb by His hand, blessed with human frailties so deep and pervasive as to have cost the life of God himself, I was led to God's feet.

He who is Love has given me the gift of love. It was given for nothing I have done or been. I was sinful even while confessing my sin. There was no need to beg for love. He loves me more than life. There is nothing I may do to thank Him or repay Him except by my free will to accept this gift He gives that it not be given in vain.

ROM 5:17 For if by one man's offence death reigned by one; much more they which receive abundance of grace and of the gift of righteousness shall reign in life by one, Jesus Christ. 18 Therefore as by the offence of one judgment came upon all men to condemnation; even so by the righteousness of one the free gift came upon all men unto justification of life. 19 For as by one man's disobedience many were made sinners, so by the obedience of one shall many be made righteous. 20 Moreover the law entered, that the offence might abound. But where sin abounded, grace did much more abound: 21 That as sin hath reigned unto death, even so might grace reign through righteousness unto eternal life by Jesus Christ our Lord. 6:1 What shall we say then? Shall we continue in sin, that grace may abound? 2 God forbid. How shall we, that are dead to sin, live any longer therein?

ROM 6:14 For sin shall not have dominion over you: for ye are not under the law, but under grace. 15 What then? shall we sin, because we are not under the law, but under grace? God forbid. 16 Know ye not, that to whom ye yield yourselves servants to obey, his servants ye are to whom ye obey; whether of sin unto death, or of obedience unto righteousness?

For I have attempted to keep myself from sin and sinning and repeatedly failed, utterly. Trying to run or hide from my fallen nature and always finding me with me and never leaving or losing one iota of me, I gave up trying to change me and laid down before Him any hope of my own righteousness. I count myself the only sinner and have received firm rejection from the church, being unable, for any time, to stay me from sinning. Yet, I still feel His spirit welling up within me. But now, there is nowhere to go but to His heart, alone.

You do not have to be perfect. Perfection is not what Christianity is all about. You do your best and God does the "righteousing".   Dr. Gene Scott.

1CO 15:10 But by the grace of God I am what I am: and his grace which was bestowed upon me was not in vain; but I laboured more abundantly than they all: yet not I, but the grace of God which was with me.

2CO 4:14 Knowing that he which raised up the Lord Jesus shall raise up us also by Jesus, and shall present us with you. 15 For all things are for your sakes, that the abundant grace might through the thanksgiving of many redound to the glory of God. 16 For which cause we faint not; but though our outward man perish, yet the inward man is renewed day by day.

JAM 1:1 James, a servant of God and of the Lord Jesus Christ, to the twelve tribes, which are scattered abroad, greeting. 2 My brethren, count it all joy when ye fall into divers temptations; 3 Knowing this, that the trying of your faith worketh patience. 4 But let patience have her perfect work, that ye may be perfect and entire, wanting nothing.

ZEC 4:6 Then he answered and spake unto me, saying, This is the word of the LORD unto Zerubbabel, saying, Not by might, nor by power, but by my spirit, saith the LORD of hosts. 7 Who art thou, O great mountain? before Zerubbabel thou shalt become a plain: and he shall bring forth the headstone thereof with shoutings, crying, grace, grace unto it.

Having been shown His grace, by His grace, I at once saw my shortcomings and needs and was drawn to know a basic wrongness in me. I now hold on with my life, for my life, to the grace of God, knowing He who made me knew me and still loved me enough to woo me, with His prevenient grace, by His spirit, back to Him. And if He could and would do this, that by His longsuffering and forgiveness, He would keep loving me to the very end, seeing that He knew all I would be and do before He saved me. By doing this, He is keeping me for Himself until that day I may be made perfect, over there.

WHAT IS GRACE?

Only by the grace of God can salvation and the communion we seek take place. We may ask. We may beg. But, it is only in watchful waiting that we will receive. His grace is sufficient and the only vehicle by which salvation and communion with God is granted. But what is grace?

Grace is a blessing, a blessing that is undeserved, unsolicited and unexpected, a blessing that brings a sense of the divine order of things into our lives. The ways of grace are mysterious, we cannot always figure them out. But we know grace by its fruits, by the blessings of its works. We would expect to be startled when grace manifests itself. The opposite is true. It doesn't startle us at all, for grace is everywhere. We may not discern it; we may not recognize it for we are inclined to take it for granted. "Living with Grace" by Rev. Peter Fleck

If we are walking, dancing, eating, teaching, preaching, meditating, being, we are rid of the impediments which hinder our free movement. We are rid of all the obstacles that block us from being who we are meant to be. This is grace. A grace that indicates not an addition, but rather a subtraction and removal of those things that may hinder us from being who we are. This is grace. Reverend Bill Clark

Grace "is an attitude on God's part that proceeds entirely from within Himself, and that is conditioned in no way by anything in the objects of His favor." Burton Scott Easton in The International Standard Bible Encyclopedia.

When a thing is said to be of 'grace' we mean that the recipient has no claim upon it, that it was in no-wise due him. It comes to him as pure charity, and, at first, unasked and undesired. A.W. Pink Attributes of God

In a time before his death, Mr. McLaren, minister of the Tolboth church, said, "I am gathering together all my prayers, all my sermons, all my good deeds, all my ill deeds; and I am going to throw them all overboard and swim to glory on the plank of Free Grace."

There is one work which is right and proper for us to do, and that is the eradication of self. But however great this eradication and reduction of self may be, it remains insufficient if God does not complete it in us. For our humility is only perfect when God humbles us through ourselves. Only then are they and the virtue perfected, and not before.   Meister Eckhart

If I were good and holy enough to be elevated among the saints, then the people would discuss and question whether this was by grace or nature and would be troubled about it. But this would be wrong of them. Let God work in you, acknowledge that it is his work, and do not be concerned as to whether he achieves this by means of nature or beyond nature. Both nature and grace are his. What is it to you which means he best uses or what he performs in you or in someone else? He should work how and where and in what manner it suits him to do so. Meister Eckhart

The self-righteous, relying on the many good works he imagines he has performed, seems to hold salvation in his own hand, and considers Heaven as a just reward of his merits. In the bitterness of his zeal he exclaims against all sinners, and represents the gates of mercy as barred against them, and Heaven as a place to which they have no claim. What need have such self-righteous persons of a Saviour? They are already burdened with the load of their own merits. Oh, how long they bear the flattering load, while sinners divested of everything, fly rapidly on the wings of faith and love into their Saviour's arms, who freely bestows on them that which he has so freely promised! Jeanne-Marie Bouvier de la Motte-Guyon

Humility is a grace in the soul... It is indescribable wealth, a name and a gift from God. Learn from Me, He said; that is, not from an angel, not from a man, not from a book, but from Me, that is from My dwelling within you, from My illumination and action within you, for I am gentle and meek of heart in thought and in spirit, and your souls will find rest from conflicts and relief from evil thoughts.   John Climacus

Our activity consists of loving God and our fruition of enduring God and being penetrated by his love. There is a distinction between the love and fruition, as there is between God and his Grace. John Ruusbroec

Jesus, are you not my mother? Are you not even more than my mother? My human mother after all labored in giving birth to me only for a day or night;

you, my tender and beautiful lord, labored for me over 30 years.   Marguerite of Oingt

We are only here and possess what we have because of the timing and grace of God. Whether we have little or we have much, we have it because of God. The love in our hearts and all things we have and feel are because He made us as we are. He sets our path and places us on the path at His time. The people we meet and places we go and thus the situations springing from them are in our lives because we were born at such a time as this. Gratitude keeps our arrogance and pride in check. It assigns all of what we are and all we have to God who made all things and keeps them in existence. Gratitude is the balance point between God and man. Thankfulness is a measure of our dependence on God and our obedience to Him. It is the path that our prayers walk to get to God. Gratitude is how we approach Him. It is said there are only two things that motivate us to do things: desire and desperation. It is said, "gratitude comes from desire". This is the idea of some philosophers, but there is a higher gratitude not understood by the world.

There is a gratitude springing from the realization that one has no desires, no needs, nothing lacking. It is gratitude from epiphany. Insight brought on by grace enables us to see how God is providing our path and all things on it. It does not mean we have riches or even health, but that we are where we are supposed to be. Even in our lack or pain, we see somehow we are exactly where God would have us to be. It is the gratitude of knowing what we need to fulfill our purpose will be provided on God's path for God's purpose. All things are seen in a state of grace and balance and we are here for a purpose; God's purpose.

Joseph Lumpkin

FAITH

Faith is the key we turn to enter through the door of salvation. It unlocks the door of heaven and the presence of God.

EPH 2:8 For by grace are ye saved through faith; and that not of yourselves: it is the gift of God: Not of works, lest any man should boast.

Faith is action based upon belief, sustained by confidence.   Dr Gene Scott

You may ask why I have chosen to discuss faith at this point in a book that is seemingly dedicated to knowing God in a personal sense. After all, knowing trumps faith, doesn't it? No. It does not. There will be times of darkness and trouble in our journey when we will doubt we ever heard the voice of God. It is in these times the faith will triumph. However, neither faith nor knowing can come first. God's grace must come first. God must first open our eyes to our own inadequacies and reveal to us our need for Him. God must draw us to Him in a sovereign act of grace. He must then give us the faith by which we are saved. Faith and Grace are the two powers yoked together to pull us out of this world and into eternity.

ROM 12:3 For I say, through the grace given unto me, to every man that is among you, not to think of himself more highly than he ought to think; but to think soberly, according as God hath dealt to every man the measure of faith.

Yes, even our faith is a gift from God. Faith is manifest in the act of believing in someone we have not yet met and believing He is who He said He is, the only begotten Son of God. Faith comes to us from God by grace. We worship Him but He enables us to do so. He enables us to believe. He gives us the faith to be saved. He opens our eyes and our hearts to His word and draws us by His spirit. It is by faith we come to God and by faith we live. It is better to believe than to know, for knowing can be shaken in those times when we reach for God and cannot find Him. In those times He is silent and our souls are tested with darkness, it is only by faith we will survive. As a child whose father has left on a long journey, we no longer see Him, but we have faith He will return. We have faith He is there, still loving us. It is faith given as an act of love and grace that allows us to await His return.

HAB 2:3 For the vision is yet for an appointed time, but at the end it shall speak, and not lie: though it tarry, wait for it; because it will surely come, it will not tarry. 4 Behold, his soul which is lifted up is not upright in him: but the just shall live by his faith.

ACT 26:18 To open their eyes, and to turn them from darkness to light, and from the power of Satan unto God, that they may receive forgiveness of sins, and inheritance among them which are sanctified by faith that is in me.

ROM 1:16 For I am not ashamed of the gospel of Christ: for it is the power of God unto salvation to every one that believeth; to the Jew first, and also to the Greek. 17 For therein is the righteousness of God revealed from faith to faith: as it is written, The just shall live by faith.

ROM 3:21 But now the righteousness of God without the law is manifested, being witnessed by the law and the prophets; 22 Even the righteousness of God which is by faith of Jesus Christ unto all and upon all them that believe: for there is no difference: 23 For all have sinned, and come short of the glory of God; 24 Being justified freely by his grace through the redemption that is in Christ Jesus: ROM 3:25 Whom God hath set forth to be a propitiation through faith in his blood, to declare his righteousness for the remission of sins that are past, through the forbearance of God; 26 To declare, I say, at this time his righteousness: that he might be just, and the justifier of him which believeth in Jesus.

ROM 3:28 Therefore we conclude that a man is justified by faith without the deeds of the law.

ROM 4:16 Therefore it is of faith, that it might be by grace; to the end the promise might be sure to all the seed; not to that only which is of the law, but to that also which is of the faith of Abraham; who is the father of us all, ROM 4:23 Now it was not written for his sake alone, that it was imputed to him; 24 But for us also, to whom it shall be imputed, if we believe on him that raised up Jesus our Lord from the dead; 25 Who was delivered for our offences, and was raised again for our justification. 5:1 Therefore being justified by faith, we have peace with God through our Lord Jesus Christ: 2 By whom also we have access by faith into this grace wherein we stand, and rejoice in hope of the glory of God.

GAL 2:16 Knowing that a man is not justified by the works of the law, but by the faith of Jesus Christ, even we have believed in Jesus Christ, that we might be justified by the faith of Christ, and not by the works of the law: for by the works of the law shall no flesh be justified.

GAL 3:24 Wherefore the law was our schoolmaster to bring us unto Christ, that we might be justified by faith. 25 But after that faith is come, we are no longer under a schoolmaster. For ye are all the children of God by faith in Christ Jesus.

1TI 6:12 Fight the good fight of faith, lay hold on eternal life, whereunto thou art also called, and hast professed a good profession before many witnesses.

HEB 11:1 Now faith is the substance of things hoped for, the evidence of things not seen. 2 For by it the elders obtained a good report. 3 Through faith we understand that the worlds were framed by the word of God, so that things which are seen were not made of things which do appear. 4 By faith Abel offered unto God a more excellent sacrifice than Cain, by which he obtained witness that he was righteous, God testifying of his gifts: and by it he being dead yet speaketh. 5 By faith Enoch was translated that he should not see death; and was not found, because God had translated him: for before his translation he had this testimony, that he pleased God. 6 But without faith it is impossible to please him: for he that cometh to God must believe that he is, and that he is a rewarder of them that diligently seek him.

HEB 11:7 By faith Noah, being warned of God of things not seen as yet, moved with fear, prepared an ark to the saving of his house; by the which he condemned the world, and became heir of the righteousness which is by faith. 8 By faith Abraham, when he was called to go out into a place which he should after receive for an inheritance, obeyed; and he went out, not knowing whither he went. 9 By faith he sojourned in the land of promise, as in a strange country, dwelling in tabernacles with Isaac and Jacob, the heirs with him of the same promise: 10 For he looked for a city which hath foundations, whose builder and maker is God. HEB 11:11 Through faith also Sara herself received strength to conceive seed, and was delivered of a child when she was past age, because she judged him faithful who had promised. 12 Therefore sprang there even of one, and him as good as dead, so many as the stars of the sky in multitude, and as the sand which is by the sea shore innumerable. 13 These all died in faith, not having received the promises, but having seen them afar off, and were persuaded of them, and embraced them, and confessed that they were strangers and pilgrims on the earth.

Even with this most holy of things, faith in God, one can supplant the creator with the creature and fall victim to believing in faith itself. If we place faith in our ability to have faith it lessens our perceived dependence on God. I say perceived dependence because we have just crossed the line into the great lie by thinking we can fulfill our needs and do it better than God. Faith in faith is not faith in God. If we do not fully understand our faith comes from God, given by Him in his measure to us, we can come to believe that we have some work or contribution in this faith of ours. This belief, added to the false concept that God must respond to faith, has yielded up a doctrine that is akin to witchcraft. The doctrine of many sects of Wicca states, "As My will, so may it be." This is not so different from the "hyper-faith" concept of having enough faith to compel God to act on behalf of the one with faith. One should always stretch a truth to see if it will break. If it breaks down it is not a truth. This one does not take much stretching to come apart and not much examination to see the cracks.

What ill-thought heresy would pit Christian against Christian in a battle of faith with God as a puppet in between? This is what would happen if the concept were to be practiced by two people competing for the same job, position, raise, or possession. What right have we to expect our prayers to change the mind or path of another person? Even God allows free will, yet some expect their prayers to influence others. Worldly perspective, arrogance, pride, and greed have brought the simple concept of faith and grace into a place of wish-craft bordering on witchcraft. The "Think and Grow Rich" idea of Napoleon Hill has made its way into our churches and has destroyed our view of God's faith, replacing it with faith in faith and faith in some ability of ours to wield a wand-like power contained in our belief in ourselves. Anything that takes our spiritual eyes off of Jesus as the only source of our salvation and spiritual power is wrong. To have Him we must rely on Him.

First, you must make Him your dwelling place.   Dr. Gene Scott

Our banner and cry should be, By faith alone through His grace.

PRAYER AND FAITH

Why do we pray? Do we dare believe that we know what is better for us than God himself? Do we not believe God has our best interest at heart? If He does not want what is best for us, what good would our prayer be? Why bother a vengeful God if He does not have our best interest at heart? Does He not love us? But, if God wants what is best for us, should we not let His will be done? Does this mean keeping our opinion to ourselves? (As if He does not know it already.)

Of the most error ridden views of prayer, the most erroneous comes from a group of very wealthy preachers heading up a new movement. This new movement is a theology called by many names – Kingdom Now, Word of Faith, Dominion, Name it and Claim it, Positive Confession, and others. But the gab it and grab it theology of today is based in covetousness. This type of theology couldn't exist in socialist or communist countries. The society of sharing presented in the Book of Acts, where all people held all possessions in common, flies in the face of this thinking.

Men and women preaching this kind of prayer for pay could only survive in capitalistic or greed driven societies. The countries do not have to be especially rich. The followers simply have to be desperate or lacking contentment to a point that they can be persuaded to set aside logic and become delusional.

The primus is a simple one. If you pray for something with unwavering faith God is obliged to give it to you – no matter what.

Prosperity, health, victory, all would be never ending. But it does not take much of a leap in logic to conclude that if only one person could actually achieve this kind of faith he or she could extinguish all illness and poverty. Even death would no longer exist, since by faith the dead are raised. The universe has never worked like that, but to entertain that fact is to let one's faith waiver. Thus the theology becomes a circular trap.

This kind of theology usually comes with a price. The followers must give – give – give, because they believe God will give back to them. Who are they giving to? The preacher, of course. He, in turn, becomes wealthy and can then tell his followers to have faith like he has faith, for God has made him rich.

When the theology of preachers has become so repulsive that it brings laughter and ridicule it is time for an examination.

"Mercedes Benz" by JANIS JOPLIN

Oh Lord, won't you buy me a Mercedes Benz ?
My friends all drive Porsches, I must make amends.
Worked hard all my lifetime, no help from my friends,
So Lord, won't you buy me a Mercedes Benz ?

Oh Lord, won't you buy me a color TV ?
Dialing For Dollars is trying to find me.
I wait for delivery each day until three,
So oh Lord, won't you buy me a color TV ?

Oh Lord, won't you buy me a night on the town ?
I'm counting on you, Lord, please don't let me down.
Prove that you love me and buy the next round,
Oh Lord, won't you buy me a night on the town ?

Everybody!
Oh Lord, won't you buy me a Mercedes Benz ?
My friends all drive Porsches, I must make amends,
Worked hard all my lifetime, no help from my friends,
So oh Lord, won't you buy me a Mercedes Benz ?

That's it!

But where did this strange new theology of prayer and incantation begin? In 1846 Ethan O. Allen was traveling the US building a reputation as

America's first full-time faith-healer. By the 1950s, a hundred years later, seeds were planted that would produce a legion (I chose that word on purpose) of faith-healers. Each one attempted to distinguish themselves in some fashion by "personalizing" their approach and theology. Many emphasized prosperity, healing, material acquisition, the power of faith to compel God to do one's bidding, and the divinity of man. The age of mass communications had arrived and radio and television were easier and more financially productive than tent revivals, so the preachers took to the air. Shows spread their prosperity doctrine to hundreds of millions of people, first across the US, then across the world.

Sadly, today this "Faith" or "Word" theology is among the fastest growing segment of Christianity.

It has involved three distinct but closely related factions: Napoleon Hill "Think and Grow Rich", the Norman Vincent Peale /Robert Schuller "Positive-Possibility thinkers/Positive Mental Attitude", with their roots in "New Thought"; and the Kenneth Hagin/Kenneth Copeland "Positive Confession and Word-Faith" groups, which have their roots in E.W. Kenyon, William Branham, and the "Manifest Sons of God/Latter Rain" movement.

E.W. Kenyon (1867-1948) applied for ordination through the Southern Californa District of the Assemblies of God around 1925. In his application Kenyon stated that he spoke in tongues and that his teachings were in accordance with those of the Assemblies of God denomination. However, Kenyon's application was turned down due to negative references given by A.G. evangelist, May Eleanore Frey in a letter to General Chairman John William Welch, dated Jan 31, 1925. In addition to the poor personal reference, he was accused of personal contacts with the Ku Klux Klan. The letter went on to say that in spite of his testimony to the opposite – had not received Pentecostal Spirit baptism. Because of this rejection, he never thought of himself as a Pentecostal. Kenyon became an independent Baptist pastor, radio teacher, and author, developing a "metaphysical mixture" of fundamentalist, faith-cure, and transcendentalism. Ironically, Kenyon's teachings helped metaphysical religious concepts penetrate Christianity.

Many religious groups had responded to people's continued desire for the supernatural by demonstrating "miraculous" healings, but Kenyon believed he could go beyond even that. Kenyon claimed that he had found "Reality," higher than even the "Higher Life" movement from which he emerged. This movement was sweeping through England when he was there. In the Higher Life movement Christians should experience a second work of God in his life. This work of God is called "the second blessing," "the latter rain," or "being filled with the Holy Spirit." Higher Life teachers promoted the idea that Christians who had received this blessing from God could live a more holy, less sinful or even a sinless, life.

But Kenyon's "Reality was higher, better, more. This would be the solution to all of humanity's problems; in every arena of life, the believer could be absolute master by achieving and maintaining the right consciousness. This was Kenyon's pathway to the full realization of human potential.

Kenyon's promotion of his religious philosophy was a curious blend of biblical fundamentalism and metaphysical mind control. It represents one of the earliest major penetrations of the conservative American Christianity by mind-science.

Kenyon always considered himself a champion of biblical Christianity, and made clear his intention to remedy the menace of the competing metaphysical religions (like Christian Science and New Thought) by offering a superior alternative for seekers of Reality. Yet, ironically, the popular acceptance of his system, which we will show to be a "metaphysical mixture," resulted in a wide dissemination of mind-cure concepts, contrary to his intent.

His teachings on healing through "positive confession" or affirmations were posthumously popularized by American healing-revivalists, and again by independent charismatic movements.

Kenyon's views are now promoted by proponents of what has been called the "Health and Wealth" or "Faith" movement. His inspiration may have been taken in part from the Keswickean Higher Life movement. Some research has even suggested roots within Christian Science, New Thought, and Plymouth Brethren. His odd mixture of Christianity and "wishcraft" are promoted today by Kenneth Hagin and Kenneth Copeland.

Napoleon Hill (October 26, 1883 – November 8, 1970) was one of the earliest producers of the modern genre of personal success books. His book, "Think and Grow Rich" is one of the best-selling books of all time. Hill's works examined the power of personal beliefs, and the role they play in personal success. "What the mind of man can conceive and believe, it can achieve," is one of Hill's hallmark expressions. Hill was greatly influenced by Andrew Carnegie. Hill discovered that Carnegie believed that the process of success could be explained in a simple formula that could be duplicated by the average person. Carnegie commissioned Hill with letters of reference to interview over 500 successful men and women in order to discover and publish this formula for success. Hill published initially in 1928 as a study course called, The Law of Success. The Achievement formula was detailed further and, until 1941, was published in home-study courses, including the seventeen-volume "Mental Dynamite" series.

Hill later called his personal success teachings "The Philosophy of Achievement" and he considered freedom, democracy, capitalism, and harmony to be important contributing elements. For without these foundations to build upon, as Hill demonstrated throughout his writings, successful personal achievements are not possible. Negative emotions, fear and selfishness among others, had no part to play in his philosophy, and Hill considered them to be the source of failure for unsuccessful people. (Information gleaned from Wikipedia and other sources.)

Dr. Norman Vincent Peale (May 31, 1898 – December 24, 1993) was a Protestant preacher and author of The Power of Positive Thinking and a progenitor of the theory of "Positive Thinking."

Robert Schuller is the televangelist who built the Crystal Cathedral Church, from where he hosted a weekly TV show called "The Hour of Power." Schuller was strongly influenced by his mentor, Norman Peale. Schuller chose to focus on what he believes are the positive aspects of the faith. He deliberately avoids condemning people and he encourages Christians (and non-Christians) to achieve great things through Positive Thinking.

By Christianizing the concepts of Hill and Peale, Schuller took the "Think and Grow Rich" and "The Power of Positive Thinking" philosophies and produced "The Hour of Power." His ideas were forced into a rather tenuous theology that could be labeled "Pray, Pay, and someone will Grow Rich."

Well-known leaders in this new riches and wealth theology are E.W. Kenyon, Charles Capps, Kenneth Hagin, Kenneth Copeland, Frederick K.C. Price, Robert Tilton, and David Cho, to name a few.

Kenneth E. Hagin (1917 - 2004) preached and focused on the power of the spoken word. This idea came from E. W. Kenyon and W. M. Branham. In 1974 Hagin founded Rhema Bible Training Centre in an attempt to bring new preachers under his ministry by teaching the Faith or Word principles using Kenyon's Rhema doctrine. Hagin's message promised a return on investments made to God that were given to the church. This is where many Christians go astray. A tithe, in the modern sense, is an investment in those who run the church, ministry, or religious entertainment you attend and not to God. The income of Hagin's ministries proves the point.

Kenneth Hagin, Oral Roberts, Frederick Price, Kenneth Copeland, Don Gossett, Charles Capps and other leading proponents in this movement all directly inherited their theology from Kenyon and his contemporaries. This new generation of televangelists have enjoyed the ability to propagate the Prosperity message by means of extensive and expensive media ministries, fully funded by followers giving to their organization in response to their message, thus perpetuating the influx of funds.

Cho teaches that Christians can get anything they want by calling upon the spirit world in the "fourth dimension" and envisioning (visualizing) their felt needs, no matter how crass and gross. Cho teaches that positive thinking, positive speaking, and positive visualization are the keys to success, and that anyone can literally "incubate" and give birth to physical reality by creating a vivid image in his or her mind and focusing upon it.

Oral Granville Roberts (1918 -), was considered by many to be the most prominent Pentecostal in the world in the 1980's. In 1956 Roberts was mailing his monthly magazine, Abundant Life, to over a million people. In 1969 he was reaching 64 million viewers with prime-time television programs. By 1981 he was able to open his $250 million dollar "City of Faith Medical and Research Centre," to combine the healing power of faith with medicine. Roberts' basic presuppositions were, firstly, that God is good; and, secondly, that God therefore wills to heal and prosper his people. Roberts taught that monetary giving to the church was a "seed of faith" that would return a harvest of wealth for those who had complete faith in God. This was basically the same doctrine that Hagin preached.

Charles Emmitt Capps (1934 -) is a current proponent of the Prosperity movement. After being healed under Hagin's teachings in 1969, he began teaching that words are the most powerful things in the universe. If spoken in faith, Capps taught, words carry creative power by releasing God's ability within you. He set out his message in "The Tongue, a Creative Force" (1976), and in 1980, he was ordained into the "faith ministry" by K. Copeland.

Kenneth Copeland (1937 -) is perhaps the leading proponent of the Word of Faith gospel today. In his early days, Kenneth Hagin and Oral Roberts had a life changing impact on Copeland. He enrolled in Oral Roberts University while attending Kenneth Hagin's Tulsa seminars. He also sought out the teachings of E. W. Kenyon, which had a determining influence on his theology. In 1973 Copeland began publishing "Believer's Voice of Victory." Like his spiritual fathers, Copeland emphasizes complete prosperity – spirit, soul and body – through total commitment to God's will, demonstrated by the spoken word. Like John G. Lake, M. B. Eddy and P.P. Quimby before them, Copeland's teaching raises the status of humanity to a God-like level by teaching that believers possess the ability to rescue themselves from trouble by use of their "divine right." It was Copeland who said, "You impart humanity into a child that's born of you. Because you are a human, you have imparted the nature of humanity into that born child. That child wasn't born a whale. It was born a human. Well, now, you don't have a God in you. You are one."

Although the Word of Faith movement is currently controversial and even repudiated by some sections within Pentecostalism, the key figures who were influential in creating the underlying doctrines of this movement were all Pentecostal.

Like the emphasis on Divine Healing within the Holiness movement, which naturally carried over into Pentecostalism when it emerged, the emphasis of Positive Confession theology, which pre-existed Pentecostalism, carried over into the movement from its origin because those who were key proponents of this doctrinal emphasis became Pentecostals and continued to be leaders within the movement.

Even though many Pentecostals reject some aspects of the foundational doctrines of the Word of Faith movement, general acceptance has occurred of the overall emphasis on material abundance, positivity and the power of the spoken word, and what they term, "victorious Christian living."

The leaders of this group have been successful in creating great wealth and amassing large congregations, but their movement does not yet constitute a new denomination, however it certainly represents teachings outside of orthodox Christianity.

D.R. McConnell points out that "any new religious movement [within Protestantism] must bear the scrutiny of two criteria: biblical fidelity and historical orthodoxy." Regrettably, the Positive Confession movement fails on both counts. The historical roots of this movement (which Charles Farah has called "Faith Formula Theology") lie in the occult, and most recently, in New Thought and its off-shoot, the Mind Science cults.

Its Biblical basis is found only in the peculiar interpretations of its own leaders, not in generally accepted Christian theology. This movement teaches that faith is a matter of what we say more than whom we trust or what God you affirm in your heart. The term "positive confession" refers to the teaching that words have creative power. What you say, Word-Faith teachers claim, determines everything that happens to you. Your "confessions," that is, the things you say -- especially the favors you demand of God -- must all be stated positively and without wavering. Then God is obligated to answer. Word-Faith believers deliver their positive confessions as an incantation by which they can conjure up anything they desire: "Believe it in your heart; say it with your mouth and it will happen. That is the principle of faith. You can have what you say" (Charismatic Chaos, pp. 281, 285). This is at the heart of the Positive Confession movement today, also known as the "name-it-and-claim-it" gospel. However, it is also the foundational message of witchcraft, as they proclaim, "As I will, so it will be!"

The Positive Confession movement is a Charismatic and sometimes Pentecostal form of Christian Science. There are great parallels in their common beliefs.

Faith is a force that both God and man can use: "Faith is a force just like electricity or gravity" (Copeland). "It is the substance out of which God creates whatever is" (Capps). "God uses faith, and so may we in exactly the same way in order to produce the same results through obedience to the same laws of faith that God applied in creation. "(Capps). "You have the same ability as God has dwelling or residing on the inside of you" (Capps). "We have all the capabilities of God. We have His faith" (Copeland).

Faith's force is released by speaking words: "Words are the most powerful thing in the universe because they are containers that "carry faith or fear and they produce after their kind" (Capps). "God had faith in His own words ... God had faith in His faith, because He spoke words of faith and they came to pass. That faith force was transported by words ... the God-kind-of-faith ... is released by the words of your mouth" (Hagin). "Creative power was in God's mouth. It is in your mouth also" (Capps).

Man is a "god": "Man was designed or created by God to be the god of this world" (Tilton, Hagin, Capps). "Adam was the god of this world ... but he sold out to Satan, and Satan became the god of this world" (Hagin). "We were created to be gods over the earth, but remember to spell it with a little 'g'." (Tilton, Hagin, Capps). Man was created in the God class ... We are a class of gods ... God himself spawned us from His innermost being ... We are in God; so that makes us part of God. Look at 2 Cor 5:17." (Copeland).

Anyone can use the faith. "Because man is a little god in God's class: very capable of operating on the same level of faith as God". (Capps) "All men are spirit beings." (Hagin) "Whether Christian or pagan, man can release this "faith force" by speaking words if he only believes in his words as God believes in His." (Hagin). "Everything you say [positive or negative] will come to pass" (Capps). "Spiritual things are created by WORDS. Even natural, physical things are created by WORDS" (Hagin).

You get what you confess: "You get what you say." (Hagin, Hunter). "Only by mouth confession can faith power be released, allowing tremendous things to happen" (Cho). "Remember, the key to receiving the desires of your heart is to make the words of your mouth agree with what you want." (Copeland). "Whatever comes out of your mouth shall be produced in your life" (Tilton).

Never make a negative confession: "The tongue can kill you, or it can release the life of God within you ... whether you believe right or wrong, it is still the law" (Capps). There is power in "the evil fourth dimension" (Cho). If you confess sickness you get it, if you confess health you get it; whatever you say you get" (Hagin). "Faith is as a seed ... you plant it by speaking it" (Capps). "The spoken word ... releases power -- power for good or power for evil" (Bashan).

So – I ask again, Why do we pray, if not for health and wealth and all of those toys we desire?

The Christian faith demands union and communion with the creator wherein He teaches us, guides us, and loves us. Through meditation, adoration, and prayer we are joined with Him and transformed from within. Such love and transformation engendered by this relationship can reunite Christians with the power, courage, and glory needed to survive in a world, which is becoming increasingly hostile to them.

With most people, and sadly, with most Christians, a crucial gap remains between God and man. What is needed is not the teaching of doctrine, law, or church tradition, nor is it any social or moral message. We need a heart-to-heart dialogue with God. We need and long for a relationship with our creator in which He loves and teaches us as a father would a child. A child knows he is loved by the kiss on his cheek, the words, the touch, and the embrace. It is in this type of communion we "know" God. He has bid us come, but the modern church has forgotten the path. It is still there, beneath the hedges of religion and pride. The hedges must be cleared away to find the path.

Prayer is not for us to change the mind of God. It is to allow Him to mold and strengthen our souls to endure His will. Prayer is not for us to beg the Almighty for favors and trinkets. Prayer is a vehicle of communion with God, in which we may sit in His presence and, in some small way, know who He is. In knowing Him, we shall know how to live closer to Him. Paul tells us to "pray without ceasing." This is not the prayer of beggary. It is the prayer of communion; it is not a discursive prayer, but one of silence and listening.

We must strive to keep our prayer life in balance between Discursive prayer and Contemplative prayer. In discursive prayer we carry on a dialogue between the Lord and ourselves. The problem in this type of prayer is we tend to do all of the talking. We bring a wish list before the throne. We repeat our requests as if He did not hear us the first time. We beg God to fill our requests, as if we could possibly know what is best in the light of eternity. We seldom listen to His answer. In contemplative prayer we stay silent and listen to the Lord. We think about Him and His glory. We learn to be still inside so we may hear His soft, beckoning voice.

Prayer is not for us to change the mind of God, but for us to be conformed to His will.

This is a state of Grace.

Anything attained here is grace. It is not dependant on our wealth or health, only our desire to know and experience Him.

In a time before his death, Mr. McLaren, minister of the Tolboth church, said, "I am gathering together all my prayers, all my sermons, all my good deeds, all my ill deeds; and I am going to throw them all overboard and swim to glory on the plank of Free Grace."

Thus, it is not acquisition that couples us with God, but it is gratitude. Gratitude is the balance point between God and man. Thankfulness is a measure of our dependence on God and our obedience to Him. It is the path that our prayers walk to get to God. Gratitude is how we approach Him. It is said there are only two things that motivate us to do things: desire and desperation. It is said, "gratitude comes from desire". This is the idea of some philosophers, but there is a higher gratitude not understood by the world.

There is a gratitude springing from the realization that one has no desires, no needs, nothing lacking. Even though we are imprisoned, if God is All then we have all. It is gratitude from epiphany. Insight brought on by grace enables us to see how God is providing our path and all things on it. It does not mean we have riches or even health, but that we are where we are supposed to be. Even in our lack or pain, we see somehow we are exactly where God would have us to be. It is the gratitude of knowing what we need to fulfill our purpose will be provided on God's path for God's purpose. All things are seen in a state of grace and balance, and we are here for a purpose; God's purpose.

The faith we seek is not in the form of belief in our own incantation, but it is faith in Him. We must know that it is first by Him and through Him that we could have any measure of faith at all. Faith is the key we turn to enter through the door of salvation. It unlocks the door of heaven and the presence of God. But it is not faith in words, or faith in faith, it is simply the faith in a father – God who knows what is best for his spoiled children.

Joseph Lumpkin

EPH 2:8 For by grace are ye saved through faith; and that not of yourselves: it is the gift of God: Not of works, lest any man should boast.

Faith is action based upon belief, sustained by confidence.   Dr. Gene Scott

Faith has its proper place. Faith turns the key of salvation and allows us entry into Heaven. There will be times of darkness and trouble in our journey when we will doubt we ever heard the voice of God. It is in these times that faith will triumph. However, neither faith nor knowing can come first. God's grace must come first. God must first open our eyes to our own inadequacies and reveal to us our need for Him. God must draw us to Himself in a sovereign act of grace. He must then give us the faith by which we are saved. Faith and Grace are the two powers yoked together to pull us out of this world and into eternity.

ROM 12:3 For I say, through the grace given unto me, to every man that is among you, not to think of himself more highly than he ought to think; but to think soberly, according as God hath dealt to every man the measure of faith.

Yes, even our faith is a gift from God. Faith is manifest in the act of believing in someone we have not yet met and believing He is who He said He is, the only begotten Son of God. Faith comes to us from God by grace. We worship Him but He enables us to do so. He enables us to believe. He gives us the faith to be saved. He opens our eyes and our hearts to His word and draws us by His spirit. It is by faith we come to God and by faith we live. It is better to believe than to know, for knowing can be shaken in those times when we reach for God and cannot find Him. In those times He is silent and our souls are tested with darkness, it is only by faith we will survive. As a child whose father has left on a long journey, we no longer see Him, but we have faith He will return. We have faith He is there, still loving us. It is faith given as an act of love and grace that allows us to await His return.

HAB 2:3 For the vision is yet for an appointed time, but at the end it shall speak, and not lie: though it tarry, wait for it; because it will surely come, it will not tarry. 4 Behold, his soul which is lifted up is not upright in him: but the just shall live by his faith.

ACT 26:18 To open their eyes, and to turn them from darkness to light, and from the power of Satan unto God, that they may receive forgiveness of sins, and inheritance among them which are sanctified by faith that is in me.

ROM 1:16 For I am not ashamed of the gospel of Christ: for it is the power of God unto salvation to every one that believeth; to the Jew first, and also to the Greek. 17 For therein is the righteousness of God revealed from faith to faith: as it is written, The just shall live by faith.

ROM 3:21 But now the righteousness of God without the law is manifested, being witnessed by the law and the prophets; 22 Even the righteousness of God which is by faith of Jesus Christ unto all and upon all them that believe: for there is no difference: 23 For all have sinned, and come short of the glory of God; 24 Being justified freely by his grace through the redemption that is in Christ Jesus: ROM 3:25 Whom God hath set forth to be a propitiation through faith in his blood, to declare his righteousness for the remission of sins that are past, through the forbearance of God; 26 To declare, I say, at this time his righteousness: that he might be just, and the justifier of him which believeth in Jesus.

ROM 3:28 Therefore we conclude that a man is justified by faith without the deeds of the law.

ROM 4:16 Therefore it is of faith, that it might be by grace; to the end the promise might be sure to all the seed; not to that only which is of the law, but to that also which is of the faith of Abraham; who is the father of us all, ROM 4:23 Now it was not written for his sake alone, that it was imputed to him; 24 But for us also, to whom it shall be imputed, if we believe on him that raised up Jesus our Lord from the dead; 25 Who was delivered for our offences, and was raised again for our justification. 5:1 Therefore being justified by faith, we have peace with God through our Lord Jesus Christ: 2 By whom also we have access by faith into this grace wherein we stand, and rejoice in hope of the glory of God.

GAL 2:16 Knowing that a man is not justified by the works of the law, but by the faith of Jesus Christ, even we have believed in Jesus Christ, that we might be justified by the faith of Christ, and not by the works of the law: for by the works of the law shall no flesh be justified.

GAL 3:24 Wherefore the law was our schoolmaster to bring us unto Christ, that we might be justified by faith. 25 But after that faith is come, we are no longer under a schoolmaster. For ye are all the children of God by faith in Christ Jesus.

1TI 6:12 Fight the good fight of faith, lay hold on eternal life, whereunto thou art also called, and hast professed a good profession before many witnesses.

HEB 11:1 Now faith is the substance of things hoped for, the evidence of things not seen. 2 For by it the elders obtained a good report. 3 Through faith we understand that the worlds were framed by the word of God, so that things which are seen were not made of things which do appear. 4 By faith Abel offered unto God a more excellent sacrifice than Cain, by which he obtained witness that he was righteous, God testifying of his gifts: and by it he being dead yet speaketh. 5 By faith Enoch was translated that he should not see death; and was not found, because God had translated him: for before his translation he had this testimony, that he pleased God. 6 But without faith it is impossible to please him: for he that cometh to God must believe that he is, and that he is a rewarder of them that diligently seek him.

HEB 11:7 By faith Noah, being warned of God of things not seen as yet, moved with fear, prepared an ark to the saving of his house; by the which he condemned the world, and became heir of the righteousness which is by faith. 8 By faith Abraham, when he was called to go out into a place which he should after receive for an inheritance, obeyed; and he went out, not knowing whither he went. 9 By faith he sojourned in the land of promise, as in a strange country, dwelling in tabernacles with Isaac and Jacob, the heirs with him of the same promise: 10 For he looked for a city which hath foundations, whose builder and maker is God. HEB 11:11 Through faith also Sara herself received strength to conceive seed, and was delivered of a child when she was past age, because she judged him faithful who had promised. 12 Therefore sprang there even of one, and him as good as dead, so many as the stars of the sky in multitude, and as the sand which is by the sea shore innumerable. 13 These all died in faith, not having received the promises, but having seen them afar off, and were persuaded of them, and embraced them, and confessed that they were strangers and pilgrims on the earth.

This verse needs repeating in other forms so that it might settle in us, understood and apprehended. Those who had great faith walked through life in animal skins, tortured, persecuted, beaten, and the world was not worthy of them. Some saw miracles. Some did not. Some saw death. Some did not. But all, through faith, were looking forward to greater things, which they did not see here on this Earth.

Prosperity preaching does not work very well when one can look out their window and see men and women of faith being dipped in tar and set on fire to light the courtyard of Caesar, beaten to death or shot in a city park, or forced at threat of death to sing and pray to despot and debauched emperors of second class countries. Spare us the selfish theologies when there are those dying for the faith.

WHAT IS FAITH? FAITH IS PUTTING IT ALL ON THE LINE. IT IS HANGING YOUR BODY ON YOUR BELIEFS, EVEN THOUGH YOU SEE THEM AFAR OFF AND MAY NOT REACH THEM BEFORE YOU DIE.

Hebrews 11 (The Message)

" 32-38 I could go on and on, but I've run out of time. There are so many more – Gideon, Barak, Samson, Jephthah, David, Samuel, the prophets....Through acts of faith, they toppled kingdoms, made justice work, took the promises for themselves. They were protected from lions, fires, and sword thrusts, turned disadvantage to advantage, won battles, routed alien armies. Women received their loved ones back from the dead. There were those who, under torture, refused to give in and go free, preferring something better: resurrection. Others braved abuse and whips, and, yes, chains and dungeons.

We have stories of those who were stoned, sawed in two, murdered in cold blood; stories of vagrants wandering the earth in animal skins, homeless, friendless, powerless – the world didn't deserve them! – making their way as best they could on the cruel edges of the world.

39-40Not one of these people, even though their lives of faith were exemplary, got their hands on what was promised. God had a better plan for us: that their faith and our faith would come together to make one completed whole, their lives of faith not complete apart from ours."

Even with this most holy of things, faith in God, one can supplant the creator with the creature and fall victim to believing in faith itself. If we place faith in our ability to have faith it lessens our perceived dependence on God. I say perceived dependence because we have just crossed the line into the great lie by thinking we can fulfill our needs and do it better than God. Faith in faith is not faith in God. If we do not fully understand our faith comes from God, given by Him in his measure to us, we can come to believe that we have some work or contribution in this faith of ours. This belief, added to the false concept that God must respond to faith, has yielded up a doctrine that is akin to witchcraft. The doctrine of many sects of Wicca states, "As I will, so may it be." This is not so different from the "hyper-faith" concept of having enough faith to compel God to act on behalf of the one with faith. One should always stretch a truth to see if it will break. If it breaks down it is not a truth. This one does not take much stretching to come apart and not much examination to see the cracks.

What ill-thought heresy would pit Christian against Christian in a battle of faith with God as a puppet in between? This is what would happen if the concept were to be practiced by two people competing for the same job, position, raise, or possession. What right have we to expect our prayers to change the mind or path of another person? Even God allows free will, yet some expect their prayers to influence others. Worldly perspective, arrogance, pride, and greed have brought the simple concept of faith and grace into a place of wish-craft bordering on witchcraft. The "Think and Grow Rich" idea of Napoleon Hill has made its way into our churches and has destroyed our view of God's faith, replacing it with faith in faith and faith in some ability of ours to wield a wand-like power contained in our belief in ourselves. Anything that takes our spiritual eyes off of Jesus as the only source of our salvation and spiritual power is wrong. To have Him we must rely on Him. "First, you must make Him your dwelling place."

Dr. Gene Scott.

So, why do we pray? It is to come into His presence and be changed. Thus, I sit waiting for the guest. It is the longing that does the work. It is because of this that our banner and cry should always be, "It is by grace alone!"

Sources: Beyond Seduction (pp. 51-53) , Wikipedia

The Seduction of Christianity (pp. 28, 217).

MIND, MIGHT, AND MASTERY: HUMAN POTENTIAL IN METAPHYSICAL RELIGION AND E. W. KENYON, By Kevin Scott Smith

DESIRE, SIN, and EVIL

The Mystery of Sin

It seems fundamentally axiomatic that a creature cannot supercede its creator. After all, if one creates something one should be able to control that thing which is created. God created man and is obviously above him. Then man with his carnal nature created sin. Yet, now man is controlled by sin. One may say man is a slave to sin. This is a great mystery. The mystery of sin is that somehow the creation has become lord over the creator. Never before and never since in the history of creation has this happened. Only God himself who created man can set this straight. Only in God, the creator of all things, can the great mystery of sin be solved. He who created all things can save man from all things.

One may argue that sin was created before man through the actions of Satan. This would be true of a spiritual plan where angels tread and demons fall. One may say if God created all things then God also created sin. In this case I would like to use a mundane example and simply say God created man who created the shirt I am wearing. The shirt is made by man but man was made by God. One may say the decisions of man simply allowed sin into mankind. But on a much more individual level and a level concerning mankind itself, sin was created for mankind by man. In a way we all create sin in ourselves and in our world by our actions, thoughts, and decisions. Whether sin is created personally or unleashed personally at the point it is manifest it is out of man's control.

Sin demands payment in the form of the life of the person who sinned. Once we have sinned we are dead. Once we are spiritually dead we have no control over spiritual matters such as the revocation of sin. More like a bomb than any other creations, the destruction cannot be recalled. In the carnage of an exploded bomb, even though man created it, he cannot destroy its destruction. Any hope is up to redeemer to pay the price and recover our loss that we may be in control again of our spiritual destinies. The great mystery of sin is that it is the only thing created that controls the one who creates it.

Joseph Lumpkin

1CO 15:21 For since by man came death, by man came also the resurrection of the dead. 22 For as in Adam all die, even so in Christ shall all be made alive.23 But every man in his own order: Christ the first fruits; afterward they that are Christ's at his coming. 1CO 15:45 And so it is written, The first man Adam was made a living soul; the last Adam was made a quickening spirit. 46 How be it that was not first which is spiritual, but that which is natural; and afterward that which is spiritual. 47 The first man is of the earth, earthy; the second man is the Lord from heaven.

There is within the human heart a tough fibrous root of fallen life whose nature is to possess, always to possess. It covets 'things' with a deep and fierce passion. The pronouns 'my' and 'mine' look innocent enough in print, but their constant and universal use is significant. They express the real nature of the old Adamic man better than a thousand volumes of theology could do... The roots of our hearts have grown down into things, and we dare not pull up one rootlet lest we die. Things have become necessary to us, a development never originally intended. God's gifts now take the place of God, and the whole course of nature is upset by the monstrous substitution.
A. W. Tozer

Souls in deadly sin look to nothing but how they might find nourishment in the earth. Their appetite is insatiable, but they are never satisfied. They are insatiable and insupportable to their very selves. But it is quite fitting that they should be forever restless, because they have set their desire and will on what will give them nothing but emptiness.

...This is why they can never be satisfied: They are always hankering after what is finite. But they are infinite in the sense that they will never cease to be, even though because of their deadly sin they have ceased to be in grace.
Catherine of Siena

Desire is a direct result of man's infinitely expanding appetite. Our stomachs, like our carnal souls, stretch to accommodate an ever-growing desire for more, faster, higher, better... Desire gives way to hunger and a starving man is a fool. Foolishness leads us to sin. Sin takes you farther than you want to go, makes you stay longer than you want to stay, and makes you pay more than you want to pay. Of this, I speak with authority, being a sinner, counting myself as a slave kept against my will, drug back at each escape, still in chains but straining daily against them. I await Him who will free me from my captivity once and for all. He is my hope, both in glory and in this present time, Christ Jesus.

No creature is higher than its creator, but all creatures are lower and more base than their creator. God created man and in his animal nature man created sin. Sin, then, is lower than the animals. What have we done? The creature had been given dominion over its creator. Man is lost in a sea of his own making. We await our redemption from this condition. We await Christ Jesus.

ISA 40:31 *But they that wait upon the LORD shall renew their strength; they shall mount up with wings as eagles; they shall run, and not be weary; and they shall walk, and not faint. 41:1 Keep silence before me, O islands; and let the people renew their strength: let them come near; then let them speak: let us come near together to judgment.*

ROM 7:14 *For we know that the law is spiritual: but I am carnal, sold under sin. 15 For that which I do I allow not: for what I would, that do I not; but what I hate, that do I. 16 If then I do that which I would not, I consent unto the law that it is good. 17 Now then it is no more I that do it, but sin that dwelleth in me. 18 For I know that in me (that is, in my flesh,) dwelleth no good thing: for to will is present with me; but how to perform that which is good I find not. 19 For the good that I would I do not: but the evil which I would not, that I do. 20 Now if I do that I would not, it is no more I that do it, but sin that dwelleth in me.*

ROM 7:21 *I find then a law, that, when I would do good, evil is present with me. 22 For I delight in the law of God after the inward man: 23 But I see another law in my members, warring against the law of my mind, and bringing me into captivity to the law of sin which is in my members. 24 O wretched man that I am! who shall deliver me from the body of this death? 25 I thank God through Jesus Christ our Lord. So then with the mind I myself serve the law of God; but with the flesh the law of sin. 8:1 There is therefore now no condemnation to them which are in Christ Jesus, who walk not after the flesh, but after the Spirit. 2 For the law of the Spirit of life in Christ Jesus hath made me free from the law of sin and death.*

For those who are Christians, sin is temporary insanity. Call it disassociation or psychosis of the spirit. We know what we are about to do is wrong, destructive, and in violation of God's law. We know we are likely to fall but onward we rush, headlong into perdition, driven by some silent force, which is part of us but apart from us. Sin is a most malicious schizophrenia. Who can heal my broken mind? Not I, for when I try to heal my broken mind with my broken mind I fall into great confusion and despair. I pressure myself to do what I know is right, and in placing pressure on my troubled mind I widen the pit of torment within me, giving way to that hated weakness. I fall yet again. I dare not move. I cannot even love God as He has commanded without His help. My mind wars against being fixed on Him. In my prayers it runs to and fro into carnal places and refuses rescue. My strength with which I seek to serve the Lord is used up on this rebellious member. I cry out to the Lord for help. I wait for Him who can remake my mind. I seek the MIND OF CHRIST.

MAR 12:30 And thou shalt love the Lord thy God with all thy heart, and with all thy soul, and with all thy mind, and with all thy strength: this is the first commandment.

ROM 7:22 For I delight in the law of God after the inward man: 23 But I see another law in my members, warring against the law of my mind, and bringing me into captivity to the law of sin which is in my members. 24 O wretched man that I am! who shall deliver me from the body of this death?

ROM 8:6 For to be carnally minded is death; but to be spiritually minded is life and peace. 7 Because the carnal mind is enmity against God: for it is not subject to the law of God, neither indeed can be.

ROM 12:1 I beseech you therefore, brethren, by the mercies of God, that ye present your bodies a living sacrifice, holy, acceptable unto God, which is your reasonable service. 2 And be not conformed to this world: but be ye transformed by the renewing of your mind, that ye may prove what is that good, and acceptable, and perfect, will of God.

ISA 26:2 Open ye the gates, that the righteous nation which keepeth the truth may enter in. 3 Thou wilt keep him in perfect peace, whose mind is stayed on thee: because he trusteth in thee. 4 Trust ye in the LORD forever: for in the LORD JEHOVAH is everlasting strength:

1CO 2:16 For who hath known the mind of the Lord, that he may instruct him? But we have the mind of Christ. 3:1 And I, brethren, could not speak unto you as unto spiritual, but as unto carnal, even as unto babes in Christ. 2 I have fed you with milk, and not with meat: for hitherto ye were not able to bear it, neither yet now are ye able. 3 For ye are yet carnal: for whereas there is among you envying, and strife, and divisions, are ye not carnal, and walk as men?

ORIGINAL SIN

The term "Original Sin" did not come into existence until Augustine (c. 354-430). The idea may have been touched upon in the writings of Tertullian, but it was in Augustine's works that the idea became entrenched. Prior to this the theologians of the early church used different terminology indicating a contrasting way of thinking about Adam's fall, its effects and God's response to it. The phrase the Greek Fathers used to describe the tragedy in the Garden is "Ancestral Sin."

"Ancestral Sin" has a specific meaning. The Eastern Church, unlike its Western counterpart, never speaks of guilt being passed from Adam and Eve to their progeny, as did Augustine. Instead, it is assumed that each person bears the guilt of his or her own sin. The question becomes, "What then is the inheritance of humanity from Adam and Eve, if it is not guilt?" The Orthodox Fathers' answer is death. "Man is born with the parasitic power of death within him." Fr. Romanides Cyril of Alexandria teaches, "Our nature, became diseased…through the sin of one." It is not guilt that is passed on. It is a condition and a disease. It is death itself.

2 Chronicles 25:4 (King James Version)

4But he slew not their children, but did as it is written in the law in the book of Moses, where the LORD commanded, saying, The fathers shall not die for the children, neither shall the children die for the fathers, but every man shall die for his own sin.

Ezekiel 18:20 (King James Version)

20The soul that sinneth, it shall die. The son shall not bear the iniquity of the father, neither shall the father bear the iniquity of the son: the righteousness of the righteous shall be upon him, and the wickedness of the wicked shall be upon him.

Romans 5 (See Amplified Bible and Young's Translation.)

12Therefore, as sin came into the world through one man, and death as the result of sin, so death spread to all men, [no one being able to stop it or to escape its power] because all men sinned. (Young reads: in which man all men sinned.)

13[To be sure] sin was in the world before ever the Law was given, but sin is not charged to men's account where there is no law [to transgress].

14Yet death held sway from Adam to Moses [the Lawgiver], even over those who did not themselves transgress [a positive command] as Adam did. Adam was a type (prefigure) of the One Who was to come [in reverse, the former destructive, the Latter saving].

15But God's free gift is not at all to be compared to the trespass [His grace is out of all proportion to the fall of man]. For if many died through one man's falling away (his lapse, his offense), much more profusely did God's grace and the free gift [that comes] through the undeserved favor of the one Man Jesus Christ abound and overflow to and for [the benefit of] many.

How can the above verses be reconciled? If the sin of the father is not visited upon the son, nor is the sin of the father counted or paid by the son, and all mankind is the descendant of Adam, how can Adam's sin be on us? It is not. It is not sin that is being addressed here. It is the result of Adam's sin and not the punishment for it that is discussed by Paul in Romans. The effect is not the same as the punishment.

We are given these clues to distinguish between sin and death:

Sin cannot be sin until there is a law to break. Yet, between Adam, the sinner and Moses, the lawgiver, there was no law, thus no sin, but all men died. God spoke directly to the individual before the law came. God's command to the person was a personal law. Adam was given a command directly by God, which he broke, having eaten from the tree forbidden by God for him to touch. Cain failed when he murdered his brother, Abel. There was no law, but when Cain lied God was not amused and cursed Cain for his actions. It seemed that even then, if there were truth and repentance there was hope. These were personal crimes, not sins against the law. However, all men from Adam to Moses died. So, much like a man setting a wildfire, the result of Adam's sin brought death into the world because the result was the expulsion of Adam and Eve from the Garden before they could partake of the Tree of Life.

The aim of God was for Adam and Eve to be sin free and live eternally. God never restricted them from the tree of life. Their descendants would have inherited immortality. Yet, free will would have lived within each person, as it did in Adam and Eve. To live forever in sin would have indeed been a curse. The result of Adam's disobedience was mortality. God removed them from the garden before they could become immortal by eating of the tree of life. When the Young translation reads:" in which man all men sinned." The translator is attempting to point out that the punishment of death is a result of one man's sin.

Genesis 3 (The Message) 22 God said, "The Man has become like one of us, capable of knowing everything, ranging from good to evil. What if he now should reach out and take fruit from the Tree-of-Life and eat, and live forever? Never – this cannot happen!"

23-24 So God expelled them from the Garden of Eden and sent them to work the ground, the same dirt out of which they'd been made. He threw them out of the garden and stationed angel-cherubim and a revolving sword of fire east of it, guarding the path to the Tree-of-Life.

Since Adam and Eve were created with the purpose of communing with God: "They needed to mature, to grow to awareness by willing detachment and faith, a loving trust in a personal God" (Clement, 1993, p. 84). Theophilus of Antioch (2nd Century) believed that Adam and Eve were created neither immortal nor mortal. They were created with the potential to become either through obedience or disobedience (Romanides, 2002). The maturing and the choice of being mortal or immortal was given to them by the apparatus of free will. In the Garden there were two trees. One was the Tree of Life and the other the Tree of Knowledge. Only the Tree of Knowledge was forbidden. They could have eaten from the Tree of Life at any time without punishment. It was left untouched, while they chose to eat the forbidden fruit.

The freedom to obey or disobey belonged to our first parents, "For God made man free and sovereign" (Romanides, 2002, p. 32). To embrace their God-given vocation would bring life, to reject it would bring death, but not at God's hands. Theophilus continues, "…should he keep the commandment of God he would be rewarded with immortality…if, however, he should turn to things of death by disobeying God, he would be the cause of death to himself" (Romanides, 2002, p. 32)

"Sin reigned through death." (Romans 5:21) Death is the natural result of turning aside from God.

Adam and Eve were overcome with the same temptation that afflicts all humanity: to be autonomous, to go their own way, to realize the fullness of human existence without God. According to the Orthodox fathers, sin is not a violation of an impersonal law or code of behavior, but a rejection of the life offered by God (Yannaras, 1984). This is the mark, to which the word amartia - sin - (missing the mark) refers. Fallen human life is above all else the failure to realize the God-given potential of human existence, which is, as St. Peter writes, to "become partakers of the divine nature" (II Peter 1:4). St. Basil writes; "Humanity is an animal who has received the vocation to become God" (Clement, 1993, p. 76).

In Orthodox thought, God did not threaten Adam and Eve with punishment nor was He angered or offended by their sin; He was moved to compassion. The expulsion from the Garden and from the Tree of Life was an act of love and not vengeance so that humanity would not "become immortal in sin"

(Romanides, 2002, p. 32). Thus began the preparation for the Incarnation of the Son of God and the solution that alone could rectify the situation: the destruction of the enemies of humanity and God, death (I Corinthians 15:26, 56), sin, corruption and the devil (Romanides, 2002).

Adam was the first man to sin. Through him, death came to mankind. No one can escape it.

This is not to say that the fall of Adam did not affect man. It did. His disobedience is mimicked in us all. As his children, we have free will and rebellion flowing in our blood. But, at any time, free will and the choice not to sin can win out. This is the most important factor. We have the choice not to sin. Adam sinned and paradise was lost. Death was introduced to man. But it is for our own sin that we are responsible. The specific act of the Original or first Sin was the sin of Adam. It is not the responsibility of all humanity. Instead, the consequences of that act exist and plague the world. Original Sin created an environment in which God withdrew His personal communion as it was in the Garden of Eden. Now it is simply not possible without direct Divine intervention for a human being to avoid committing sin some time in his or her life. When God no longer communed with man, but withdrew, man lost his way and began to decline into "spiritual illness." Thus, the world's first sin, or the "Original Sin" is not inherited guilt. It is inherited death. People do not bear personal responsibility for the acts of Adam, no more than they are responsible for the sins of their great-grandfather, although his sins affect his offspring. In the fallen state of the world, it is impossible for anyone not to sin, but until they do… and they will… they are not sinners.

By attempting to interpret Original Sin to mean that we are all born sinners, the church has been forced, out of its own conscience, to embrace an escape clause, which is the creation of a humane yet non-biblical domain. By assuming the full results of this view of Original Sin, we have to assume all children are destined to hell. If newborns are born sinners and have not accepted Jesus as their savior, they will burn forever in hell. This is not very palatable, especially for people seeking to worship a God of love and kindness.

Protestants claim to believe in Original Sin, but do not believe in infant baptism. With no way to relieve the sinful state there is no way to remove Original Sin. In this situation it becomes blindingly obvious that through the simple logic of Original Sin, Protestants have condemned all children below the age of consent to Hell. For Protestants, Infant Baptism does not remove Original Sin; therefore, we must reconsider the meaning of Original Sin. In truth, Protestants believe in an age of accountability where the person is aware of the consequences of actions, wherein the conscience "convicts" the person of wrongdoing. This is more closely attuned to the Orthodox view of Original Sin. However, the view does lay open the problem of sociopaths and others with conditions rendering them "conscienceless."

To get around the atrocity of sending newborns to hell, the Catholic Church began to baptize small children. This is now called infant baptism and is said to remove Original Sin, allowing the child to attain heaven if he or she dies before the age of reason. Why is there an age of reason if Baptism has already removed Original Sin? Beats me... But by the age of twelve or so, the child will have gone through a series of indoctrinations or courses, and will be sprinkled, blessed and confirmed as an adult.

But infant mortality was very high and quite often the newborn died before the priest could perform baptism. The result was the creation of an entire realm, called Limbo.

The Limbo of Infants (Latin limbus infantium) is a hypothesis about the permanent status of the unbaptized who die in infancy, too young to have committed personal sins, but not having been freed from Original Sin. Since the time of Augustine, theologians considered baptism to be necessary for salvation. Some who hold this theory regard the Limbo of Infants as a state of maximum natural happiness, others as one of "mildest punishment" consisting at least of privation of the beatific vision and of any hope of obtaining it. This theory, in any of its forms, has never been dogmatically defined by the Church, but it is permissible to hold it.

905 A.D.: Pope Pius X made a definitive declaration confirming the existence of Limbo. However, this was not an infallible statement by the Pope:

"Children who die without baptism go into limbo, where they do not enjoy God, but they do not suffer either, because having Original Sin, and only that, they do not deserve paradise, but neither hell or purgatory."

Recently, within the last decade, the Catholic Church has declared Limbo non-existent and has stressed the hope that these infants may attain heaven instead of the supposed state of Limbo; however, the directly opposed theological opinion also exists, namely that there is no intermediate afterlife state between salvation and damnation, and that all the unbaptized are damned. With this, the Catholic Church has placed itself in the throws of re-examination of its own concept of inherited Original Sin and its power to send all unbaptized children to hell.

From The Times

October 4, 2006

"The Pope will cast aside centuries of Catholic belief later this week by abolishing formally the concept of limbo, in a gesture calculated to help win the souls of millions of babies in the developing world for Christ.

All the evidence suggests that Benedict XVI never believed in the idea anyway. But in the fertile evangelization zones of Africa and Asia, the Pope — an acknowledged authority on all things Islamic — is only too aware that Muslims believe the souls of stillborn babies go straight to Heaven. For the Church, looking to spread the faith in countries with a high infant mortality rate, now is a good time to make it absolutely clear that stillborn babies of Christian mothers go directly to Heaven, too.

Anyone who deludes themselves that Muslims do not know about limbo would be wrong. Dante put Jerusalem's conqueror Saladin in limbo in his Inferno, along with Ovid and Homer and other pre-Christian villains and heroes.

Even though it has never been part of the Church's doctrine formally, the existence of limbo was taught until recently to Catholics around the world. In Britain it was in the Penny Catechism, approved by the Catholic Bishops of England and Wales, that declared limbo "a place of rest where the souls of the just who died before Christ were detained".

But its lack of doctrinal authority has long failed to impress the Pope, who was recorded as saying before his election: "Personally, I would let it drop, since it has always been only a theological hypothesis."

(Oct. 4, 2008) This week a 30-strong Vatican international commission of theologians, which has been examining limbo, began its final deliberations. Vatican sources said it had concluded that all children who die, do so in the expectation of "the universal salvation of God" and the "mediation of Christ", whether baptised or not.

The theologians' finding is that God wishes all souls to be saved, and that the souls of unbaptised children are entrusted to a "merciful God" whose ways of ensuring salvation cannot be known. "In effect, this means that all children who die go to Heaven," one source said.

The commission's conclusions will be approved formally by the Pope on Friday.

Christians hold that Heaven is a state of union with God, while Hell is separation from God. They have long wrestled, however, not only with the fate of unbaptised children, but also with the conundrum of what happened to those who lived a "good life" but died before the time of Jesus.

The answer since the 13th century has been limbo. What remains in an uncertain state, though, is the status of all the pre-Christian and unbaptised adult souls held by some still to be in this halfway house between Heaven and Hell.

The Pope is expected to abolish only "limbus infantium", where the souls of unbaptised infants go. The precise status of "limbus patrum", where the good people went who lived before Christ remains . . . well, in limbo.

Although it is the latter that has been subject to such dramatic representation in art and literature, no Christian mother today who miscarries, has a stillborn child or otherwise loses a baby before baptism can bear to view without a purgatorial shudder the traditional images, such as those by Giotto, of Christ freeing Old Testament figures from limbo.

In propelling limbo out of its own uncertain state, the Pope is merely acknowledging the distress its half-existence causes to millions and is bringing his characteristic Teutonic sense of righteous clarity to the matter.

One of the reasons Baptists and some other Protestant denominations resist infant baptism is because they believe the souls of babies are innocent and that it is for adults to choose a life in Christ or otherwise. The early church father Tertullian opposed infant baptism on these grounds. But the teachings that took hold of the imagination and the faith of the early Christians were those of the Greek fathers such as Gregory of Nazianzus who wrote: "It will happen, I believe . . . that those last mentioned [infants dying without baptism] will neither be admitted by the just judge to the glory of Heaven nor condemned to suffer punishment, since, they are not wicked."

This seems lenient compared with St Augustine, who in 418 persuaded the Council of Carthage to condemn the British Pelagian heresy that there was an "in between" place for unbaptised babies. He persuaded the council that unbaptised babies share the general misery of the damned. The most he would concede was that their misery was not quite as bad as that of wicked dead adults. (Augustine was such an ass.)

Many of Augustine's views are losing support today. His harsh and restrictive views on sex, marriage, and innocent babies burning in hell has gripped and molded the Catholic Church for many years. Of all his doctrines, the most ill-conceived was his application of Original Sin and infant hell. But, if we hold to the belief that we all are born with Original Sin and are thus destined for hell, the fact that all stillborn and unbaptized children are hell bound is the only logical conclusion. Indeed, if one does not accept that the sprinkled water of a priest can remove such a stain, we are all destined to hell, at least until the age of understanding, after which we can apply faith to the equation for ourselves.

In this light, it is easy to see how our understanding of Original Sin may be incorrect. No sin can be inherited, neither from father to son, nor from Adam to modern man. Yet the state of the world fell and paradise was lost. God withdrew His communion with man as man sought to use his free will, refusing God's plan. As we inherit traits from our parents, so we inherit the propensity to sin. All will sin, just as all will breathe, but until we do sin, we are not sinners.

The piety and devotion of Augustine is largely unquestioned by Orthodox theologians, but his conclusions on the Atonement are not (Romanides, 2002). Augustine, by his own admission, did not properly learn to read Greek and this was a liability for him. He seems to have relied mostly on Latin translations of Greek texts.

His misinterpretation of a key scriptural reference, Romans 5:12, is a case in point (Meyendorff, 1979). In Latin the Greek idiom "eph ho" which means "because of" was translated as "in whom." Saying that all have sinned in Adam is quite different than saying that all sinned because of him. Augustine believed and taught that all humanity has sinned in Adam (Meyendorff, 1979, p. 144). The result is that guilt replaces death as the ancestral inheritance (Augustine, 1956b). Therefore the term Original Sin conveys the belief that Adam and Eve's sin is the first and universal transgression in which all humanity participates.

Admittedly, the idea of salvation as a process is not absent in the West. (One can call to mind the Western mystics and the Wesleyan movement as examples.) However, the underlying theological foundations of Eastern Church and Western Church in regard to ancestral or Original Sin are dramatically opposed. The difference is apparent when looking at the understanding of ethics itself. For the Western Church, ethics often seems to imply adherence to an external code; for the Eastern Church, ethics implies "the restoration of life to the fullness of freedom and love" (Yannaras, 1984, p. 143).

Sin is missing the mark or, put another way, it is the failure to realize the full potential of the gift of human life, and calls for a gradual approach to pastoral care. The goal is nothing less than an existential transformation from within through growth in communion with God. Daily sins are more than moral infractions; they are glimpses into the brokenness of human life and evidence of personal struggle. "Repentance means rejecting death and uniting ourselves to life" (Yannaras, 1984, 147-148).

A young monk was once asked, "What do you do all day in the monastery?" He replied, "We fall and rise, fall and rise."

Death has caused a change in the way we relate to God, to one another and to the world. Our lives are dominated by the struggle to survive. Yannaras writes that we see ourselves not as persons sharing a common nature and purpose, but as autonomous individuals who live to survive in competition with one another. Thus, set adrift by death, we are alienated from God, from others and also from our true selves (Yannaras, 1984).

Yannaras writes that the message of the Church for humanity, wounded and degraded by the 'terrorist God of juridical ethics' is precisely this: "what God really asks of man is neither individual feats nor works of merit, but a cry of trust and love from the depths." The cry comes from the depth of our need to the unfathomable depth of God's love; the Prodigal Son crying out, "I want to go home" to the Father who, seeing his advance from a distance, runs to meet him. (Luke 15:11-32)

The Apostle Paul struggled daily with his inability to be consistent in his works and deeds.

"I do not understand my own actions. For I do not do what I want, but I do the very thing I hate. Now if I do what I do not want, I agree that the law is good. So then it is no longer I that do it, but sin which dwells within me. For I know that nothing good dwells within me, that is, in my flesh. I can will what is right, but I cannot do it. For I do not do the good I want, but the evil I do not want is what I do. Now if I do what I do not want, it is no longer I that do it, but sin which dwells within me. So I find it to be a law that when I want to do right, evil lies close at hand. For I delight in the law of God, in my inmost self, but I see in my members another law at war with the law of my mind and making me captive to the law of sin which dwells in my members. Wretched man that I am! Who will deliver me from this body of death?" (Romans 7:15-24)

The solution to this dilemma is stated by Paul in these terms: "For God has done what the law, weakened by the flesh, could not do: sending his own Son in the likeness of sinful flesh and for sin, he condemned sin in the flesh, in order that the just requirement of the law might be fulfilled in us, who walk not according to the flesh but according to the Spirit." (Romans 8:3-4)

What this divine/human relationship will produce, God knows, but we place ourselves in His loving hands and not without some trepidation because "God is a loving fire… for all: good or bad" (Kalomiris, 1980, p. 19). The knowledge that salvation is a process makes our failures understandable. The illness that afflicts us demands access to the grace of God often and repeatedly. We offer to Him the only things that we have, our weakened condition and will. Joined with God's love and grace it is the fuel that breathed upon by the Spirit of God, breaks the soul into flame.

In our purification the Spirit of God works within us over time in such a way that we sin less and less over great and greater periods of time. This is the work of the Spirit in us whether we are sprinkled or dunked in the Catholic Church, the Church of Christ, or just a little countryside Baptist Church.

Much of the information used in this chapter is derived from the writings of Antony Hughes, M.Div., the rector of St. Mary's Orthodox Church in Cambridge, MA, as well as Wikipedia, the BBC, Times Magazine, and other sources.

SALVATION: A STANDING, A STATE OF MIND

The Spirit of God opens our eyes to what we are and who He is. In that instant we are convicted in our hearts. We are guilty of sins and crimes against God. We regret the decisions and choices that lead us to do those things. When we see his righteousness we feel shame for being the proud, unrighteous, and sinful creatures we are. He has judged us guilty of sin and we stand ready to be condemned with no excuse and no justification. Then Jesus comes! "Father God", He says. "I have died for this one and have paid the price for his crime. I have been condemned for him and have suffered death for him that he may live. My blood was spilled that he may be forgiven."

Our acceptance of Christ's death for us is salvation. Salvation is attained when we accept Christ's perfect life given in exchange for our imperfect life. We are justified through or because of Him, but we are not exonerated. We are not found innocent. We are found guilty but Jesus Christ has served our sentence. The law no longer has rule over us. The law has been fulfilled because the payment for breaking the law has been upheld and collected. He paid it for me. I am no longer a slave to sin or the law.

From this point on we must live in the present. Those sins of the past are now behind us. They are forgiven. We must only think of them to learn from our mistakes. They should in no way hold us back. We cannot cling to them. It would be like holding on to an anchor. They would drag us down. We cannot hope to carry the guilt and shame. They will impede and exhaust us. Guilt, shame, and regret must all be left at the foot of the cross where Jesus died; the price for our sins was paid. We now stand before God as free persons.

The blood of an innocent man has been given as payment for our crimes against God. His life has paid the price for our sins. The cost of sin is death. Thus He who had no sin was sacrificed to pay the price, for if a sinner died he would only be paying for his own sins. The payment had to be innocent and sinless blood. There is only one man perfect and sinless; Christ Jesus, the Son of God. Now we are cleansed of our sins. Our standing is now sinless in the sight of God, yet in this world we are what we were. Not one molecule has changed. Barring a miracle of healing or transfiguration our state has not changed; but it will. Now, the Spirit of God has come to indwell us, teach us, lead us, change us. We will never be sinless or perfect, but we can be better instruments of God. Now we can stand before God and commune with Him.

Now being made sinless in the sight of God by Christ, who also intervened as mediator and priest on our behalf, we can boldly approach the throne.

HEB 4:14 Seeing then that we have a great high priest, that is passed into the heavens, Jesus the Son of God, let us hold fast our profession. 15 For we have not an high priest which cannot be touched with the feeling of our infirmities; but was in all points tempted like as we are, yet without sin. 16 Let us therefore come boldly unto the throne of grace, that we may obtain mercy, and find grace to help in time of need.

God exists only in the NOW. God is only in the present. We must be here now. This means we can't be held back by regret, guilt, or shame. These things drag our hurting and sorrowful minds back to the past; back to the time and place of the pain and sin. Our minds and hearts must be clear of conviction and condemnation. The clear and clean eternal now is where our God resides. All paths have led us to this one point in time when we can lay all burdens of regret, guilt, and shame aside.

God has brought us here. He set divergent paths on our road of sin and each divergent path has led to Him. When our eyes were opened we cried, "Lord I am guilty and ashamed! What must I do to be saved?" Now our heart yearns to be with the one who loved us enough to save us. Now we seek the beloved! We must not seek Him in the past. We cannot seek Him in the future. We must seek Him in the present by being totally in the present – here – with Him. He is here in the infinite now. We cannot worry about the future. It is a matter of trust. This is not to say we should be lax or dismissive in our work, but we should trust God to make a way for us to make our way. A road will be provided for us to walk.

MAT 6:26 Behold the fowls of the air: for they sow not, neither do they reap, nor gather into barns; yet your heavenly Father feedeth them. Are ye not much better than they?

MAT 6:31 Therefore take no thought, saying, What shall we eat? or, What shall we drink? or, wherewithal shall we be clothed? 32 (For after all these things do the Gentiles seek:) for your heavenly Father knoweth that ye have need of all these things. 33 But seek ye first the kingdom of God, and his righteousness; and all these things shall be added unto you.

LUK 11:13 If ye then, being evil, know how to give good gifts unto your children: how much more shall your heavenly Father give the Holy Spirit to them that ask him?

The past is gone. The future is not yet here. All we have is now. Without looking forward or back, we worship God now. We praise Him for who He is and what is happening now. He is saving us and showering us with His grace, even now. Let us be completely focused on God at this moment, in the ETERNAL NOW.

THE PRESENCE OF GOD

There is the omnipresence of God and the manifest presence of God. Although God is everywhere all the time, we wish His presence manifested in our lives. This can only be done by His permission and through His grace. With eyes opened and heart on fire we understand the sovereignty of God and cry, "GRACE! GRACE! IT IS BY GRACE ALONE!" We were wooed, convicted, and saved from condemnation because He is gracious. He did not have to do it. We did not deserve it, but He did it anyway.

Now what God wants is a relationship with us, as a father would want to love and nurture a child. We know God is everywhere but He only reveals Himself as He wishes. He may manifest through miracles, visions, but through faith He is manifested in our hearts. Visions are splendid, but they pass quickly. Miracles come so seldom. Jesus is in us forever. It is less spectacular than seeing visions. It is not as awe inspiring as a miracle. It is the power of God in salvation and in life changing action. The manifest presence of God is when God reveals Himself to us. We may seek those moments of visions and miracles as if they will give us the faith to believe more deeply, but signs will not change a person. Only God in us will do that. This is the most powerful manifest presence of God.

MAT 12:38 Then certain of the scribes and of the Pharisees answered, saying, Master, we would see a sign from thee. 39 But he answered and said unto them, An evil and adulterous generation seeketh after a sign; and there shall no sign be given to it, but the sign of the prophet Jonas: 40 For as Jonas was three days and three nights in the whale's belly; so shall the Son of man be three days and three nights in the heart of the earth.

MAT 16:1 The Pharisees also with the Sadducees came, and tempting desired him that he would shew them a sign from heaven. 2 He answered and said unto them, When it is evening, ye say, It will be fair weather: for the sky is red.   3 And in the morning, It will be foul weather to day: for the sky is red and lowering. O ye hypocrites, ye can discern the face of the sky; but can ye not discern the signs of the times?

1CO 1:22 For the Jews require a sign, and the Greeks seek after wisdom: 23 But we preach Christ crucified, unto the Jews a stumbling block, and unto the Greeks foolishness; 24 *But unto them which are called, both Jews and Greeks, Christ the power of God, and the wisdom of God.*

MARY: Immaculate Conception, Assumption, Co-Redeemer

Seeing as how we have been on the topic of Original Sin, it seems appropriate that we now look at the doctrine of The Immaculate Conception.

Many of my Protestant friends will affirm their belief that Jesus was conceived by the Holy Spirit and born without Original Sin, but that is not what this doctrine concludes. The doctrine of The Immaculate Conception states that Mary, the mother of Jesus, was born without sin.

To think that the Catholic Church believes that Mary was prepared as a vessel for Jesus and was born sinless may come as a surprise.

The Catholic doctrine of Immaculate Conception asserts that Mary, the mother of Jesus, was preserved by God from the stain of original sin at the time of her own conception. (That is, at the time of copulation between the parents of Mary, God interceded and stopped the transference of Original Sin to the soul that would become Mary.) According to the dogma, Mary was conceived by normal biological means, but her soul was acted upon by God (kept "immaculate") at the time of her conception.

Let us stop here and ask the obvious question. If Jesus needed an immaculate vessel, and Mary needed to be immaculate, why wouldn't Mary's mother also need to be immaculate, ad infinitum until Eve herself would have been immaculate.

The Catholic Church believes the dogma is supported by the scripture of her being greeted by Angel Gabriel as "full of Grace", as well as either directly or indirectly by the writings of many of the Church Fathers, and is often called "Mary the Blessed Virgin" (Luke 1:48). Catholic theology maintains that since Jesus became incarnate of the Virgin Mary, she needed to be completely free of sin to bear the Son of God, and that Mary is "redeemed 'by the grace of Christ' but in a more perfect manner than other human beings."

The formation of Mariology has been maturing in the Catholic and Orthodox Churches from the beginning of the church. Yet, it was not until 1854 that Pope Pius IX declared the Immaculate Conception as an official doctrine.

The Orthodox Church has rejected this doctrine since the church does not believe in Original Sin. Eastern Orthodox theologians suggest that the references among the Greek and Syrian Fathers to Mary's purity and sinlessness may refer not to an "a priori state," but to her conduct after birth.

The Conception of Mary was celebrated in England from the ninth century. Aquinas and Bonaventure, for example, believed that Mary was completely free from sin, but that she was not given this grace at the instant of her conception.

Joseph Lumpkin

The Feast of the Immaculate Conception of Mary had been established in 1476 by Pope Sixtus IV who stopped short of defining the doctrine as a dogma of the Catholic Faith.

The Feast of the Immaculate Conception, was consecrated by Pope Pius XII in 1942.

In principle this doctrine was a part of the Roman Catholic and Byzantine thinking in the Middle Ages. The apostolic constitution Munificentissimus Deus, promulgated by Pius XII on November 1, 1950, made it a doctrine necessary for salvation, stating, "The Immaculate Mother of God, the ever-Virgin Mary, having completed the course of her earthly life, was assumed body and soul into heavenly glory."

Although this is not a dogma in the Orthodox Church, there is the universal belief that there was a pre-sanctification of Mary at the time of her conception, similar to the conception of Saint John the Baptist. (Wait... What!? John flipped and jumped in the womb when Mary and Elizabeth met, and were both pregnant, but John had a special sanctification? Really?)

Another misunderstanding is that with her immaculate conception, Mary did not need a savior. On the contrary, when defining the dogma, Pope Pius IX represented Catholic tradition by affirming that Mary was redeemed in a manner more sublime. He stated that Mary, rather than being cleansed after sin, was completely prevented from contracting original sin in view of the foreseen merits of Jesus Christ, the Savior of the human race.

In a furtherance of the doctrine of Immaculate Conception, the Assumption of Mary into heaven was embraced.

In Roman Catholic doctrine, the Assumption means that Mary, the mother of Jesus, was taken (assumed) bodily into heavenly glory when she died.

Gregory of Tours in his De Gloria Martyrum of the sixth century quotes an unfounded legend about Mary's assumption. As the story became popular in both East and West it took two forms. The Coptic version describes Jesus appearing to Mary to foretell her death and bodily elevation into heaven, while the Greek, Latin, and Syriac versions picture Mary calling for the apostles, who are transported to her miraculously from their places of service. Then Jesus, after her death, conveyed her remains to heaven. The doctrine was first treated in deductive theology about 800 A.D. Benedict XIV (d. 1758) proposed it as a probable doctrine.

In the Orthodox church, the koimesis, or dormition ("falling asleep"), of the Virgin began to be commemorated on August 15 in the 6th century. The observance gradually spread to the West, where it became known as the Feast of the Assumption. By the 13th century, the belief was accepted by most Catholic theologians, and it was a popular subject with Renaissance and

Baroque painters. The Assumption was declared a dogma of the Roman Catholic faith by Pope Pius XII in 1950.

Assumption of the Virgin (Latin assumere,"to take up") in the Roman Catholic church and the Orthodox church is the doctrine that after her death the body of Mary, the mother of Christ, was taken into heaven and reunited with her soul. Defined as an article of faith by Pope Pius XII in 1950, the assumption was first commemorated as the Feast of the Dormition (falling asleep) of Mary in the 6th century. This feast later developed into the Feast of the Assumption, now celebrated in the Roman Catholic Church on August 15 every year.

Feasts celebrating the death of Mary date from the fifth century. In the East the late seventh century feasts included the assumption. After the eighth century the West followed suit. Nicholas I by edict (863 A.D.) placed the Feast of the Assumption on the same level as Easter and Christmas. Cranmer omitted it from the Book of Common Prayer and it has not since been included.

The 1950 action regarding the assumption of Mary is built upon the declaration of "The Immaculate Conception" (Dec. 8, 1854), which declared Mary free from original sin. Both issue from the concept of Mary as the "Mother of God." Her special state, Pius XII felt, demanded special treatment. If Mary is indeed "full of grace" (cf. Luke 1:28, 44) the assumption is a logical outcome. Like Jesus, she is sinless, preserved from corruption, resurrected, received into heaven, and a recipient of corporeal glory. Thus Mary is crowned Queen of Heaven and assumes the roles of intercessor and mediator.

The argument in Munificentissimus Deus develops along several lines. It emphasizes Mary's unity with her divine Son, for she is "always sharing His lot." Since she shared in the past in His incarnation, death, and resurrection, now, as His mother, she is the mother of his church, which is His body. Rev. 12:1 is applied to Mary; she is the prototype of the church, for she has experienced anticipatorially corporeal glorification in her assumption. In a strange and convoluted incestuous twist, three times Mary is referred to as the "New Eve," working again the parallel of Christ as the new Adam and presenting the glorified Christ as one with the new Eve.

There is now an ongoing push within the Catholic Church to take the last step in the adoration and deification of Mary by declaring her as Co-Redeemer along side Jesus.

Pope John Paul II publicly used the term "Coredemptrix" at least six times in his pontificate, and at one point Miravalle predicted that he would proclaim the dogma before the millennial year of 2000.

By far the most significant criticism, if only on account of its source, has been that of Cardinal Joseph Ratzinger, now Pope Benedict.

Ratzinger told a German interviewer in 2000 that the "formula `Co-redemptrix' departs to too great an extent from the language of Scripture and of the (church) Fathers and therefore gives rise to misunderstandings," threatening to "obscure" the status of Christ as the source of all redemption.

"I do not think there will be any compliance with this demand (for papal proclamation of the dogma) within the foreseeable future," he said at the time.

For many Christians the story of Mary holds within it, several deep lessons for the Christian mystic. Even before the great schism between the Orthodox and Roman churches, Mary held a place in the minds and hearts of the Christian church. Later, in church history, in a move to balance what was felt to be an over-emphasis on Mary and her status, the Protestant church began to diminish her status until she is now considered little more than a willing incubator for Jesus. Polarization is an all too human reaction, which leads us, in many cases, to fully reject a doctrine and even a person when we believe it, or they, are in error. The error may hold only a part of what is presented, but the rejection is full. Thus large areas of truth are thrown out with areas of error.

The Bible tells us she will be called blessed, but many do not call her anything at all. The majority of Protestant believers ignore Mary. It is the overcompensation to avoid the recurrence of the error. Throwing truth out with error, the baby that got tossed out in the bathwater of error this time happened to be the Mother of Jesus. I do not support an extreme elevation or veneration of Mary or of any creature for that matter, since such a view would cloud the vision of the preeminence of Christ. But, neither do I agree with the place to which most Protestant churches have resigned her.

Although it is true, grace shed on someone does not indicate moral or spiritual status, it is also true God had a plan for salvation from the foundations of the world and in His plan, Mary had a place. As people of faith, Mary's story has a deep and significant meaning for us. Grace is given without, and many times, in spite of spiritual condition. It was not Mary's state or condition but the willingness of her decision that drew the sovereign will of God. In this vein the early fathers found something so fascinating and deeply spiritual about the story of Mary they elevated her to a venerated status. As we look closer into the story of Mary we will see she is the template and prototype of the true mystical experience. Her experience is the key and summation of the entire Christian process. In her we find our spiritual likeness, our history, and our story. In the story of Mary the mystical life is foretold.

LUKE 1:35 And the angel answered and said unto her, The Holy Ghost shall come upon thee, and the power of the Highest shall overshadow thee: therefore also that holy thing which shall be born of thee shall be called the Son of God. 37 For with God nothing shall be impossible. 38 And Mary said, "Behold the handmaid of the Lord; be it unto me according to thy word." And the angel departed from her. 41 And it came to pass, that, when Elisabeth heard the salutation of Mary, the babe leaped in her womb; and Elisabeth was filled with the Holy Ghost: 42 And she spake out with a loud voice, and said, Blessed art thou among women, and blessed is the fruit of thy womb. 43 And whence is this to me, that the mother of my Lord should come to me? 44 For, lo, as soon as the voice of thy salutation sounded in mine ears, the babe leaped in my womb for joy. 45 And blessed is she that believed: for there shall be a performance of those things, which were told her from the Lord. 46 And Mary said, My soul doth magnify the Lord, 47 And my spirit hath rejoiced in God my Saviour.

LUK 1:48 For he hath regarded the low estate of his handmaiden: for, behold, from henceforth all generations shall call me blessed. 49 For he that is mighty hath done to me great things; and holy is his name. 50 And his mercy is on them that fear him from generation to generation. 51 He hath shewed strength with his arm; he hath scattered the proud in the imagination of their hearts. 52 He hath put down the mighty from their seats, and exalted them of low degree.

In His grace, God chose Mary, a young woman with no obvious attributes that set her apart from hundreds of others. In her own words, she was someone who counted herself as a lowly maiden. In His power and mercy He came to her. His spirit was on her and in her and He communed with her within her heart and soul. God, being out of time and space, had a plan for creation before He created. This also includes the incarnation. Creation was created for Jesus and through Jesus. The plan for creation was completed in the mind of God before the act of creating. Therefore, Mary was in God's plan for the birth of Jesus before creation, but because of free will she had acquiescence. It was because of her free will and the obedience that followed from it she was blessed. We cannot know why Mary was chosen and set apart. God has always used men and women who seemed common and ordinary to do great things. So it was with the mother of God. Mary, by believing the child in her was indeed sent and fathered by the Holy Spirit of God and set in her virgin body for the redemption of man, became the first Christian.

" The Holy Ghost shall come upon thee, and the power of the Highest shall overshadow thee: therefore also that holy thing which shall be born of thee shall be called the Son of God." Luke 1:35

It was not through doctrine or church that they met but through a real and powerful personal communion. This is the essence of the mystical experience. God draws us and woos us to Him and in our desire to be with Him we are allowed an intimate communion with Him. In this spiritual state of togetherness with God, the Holy Spirit of God implants Christ in our spiritual wombs. Christ forms in us, grows in us, moves in us and through us until we give birth to Him through our hearts and souls and show Him to the world in our love and actions with spontaneous acts of love and serving. It is through a heart and mind that calls out to Him and declares, "Behold the handmaid of the Lord; be it unto me according to thy word." Only in this can we contain God's Spirit. Only in this can God hold us. By this alone comes the world's greatest experience. What we do not realize in our simplicity is each time Christ is birthed in us we are experiencing the mystical equivalent of the incarnation once again. Each time we nurture Him in us and show Him forth to others, we have become Mary and the great incarnation has come upon us.

ISA 9:6 For unto us a child is born, unto us a son is given: and the government shall be upon his shoulder: and his name shall be called Wonderful, Counsellor, The mighty God, The everlasting Father, The Prince of Peace. 7 Of the increase of his government and peace there shall be no end, upon the throne of David, and upon his kingdom, to order it, and to establish it with judgment and with justice from henceforth even for ever. The zeal of the LORD of hosts will perform this.

It is for this event that even if man had not fallen, still Christ would have come. He is the crown of mankind. He is the crowning of creation. He was destined from the foundation of creation to be the one and only avenue for the union of God and man. Such a union going far beyond any understanding communion could bring. Thus, we may commune with God but Christ lives in us, in a state that is distinct yet in union.

Sources: Cambridge Encyclopedia, Encyclopedia.StateUniversity.com, Wikipedia, EWTN Catholic Television Network, Catholic.org, mb-soft.com, Religious News, "Dark Night of the Soul" by Joseph Lumpkin, and other sources.

BAPTISM

Is baptism a type, shadow, and symbol, or is it actually necessary for salvation? Can one be sprinkled with water or is complete submersion needed?

Should the words of some Bible verses be taken literally, even though in other passages differing ideas may be expressed? Can some passages be viewed in a completely literal sense while others are said to be symbolic?

There are deeply disturbing problems when taking literally those passages regarding the need of baptism to be saved. A logical dissonance immediately becomes apparent between how some churches view transubstantiation and how they view baptism. With passages like the one below, it is easy to see the statement is clear and straightforward. Jesus himself is proclaiming that the bread is His body and the cup contains His blood. This is a direct statement without any equivocation on the part of the Son of God. Yet, most churches do not take this statement literally.

Matthew 26 (King James Version)

26 And as they were eating, Jesus took bread, and blessed it, and brake it, and gave it to the disciples, and said, Take, eat; this is my body. 27 And he took the cup, and gave thanks, and gave it to them, saying, Drink ye all of it; 28 For this is my blood of the new testament, which is shed for many for the remission of sins.

Some churches have doctrines, which even though dismissing the above statement, hold fast to the need to be baptized before one can see the heavenly gates. What's more, all of these denominations insist that only their preachers, pastors, or priests can perform this magic, which, by the mumbling of some words and the application of tap water, may change the soul from sinful to sanctified in a blessed instant.

The questions raised are two-fold. Can one man, in any way, change another man's soul? What is being baptized, the body or the soul? It is the soul that will see judgment. If we baptize the body, how can it affect the soul?

This colloquy is in no way an argument for transubstantiation but is instead an argument against arbitrary literalism as applied to biblical interpretation and therefore to doctrine.

Joseph Lumpkin

First, let us look at the cornerstone verse that supports the "Baptism for Salvation" doctrine.

Mark 16 (New International Version)

15He said to them, "Go into all the world and preach the good news to all creation. 16Whoever believes and is baptized will be saved, but whoever does not believe will be condemned. 17And these signs will accompany those who believe: In my name they will drive out demons; they will speak in new tongues; 18they will pick up snakes with their hands; and when they drink deadly poison, it will not hurt them at all; they will place their hands on sick people, and they will get well."

But wait! Wasn't this chapter one of those passages we discussed earlier in the book? This is one of the chapters we can prove beyond a reasonable doubt was added later and did not occur in the older manuscripts. Let's look at exactly where the more reliable witnesses (manuscripts) end.

According to the New International Version (NIV): "The most reliable early manuscripts and other ancient witnesses do not have Mark 16:9-20."

The following is Mark 16:9-20 and is NOT included in the most reliable versions.

9When Jesus rose early on the first day of the week, he appeared first to Mary Magdalene, out of whom he had driven seven demons. 10She went and told those who had been with him and who were mourning and weeping. 11When they heard that Jesus was alive and that she had seen him, they did not believe it. 12 Afterward Jesus appeared in a different form to two of them while they were walking in the country. 13 These returned and reported it to the rest; but they did not believe them either. 14 Later Jesus appeared to the Eleven as they were eating; he rebuked them for their lack of faith and their stubborn refusal to believe those who had seen him after he had risen. 15 He said to them, "Go into all the world and preach the good news to all creation. 16 Whoever believes and is baptized will be saved, but whoever does not believe will be condemned. 17 And these signs will accompany those who believe: In my name they will drive out demons; they will speak in new tongues; 18 they will pick up snakes with their hands; and when they drink deadly poison, it will not hurt them at all; they will place their hands on sick people, and they will get well." 19 After the Lord Jesus had spoken to them, he was taken up into heaven and he sat at the right hand of God. 20Then the disciples went out and preached everywhere, and the Lord worked with them and confirmed his word by the signs that accompanied it.

Thus, the verse on which the "baptism for salvation" doctrine is based does not appear in reliable versions.

It is amazing and very sad that at least two major denominations have been so influenced by verses added after the apostle wrote the book. The accepted theory as to why the addition occurred concludes that the pages at the end of the book of Mark were somehow destroyed. Scribes, wishing for an ending of exhortation, devised the ending sometime in the second century. For more information on the Book of Mark and other endings found in various manuscripts see Appendix "B."

"Let my pastor baptize you or you will go to hell." Such harsh views have not disappeared over time as one might think people or denominations would mature and become more reasonable. Such gravity is placed on baptism in some denominations that churches split over such trivial matters as how long to keep the water in the baptismal pool before draining the "swamp." Is it the stagnant water that saves? If not, then is it the power of the man who dips the sinner that might be enough to save? If it is not the power of water or man that saves then we must re-assess and re-ask, "Is baptism a symbol or does the act actually save us?"

What is baptism? It is an act symbolizing our death, burial, and resurrection in Christ. In this type and symbol, complete submersion comes closest, whereas sprinkling takes on an Old Testament type of sprinkling the blood of the sacrificed animal on the people to cover their sins or to form a covenant.

Compare these verses of baptism and sprinkling.

Romans 6 (King James Version)

1What shall we say then? Shall we continue in sin, that grace may abound? 2 God forbid. How shall we, that are dead to sin, live any longer therein? 3 Know ye not, that so many of us as were baptized into Jesus Christ were baptized into his death? 4 Therefore we are buried with him by baptism into death: that like as Christ was raised up from the dead by the glory of the Father, even so we also should walk in newness of life. 5 For if we have been planted together in the likeness of his death, we shall be also in the likeness of his resurrection: 6 Knowing this, that our old man is crucified with him, that the body of sin might be destroyed, that henceforth we should not serve sin. 7 For he that is dead is freed from sin. 8 Now if we be dead with Christ, we believe that we shall also live with him: 9 Knowing that Christ being raised from the dead dieth no more; death hath no more dominion over him. 10 For in that he died, he died unto sin once: but in that he liveth, he liveth unto God. 11 Likewise reckon ye also yourselves to be dead indeed unto sin, but alive unto God through Jesus Christ our Lord.

Exodus 24 (New International Version)

The Covenant Confirmed

1 Then he said to Moses, "Come up to the LORD, you and Aaron, Nadab and Abihu, and seventy of the elders of Israel. You are to worship at a distance, 2 but Moses alone is to approach the LORD; the others must not come near. And the people may not come up with him."

3 When Moses went and told the people all the LORD's words and laws, they responded with one voice, "Everything the LORD has said we will do." 4 Moses then wrote down everything the LORD had said. He got up early the next morning and built an altar at the foot of the mountain and set up twelve stone pillars representing the twelve tribes of Israel. 5 Then he sent young Israelite men, and they offered burnt offerings and sacrificed young bulls as fellowship offerings (a) to the LORD. 6 Moses took half of the blood and put it in bowls, and the other half he sprinkled on the altar. 7 Then he took the Book of the Covenant and read it to the people. They responded, "We will do everything the LORD has said; we will obey." 8 Moses then took the blood, sprinkled it on the people and said, "This is the blood of the covenant that the LORD has made with you in accordance with all these words."

(a)-Traditionally peace offerings

Let us keep in mind that before the death of Jesus, the world was under the old covenant. Things worked differently. Under the Old Covenant types and symbols painted a picture for the practitioner of the real substance to come. In the case of Baptism, as in the entire Bible, water represents the spirit of God and the cleansing of the person.

After the death of Jesus, the spirit of God began to work in a new capacity. No longer was the spirit confined to a prophet here or a person there. The Spirit of God would be in and with all believers. No longer were types and symbols used as a picture of the true substance. Once Jesus said that no one can enter heaven unless he has been born again of water and the Holy Spirit (John 3:5). Now, after His death, the ceremony of Water baptism was placed in an inferior and obsolete role when the resurrected Jesus explained that the symbol was about to become real.

Acts 1:4-6 (New International Version)

4 On one occasion, while he was eating with them, he gave them this command: "Do not leave Jerusalem, but wait for the gift my Father promised, which you have heard me speak about. 5 For John baptized with water, but in a few days you will be baptized with the Holy Spirit."

No longer was there a need for water to be used as a picture of the Spirit, of cleansing, or of the resurrection of the soul. The Spirit was coming. From that point on, believers were given the Spirit of God and raised into life.

Baptism is a symbol of where the person is, that is saved by the spirit, not where they are going, saved after being submerged in water by a man. We are baptized to show the world the testimony of what we believe; that our old self is dead and buried and that just as rising out of the water signifies resurrection, we will "reckon" ourselves to be dead indeed unto sin, but alive unto God through Jesus Christ our Lord.

We reckon ourselves to be dead. The word "reckon" is to conclude after calculation, or to be of an opinion. In other words, nothing has changed but our opinion. This is because symbols do not change us. Only the Spirit of God does that.

Baptism is not needed for salvation or church membership.

Joseph Lumpkin

PREDESTINATION AND FOREKNOWLEDGE

"Hath not the potter power over the clay, of the same lump to make one vessel unto honour, and another unto dishonour?" (Romans 9:21).

The path from the mind of God to the mind of man contains a sheer precipice, which no human can ascend. Mankind is not able to apprehend the purpose or design of creation or judgment. We view the questions of predestination and foreknowledge with half-blind eyes.

How God's plan and man's free will fit together is the greatest paradox of theology. Within the enigma are the puzzle pieces of the sacrificial death of Jesus, the scope and power of that atonement, the fall of man, the grace of God, and hell itself. Yet, there are those who are so sure they understand how predestination, foreknowledge, and free will combine in God's plan that there is no place in their minds for discussion. I will tell you now I am not one of these.

Let us examine some ways men have attempted to solve the paradox. A few solutions may surprise you.

By the way – Were you destined to read this book or was it by chance you chose it? If it was predestined for you to read, for what purpose did God intend it.

JAMES MADISON:

Who does not see that the same authority which can establish Christianity, in exclusion of all other religions, may establish with the same ease any particular sect of Christians, in exclusion of all other sects?

Memorial and Remonstrance

There are few controversies that have divided more and burned as hot as the one between views of predestination and foreknowledge.

If God is omnipotent what He knows will happen is destined to happen. Yet, this knowledge is not the same as actively guiding an outcome. However, if God knows the outcome then the outcome cannot be altered, thus it is predestined.

If predestination is taken to its full conclusion, man has no free will at all and even those choices he believes he is making are predetermined. This flies in the face of personal responsibility. Thus if one holds fast to this argument, one must ask why we would punish anyone for an infraction of the law, say murder or rape, seeing that it was choreographed before his or her birth.

What are the rightful places for God's sovereignty and man's free will? What is man's responsibility for personal sin?

From the days of Judaism, religious men have believed that God had a plan, which He was causing to unfold. This belief in predestination was brought into Christianity from its very foundation. This is because the scripture states that Jesus was "purposed to die" from the very beginning.

Yet, Jesus asked God if the plan could be altered so that his torture and death could be avoided. Does this mean predestined plans can be changed?

Acts 2:23 (New International Version)

23This man was handed over to you by God's set purpose and foreknowledge; and you, with the help of wicked men put him to death by nailing him to the cross.

1 Peter 1 (New International Version)

17Since you call on a Father who judges each man's work impartially, live your lives as strangers here in reverent fear. 18For you know that it was not with perishable things such as silver or gold that you were redeemed from the empty way of life handed down to you from your forefathers, 19but with the precious blood of Christ, a lamb without blemish or defect. 20He was chosen before the creation of the world, but was revealed in these last times for your sake. 21Through him you believe in God, who raised him from the dead and glorified him, and so your faith and hope are in God.

So, God chose Jesus before the world was formed, and had a purpose for Him and foreknowledge of His death.

Does this mean it was set and could not be changed?

Matthew 26 (King James Version)

38 Then saith he unto them, My soul is exceeding sorrowful, even unto death: tarry ye here, and watch with me.

39 And he went a little farther, and fell on his face, and prayed, saying, O my Father, if it be possible, let this cup pass from me: nevertheless not as I will, but as thou wilt.

40 And he cometh unto the disciples, and findeth them asleep, and saith unto Peter, What, could ye not watch with me one hour?

41 Watch and pray, that ye enter not into temptation: the spirit indeed is willing, but the flesh is weak.

42 He went away again the second time, and prayed, saying, O my Father, if this cup may not pass away from me, except I drink it, thy will be done.

From this passage we see that Jesus assumed that God could change the future, even if it had been planned from the creation of the world. A predestined event may not be set in stone. Jesus was openly battling to make His free will conform to the Father's will. He wished not to be tortured and killed but submitted to God's will anyway. In some fashion, not fully understood by mankind, free will and predestination must co-exist. With this in mind let us look into the matter.

The proponents of predestination cannot agree on the exact order of events. In general it is thought that God creates us, selects from His creation who He will send to heaven and who He will not. He then allows the predestined event to unfold. The exact sequence of events gives way to differing doctrines with very long names.

Supralapsarianism

    God calls the elect to salvation.

    He elects some and condemns the rest.

    God creates mankind.

    God permits the Fall of Man.

    God provides salvation for elect.

    (Note that in this theory, God actively saves and actively condemns.)

Infralapsarianism

    God creates mankind.

    God permits the Fall of Man.

    God elects some but passes over the rest.

    God provides salvation for elect.

    God calls the elect to salvation.

    (In this theory God, actively chooses some and passively skips others.)

Amyraldism

    God creates mankind.

    God permits the Fall of Man.

    God provides salvation sufficient for all

    God elects some and passes over the rest.

    God calls the elect to salvation.

    (This is another theory that calls for active selection of some while others are passively ignored.)

Universalism

    God creates mankind.

    God permits the Fall of Man.

    God provides salvation for all.

    God calls all to salvation.

God will either save all, no matter their wish, or He will reveal Himself to all in such a way that all of mankind will wish to be saved.

(It is not clear on the surface, but Universalism can be looked at as a type of predestination as well. This is because the doctrine states that all will be saved or chosen, even those who have chosen to oppose God in their lives.)

Arminianism is a free will doctrine. It has within its systems a single statement that sets it apart from all others. "God elects those who believe." This means the "believer" has a part in his or her destiny.

Arminianism

    God creates mankind.

    God permits the Fall of Man.

    God provides salvation for all.

    God calls all to salvation.

    God elects those who believe in Him.

(In this theory, all are actively chosen by God, but their destiny depends on the believer's active choice.)

The traditional church view has always been that a person must be a Christian, must belong to their particular sect or denomination, and must follow those rules set out by the denomination and local church to be "accepted" and go to heaven. Universalism seems to have no place in the traditional church, yet there are scriptures supporting this belief. The question becomes; has God predestined humanity to be saved by sacrificing all and paying all to save all? Is it true that Jesus died to save mankind? Is it true God wishes for all men and women to be saved.

Colossians 1:15-20

15 He is the image of the invisible God, the firstborn over all creation. 16 For by Him all things were created that are in heaven and that are on earth, visible and invisible, whether thrones or dominions or principalities or powers. All things were created through Him and for Him. 17 And He is before all things, and in Him all things consist. 18 And He is the head of the body, the church, who is the beginning, the firstborn from the dead, that in all things He may have the preeminence. 19 For it pleased the Father that in Him all the fullness should dwell, 20 and by Him to reconcile (apokatallasso) all things to Himself, by Him, whether things on earth or things in heaven, having made peace through the blood of His cross.

1 Timothy 2:3-6 (KJV)

3 For this is good and acceptable in the sight of God our Saviour; 4 Who will have (thelo) all men to be saved, and to come unto the knowledge of the truth. 5 For there is one God, and one mediator between God and men, the man Christ Jesus; 6 Who gave himself a ransom for all, to be testified in due time.

Romans 5:18-19

18 Therefore, as through one man's offense judgment came to all men, resulting in condemnation, even so through one Man's righteous act the free gift came to all men, resulting in justification of life.

John 12:32

"And I, if I am lifted up from the earth, will draw all peoples to Myself."

But what does "predestination" mean? What exactly is being guided or chosen so as to be predestined?

The Greek word translated predestine is the word from which we get our English word horizon. The Greek word horizo means to establish or set boundaries. Pre – destination is literally pre-horizon or to preset boundaries. To set the boundaries or to draw lines, or to establish the limits of something is to determine what will be. To do so ahead of time is to predestine.

Romans 8:29 (New International Version)

29 For those God foreknew he also predestined to be conformed to the likeness of his Son, that he might be the firstborn among many brothers.

The predestination of Romans 8:29 means that in eternity past, God drew some lines. He established a horizon or a set of limits around each person He had foreknown.

Here, we must decide if the limits were to restrict or to protect. Were they active and was the choice not to choose some also active or simply a passive "dismissiveness."

Remember that some doctrines of predestination have God choosing who will go to hell and some have Him choosing who will enter heaven while leaving the others to their own devices. The distinction is subtle but one is actively sending folks to hell and the other simply ignores them until they die and go there on their own.

They enter into hell on their own because they never come to know God. They do not know Him because He never called them to an awakening of their fallen state and their need for Him.

While Arminianism has all men being called by God at one time or another throughout their lives in an act called "prevenient" grace, Calvinism has only the chosen being called by "irresistible" grace.

In the fallen state, humanity is blind to the things of God, and is not aware of its spiritual needs. Before God opens their eyes, men and women are atheists, unaware they need God. They cannot love the God they do not know. They do not fear the God who they do not know exists. The state of unsaved man is summed up; "all the imaginations of the thoughts of his heart" are still "evil, only evil," continually." Scripture is clear that in our "natural state," we cannot even call out to God because we neither feel nor believe in God. Thus God must first act on the heart of man before the person can comprehend his state of depravity. "No man can come to me, except the Father which hath sent me draw him." John. 6:44.

The spirit of God awakens the person to their lost state and draws their heart to Him. The next question concerns the person's ability to resist the action of this drawing grace. Is it irresistible or not? Does the person have a say so, or are they overwhelmed by the experience? In other words, does man maintain his free will and thus have a choice to be saved or is he chosen and must obey? Calvinism is based on the "TULIP" principle outlined below.

The Synod of Dort clearly defined, in five simple points, the steps of Calvinism toward salvation.

T   Humanity is by nature Totally depraved and unable to merit salvation.

U   Some people are Unconditionally elected by God's saving grace.

L   God's atonement in Christ is Limited in its efficacy to the salvation of the Elect.

IGod's transforming grace, ministered by the Holy Spirit, is Irresistible on the part of humans.

P   The saints must Persevere in faith to the end, but none of the elect can finally be lost.

(I do not know why we must persevere if we are assured salvation. It just seems like the right thing to do.)

In the minds of those who believe in predestination, God chooses, God draws, God saves, God keeps. When it comes to salvation, man has little to say about his destiny.

In the Wesleyan way of viewing the world, the grace of God may be resisted by the will of the individual. The decision is in the hearts and minds of each person.

There is no way to prove which is the truth, for if our paths are chosen from the beginning, or if the will of God becomes our will, we would never know it. Automatons may believe they are following their own will, but it is pre-programmed into them and is therefore their natural path.

Let us assume that the question of free will is only for salvation and that we have free will in other parts of our lives. Calvinism taken to its conclusion can yield Determinism. The dictionary says Determinism is, "a doctrine that all facts and events exemplify natural laws." If Determinism is true, then we are not free but only think we are. Since we are all subject to the laws that govern the universe, we may "feel" as though we are free to do as we please, we are actually determined to act as we do based on the way the world was created, and they way we were created. That is, the way God created and thus pre-programmed us.

This means God decided before we were made who would go to heaven and who would go to hell. Determinism rules all human actions. If Determinism is true, then we have no choice to act any other way than we do, regardless of the illusion of free will.

To recap, we have various thoughts on predestination. Some have God actively or passively choosing who will go to hell. Some think God could actually set our life path before we are born. There are various flavors of the belief and they vary in how much free will we may have. Some believe our entire life is predetermined. Some believe it is only our salvation that is a fore drawn conclusion. Then there is a faction who believes that man has a say so in choosing heaven or hell. God woos us and calls us but we choose to accept the invitation or not.

But we still have not answered the first question of the limits. If predestination means to pre-set limits or boundaries, and it seems those limits or boundaries block or permit the person to know, love, and believe in God, what could this limitation be? Could it be in us and with us from our birth?

Excerpts from Times Magazine: Posted Monday, Oct. 25, 2004 –

"Ask true believers of any faith to describe the most important thing that drives their devotion, and they'll tell you it's not a thing at all but a sense--a feeling of a higher power far beyond us. Western religions can get a bit more doctrinaire: God has handed us laws and lore, and it's for us to learn and practice what they teach. For a hell-raising species like ours, however--with too much intelligence for our own good and too little discipline to know what to do with it--there have always been other, more utilitarian reasons to get religion. Chief among them is survival. Across the eons, the structure that religion provides our lives helps preserve both mind and body. But that, in turn, has raised a provocative question, one that's increasingly debated in the worlds of science and religion: Which came first, God or the need for God? In other words, did humans create religion from cues sent from above, or did evolution instill in us a sense of the divine so that we would gather into the communities essential to keeping the species going?

Nowhere has that idea received a more intriguing going-over than in the recently published book, "The God Gene: How Faith Is Hardwired into Our Genes" (Doubleday; 256 pages), by molecular biologist Dean Hamer. Chief of gene structure at the National Cancer Institute, Hamer not only claims that human spirituality is an adaptive trait, but he also says he has located one of the genes responsible, a gene that just happens to also code for production of the neurotransmitters that regulate our moods. Our most profound feelings of spirituality, according to a literal reading of Hamer's work, may be due to little more than an occasional shot of intoxicating brain chemicals governed by our DNA. "I'm a believer that every thought we think and every feeling we feel is the result of activity in the brain," Hamer says. "I think we follow the basic law of nature, which is that we're a bunch of chemical reactions running around in a bag."

"Hamer began looking in 1998, when he was conducting a survey on smoking and addiction for the National Cancer Institute. As part of his study, he recruited more than 1,000 men and women, who agreed to take a standardized, 240-question personality test called the Temperament and Character Inventory (TCI). Among the traits the TCI measures is one known as self-transcendence, which consists of three other traits: self-forgetfulness, or the ability to get entirely lost in an experience; transpersonal identification, or a feeling of connectedness to a larger universe; and mysticism, or an openness to things not literally provable. Put them all together, and you come as close as science can to measuring what it feels like to be spiritual. "This allows us to have the kind of experience described as religious ecstasy," says Robert Cloninger, a psychiatrist at Washington University in St. Louis, Mo., and the designer of the self-transcendence portion of the TCI."

"Hamer decided to use the data he gathered in the smoking survey to conduct a little spirituality study on the side. First he ranked the participants along Cloninger's self-transcendence scale, placing them on a continuum from least to most spiritually inclined. Then he went poking around in their genes to see if he could find the DNA responsible for the differences. Spelunking in the human genome is not easy, what with 35,000 genes consisting of 3.2

billion chemical bases. To narrow the field, Hamer confined his work to nine specific genes known to play major roles in the production of monoamines--brain chemicals, including serotonin, norepinephrine and dopamine, that regulate such fundamental functions as mood and motor control. It's monoamines that are carefully manipulated by Prozac and other antidepressants. It's also monoamines that are not so carefully scrambled by ecstasy, LSD, peyote and other mind-altering drugs--some of which have long been used in religious rituals.

Studying the nine candidate genes in DNA samples provided by his subjects, Hamer quickly hit the genetic jackpot. A variation in a gene known as VMAT2--for vesicular monoamine transporter--seemed to be directly related to how the volunteers scored on the self-transcendence test. "

"At least one faith, according to one of its best-known scholars, formalizes the idea of gene-based spirituality and even puts a pretty spin on it. Buddhists, says Robert Thurman, professor of Buddhist studies at Columbia University, have long entertained the idea that we inherit a spirituality gene from the person we were in a previous life. Smaller than an ordinary gene, it combines with two larger physical genes we inherit from our parents, and together they shape our physical and spiritual profile. Says Thurman: "The spiritual gene helps establish a general trust in the universe, a sense of openness and generosity."

"Other researchers have taken the science in a different direction, looking not for the genes that code for spirituality but for how that spirituality plays out in the brain. Neuroscientist Andrew Newberg of the University of Pennsylvania School of Medicine has used several types of imaging systems to watch the brains of subjects as they meditate or pray. By measuring blood flow, he determines which regions are responsible for the feelings the volunteers experience. The deeper that people descend into meditation or prayer, Newberg found, the more active the frontal lobe and the limbic system become. The frontal lobe is the seat of concentration and attention; the limbic system is where powerful feelings, including rapture, are processed. More revealing is the fact that at the same time these regions flash to life, another important region--the parietal lobe at the back of the brain--goes dim. It's this lobe that orients the individual in time and space."

"Of course, concepts of God reside in the brain. They certainly don't reside in the toe," says Lindon Eaves, director of the Virginia Institute for Psychiatric and Behavioral Genetics at Virginia Commonwealth University in Richmond. "The question is, To what is this wiring responsive? Why is it there?"

Says Paul Davies, professor of natural philosophy at Macquarie University in Sydney, Australia: "I think a lot of people make the mistake of thinking that if you explain something, you explain it away. I don't see that at all with religious experience."

"Those religious believers who are comfortable with the idea that God genes are the work of God should have little trouble making the next leap: that not only are the genes there but they are central to our survival, one of the hinges upon which the very evolution of the human species turned. It's an argument that's not terribly hard to make."

"One of the best examples of religion as social organizer, according to Binghamton University's Wilson, is early Calvinism. John Calvin rose to prominence in 1536 when, as a theologian and religious reformer, he was recruited to help bring order to the fractious city of Geneva. Calvin, perhaps one of the greatest theological minds ever produced by European Christianity, was a lawyer by trade. Wilson speculates that it was Calvin's pragmatic genius to understand that while civil laws alone might not be enough to bring the city's deadbeats and other malefactors into line, divine law might be."

"Nonetheless, sticking points do remain that prevent genetic theory from going down smoothly. One that's particularly troublesome is the question of why Hamer's God gene--or any of the others that may eventually be discovered--is distributed so unevenly among us. Why are some of us spiritual virtuosos, while others can't play a note? Isn't it one of the central tenets of religion that grace is available to everybody? At least a few scientists shrug at the question. "Some get religion, and some don't," says Virginia Commonwealth University's Eaves…" --With reporting by Jeff Chu/ London, Broward Liston/ Orlando, Maggie Sieger/ Chicago and Daniel Williams/ Sydney

Some get religion and some do not. The gene is distributed unequally among people. Is this the "boundary" spoken of in the scriptures? Is this the tool of predestination? Is this God's mark for heaven or hell? We would believe we have free will. It would feel as if we do. Yet, from our birth, and maybe from the very thought of us by God in the beginning of time, we were predestined to be with or without The God Gene.

PARADOX OF THE WAY

Individual Will, Predestination, and God's Path for our Lives

MAT 5:44 *But I say unto you, Love your enemies, bless them that curse you, do good to them that hate you, and pray for them which despitefully use you, and persecute you; 45 That ye may be the children of your Father, which is in heaven: for he maketh his sun to rise on the evil and on the good, and sendeth rain on the just and on the unjust.*

EPH 1:3 *Blessed be the God and Father of our Lord Jesus Christ, who hath blessed us with all spiritual blessings in heavenly places in Christ: 4 According as he hath chosen us in him before the foundation of the world, that we should be holy and without blame before him in love: 5 Having predestinated us unto the adoption of children by Jesus Christ to himself, according to the good pleasure of his will, 6 To the praise of the glory of his grace, wherein he hath made us accepted in the beloved.*
EPH 1:8 *Wherein he hath abounded toward us in all wisdom and prudence; 9 Having made known unto us the mystery of his will, according to his good pleasure which he hath purposed in himself: 10 That in the dispensation of the fullness of times he might gather together in one all things in Christ, both which are in heaven, and which are on earth; even in him: 11 In whom also we have obtained an inheritance, being predestinated according to the purpose of him who worketh all things after the counsel of his own will: 12 That we should be to the praise of his glory, who first trusted in Christ.*

With limited insight and finite minds, we enter into arguments about God and his infinite plan. We debate and denominations split over our feeble ideas of free will, foreknowledge, predestination, and self-determination. Never could we hope to understand the depth and complexity of God, but argue it passionately, we will.

Does God have a plan for us? Did He make us for a reason? Are we here to fulfill His plan of salvation and light in the world? I am not asking if God "needs" us to fulfill His plan. I am asking if we have a place in His plan? Do we have an individual purpose? Is obedience a choice? Does one have free will? Is free will necessary in order to love? It seems that both views, predestination and foreknowledge, must be correct. As mutually exclusive as predestination and foreknowledge may appear upon first sight, they must somehow co-exist in the plan of God. Like a river flowing through a valley, we live on the path we are placed upon from birth. Along this path of life we encounter people and circumstances related to the timing of our birth and path. We have no acquiescence in this. Our starting point in time, place of birth, social placement, financial status, abilities, intelligence range, and other items are things we cannot control. They are functions of timing, circumstances, or genetics.

We are born into a family at a time and in a place with certain strengths and weaknesses none of which we can control. We are set on a general path of life based on these attributes and resources. Some of these determine what life has in store for us. Like the landscape, terrain, rocks, boulders, eddies, and currents of the river, we will endure what happens to us along the way. The way we flow with or in spite of the obstacles is up to us. Although we are made in a certain way, we know we may choose to give in to sin or resist the Devil. There are six billion people on this planet. Each one of them has free will, although one may argue to what degree. Six billion people make choices throughout the day that affect others. From our vantage point it may look as if we spin our wheel of fortune and take what life has to offer. Indeed, that is how life affects us at times, but our view is a microcosmic myopia. From a heavenly arena it may be in perfect order. Some would say with faith, grace, and salvation issuing from the throne of God, all things are in His hands. It is true nothing in the plan of salvation is left undone.

David, looking ahead into the brilliant light of God's plan wrote: *PSA 116:12 What shall I render unto the LORD for all his benefits toward me? 13 I will take the cup of salvation, and call upon the name of the LORD.*

Thus we take and drink the cup of His salvation and we call upon the name of the Lord.

ROM 10:13 For whosoever shall call upon the name of the Lord shall be saved.

One could easily cross into a fatalistic predestinationalism if it weren't for the fact that our response to the plight of the world is in our hands. We exercise our choice to forgive, hate, love, help, or hinder each moment of every day. It is our free will. A plan must be put to use - and that is our place in God's plan, to take what is offered and decide to forgive, have gratitude, and love.

This can be a most difficult thing when facing the death or injury of a loved one, or betrayal from a friend. I cannot say with certainty that any of those things are in God's plan. I can say they came from the interactions of the free will of men. The one thing I am certain of is that God is leading us in the direction of salvation and relationship with Him. If God's plan for us is general and expansive, such as to love others and to love Him, then in those times of trials we should run to Him for solace and strength. If His plan is specific, such as a particular profession, marriage to a particular person, and such, we should run to Him for advice. In either case, our place is with God.

This is how the plan of salvation and man's place therein seem to fit together in a tapestry of predestination and foreknowledge, but in the end we must admit our inability to know the mind of God. Did God make us to succeed or fail? Did He create some to endure hell forever while giving some eternal life from the start? As the scriptures read, (reading more accurately in the ancient Greek), He has predestined salvation for us in Christ. It does not say He predestined us for salvation. How much control we have and how much is all in the hands of God, we will not know until we can view our life in one long scene from the portals of heaven and ask God face to face. I have a feeling at that point it will not really matter. These issues have forced us off task too often. They have clogged our minds with "unknowables" and, through our pride, we have been led to take sides and travel side roads, and defend our vague ideas to the point we have lost sight of Him whose plan we argue.

1CO 8:1 ... Knowledge puffeth up, but charity edifieth. 2 And if any man think that he knoweth any thing, he knoweth nothing yet as he ought to know. 3 But if any man love God, the same is known of him.

LUK 11:42 But woe unto you, Pharisees! for ye tithe mint and rue and all manner of herbs, and pass over judgment and the love of God: these ought ye to have done, and not to leave the other undone. 43 Woe unto you, Pharisees! for ye love the uppermost seats in the synagogues, and greetings in the markets. 44 Woe unto you, scribes and Pharisees, hypocrites! for ye are as graves which appear not, and the men that walk over them are not aware of them. 45 Then answered one of the lawyers, and said unto him, Master, thus saying thou reproachest us also. 46 And he said, Woe unto you also, ye lawyers! for ye lade men with burdens grievous to be borne, and ye yourselves touch not the burdens with one of your fingers.

HEB 5:11 Of whom we have many things to say, and hard to be uttered, seeing ye are dull of hearing .12 For when for the time ye ought to be teachers, ye have need that one teach you again which be the first principles of the oracles of God; and are become such as have need of milk, and not of strong meat. 13 For every one that useth milk is unskillful in the word of righteousness: for he is a babe. 14 But strong meat belongeth to them that are of full age, even those who by reason of use have their senses exercised to discern both good and evil. 6:1 Therefore leaving the principles of the doctrine of Christ, let us go on unto perfection; not laying again the foundation of repentance from dead works, and of faith toward God, 2 Of the doctrine of baptisms, and of laying on of hands, and of resurrection of the dead, and of eternal judgment. 3 And this will we do, if God permit.

ROM 3:19 *Now we know that what things soever the law saith, it saith to them who are under the law: that every mouth may be stopped, and all the world may become guilty before God. 20 Therefore by the deeds of the law there shall no flesh be justified in his sight: for by the law is the knowledge of sin. 21 But now the righteousness of God without the law is manifested, being witnessed by the law and the prophets; 22 Even the righteousness of God which is by faith of Jesus Christ unto all and upon all them that believe: for there is no difference:23 For all have sinned, and come short of the glory of God; 24 Being justified freely by his grace through the redemption that is in Christ Jesus*

We have set in place doctrines with names to keep out those who disagree with things we cannot prove. We create denominations each time we accent a piece of the truth to the exclusion of the whole. We part ways through politics and power as disagreements arise as to who should control the church or how control is maintained. Where is God in all of this? He is not in the work we do to convert others to our denomination or convince others of our way. He is in His word, working to save the lost soul, and He is in the hearts of those who believe in Him. Denominationalism is not Christianity. It is a study of the beliefs of a group usually based on the views of a single man.

Furthermore, denominations are based partly on personality and preferences. In a general way, there are certain personalities drawn toward certain denominations. Many times we are raised in a denomination or church and there we stay out of a sense of family or loyalty, but if people were to be set free from those things we would find like attracts like. It is simply a function of personality that a kinetic, effusive person is not going to be comfortable in a quiet, liturgically driven church. Likewise, an orderly, structured, quiet person will find a noisy, free flowing, spontaneous service disturbing. Some churches have overcome this problem by having two or more services of differing types. The beliefs are that same, they are simply expressed differently. In this natural grouping it can be seen denominations can be a matter of how to express one's beliefs as much as what the beliefs are.

Some churches break down membership across socio-economic levels where the wealthy tend to gather in one church and the poor attend another church. It is a generally accepted rule of society that most individuals tend to stay within one or two social classes of their upbringing. This assumes a five to seven class system of income and lifestyle. The five class system breakdown is comprised of lower, lower-middle, middle, upper-middle, and upper classes. Since it tends to stress most people to ascend or descend more than two social levels, it stands to reason intermingling for any length of time would be uncomfortable to some. We tend to stay with our own kind, and that tends to include class groups also. This is the worldly man, who judges according to riches, and not the spiritual man, who sees the love of God in others equally. None of this is to say there are not more errors and heresies in certain sects and denominations. Some have more solid theologies than others, however, keeping with the basics of the creed presented will help avoid pitfalls of theology and bring most other issues to a point of view or political structure.

JAM 2:2 For if there come unto your assembly a man with a gold ring, in goodly apparel, and here come in also a poor man in vile raiment; 3 And ye have respect to him that weareth the gay clothing, and say unto him, Sit thou here in a good place; and say to the poor, Stand thou there, or sit here under my footstool: 4 Are ye not then partial in yourselves, and are become judges of evil thoughts? 5 Hearken, my beloved brethren, Hath not God chosen the poor of this world rich in faith, and heirs of the kingdom which he hath promised to them that love him? 6 But ye have despised the poor. Do not rich men oppress you, and draw you before the judgment seats? 7 Do not they blaspheme that worthy name by the which ye are called? 8 If ye fulfil the royal law according to the scripture, Thou shalt love thy neighbour as thyself, ye do well:

Denominations and church attendance can fall into man-made categories. Categories and denominations sprang from man, not God. Our purpose is not to belong to a denomination. It is to belong to God. Again, man falls into a Pharisee mindset, ignoring the reason of our salvation and arguing the minutiae.

This is not to say we should avoid church. We need the reinforcement and support of fellow Christians. In our churches, let us stand out as those who love and support others in their search for God.

HEB 10:23 Let us hold fast the profession of our faith without wavering; (for he is faithful that promised;) 24 And let us consider one another to provoke unto love and to good works: 25 Not forsaking the assembling of ourselves together, as the manner of some is; but exhorting one another: and so much the more, as ye see the day approaching.

It is in this vein I find myself stopped short and lacking. Having letters of someone learned and having seen the zeal to study doctrine day and night, I became as one having a tourniquet around his neck, with head and heart separate, I had no ability to transmute knowledge into wisdom.

2TI 3:7 Ever learning, and never able to come to the knowledge of the truth.

It is because knowledge of anything other than Christ can become superfluous. We must strive to keep the three legs of our Christian journey in balance. The three legs of Christian life are Worship, Study, and Prayer. Our worship must be pure and upward reaching, not simply entertainment, good music, or fiery preaching but full of the passion of His passion, His life, His purpose, His nature, and His words. Our study should be more about Him and His character and less about social ideas. Our prayers should be a never-ceasing desire to commune with God and to know Him and His will. With God's character in us, we will know what He would have us do.

We should avoid useless and divisive doctrine, which is impossible to prove as well as those having little or nothing to do with our relationship to God and salvation. We should ask ourselves as an example, "If the doctrine of predestination or foreknowledge was true, would I still serve Him?" If the answer is yes, it is not worth spending much time to study it. The time used to read about others opinions on that subject should be used to seek God.

We must strive to keep our prayer life in balance between Discursive prayer and Contemplative prayer. In discursive prayer we carry on a dialogue between the Lord and ourselves. The problem in this type of prayer is we tend to do all of the talking. We bring a wish list before the throne. We repeat our requests as if He did not hear us the first time. We beg God to fill our requests, as if we could possibly know what is best in the light of eternity. We seldom listen to His answer. In contemplative prayer we stay silent and listen to the Lord. We think about Him and His glory. We learn to be still inside so we may hear His soft, beckoning voice.

Prayer is not for us to change the mind of God, but for us to be conformed to His will.

THE BINARY PROBLEM
Heaven, Hell and War

Muslims see the world in only one of two conditions – A world at peace - A world at war. The world will be at war until every person is converted, by force if necessary. A world at peace is a world totally under Islamic law. The Koran declares that all people must be converted or killed. It depends on the person reading the book as to how literally they wish to interpret and carry out the command. It is an abominable command to non-Muslims.

Are you saved? Are you lost? Some believe that salvation is an instantaneous event. Some believe you awaken to the truth and grow into it. Yet, regardless of the definition of salvations, most hold to the thought that in the end, there will be only the Christian righteous left, for the hand of God will annihilate all others. Of course, during the crusades Christians took the will of God into their own hands, killing everyone who refused to convert. Muslims of the time found this to be an abominable act.

There is a difference between the two occurrences. The crusades were fueled by men of greed twisted the loving and gracious words of beatitudes into hate and murder, but the Bible, unaltered, preaches love and forgiveness. In the case of Islam, men of reason temper a message of violence into a religion acceptable to some. Yet, the Koran remains unaltered in the message of hate, which many follow to the letter.

In the end, regardless of the religion, all but the righteous will die. Holy men of Islam incite murder of all non-Muslims. Holy men of Christianity pray for world conversion, being certain that God will kill all that are not saved.

All three major religions issuing from the Abrahamic root are binary systems. You are either Christian or not. You are either Muslim or not. You are either Jewish or not.

When we come to this point of a binary state, implosions usually occur. The definition of what it takes to be a Jew, Christian, or Muslim becomes of absolute importance. If there is disagreement on points of entry splintering results as one group declares the other to be heretics and infidels.

Christianity split along lines of papists and non-papists. Interestingly, Islam split along the same lines, since the difference between the Shiah and Suuni Muslims boils down to one of succession and power.

The division between Shia and Sunni dates back to the death of the Prophet Muhammad, and the question of who was to take over the leadership of the Muslim nation.

Sunni Muslims believed that the new leader should be elected from among those capable of the job. With this type of election by the high clergy, the Prophet Muhammad's close friend and advisor, Abu Bakr, was chosen to become the first Caliph of the Islamic nation.

Shia believe that leadership should have stayed within the Prophet's family. The Shia Muslims believe that following the Prophet Muhammad's death, leadership should have passed directly to his cousin, who was also a son-in-law. 'Ali was Muhammad's first cousin and closest living male relative, as well as his son-in-law, having married his daughter Fatimah. 'Ali would eventually become the fourth Muslim caliph.

'Ali's rule over the early Muslim community was often contested. As a result, he had to struggle to maintain his power, waging "increasingly unsuccessful wars." After Ali's murder in 661 CE, his main rival Mu'awiya claimed the caliphate.

'Ali ruled from 656 CE to 661 CE, when he was assassinated. The dispute over the right successor to Muhammad resulted in the formation of two main sects, the Sunni, and the Shia.

The persecution of Shias throughout history by Sunni co-religionists has often been characterized by brutal and genocidal acts. Comprising only about 10-15% of the entire Muslim population, to this day, the Shia remain a marginalized community in many Sunni Arab dominant countries without the rights to practice their religion and organize.

Joseph Lumpkin

But, before we point a finger and declare ourselves somehow better, let us remember the trouble in Northern Ireland. "The Troubles" refers to approximately three decades of violence, 1960s to 1990s, between elements of Northern Ireland's nationalist Roman Catholic community and Protestant unionist community.

The mentality of fundamentalism is by no means an exclusive property of orthodoxy. Its attitudes are found in every branch of Christendom: the quest for negative status, the elevation of minor issues to a place of major importance, the use of social mores as a norm of virtue, the toleration of one's own prejudice but not the prejudice of others, the confusion of the church with a denomination, and the avoidance of prophetic scrutiny by using the Word of God as an instrument of self-security but not self-criticism. The mentality of fundamentalism comes into being whenever a believer is unwilling to trace the effects of original sin in his own life. And where is the believer who is wholly delivered from this habit? --E.J. Carnell

As editor of the largest newspaper in West Virginia, I scan hundreds of reports daily and I am amazed by the frequency with which religion causes people to kill each other. It is a nearly universal pattern, undercutting the common assumption that religion makes people kind and tolerant. - James Haught

Every other sect supposes itself in possession of the truth, and that those who differ are so far in the wrong. Like a man traveling in foggy weather they see those at a distance before them wrapped up in a fog, as well as those behind them, and also people in the fields on each side; but near them, all appears clear, though in truth they are as much in the fog as any of them. --Benjamin Franklin

CHRIST and THE INCARNATION

It is at this point, most blessed, that we stumble. It is here at Christ's feet we fall and fail. It is with the words of adoration, love, and the description of Jesus that we perish in our intent. Even the Holy scriptures, though not in error, because of restrictions of word and language, fall so short as to utterly fail in any possible description of whom He is. Here, we destroy our own goals by attempting to somehow qualify or quantify His glory. With any words, no matter how well written, there will be an image formed, an idea set, a concept put in place, all of which will be incomplete and inadequate, and all of which must be transcended and un-known if His fullness is to be tasted.

Anything written will lead the reader into failure of knowing Him completely by placing in our feeble minds some restricted image even if it be holy and powerful. A description is no more the thing being described than a painting is the real sky or sea. One may point to something, describe it in detail, or paint a picture of it and still the image and words are completely useless when compared to the real and authentic item or the utility of the thing. It is more so with God, for He is infinite and cannot be captured in finite language, word, or color. Yet, for those who have not met Him, and for those who know Him only from others, I submit these lines as an enticement in hopes of encouraging you into a personal relationship of communion with Him. We must remember what He said of Himself. "TELL THEM, I AM."

When you hear that Jesus is begotten of God, beware lest the words make some inadequate thoughts of the flesh appears before your mind's eye.   The Tree of Life by St. Bonaventure

GEN 15:1 After these things the word of the LORD came unto Abram in a vision, saying, Fear not, Abram: I am thy shield, and thy exceeding great reward.

EXO 3:13 And Moses said unto God, Behold, when I come unto the children of Israel, and shall say unto them, The God of your fathers hath sent me unto you; and they shall say to me, What is his name? what shall I say unto them?

EXO 3:14 And God said unto Moses, I AM THAT I AM: and he said, Thus shalt thou say unto the children of Israel, I AM hath sent me unto you.

(In the person of Christ} a man has not become God; God has become man. (Cyril of Alexandria: Select Letters)

... for the Only Begotten Word of God has saved us by putting on our likeness. Suffering in the flesh, and rising from the dead, He revealed our nature as greater than death or corruption. What He achieved was beyond the ability of our condition, and what seemed to have been worked out in human weakness and by suffering was really stronger than men and a demonstration of the power that pertains to God. ...This was how He would be revealed as ennobling the nature of man in Himself by making {human nature} participate in his own sacred and divine honors. ... We must not think that He who descended into the limitation of manhood for our sake lost his inherent radiance and that transcendence that comes from his nature. No, He had this divine fullness even in the emptiness of our condition, and He enjoyed the highest eminence in humility, and held what belongs to him by nature (that is, to be worshipped by all) as a gift because of his humanity. Cyril of Alexandria

Now, everything is holy which is free of this world's defilement. And {such holiness} is in Christ by His very nature, just as it is in the Father; but in the holy disciples it is something adventitious, introduced from outside {through their participation in the Holy Spirit}, by means of the sanctification that comes by way of grace, and by means of splendid, virtuous living; for this is the manner in which one is fashioned to the divine, supramundane image. (The Image of God in Man according to Cyril of Alexandria)

Secrets of the incomprehensible wisdom of God, unknown to any beside Himself! Man, sprung up only of a few days, wants to penetrate, and to set bounds to it. Who is it that hath known the mind of the Lord, or who hath been His counselor? Quotations from Jeanne-Marie Bouvier de la Motte-Guyon

The Incarnation is not a union of wills dependent upon some fragile and inconsistent human response toward Christ. Grace cannot depend upon anything, certainly not the deficiencies of the best of human will. Grace must be unconditional, depending on nothing from, in, or of us. The Incarnation must therefore be an amalgam of Christ with man. This union, although never forced upon us, must be stronger than we and stronger further than any human act or choice. The incarnate Word coming into human conditions and limitations was enacted in order to radically change, alter, and restore them, without destroying them.

God remains God and his man is still man, but after Christ has come upon us we are charged with divine power. Only then are we, the believer, capable of restoring or being restored to the fullness of life as we share in it sacramentally with Him. It then becomes the ultimate paradox that in the strictest Trinitarian view, God offers praise and prayer to himself through us. But, then, who else would be worthy to praise Him and commune with Him except it be He? God in us as Christ has imbued us with Himself through perfect grace has now made it possible for us to approach the Father in love and adoration.

... He transmits the grace of sonship even to us..., insofar as human nature had first achieved this possibility in Him. (On the Unity of Christ)

THE DARK NIGHT

In anguish, our soul cries out to God, but He does not answer. In despair we sit alone and empty, in search of Him. We wish to die for Him. We wish to die to self. Our stubborn carnal hearts keep beating. We died because we cannot die. That is to say, we die inside through sin and sorrow because we refuse to die to self. We struggled to lay ourselves down and pick up His Cross, His glory, His life in us. But the old man resists, fighting for each spiritual breath. This "not dying" is agony. We long for Him, waiting for Him with each breath we take, trying to get out of his way. Yet, no matter how we move ourselves we are still in our own way.

The soul cries out but God seems not to hear. Our hearts cry out for the beloved, but He cannot be found. We are poured out like water. Our hearts are like wax melted and running away. We have waited for Him, prayed for Him, meditated on Him, beckoned Him, cried for Him, wept for Him, hurt for Him, and now we are in agony for Him. He is behind the Cloud, we cannot see Him nor can we feel Him. How can one who is everywhere be so far away? But He is. With prayer and desire we beat against the Cloud, the wall that keeps us from God. We cannot get through the wall.

There is no night darker than this. Sorrow is a knife cutting the soul deeper and deeper and so it becomes a bowl, capable of holding more joy when finally there is the joy of His coming. There is no night more sorrowful…but Joy cometh in the morning. We can do nothing but to await the Son. If we endure, this sorrow, this most deep and personal tribulation, will give way to patience and stillness.

LUK 21:19 In your patience possess ye your souls.

Desire will die and obedience will take its place.

ROM 6:16 Know ye not, that to whom ye yield yourselves servants to obey, his servants ye are to whom ye obey; whether of sin unto death, or of obedience unto righteousness?

Grace will be shed on us in obedience to God, and our hearts will receive his fullness.

ROM 5:2 By whom also we have access by faith into this grace wherein we stand, and rejoice in hope of the glory of God. 3 And not only so, but we glory in tribulations also: knowing that tribulation worketh patience; 4 And patience, experience; and experience, hope: 5 And hope maketh not ashamed; because the love of God is shed abroad in our hearts by the Holy Ghost which is given unto us. 6 For when we were yet without strength, in due time Christ died for the ungodly. 7 For scarcely for a righteous man will one die: yet peradventure for a good man some would even dare to die. 8 But God commendeth his love toward us, in that, while we were yet sinners, Christ died for us. 9 Much more then, being now justified by his blood, we shall be saved from wrath through Him.

…with no other light or guide than the one that burned in my heart.

The Dark Night by St John of the Cross

Where have you hidden, Beloved, and left me moaning? You fled like the stag after wounding me; I went out calling you but you were gone. Spiritual Canticle by St John of the Cross.

God, who is all perfection, wars against all imperfect habits of the soul, and, purifying the soul with the heat of his flame, he approves its habits from it, and prepares it, so that at last he may enter it and be united with it by his sweet, peaceful, and glorious love, as is the fire when it has entered the wood. St. John of the Cross

What satisfies love best of all is that we be wholly stripped of all repose, whether in strangers, or in friends, or even in love herself. And this is a frightening life love wants, that we must do with the satisfaction of love in order to satisfy love. They who are thus drawn and accepted by love, and fettered by her, are the most indebted to love, and consequently they must continually stand subject to the great power over strong nature, to content her. And that life is miserable beyond all that the human heart can bear. Hadewijch of Antwerp

Our task is to offer ourselves up to God like a clean smooth canvas and not bother ourselves about what the God may choose to paint on it, but, at every moment, feel only for stroke of his brush. It is the same piece of stone. Each blow from the chisel of the sculptor makes it feel -- if it could feel -- as if it were being destroyed. As blow after blow rings down on it, the stone knows nothing about how the sculptor is shaping it. All it's feels is the chisel hacking away at it's, savaging it and mutilating it. Jean Pierre Caussadede

When God is seen in darkness it does not bring a smile to the lips, nor devotion, or ardent love; neither does the body with the soul tremble or move as at other times; the soul sees nothing and everything; the body sleeps and speech is cut off. Angela of Floigno

HEB 11:32 And what shall I more say? for the time would fail me to tell of Gedeon, and of Barak, and of Samson, and of Jephthae; of David also, and Samuel, and of the prophets: 33 Who through faith subdued kingdoms, wrought righteousness, obtained promises, stopped the mouths of lions. 34 Quenched the violence of fire, escaped the edge of the sword, out of weakness were made strong, waxed valiant in fight, turned to flight the armies of the aliens.35 Women received their dead raised to life again: and others were tortured, not accepting deliverance; that they might obtain a better resurrection: 36 And others had trial of cruel mockings and scourgings, yea, moreover of bonds and imprisonment: 37 They were stoned, they were sawn asunder, were tempted, were slain with the sword: they wandered about in sheepskins and goatskins; being destitute, afflicted, tormented; HEB 11:38 (Of whom the world was not worthy:) they wandered in deserts, and in mountains, and in dens and caves of the earth. 39 And these all, having obtained a good report through faith, received not the promise: 40 God having provided some better thing for us, that they without us should not be made perfect. 12:1 Wherefore seeing we also are compassed about with so great a cloud of witnesses, let us lay aside every weight, and the sin which doth so easily beset us, and let us run with patience the race that is set before us, 2 Looking unto Jesus the author and finisher of our faith; who for the joy that was set before Him endured the cross, despising the shame, and is set down at the right hand of the throne of God. 3 For consider him that endured such contradiction of sinners against himself, lest ye be wearied and faint in your minds. 4 Ye have not yet resisted unto blood, striving against sin.

NO PLACE FOR EGO

We are separate and individual creatures, wishing to fit in, wishing to be unique; wishing to be united, wishing to be distinct. We vacillate between the positions, thinking they are opposites. They are not. The wall in our psyche allowing us to distinguish ourselves from others around us is called the ego boundary. Our egos stubbornly refuse to yield, even to God. Pride and self-protection keeps us separate and distinct but we are not complete or whole. The effects of breaching the ego boundary can be seen in those moments of spiritual or sexual bliss. In the union of husband and wife, in those moments of complete tenderness and giving, when distinction between the lover and beloved is lost, and for a space of time it becomes impossible to know where the emotional and physical lines exist between you and the other. There is no fear of losing self but instead a sense of being poured into the other body and soul in a union both separate and together; individual and united, resulting in tears of joy and a river of emotional release as one is being cleansed as if a flood was washing through the soul.

So it is with the union of God and man. When man's ego boundary is finally lowered and man gives himself, even his self-hood, completely up to God. Man and his individuality are not lost but are borne upon the wings of God's love, washing man clean in a river of love. Breaching the ego boundary is a spontaneous act uncontrolled by man. It is made possible by trust and love deep enough to surrender life and self.

TO REACH THE MOUNTAIN, FIRST CLEAR THE PATH

Up to this point, we have spent time clarifying who God is and what we believe. Even Satan and his demons know who Christ is but this knowledge has not freed them. The knowledge never made it from head to heart. Their knowledge never became truth. Will we take the knowledge and make it truth in our lives? Will we become more righteous than Satan?

MAT 7:21 Not every one that saith unto me, Lord, Lord, shall enter into the kingdom of heaven; but he that doeth the will of my Father which is in heaven. 22 Many will say to me in that day, Lord, Lord, have we not prophesied in thy name? and in thy name have cast out devils? and in thy name done many wonderful works? 23 And then will I profess unto them, I never knew you: depart from me, ye that work iniquity.

MAR 5:2 And when he was come out of the ship, immediately there met him out of the tombs a man with an unclean spirit, 3 Who had his dwelling among the tombs; and no man could bind him, no, not with chains: 4 Because that he had been often bound with fetters and chains, and the chains had been plucked asunder by him, and the fetters broken in pieces: neither could any man tame him. 5 And always, night and day, he was in the mountains, and in the tombs, crying, and cutting himself with stones. 6 But when he saw Jesus afar off, he ran and worshipped him, 7 And cried with a loud voice, and said, What have I to do with thee, Jesus, thou Son of the most high God? I adjure thee by God, that thou torment me not.

Knowledge of God alone does nothing to change the heart of man or demon. Only being with God and communing with Him will alter our natures and only then according to our ability to yield to His spirit through obedience. Acting on knowledge as truth is faith, and faith is the key to heaven. Satan knows the truth of who God is but He does not act on it. Satan knows God but has no faith.

In espousing the following point I know I will incur the wrath of many. However, if we think about it carefully we will find it to be true. Church attendance, obedience to the law, knowledge of the Scriptures, prayer if empty repetition, even worship if it is empty of spirit, will not change the heart of man. Only by being in God's presence can we hope to get to know Him intimately and be changed by exposure to Him; as a child is changed and molded by the parent. Our churches have lost the way back to God. The people are not being told what it takes to live a full spiritual life. Because of this our churches are dying and people are suffering. We go to church, assemble together, read scripture, sing songs, pray, and leave. Seldom, if ever, do we simply sit and wait on the Spirit to come, to speak, to work in us.

We have been glimpsing God through Holy Scripture and doctrine. This is like trying to know someone by looking at his portrait or reading his letters. It is a facsimile and not the real person. We can get to know certain things about them and only those on a superficial level. We can come to admire them and even understand certain traits of their nature, but it is not the same as having a conversation and spending time with them. Most people, even ministers and priests, have reduced a relationship with God to a study session. Their time in prayer is when they tell God their troubles, needs, and greed. It takes time to listen and we don't seem to have time for God these days. This is not the way our relationship with God was intended to be. However, now that we have an understanding as to who He is and what He is like, we can make a decision if we wish to know Him better. We can, if we choose, extend our relationship to a state of intimacy. Knowing by experience is quite different than knowing by reading. The things we have learned about God and His nature will help lead us toward Him and keep us on the right path.

Scripture and the doctrine that springs from it are to inform man of the plan, purpose, and person of God and to direct, guide, and inspire man.

But, if scripture and doctrine were enough we could have kept the law and could have been justified by the law. Having no sin found in man under the law, there would have been no need for Christ to have come and die. But, scripture and doctrine are not enough and the heart of man has not changed. Even Adam, who spent time with God and had a relationship with Him fell, sinned, and died. What chance do we have? We have someone who paid the price of death for us and we have the spirit of God moving inside us, working to guide us and make us into His image. We have hope because we have forgiveness.

HEB 2:17 Wherefore in all things it behooved him to be made like unto his brethren, that he might be a merciful and faithful high priest in things pertaining to God, to make reconciliation for the sins of the people. 18 For in that he himself hath suffered being tempted, he is able to succour them that are tempted.

We no longer have to rely on ourselves to keep the law. We rely on the one who gave the law to keep us. Now we study the word to know about Him and His ways because we love the one who saved us. Scripture now takes on a new dimension.

2TI 3:16 *All scripture is given by inspiration of God, and is profitable for doctrine, for reproof, for correction, for instruction in righteousness: 17 That the man of God may be perfect, thoroughly furnished unto all good works.*

2TI 4:1 *I charge thee therefore before God, and the Lord Jesus Christ, who shall judge the quick and the dead at his appearing and his kingdom; 2 Preach the word; be instant in season, out of season; reprove, rebuke, exhort with all longsuffering and doctrine. 3 For the time will come when they will not endure sound doctrine; but after their own lusts shall they heap to themselves teachers, having itching ears; 4 And they shall turn away their ears from the truth, and shall be turned unto fables.*

DEU 32:1 *Give ear, O ye heavens, and I will speak; and hear, O earth, the words of my mouth. 2 My doctrine shall drop as the rain, my speech shall distil as the dew, as the small rain upon the tender herb, and as the showers upon the grass: 3 Because I will publish the name of the LORD: ascribe ye greatness unto our God. 4 He is the Rock, his work is perfect: for all his ways are judgment: a God of truth and without iniquity, just and right is he.*

PRO 4:1 *Hear, ye children, the instruction of a father, and attend to know understanding. 2 For I give you good doctrine, forsake ye not my law. 3 For I was my father's son, tender and only beloved in the sight of my mother. 4 He taught me also, and said unto me, Let thine heart retain my words: keep my commandments, and live. 5 Get wisdom, get understanding: forget it not; neither decline from the words of my mouth. 6 Forsake her not, and she shall preserve thee: love her, and she shall keep thee.*

MAR 4:1 *And he began again to teach by the seaside: and there was gathered unto him a great multitude, so that he entered into a ship, and sat in the sea; and the whole multitude was by the sea on the land. 2 And he taught them many things by parables, and said unto them in his doctrine,*

MAR 12:38 *And he said unto them in his doctrine, Beware of the scribes, which love to go in long clothing, and love salutations in the marketplaces, 39 And the chief seats in the synagogues, and the uppermost rooms at feasts: 40 Which devour widows' houses, and for a pretence make long prayers: these shall receive greater damnation.*

JOH 7:16 *Jesus answered them, and said, My doctrine is not mine, but his that sent me. 17 If any man will do his will, he shall know of the doctrine, whether it be of God, or whether I speak of myself. 18 He that speaketh of himself seeketh his own glory:*

but he that seeketh his glory that sent him, the same is true, and no unrighteousness is in him.

ACT 2:41 Then they that gladly received his word were baptized: and the same day there were added unto them about three thousand souls. 42 And they continued steadfastly in the apostles' doctrine and fellowship, and in breaking of bread, and in prayers.

ROM 6:16 Know ye not, that to whom ye yield yourselves servants to obey, his servants ye are to whom ye obey; whether of sin unto death, or of obedience unto righteousness? 17 But God be thanked, that ye were the servants of sin, but ye have obeyed from the heart that form of doctrine which was delivered you. Being then made free from sin, ye became the servants of righteousness.

1TI 4:6 If thou put the brethren in remembrance of these things, thou shalt be a good minister of Jesus Christ, nourished up in the words of faith and of good doctrine, whereunto thou hast attained.

Joseph Lumpkin

TRAPS AND SNARES ALONG THE PATH

Hate, resentment, and anger

As we approach Him we will find our hearts will open to Him and we will begin to recognize His presence in our hearts and lives more easily. We will get to know God on an intimate level. Unfortunately, there are things that will stop us in our tracks. Hate, resentment, and anger can destroy our journey. They are contrary to the heart and wishes of God. These emotions stick like glue to the heart of man. They hang on us like weights around our necks, impeding us on the journey. They will wear us down, fatigue our steps, and halt our progress. Sadly, these things, hate, resentment and anger are some of the last obstacles to be overcome.

Anger: excessive emotion or passion aroused by a sense of injury or wrong; wrath; to provoke to resentment; excite to wrath; enrage.   Webster's New School and Office Dictionary

Hate: to dislike intensely: abhor: detest: intense aversion.   Webster's New School and Office Dictionary

Resentment: strong anger or displeasure: deep sense of injury.   Webster's New School and Office Dictionary

Hate, anger, and resentment are interwoven emotions. They eat at us and consume us slowly, like an acid; they rot us from the inside. They draw our minds to the pain from injuries done in the past. The pain holds us hostage in the past, by the pain we feel in the present. We hearken to the past and our minds dwell there. Letting go of the pain is not so easy, and although I do not want this to evolve into a book on psychology, we must realize healing and forgiveness are needed.

PHI 2:3 Let nothing be done through strife or vainglory; but in lowliness of mind let each esteem other better than themselves. 4 Look not every man on his own things, but every man also on the things of others. 5 Let this mind be in you, which was also in Christ Jesus:

JAM 3:16 For where envying and strife is, there is confusion and every evil work.

LEV 19:17 Thou shalt not hate thy brother in thine heart: thou shalt in any wise rebuke thy neighbour, and not suffer sin upon him. 18 Thou shalt not avenge, nor bear any grudge against the children of thy people, but thou shalt love thy neighbour as thyself: I am the LORD.

PSA 34:21 Evil shall slay the wicked: and they that hate the righteous shall be desolate. 22 The LORD redeemeth the soul of his servants: and none of them that trust in him shall be desolate.

MAT 5:43 Ye have heard that it hath been said, Thou shalt love thy neighbour, and hate thine enemy. 44 But I say unto you, Love your enemies, bless them that curse you, do good to them that hate you, and pray for them which despitefully use you, and persecute you; 45 That ye may be the children of your Father which is in heaven: for he maketh his sun to rise on the evil and on the good, and sendeth rain on the just and on the unjust.

LUK 6:22 Blessed are ye, when men shall hate you, and when they shall separate you from their company, and shall reproach you, and cast out your name as evil, for the Son of man's sake.

ROM 13:13 Let us walk honestly, as in the day; not in rioting and drunkenness, not in chambering and wantonness, not in strife and envying. 14 But put ye on the Lord Jesus Christ, and make not provision for the flesh, to fulfil the lusts thereof.

1JO 3:14 We know that we have passed from death unto life, because we love the brethren. He that loveth not his brother abideth in death.

ROM 12:17 Recompense to no man evil for evil. Provide things honest in the sight of all men. 18 If it be possible, as much as lieth in you, live peaceably with all men. 19 Dearly beloved, avenge not yourselves, but rather give place unto wrath: for it is written, Vengeance is mine; I will repay, saith the Lord.   20 Therefore if thine enemy hunger, feed him; if he thirst, give him drink: for in so doing thou shalt heap coals of fire on his head. 21 Be not overcome of evil, but overcome evil with good.

EPH 2:2 Wherein in time past ye walked according to the course of this world, according to the prince of the power of the air, the spirit that now worketh in the children of disobedience: 3 Among whom also we all had our conversation in times past in the lusts of our flesh, fulfilling the desires of the flesh and of the mind; and were by nature the children of wrath, even as others. 4 But God, who is rich in mercy, for his great love wherewith he loved us, 5 Even when we were dead in sins, hath quickened us together with Christ, (by grace ye are saved;) 6 And hath raised us up together, and made us sit together in heavenly places in Christ Jesus: 7 That in the ages to come he might shew the exceeding riches of his grace in his kindness toward us through Christ Jesus.

GAL 5:19 Now the works of the flesh are manifest, which are these; Adultery, fornication, uncleanness, lasciviousness, 20 Idolatry, witchcraft, hatred, variance, emulations, wrath, strife, seditions, heresies, 21 Envyings, murders, drunkenness, revellings, and such like: of the which I tell you before, as I have also told you in time past, that they which do such things shall not inherit the kingdom of God. 22 But the fruit of the Spirit is love, joy, peace, longsuffering, gentleness, goodness, faith, 23 Meekness, temperance: against such there is no law.

EPH 4:26 Be ye angry, and sin not: let not the sun go down upon your wrath: 27 Neither give place to the devil.

Anger, strife, and resentment constrict our thoughts and capture them. We dwell on the person that hurt us and not on God. We wish evil on the person. Our pain or anger pulls our thoughts back to him or her constantly. Our imagination runs to hurtful recompense. We become trapped within our malicious thoughts. It is a trap sprung on us by us and it is difficult to escape.

PSA 94:11 The LORD knoweth the thoughts of man, that they are vanity.

PSA 119:113 I hate vain thoughts: but thy law do I love.

PSA 139:23 Search me, O God, and know my heart: try me, and know my thoughts: 24 And see if there be any wicked way in me, and lead me in the way everlasting. 140:1 Deliver me, O LORD, from the evil man: preserve me from the violent man; 2 Which imagine mischiefs in their heart; continually are they gathered together for war.

JER 6:19 Hear, O earth: behold, I will bring evil upon this people, even the fruit of their thoughts, because they have not hearkened unto my words, nor to my law, but rejected it.

The minimum penalty we can hope for in this state is that our minds will be stripped of God's presence and engorged with resentment and hate. Our beloved will be taken from us by force and replaced with resentment. Our finite minds have only limited capacity and so He will be pushed out when thoughts of anger and resentment become sizable enough the intruders will crowd and push the Lord from our heart. Even if some thought of the Lord remains, the voices of hate and anger are strong and constant enough His sweet voice will not be easily heard.

Our spirit will suffer and starve. Christ is our focus and our bread. He is the food of our soul. It is He who sustains us. Let our minds dwell on the goodness of the Lord. But, be warned, we can be taken by surprise and the enemy can cause wrath and pain at the hands of others. It is not enough to be vigilant. If wounded we must be willing to forgive. Hate, resentment, and anger tie us to the past. God does not live in the past, only in the present.

We know we must forgive and forget, yet, at times it is not so easy. If there are issues to be addressed through counseling, please refer to my previous book, <u>Christian Counseling: Healing the Tribes of Man.</u> For now let us examine the spiritual side of forgiveness. It is a matter of trust in God and His plan. In the story of Joseph, son of Jacob, we see a young boy whose brothers were full of envy and hate toward him. The brothers arranged to capture him while he was away from the protection of his father and sell him into slavery. They never heard from him again and assumed he was dead. Joseph was sold as a slave in Egypt where he ended up in the house of the Pharaoh. There he showed his character and intelligence and rose to be Pharaoh's second in command. There came a famine upon the land, which Joseph had foreseen. Joseph had prepared Pharaoh's kingdom for the event. However, his brothers were in their homeland suffering. Not knowing Joseph was alive, they came into Egypt and asked to buy food. They were brought before Joseph.

GEN 45:4 And Joseph said unto his brethren, Come near to me, I pray you. And they came near. And he said, I am Joseph your brother, whom ye sold into Egypt. 5 Now therefore be not grieved, nor angry with yourselves, that ye sold me hither: for God did send me before you to preserve life. 6 For these two years hath the famine been in

Joseph Lumpkin

the land: and yet there are five years, in the which there shall neither be earning nor harvest. 7 And God sent me before you to preserve you a posterity in the earth, and to save your lives by a great deliverance. 8 So now it was not you that sent me hither, but God: and he hath made me a father to Pharaoh, and lord of all his house, and a ruler throughout all the land of Egypt.

God will weave His plan and His will into our lives and will bring good out of the evil done to us. This kind of trust is a hard thing. It demands we replace our pain with our trust in Him. He did not say the hurt would stop, but we can be assured the evil and the pain will be used for good. As the steps of a righteous man are ordered by the Lord, so the outcome of evil and pain inflicted on him also is guided by God. Why does God not prevent the fool from hurting the righteous man? Because even the fool has free will to be foolish, else how could they be saved by their faith?

REGRET, GUILT and SHAME

Regret is emotionally looking back over your shoulder. How can you clearly see your destination when you keep your sight behind you?

Regret: mental sorrow or concern for anything, as for past conduct or negligence: remorse: to remember with sorrow: to bewail the loss or want of. Webster's New School and Office Dictionary

Guilt: the state of being liable to a penalty; sin; criminality. Webster's New School and Office Dictionary

Shame: a painful sensation caused by a sense of guilt, impropriety, or dishonor; cover with disgrace. Webster's New School and Office Dictionary

Unlike guilt, regret may be more focused on what we have not done. The base issue however, may be a lack of belief God is guiding our path. The path we chose may be good and profitable, but the one we did not choose could have been glorious… or deadly. The path we walk may be filled with trials but there is a sense that we are where we need to be. It is impossible to know what decision is best since we can't walk two paths at once. We may be on a path now we do not like, but it has lessons in it no other path would have. Wherever we are, in heaven or in the belly of hell, God is there. He is with us.

Regret comes from not being satisfied with things as they are. Regret is second-guessing yourself or God. Regret comes from an unsettling feeling that we are not where we need to be. It can be tied to guilt very closely if regret is focused on a past sin or wrong done by you. So often we do things and wish we could take them back. Not to have these feelings shows us to be without conscience. To harbor these feelings of the past robs our lives of God's plans now. Regret is wishing things could have been different, ignoring the grace of today.

Even if our ways are difficult today it does not mean God isn't with us. Even if there is failure, it does not mean the Lord does not order, permit, or arrange the lessons learned. He sends us to school as we send our children to schools. Lessons along the way are instructions to the soul. We must trust God is guiding us. Even if we have disobeyed God and taken paths which we were not intended to take, the grace of God will cause the path we are on to converge with the right one somewhere down the road. Things may not be exactly as they would have, had we not diverged, but in God's grace our mission can be fulfilled. Even if we have ultimate faith God will guide our steps, it does not mean we should passively wait for indecision to overtake us and have fate force us onto a path not of our choosing. If we choose not to choose or not to act we are letting the river of life sweep us downstream and wash us up on its shore, as it will. We must have courage, listen to God's voice, or feel His hand guide us then take that course. God does not guide passively. Passivity is guided by fear.

Regret is looking back on those missteps, which can make us miss God-given opportunities in the present. Regret can be avoided by having course, commitment, and trust. It is up to God to make His path known. It is up to us to take it. We make the best choice we can based on seeking God's will. We commit fully to the path. We trust it will lead us to the place God would have us be.

LUK 9:62 *And Jesus said unto him, No man, having put his hand to the plough, and looking back, is fit for the kingdom of God.*

PSA 37:23 *The steps of a good man are ordered by the LORD: and he delighteth in his way. 24 Though he falls, he shall not be utterly cast down: for the LORD upholdeth him with his hand. 25 I have been young, and now am old; yet have I not seen the righteous forsaken, nor his seed begging bread. 26 He is ever merciful, and lendeth; and his seed is blessed.*

2SA 23:3 *The God of Israel said, the Rock of Israel spake to me, He that ruleth over men must be just, ruling in the fear of God. 4 And he shall be as the light of the morning, when the sun riseth, even a morning without clouds; as the tender grass springing out of the earth by clear shining after rain. 5 Although my house be not so with God; yet he hath made with me an everlasting covenant, ordered in all things, and sure: for this is all my salvation, and all my desire, although he make it not to grow.*

Wherever we are, we must keep our vision. To walk a path there must be two things kept in sight at all times; where we are and where we are going. Where we are includes the immediate obstacles, the tangles and briars at our feet, and what it will take to make the next step. Where we are going is our destination. This is the heart of God, His love, His Son, His way.

PRO 29:18 Where there is no vision, the people perish: but he that keepeth the law, happy is he.

No greater restraints exist on our journey to God's heart than those of guilt and shame.

For me, guilt was the great wall, the cement in my shoes, and the handcuffs around my heart. Not just an emotional but also an actual physical ailment keeping me from faith and grace. I simply cannot condense guilt to words. An impossible task. A nearly impossible burden to put down. My guilt was all wrapped up in the fact that my church hurt me very badly as a child and a young person. I may have actually felt more than just anger towards the church. In my mind, I transferred that anger to God. It was the only thing I knew to do at the time, I believe it was the way my subconscious or even my conscious mind tried to protect me from any more pain and disillusionment. So over the years the anger and guilt surrounded me. It became comfortable. If I didn't feel the love of God, I would not feel the hurt and disappointment when God let me down - after all, my church let me down and God was my church. Wasn't He? Joyce Dujardin

At times, guilt and shame can be used as weapons of control by church, family, and others. It is not that we should not feel guilt, but that we should not be controlled or beaten down by it. Guilt heaped on us by others, if accepted, cannot be relieved until the other releases us. This is a fine line since we have the scriptures to guide us and they tell us how to approach others who are in sin. We are not to harp on their sin but to come to them at most three times to turn them away from their sin and back to God. We should be careful not to be enticed by our association into their sin.

If you take a dirty cloth and a clean cloth and rub them together, the clean cloth will always get dirty, but the dirty cloth will never come clean. Be careful with whom you associate. W.R. Lumpkin

Guilt, kept in play, will damage the soul. Guilt is about what you do, but shame is about what you are. Guilt can become shame if the person is not allowed to escape the feeling imposed on him by others. This is because when we have repented, corrected course, and changed our ways but still we have guilt heaped on us, we will eventually assume the error is not in what we did but in who or what we are. When this happens we have crossed the line between guilt and shame. Shame is the most destructive of forces. Our shame caused the death of Christ. It is because of what we are He had to die.

PSA 69:6 Let not them that wait on thee, O Lord GOD of hosts, be ashamed for my sake: let not those that seek thee be confounded for my sake, O God of Israel. 7 Because for thy sake I have borne reproach; shame hath covered my face.

PSA 69:19 Thou hast known my reproach, and my shame, and my dishonour: mine adversaries are all before thee. 20 Reproach hath broken my heart; and I am full of heaviness: and I looked for some to take pity, but there was none; and for comforters, but I found none. 21 They gave me also gall for my meat; and in my thirst they gave me vinegar to drink.

I must repeat: Guilt is about what we do, but shame is about what we are.

Shame is our condition, but we have no right to put shame on others. Our only right is to know it in ourselves and to understand Christ came that we may be free of shame.

We may be guilty of doing something wrong. This is sin and we are all sinners. We CANNOT bring shame upon another. This would be breaking the only laws Christ commanded us to do; love one another as ourselves. So many of us have been taught we are bad people. This is different from people doing bad things. Indeed, we were bad people before Christ came to free us of ourselves. Our state is still sinful, but no one is more sinful than any other. In this light we shall bring judgment into our lives as we shame another.

MAT 7:1 Judge not, that ye be not judged. 2 For with what judgment ye judge, ye shall be judged: and with what measure ye mete, it shall be measured to you again. 3 And why beholdest thou the mote that is in thy brother's eye, but considerest not the beam that is in thine own eye? 4 Or how wilt thou say to thy brother, Let me pull out the mote out of thine eye; and, behold, a beam is in thine own eye? 5 Thou hypocrite, first cast out the beam out of thine own eye; and then shalt thou see clearly to cast out the mote out of thy brother's eye.

Shame destroys people, for we cannot be free of ourselves. Only Christ can set us free and only He has a right to reveal our shame. We may be guilty of sin but when the sin stops and is confessed the guilt is gone. If there is shame how can we help or correct it? Shame will be forever or until Christ reveals to the shameful ones His love and shows them their own worth in Him. Guilt is about deeds. Shame is about worth. Shame makes us feel unworthy of God's grace to the point we may refuse His salvation. This is why shame is so terrible. The love of Christ overcomes shame by showing us we are capable of being loved by God Himself. That is, if we allow Him into our hearts.

God will deal with any church, minister, counselor, or parent who has used shame to diminish or control a child or member accordingly. If you are controlled by shame you must understand we are all the same sinful creatures and no person is worth more in God's eyes than you are right now. You have complete love and worth in God's eyes, so much so that He would have come and died for you and you alone. If the entire world rejects Him and is damned, He still comes for you.

Christ forgives and forgiveness relieves guilt. Christ transforms us, and this removes shame.

Joseph Lumpkin

CONDEMNATION, CONVICTION, and JUDGING

One can be convicted without being condemned. Conviction is to be found guilty of a crime or a sin. We are all sinners yet some do not feel convicted. When the Spirit of God reveals to us our shortcomings and our faults we are convicted of them, yet we are not condemned. This is because Christ did not come to condemn us but to save us.

JOH 3:17 *For God sent not his Son into the world to condemn the world; but that the world through him might be saved. 18 He that believeth on him is not condemned: but he that believeth not is condemned already, because he hath not believed in the name of the only begotten Son of God. 19 And this is the condemnation, that light is come into the world, and men loved darkness rather than light, because their deeds were evil.*

Punishment and darkness is what we will suffer for heaping condemnation on someone else. It is not our place to condemn, only His. Christ is the great judge of all. He will judge and He will convict. If the price of sin has not been paid by believing in Him, then He will condemn. A person's standing with God is not ours to know. We cannot condemn. We cannot convict. We cannot judge the hearts of others.

JOB 21:22 *Shall any teach God knowledge? seeing he judgeth those that are high.*

JOH 5:22 *For the Father judgeth no man, but hath committed all judgment unto the Son:*

1CO 4:4 *For I know nothing by myself; yet am I not hereby justified: but he that judgeth me is the Lord. 5 Therefore judge nothing before the time, until the Lord come, who both will bring to light the hidden things of darkness, and will make manifest the counsels of the hearts: and then shall every man have praise of God.*

LUK 23:39 *And one of the malefactors which were hanged railed on him, saying, If thou be Christ, save thyself and us. 40 But the other answering rebuked him, saying, Dost not thou fear God, seeing thou art in the same condemnation?*

ROM 7:25 I thank God through Jesus Christ our Lord. So then with the mind I myself serve the law of God; but with the flesh the law of sin. 8:1 There is therefore now no condemnation to them which are in Christ Jesus, who walk not after the flesh, but after the Spirit.

JAM 4:11 Speak not evil one of another, brethren. He that speaketh evil of his brother, and judgeth his brother, speaketh evil of the law, and judgeth the law: but if thou judge the law, thou art not a doer of the law, but a judge. 12 There is one lawgiver, who is able to save and to destroy: who art thou that judgest another?

To be convicted of our sins by the Spirit of God is the beginning of grace. It is in this one premier act God draws us to Him. Seeing the truth about ourselves and the need for a redeemer is the first act of freedom. God wishes to forgive us and bring us into a relationship with Him rather than condemn us. Conviction may be painful but it is an act of grace that will save us from condemnation.

JOH 8:3 And the scribes and Pharisees brought unto him a woman taken in adultery; and when they had set her in the midst, 4 They say unto him, Master, this woman was taken in adultery, in the very act. 5 Now Moses in the law commanded us, that such should be stoned: but what sayest thou? 6 this they said, tempting him, that they might have to accuse him. But Jesus stooped down, and with his finger wrote on the ground, as though he heard them not. 7 So when they continued asking him, he lifted up himself, and said unto them, He that is without sin among you, let him first cast a stone at her. 8 And again he stooped down, and wrote on the ground. 9 And they which heard it, being convicted by their own conscience, went out one by one, beginning at the eldest, even unto the last: and Jesus was left alone, and the woman standing in the midst. 10 When Jesus had lifted up himself, and saw none but the woman, he said unto her, Woman, where are those thine accusers? hath no man condemned thee? 11 She said, No man, Lord. And Jesus said unto her, Neither do I condemn thee: go, and sin no more. 12 Then spake Jesus again unto them, saying, I am the light of the world: he that followeth me shall not walk in darkness, but shall have the light of life.

Joseph Lumpkin

BEING BOUND TOGETHER WITH GOD

Bind us together, Lord. Bind us together with cords that can not be broken. From a spiritual song

ROM 8:38 *For I am persuaded, that neither death, nor life, nor angels, nor principalities, nor powers, nor things present, nor things to come, 39 Nor height, nor depth, nor any other creature, shall be able to separate us from the love of God, which is in Christ Jesus our Lord.*

The eyes of my soul were opened, and I beheld the plenitude of God, wherein I did comprehend the whole world, both here and beyond the sea, and the abyss, and the ocean, and all things. In all these things I beheld naught save the Divine power, in a matter assuredly indescribable; so that through excess of marveling the soul cried with a loud voice, saying, "this whole world is full of God!" .... Angela of Floigno

Yet the creature does not become God, for the union takes place in God through Grace and our homeward turning love: and therefore the creature in its inward contemplation feels the distinction and the otherness between itself in God.   John Ruusbroec

Three parts of the Christian life, Worship, Study, and Prayer (communion) keep us in touch with God. Three strands making up the cord that ties us to God and keep us reaching upward to Him. They are Love, Praise, and Gratitude.

Worship is to seek and know the worth of God. What is He worth? What a strange question, you may say, but the answer underlies our actions. Is He worthy of praise? Is He worthy of our obedience? How about our study, prayers, love, gratitude... Are these areas in balance? One can love someone and not care to be with him. One can commune with someone and not love him. One can be grateful to a stranger. We can praise the actions of someone when we do not know their character. To get to know God we have Worship, Study, and Prayer. To come into His presence we have Love, Praise, and Gratitude. When all three of these attributes are brought to bear in one relationship there is fullness and joy.

Out of the three, gratitude is the most overlooked. In our world we arrogantly presume our looks, intelligence, strength, or cunning are the reasons we have success, house, car, job, health, or position. We are fools. Without thankfulness we come to believe we sustain ourselves by our own hands. What we have and what we believe we deserve takes on larger proportions and greater value than they should. We come to worship the things of this world more than the maker of all things.

ROM 1:21 Because that, when they knew God, they glorified him not as God, neither were thankful; but became vain in their imaginations, and their foolish heart was darkened. 22 Professing themselves to be wise, they became fools, 23 And changed the glory of the uncorruptible God into an image made like to corruptible man, and to birds, and four footed beasts, and creeping things.

For man, from the beginning of his creation, had been entrusted with the reins of his own volitions, with unrestricted movement towards his every desire; for the Deity is free and man had been formed after Him. (The Image of God in Man According to Cyril of Alexandria)

But, with a heart open and grateful to God we have joy and an enduring relationship.

PSA 100:2 Serve the LORD with gladness: come before his presence with singing. 3 Know ye that the LORD he is God: it is he that hath made us, and not we ourselves; we are his people, and the sheep of his pasture. 4 Enter into his gates with thanksgiving, and into his courts with praise: be thankful unto him, and bless his name. 5 For the LORD is good; his mercy is everlasting; and his truth endureth to all generations. 101:1 I will sing of mercy and judgment: unto thee, O LORD, will I sing.

Out of gratitude and love springs charity. Charity flies forth from a heart filled with thankfulness and gratitude. All things are seen, as they are, a gift from God. We clearly see His love for us. Our hearts are joyous as we share God's gifts to us with others. Charity is the result of gratitude to God and God's love in us toward our fellow man.

COL 3:14 And above all these things put on charity, which is the bond of perfectness. 15 And let the peace of God rule in your hearts, to the which also ye are called in one body; and be ye thankful.

1 COR 13:13 And now abideth faith, hope, charity, these three; but the greatest of these is charity.

What is the secret of finding the treasure? There isn't one. The treasure is everywhere. It is offered to us at every moment and wherever we can find ourselves. (In) All creatures, friends or enemies, for it is ours abundantly, and it courses through every fiber of our body and soul until it reaches the very core of our being. If we open our mouths they will be filled. Jean Pierre Caussadede

Fickle and forgetful is man that he would trip over the truth, or through grace fall headlong into it, and then rush off, forgetting all he had seen, learned, and felt in his deepest part. Not being reminded of the epiphany daily, man creeps into a mode of doubt and counts all of his communion and time with God as the dross of dreams and imaginings. In the dark nights of the soul, it is not knowledge that keeps us alive. It is faith, unshakable and tenacious. Faith trusts God is still there even if He cannot be seen. Faith knows God is there even if He cannot be felt. Faith sees the sun in the midst of night and faith waits for Joy cometh in the morning. Do you have knowledge of this faith? Is your heart fixed on God? Then the bridegroom will come and we will be one, transformed and conformed, we will be one.

PSA 57:7 My heart is fixed, O God, my heart is fixed: I will sing and give praise. 8 Awake up, my glory; awake, psaltery and harp: I myself will awake early. 9 I will praise thee, O Lord, among the people: I will sing unto thee among the nations. 10 For thy mercy is great unto the heavens, and thy truth unto the clouds. 11 Be thou exalted, O God, above the heavens: let thy glory be above all the earth.

But what passes in the union of the Spiritual Marriage is very different. The Lord appears in the centre of the soul, not through an imaginary, but through an intellectual vision …, just as He appeared to the Apostles, without entering through the door, when He said to them: "Pax vobis" (peace be unto you) the soul, I mean the spirit of this soul, is made one with God, Who, being likewise a Spirit, has been pleased to reveal the love that He has for us by showing to certain persons the extent of that love, so that we may praise His greatness.

For He has been pleased to unite Himself with His creature in such a way that they have become like two who cannot be separated from one another: even so He will not separate Himself from her.   Teresa of Avila

... it must not be thought that the faculties and senses and passions are always in this state of peace, though the soul itself is. In the other Mansions *(i.e. those mansions which are exterior to the central one in which the soul now dwells)* there are always times of conflict and trial and weariness, but they are not of such a kind as to rob the soul of its peace and stability -- at least, not as a rule. ...for it is difficult to understand how the soul can have trials and afflictions and yet be in peace... Teresa of Avila

... in this temple of God, in this Mansion of His, he and the soul alone have fruition of each other in the deepest silence. There is no reason now for the understanding to stir, or to seek out anything, for the Lord Who created the soul is now pleased to calm it and would have it look, as it were, through a little chink, at what is passing. Now and then it loses sight of it and is unable to see anything; but this is only for a very brief time   Teresa of Avila

And I am quite dazed myself when I observe that, on reaching this state, the soul has no more raptures (accompanied, that is to say, by the suspension of the senses), save very occasionally, and even then it has not the same transports and flights of the spirit. These raptures, too, happen only rarely, and hardly ever in public as they very often did before. Nor have they any connection, as they had before, with great occasions of devotion... Teresa of Avila

It is the nature of the Holy Spirit that I should be consumed in him, dissolved in him, and transformed wholly into love. ... God does not enter those who are freed from all otherness and all createdness: rather he already exits in an essential manner within them... Meister Eckhart

God is always near you and with you; leave Him not alone. ...I continued some years, applying my mind carefully the rest of the day, and even in the midst of my business, *to the presence of God,* whom I considered always *with* me, often *in* me. Brother Lawrence

... And the latter (union) comes to pass when the two wills -- namely that of the soul and that of God -- are conformed together in one, and there is naught in the one that is repugnant to the other. And thus, when the soul rids itself totally of that which is repugnant to the Divine will and conforms not with it, it is transformed in God through love.   Saint John of the Cross

In thus allowing God to work in it, the soul ... is at once illumined and transformed in God, and God communicates to it His supernatural Being, in such wise that it appears to be God Himself, and has all that God Himself has. And this union comes to pass when God grants the soul this supernatural favour, that all the things of God and the soul are one in participant transformation; and the soul seems to be God rather than a soul, and is indeed God by participation; although it is true that its natural being, though thus transformed, is as distinct from the Being of God as it was before... Saint John of the Cross

JOH 14:18 I will not leave you comfortless: I will come to you. 19 Yet a little while, and the world seeth me no more; but ye see me: because I live, ye shall live also. 20 At that day ye shall know that I am in my Father, and ye in me, and I in you. 21 He that hath my commandments, and keepeth them, he it is that loveth me: and he that loveth me shall be loved of my Father, and I will love him, and will manifest myself to him.

JOH 15:4 Abide in me, and I in you. As the branch cannot bear fruit of itself, except it abide in the vine; no more can ye, except ye abide in me. 5 I am the vine, ye are the branches: He that abideth in me, and I in him, the same bringeth forth much fruit: for without me ye can do nothing.

To abide in the one we love, what bliss this is. In the sense of husband and wife and as lover and beloved, to be in the presence of the one whom your soul loves heals and extends the soul. It fills and fulfills the soul and by this there is no more need for expressions of ecstasy because ecstasy is here. Expressions of ecstasy come as we are reaching for or entering it. When there, we become quiet and peaceful, wanting nothing more than to remain. To stay, to look upon the face of the beloved, to remain in the embrace, being bound together with God brings peace passing all understanding.

GOD, WORSHIP AND OBEDIENCE

As the world becomes more sophisticated man tends to rely on his own understanding, as limited as it may be. We invent doctrine to suit our needs and aims, as well as our preconceived ideas. In this environment, threads and smatterings of Christianity, Eastern religions, new age, and ancient beliefs mix into a stew of nonsense. One of the main beliefs to rear its old head is pantheism, the belief God is in all things and is all things. Out of this religious structure one concludes God is an all-invasive and ever-present energy. It is surprising how many Christians lean toward this conclusion.

If God is everything one can easily make the leap of logic that God is energy. He or his creations would exist as patterns of energy. Energy has no mind, no likes, no dislikes, no goals, no ability to decide, no conscience, and no love. In this world, God would not care. There would be no need to worship God since He would have no mind to care or appreciate our actions. There would be no need for obedience to the will of God since He would have no will. We would only have to worry about understanding the pattern and flow of the energy in order to use it correctly, for good or evil. Thus God becomes the same as electricity or a split atom. For maximum results, we would not want to go against the energy, whatever we would define it to be. There would be no sin because there would be no rule or opinion from God to miss or dismiss.

Pantheism makes no distinctions between the creature and the creator. They are the same. Thus God is lowered to the level of the lowest of creatures and the creature raised to the status of God. For how can God be divisible? Like water, any part of God would have the same nature as the whole. Any portion of an infinite has infinity within it. How then can we say this twig or that worm, which are without thought and love, can be God? If, however, God had just one thought, one wish, one desire, or one preference, the framework of pantheism would come tumbling down, and with it, disobedience and sin would come into being.

Joseph Lumpkin

A PLACE TO PLACE THE MIND

Thoughts, Actions, and Submission

I am not engaged to Christianity by decent forms, or saving ordinances; it is not usage, it is not what I do not understand, that binds me to it -- let these be the sandy foundations of falsehoods. What I revere and obey in it is its reality, its boundless charity, its deep interior life, the rest it gives to my mind, the echo it returns to my thoughts, the perfect accord it makes with my reason through all its representation of God and His Providence; and the persuasion and courage that come out thence to lead me upward and onward.

RALPH WALDO EMERSON, sermon, Sept. 9, 1832

1TI 4:13 Till I come, give attendance to reading, to exhortation, to doctrine. 14 Neglect not the gift that is in thee, which was given thee by prophecy, with the laying on of the hands of the presbytery. 15 Meditate upon these things; give thyself wholly to them; that thy profiting may appear to all.

PSA 63:6 When I remember thee upon my bed, and meditate on thee in the night watches. 7 Because thou hast been my help, therefore in the shadow of thy wings will I rejoice. 8 My soul followeth hard after thee: thy right hand upholdeth me.

PSA 77:12 I will meditate also of all thy work, and talk of thy doings. 13 Thy way, O God, is in the sanctuary: who is so great a God as our God? 14 Thou art the God that doest wonders: thou hast declared thy strength among the people.

At first glance, there is no difference between the meditation techniques of the Zen Buddhist masters and those of the Christian mystics. Both demand the mind be still, quiet, and focused. Both demand we lose ourselves. Both demand patience and dedication. However, there is a great distinction between the two as to where the mind is placed. The teaching of the Eastern mystics directs the student to "go within", "empty themselves", and "center the mind". Concentrate on the center of the body or on the breath. First there is focus on sound or breath, then on the center where the breath arrives, and then even that disappears into nothingness until nothing is left, not even the self; not even nothingness. The students reach inside until in the depth all disappears into all and into nothingness.

For the Christian mystic, enlightenment is not some static state of oneness, as it is to the Eastern mystic. Instead, it is an ongoing and ever-changing, living relationship between God and man. As it is in any healthy relationship we attempt to learn from and take into ourselves the better part from the other. Thus God as both father and beloved leads us, guides us, and teaches us. It is not only the mind, but the heart itself, which is focused on God. We do not seek to disappear but we seek union with Him who is the creator of all, both Him, and us together as lover and beloved. It is a great and total difference between seeking nothingness and seeking God's presence.

It is important to still the mind and stop the chaotic ramblings of thoughts so we may be fully attentive to God. We may find it necessary to implement techniques, which will help us clear and fully focus our minds. This is where the two mystical communities of East and West break. The Christian mystics use the same centering techniques of breath and sound to still and center the mind but the sound is a prayer or word that is meaningful to us in our relationship to God.

After the mind is brought under submission there is a great difference in what happens next. The Eastern mystic focuses the mind inward or more specifically on nothing, while the Christian mystic begins to reach toward the heart of God. There is a blinding yearning to be one with the spirit of God. It is a longing greater than life. Our heart is a room, a temple built for Him. We are waiting for the guest. It is the longing that does the work. We empty out our ideas of God and of ourselves. We want God to be who He is, not what we think He is. We want His fullness, not our limited idea of His fullness. No idea or imaginings can contain even the slightest portion of Him.

We reach for the Spirit without shape or form. We open the gates of our heart wide in anticipation of the arrival of the beloved. We keep the flame of our heart lit and burning, as one would light a candle to bid someone we love to enter. We wait. We wait. We wait and we reach. We reach until we find our limit. We reach until we find our hearts held down and captive under the cloud that separates us from God. It is then we begin to beat against the cloud with all of the ferocity of a lover held inside a room, away from the beloved, against their will. We have reached as high as we can reach. Like a child who holds up his arms for his father, we wait for God to come, reach down, and pick us up. We wait to be gathered into His arms.

Christian Contemplative Prayer is the opening of mind, heart, and soul to God. It is beyond thoughts and words. It is bringing God in us closer than thinking and feeling. The root of all prayer is interior silence. Only mundane and common prayer is of thoughts or feelings expressed in words. Contemplative Prayer is a prayer of silence, an experience of God's presence in us and we in Him. It is experiencing God which transcends the study of Him. Love is an experience.

SON 1:13 A bundle of myrrh is my well-beloved unto me; he shall lie all night betwixt my breasts. 14 My beloved is unto me as a cluster of campfire in the vineyards of Engedi. 15 Behold, thou art fair, my love; behold, thou art fair; thou hast doves' eyes. 16 Behold, thou art fair, my beloved, yea, pleasant: also our bed is green. 17 The beams of our house are cedar, and our rafters of fir. 2:1 I am the rose of Sharon, and the lily of the valleys. 2 As the lily among thorns, so is my love among the daughters. 3 As the apple tree among the trees of the wood, so is my beloved among the sons. I sat down under his shadow with great delight, and his fruit was sweet to my taste. 4 He brought me to the banqueting house, and his banner over me was love. 5 Stay me with flagons, comfort me with apples: for I am sick of love. 6 His left hand is under my head, and his right hand doth embrace me. 7 I charge you, O ye daughters of Jerusalem, by the roes, and by the hinds of the field, that ye stir not up, nor awake my love, till he please. 8 The voice of my beloved! behold, he cometh leaping upon the mountains, skipping upon the hills. 9 My beloved is like a roe or a young hart: behold, he standeth behind our wall, he looketh forth at the windows, shewing himself through the lattice. 10 My beloved spake, and said unto me, Rise up, my love, my fair one, and come away. SON 2:11 For, lo, the winter is past, the rain is over and gone; 12 The flowers appear on the earth; the time of the singing of birds is come, and the voice of the turtle is heard in our land; 13 The fig tree putteth forth her green figs, and the vines with the tender grape give a good smell. Arise, my love, my fair one, and come away. 14 O my dove, that art in the clefts of the rock, in the secret places of the stairs, let me see thy countenance, let me hear thy voice; for sweet is thy voice, and thy countenance is comely.

He is illusive. Our God, our lover, entices us to higher levels as we run after Him, seeking Him. We must keep Him in our hearts day and night. When we sleep He is our breath and the beating of our hearts. When awake we are ever watchful. With every fiber of our being we anticipate our next encounter. We wait and our hearts long for Him. The longing draws us to Him.

SON 3:1 By night on my bed I sought him whom my soul loveth: I sought him, but I found him not. 2 I will rise now, and go about the city in the streets, and in the broad ways I will seek him whom my soul loveth: I sought him, but I found him not. 3 The watchmen that go about the city found me: to whom I said, Saw ye him whom my soul loveth? 4 It was but a little that I passed from them, but I found him whom my soul loveth: I held him, and would not let him go, until I had brought him into my mother's house, and into the chamber of her that conceived me.

We do not turn our minds off, nor do we seek to disappear into nothingness as the Eastern mystics do. We seek Christ, the beloved. We still our hearts and minds to listen for rustle of His footsteps. We sit quietly, yearning for His approach, His breath upon our face, His fragrance as He enters the room, the mist we see covering His presence, the thin blue mist that surrounds Him. Our minds are turned outward to Him. The more quiet our hearts and minds, the sooner we will recognize Him whom we seek.

The pursuit of God will embrace the labor of bringing our total personality into conformity to His. I do not here refer to the act of justification by faith in Christ. I speak of a voluntary exalting of God to His proper station over us and a willing surrender of our whole being to the place of worshipful submission, which the Creator-creature circumstance makes proper... Let no one imagine that he will lose anything of human dignity by this voluntary sell-out of his all to his God. He does not by this degrade himself as a man; rather he finds his right place of high honor as one made in the image of his Creator. His deep disgrace lay in his moral derangement, his unnatural usurpation of the place of God. His honor will be proved by restoring again that stolen throne. In exalting God over all, he finds his own highest honor upheld...We must of necessity be servant to someone, either to God or to sin. The sinner prides himself on his independence, completely overlooking the fact that he is the weak slave of the sins that rule his members. The man who surrenders to Christ exchanges a cruel slave driver for a kind and gentle Master whose yoke is easy and whose burden is light. A. W. Tozer

Joseph Lumpkin

TO STILL THE MIND

Let the remembrance of Jesus be present with your every breath. Then indeed you will appreciate the value stillness.   John Climacus

As we begin our time of meditation and prayer we must be careful. We must first still and focus the mind. This first stage, called centering, is somewhat like techniques used in Eastern mysticism. However, objects or words used in our Christian technique should be kept completely Christ centered in their representation. As we sit in meditation and prayer, many times we find our minds in turmoil, with thoughts chasing themselves like a pack of monkeys. We must first have a way of clearing the mind of such thrashing. Before we can pray clearly we must be able to think clearly. Before we can think clearly we must stop the mind from running amok. Even in this preliminary stage of centering it takes about twenty minutes to still the mind.

Excerpts from "Five Types of Thought: By Father Thomas Keating

The most obvious thoughts are superficial ones the imagination grinds out because of its natural propensity for perpetual motion. It is important just to accept them and not pay any undue attention to them…. Sometimes they reach a point where they don't hear it at all…

The second kind of thought occurs when you get interested in something that is happening…This is the kind of thought that calls for some "reaction."… It is important not to be annoyed with yourself if you get involved with these interesting thoughts. Any annoyance that you give in to is another thought, and will take you farther away from the interior silence…

A third kind of thought arises as we sink into deep peace and interior silence. What seem to be brilliant theological insights and marvelous psychological breakthroughs, like tasty bait, are dangled in front of our mind's eye… If you acquiesce to a thought of this nature long enough to fix it in your memory you will be drawn out of the deep, refreshing waters of interior silence.

As you settle into deep peace and freedom from particular thoughts, a desire to reflect on what is happening may arise. You may think, "At last I am getting some place!" or "This feeling is just great... If you let go, you go into deeper interior silence. If you reflect, you come out and have to start over.... As soon as you start to "reflect" on an experience, it is over...The presence of God is like the air we breathe. You can have all you want of it as long as you do not try to take possession of it and hang on to it.

Any form of meditation or prayer that transcends thinking sets off the dynamic of interior purification....one may feel intense anger, sorrow or fear without any relation to the recent past. Once again, the best way to handle them is to return to the sacred word.

Once you grasp the fact that thoughts are not only inevitable, but an integral part of the process of healing and growth initiated by God, you are able to take a positive view of them. Instead of looking at them as painful distractions... Five Types of Thought: By Father Thomas Keating

It is not that we take a "positive approach to the unwanted and noisy thoughts, but we will acquire a passive approach to them. We will learn to dismiss them like twigs on the trail. We will keep walking without as much as noticing them.

...the mind should retire into itself, and recall its powers from sensible things, in order to hold pure communion with God, and be clearly illumined by the flashing rays of the Spirit, with no admixture or disturbance of the divine light by anything earthly or clouded, until we come to the source of the effulgence which we enjoy here, and regret and desire are alike stayed, when our mirrors pass away in the light of truth. Gregory of Nazianzus

TO QUIET THE MIND

Before we begin the first steps of meditation we must find a comfortable and undisturbed place. Sit quietly. Close your eyes and relax. Find in your heart a sacred word. In your heart and soul it must have a direct connection with Christ. Let the word be something special to you. Let it be grace, peace, love, hope, charity, or some word that connects you with Christ himself. Or, you may pick out some sacred object such as a cross or painting which you know will draw your heart to Him. Focus your mind and your heart upon this sacred word or object. Do not let it waiver and do not let it go.

It is common that after only a matter of moments your mind will start to wander. You'll find your focus lost, and your mind chasing itself and swirling like a storm. Your thoughts will become scattered and chaotic. Do not fret and do not worry, this is very common. It is the first obstacle to overcome in order to fully pray and meditate upon Him. God waits on the other side of chaos in our minds and hearts. This is the first step in the process of stripping away all of those things that stand in the way between our Lord and ourselves. The mind will protest and complain. It is like a stubborn mule which strains and complains against the bridle. But bridle our minds we must. It will take infinite time and patience simply to learn to quiet and control our minds so that we can pray and meditate wholly on Him.

Why does this little prayer of one syllable pierce the heavens? Surely, because it is offered with a full spirit, in the height and the depth, in the length and the breadth of the spirit of the one who prays. In the height: that is with the full might of the spirit; in the depth: for in this little syllable all the faculties of the spirit are contained; in the length: because if it could always be experienced as it is in that moment, it would cry as it does then; in the breadth: because it desires for all others all that it desires for itself.... St. John of the Cross

There are only two things in existence, the creator and created. As our minds become more still and quiet we must continually push out all of the things that try to enter in. We must allow room only for God in our hearts and minds. Whether it is height, depth, blackness, emptiness, or nothingness itself, all things but God must be pushed out of the mind and heart.

These two things that exist -- God and creation are all there is in the universe. Everything that is not God is creation. If we empty our minds and hearts of everything created what is left will be God.

As we focus our minds' eye sharply on the attributes of the ineffable Godhead, we see it as existing beyond everything created. God transcending all intellect, and all beings and is wholly outside any imagined appearance, knowledge and wisdom. "dwelling in light unapproachable."

...it is the easiest exercise of all and most readily accomplished when a soul is helped by grace in this felt desire; otherwise, it would be extraordinarily difficult for you to make this exercise. Do not hang back then, but labour in it until you experience the desire. For when you first begin to undertake it, all that you find is a darkness, a sort of cloud of unknowing; you cannot tell what it is, except that you experience in your will a simple reaching out to God [a naked intent unto God]. This darkness and cloud is always between you and your God, no matter what you do, and it prevents you from seeing him clearly by the light of understanding in your reason, and from experiencing him in sweetness of love in your affection. So set yourself to rest in this darkness as long as you can, always crying out after him whom you love. For if you are to experience him or to see him at all, insofar as it is possible here, it must always be in this cloud and in this darkness. Excerpts from The Cloud of Unknowing (James Walsh trans., New York : Paulist Press, 1981)

God is light unapproachable. We cannot gaze on him. We see *"in a glass darkly and know in part" (1 Cor 13:12)*. Deity, God, the Godhead then, is wholly incorporeal, without dimensions or size and not bounded by shape nor perturbed by them.

ROM 8:38 *For I am persuaded, that neither death, nor life, nor angels, nor principalities, nor powers, nor things present, nor things to come, 39 Nor height, nor depth, nor any other creature, shall be able to separate us from the love of God, which is in Christ Jesus our Lord.*

1 TI 6:16 *Who only hath immortality, dwelling in the light which no man can approach unto; whom no man hath seen, nor can see: to whom be honour and power everlasting. Amen.*

1 COR 13:12 *For now we see through a glass, darkly; but then face to face: now I know in part; but then shall I know even as also I am known.*

PHI 3:6 Concerning zeal, persecuting the church; touching the righteousness which is in the law, blameless.7 But what things were gain to me, those I counted loss for Christ. 8 Yea doubtless, and I count all things but loss for the excellence of the knowledge of Christ Jesus my Lord: for whom I have suffered the loss of all things, and do count them but dung, that I may win Christ, 9 And be found in him, not having mine own righteousness, which is of the law, but that which is through the faith of Christ, the righteousness which is of God by faith: 10 That I may know him, and the power of his resurrection, and the fellowship of his sufferings, being made conformable unto his death; 11 If by any means I might attain unto the resurrection of the dead.

Never let the heart cease its cry. Never let it cease its reach for its creator. Day after day this process must be repeated. As we become accustomed to this toil of forgetting all things created, we must continually reach for God with our hearts with every breath we take. Knocking, no, pounding with our heart's cry on the door that stands between God and us. This is called praying without ceasing. Because there is a separation between God and us, it is a great mystery and paradox. Even though He is with us and in us, there stands a veil of "unknowing" whose only key is grace and only door is faith. God himself must lift the veil as He wills.

1TH 5:16 Rejoice evermore. 17 Pray without ceasing. 18 In every thing give thanks: for this is the will of God in Christ Jesus concerning you. 19 Quench not the Spirit. 20 Despise not prophesying. 21 Prove all things; hold fast that which is good. 22 Abstain from all appearance of evil. 23 And the very God of peace sanctify you wholly; and I pray God your whole spirit and soul and body be preserved blameless unto the coming of our Lord Jesus Christ.

In the inner wine cellar I drank of my beloved, and, when I went abroad through all this valley I no longer knew anything, and lost the herd which I was following. St. John of the Cross

Now I occupy my soul and all my energy is in his service. I no longer tend the herd, nor have I any other work now that my every act is love. St. John of the Cross

I want to deliberately and zealously encourage a mighty and ongoing longing for God. The lack of it has brought us to our present low estate. The stiff and wooden quality of our religious lives is a result of our lack of holy desire. Complacency is a deadly foe of all spiritual growth. Acute desire must be present or there will be no manifestation of Christ to His people. He waits to be wanted. Too bad that with many of us He waits so long, so very long, in vain. A.W. Tozer.

MYSTICISM AND RECIDIVISM

MAT 13:18 Hear ye therefore the parable of the sower. 19 When any one heareth the word of the kingdom, and understandeth it not, then cometh the wicked one, and catcheth away that which was sown in his heart. This is he which received seed by the way side. 20 But he that received the seed into stony places, the same is he that heareth the word, and anon with joy receiveth it; 21 Yet hath he not root in himself, but endureth for a while: for when tribulation or persecution ariseth because of the word, by and by he is offended. 22 He also that received seed among the thorns is he that heareth the word; and the care of this world, and the deceitfulness of riches, choke the word, and he becometh unfruitful. 23 But he that received seed into the good ground is he that heareth the word, and understandeth it; which also beareth fruit, and bringeth forth, some an hundredfold, some sixty, some thirty.

Starting a journey may be easy. Finishing is not. It takes tenacity and a unique stubbornness to complete what is started. The world has tribulations and enticements to sway us from our course. Our roots of desire for God must go deeper than our roots in the world. Although the above passage is usually related to salvation it shows the trials we will go through and has within it a warning. Many fail. Be prepared to endure and push on! Knowledge of God is not the same as acknowledging God. Accepting God in our lives is only the beginning of our journey. Many do not make it to the starting line.

They hear the word and do nothing with it. Then, there are some who receive the word of God and become saved by believing in Jesus Christ. Salvation fully equips us to meet the Lord in heaven, but now, while in this world, we must decide how high up the mountain we wish to climb. Most will start this mystical journey and grow tired of judging themselves. They will fatigue in seeking God. They will become distracted by the world. They will not endure the Dark Night of the Soul. They will hide their emptiness in the pursuits of this world. They will rest at the foot of the mountain. As for me, I wish to climb the mountain and touch the face of God. It is a costly journey. It will cost time, patience, and finally it will demand from us all we are. But, think of what we will have if we can give it all away.

Most who start this journey will repeat the same step over and over. They will begin, weary, fail, wander, come back, and begin again. Caught in the midst between the emptiness they feel and the price they think they must pay to overcome. Like a seven-day fast they abort after the first day, they will walk the same rutted road again and again. This does no good. It gets us no farther than the time before. Let us make a choice before we begin. After the journey is begun it is either mysticism or recidivism.

Joseph Lumpkin

THE DANGER OF GIFTS

We are told to abandon the exterior world and seek only God, beyond form and imagination. Like brutes, we beat against the wall as if we could make our eyes see or ears hear some eternal image or voice. Longing turns to drive and yearning to impatience as we crash headlong into our limitations. No longer do we truly wait and depend on grace. We lie to ourselves, believing we have some part in this communion apart from our praying and waiting on Him who made us. Even our communion is up to Him.

Yet, our deceitful hearts, eager to be prideful of their accomplishments, will be entrapped along the way by visions and raptures both imagined and real. If imagined, it is our minds refusal to be still and wait upon the Lord. Lying beast that it is, our mind fills in the void we seek with things of its own making. It is our hearts making us believe we have accomplished something special and worthy of pride. If the visions are real in that they do not originate within us, they serve as only signposts on a long journey. By these visions and signs we can be detoured, stopped or even regressed spiritually. Visions and signs are not God. They are only another creation. They are not the creator. The road to the temple is not the temple. The sidewalk to the temple is not the temple. The bell tolling from the temple is not the temple. The stairway is not the temple. The door is not the temple. Do not stop until you reach the temple. Do you seek God? Then dreams and visions are not what you seek. Do not let them distract you from your Lord. If it is the beloved you seek, his voice or fragrance will not do. Only his presence will quench the thirst of the soul.

...They strain themselves, as though they could possibly see inwardly with their bodily eyes and hear inwardly with their ears; and so with all their senses... The result is that the devil has power to fabricate false lights or sounds, sweet smells in their nostrils, wonderful tastes in their mouths and many other strange ardors and burnings in their bodily breasts or in their entrails... Excerpts from The Cloud of Unknowing (James Walsh trans., New York : Paulist Press, 1981)

They who are in sins, and worship the creature rather than the Creator, have their heart in some way ugly and their understanding exceedingly unsightly... (The Image of God in Man According to Cyril of Alexandria)

...God is in himself so exalted that he is beyond the reach of either knowledge or desire. Desire extends further than anything that can be grasped by knowledge. It is wider than the whole of the heavens, than all angels, even though everything that lives on earth is contained in the spark of a single angel. Desire is wide, immeasurably so. But nothing that knowledge can grasp or desire can want, is God. Where knowledge and desire end, there is darkness and there God shines.   Meister Eckhart

Such a paradox as is presented here could cause one to give up, feeling hopeless and lost. Desire will drive us to His door, but the door is locked against us. One longs for God and even the longing can keep us from Him. Desire, in itself is a detriment, driving the mind to buck and run like the mule it is. At first, we desire the Lord, seeking Him openly, but if our desire could bring Him to us we would not need grace. There must be nothing of us in this. Our communion with God is in His hands alone. We can have no control in this union except to present ourselves as a willing sacrifice.

At the point we turn it all over to His divine will, God is there, waiting for us. We realize it all depends on His grace. It is because of this paradox we have such turmoil and anguish. It is here the soul is held at a distance from God. The dark night of the soul descends upon us as we work, toil, and suffer to approach Him. Morning comes only when we give up and place even our approach to Him and union with Him in His holy hands.

ROM 11:34 For who hath known the mind of the Lord? or who hath been his counsellor? 35 Or who hath first given to him, and it shall be recompensed unto him again? 36 For of him, and through him, and to him, are all things: to whom be glory for ever. Amen. 12:1 I beseech you therefore, brethren, by the mercies of God, that ye present your bodies a living sacrifice, holy, acceptable unto God, which is your reasonable service. 2 And be not conformed to this world: but be ye transformed by the renewing of your mind, that ye may prove what is that good, and acceptable, and perfect, will of God.

PSA 123:1 Unto thee lift I up mine eyes, O thou that dwellest in the heavens. 2 Behold, as the eyes of servants look unto the hand of their masters, and as the eyes of a maiden unto the hand of her mistress; so our eyes wait upon the LORD our God, until that he have mercy upon us.

1 SA 8:17 And I will wait upon the LORD, that hideth his face from the house of Jacob, and I will look for him.

ISA 40:28 Hast thou not known? hast thou not heard, that the everlasting God, the LORD, the Creator of the ends of the earth, fainteth not, neither is weary? there is no searching of his understanding. 29 He giveth power to the faint; and to them that have no might he increaseth strength. 30 Even the youths shall faint and be weary, and the young men shall utterly fall: 31 But they that wait upon the LORD shall renew their strength; they shall mount up with wings as eagles; they shall run, and not be weary; and they shall walk, and not faint.

God is here when we are wholly unaware of it. He is manifest only when and as we are aware of His Presence. On our part there must be surrender to the Spirit of God, for His work it is to show us the Father and the Son. If we co-operate with Him in loving obedience God will manifest Himself to us, and that manifestation will be the difference between a nominal Christian life and a life radiant with the light of His face.   A. W. Tozer

IN REMEMBRANCE OF HIM

It is in the remembrance, celebration, and meditation on Christ's incarnation and act of sacrifice for mankind that many fall short. On the Body and Blood we should meditate and understand the meaning and depth of the love God has for us. The meaning of the bread and wine escapes us because the full gravity of the sacrifice escapes our secular and mundane hearts. Take, for example, a worldly token such as a dollar bill. Look at the piece of paper you hold and ask yourself what it is worth. The answer is one dollar. Yet the paper and ink are worth nothing. The dollar is the value it represents. The dollar is a symbol of that amount of worth ascribed by our government to a worthless piece of paper. Thus it is with the bread and wine of our communion. Jesus himself gave us the worth of the symbols of the bread and wine when he said:

MAT 26:26 And as they were eating, Jesus took bread, and blessed it, and brake it, and gave it to the disciples, and said, Take, eat; this is my body. 27 And he took the cup, and gave thanks, and gave it to them, saying, Drink ye all of it; 28 For this is my blood of the new testament, which is shed for many for the remission of sins. 29 But I say unto you, I will not drink henceforth of this fruit of the vine, until that day when I drink it new with you in my Father's kingdom.

It is no longer I who live but Christ who lives in me. We say this, and we read this, but we do not act as if we believe it. We do not understand until His grace floods us and possesses us. It is because we have never sought to be filled to such a degree that only He exists in us. It is not the bread that is the Eucharist. It is Christ in us that is the Eucharist, for He is our Thanksgiving, and we are His, and He is the Thanksgiving of God. We should not worry about taking the Eucharist. No one is worthy to partake. But the scriptures tell us to partake worthily, the writings do not say to partake if you are worthy. Who is worthy to partake of Christ except Christ alone? We are told that we partake worthily if we discern the body and blood of Christ. Do we know who He is, and why His body and blood were given up? Then we have partaken worthily, because if we know Him, and if He is in us, then it is He who is partaking as only He can partake of something so holy as the body and blood of God Himself.

What is the value of this bread and wine? Whether one believes in transubstantiation, wherein the bread and wine literally become the physical and corporeal body and blood of Christ, or if one believes the bread and wine are symbols of the body and blood of our Lord, the value ascribed to them is what they represent and what they are worth, thus and should be treated the same. If one wishes to argue this point let us take his money and burn it since it is simply a pile of worthless paper, already printed upon. What is the worth of the Body of God? What is the worth of His blood? What is the worth of the sacrifice of a perfect man? What is the worth of the life of God? The symbols are worth the same as the things they represent because Christ himself gave them their worth. Do not be afraid for He is worthy of all praise, glory, and honor, and He is in us. This is the Eucharist of God. As Jesus is Eucharist to us, we should be Eucharist to one another. This goes back to the two commandments – love God and love our neighbor as ourselves.

1CO 11:25 After the same manner also he took the cup, when he had supped, saying, This cup is the new testament in my blood: this do ye, as oft as ye drink it, in remembrance of me. 26 For as often as ye eat this bread, and drink this cup, ye do shew the Lord's death till he come. 27 Wherefore whosoever shall eat this bread, and drink this cup of the Lord, unworthily, shall be guilty of the body and blood of the Lord. 28 But let a man examine himself, and so let him eat of that bread, and drink of that cup. 29 For he that eateth and drinketh unworthily, eateth and drinketh damnation to himself, not discerning the Lord's body.

If we could do one small piece to make ourselves worthy, we could not "count it all Grace".

The goodness of man is like children jumping to see who can come closest to the moon. What difference can an inch make in such a shortfall? Russ Martin

PRESENTING CHRIST IN US TO THE WORLD

Christ has no body now on earth but yours, no hands but yours, no feet but yours. Yours are the eyes through which Christ's compassion goes out to the world. Yours are the feet with which he goes about doing good. Yours are the hands with which he blesses men now.   St. Teresa of Avila

Christ's living in me is at the same time himself and myself. From this moment until I am united with Him in one spirit there is no longer any contradiction implied by the fact that we are different persons. He remains, naturally and physically, the son of God ... I remain the singular person that I am. But mystically and spiritually Christ lives in me from the moment that I am united to Him in his death and resurrection...   Thomas Merton

The story of Mary holds within it, several deep lessons for the Christian mystic. Even before the great schism between the Orthodox and Roman churches, Mary held a place in the minds and hearts of the Christian church. Later, in church history, in a move to balance what was felt to be an over-emphasis on Mary and her status, the Protestant church began to diminish her status until she is now considered little more than a willing incubator for Jesus. Polarization is an all too human reaction, which leads us, in many cases, to fully reject a doctrine and even a person when we believe it, or they, are in error. The error may hold only a part of what is presented, but the rejection is full. Thus large areas of truth are thrown out with areas of error.

The Bible tells us she will be called blessed, but many do not call her anything at all. The majority of Protestant believers ignore Mary. It is the overcompensation to avoid the recurrence of the error. Throwing truth out with error, the baby that got tossed out in the bathwater of error this time happened to be the Mother of Jesus. I do not support an extreme elevation or veneration of Mary or of any creature for that matter, since such a view would cloud the vision of the preeminence of Christ. But, neither do I agree with the place to which most Protestant churches have resigned her.

Although it is true grace shed on someone does not indicate moral or spiritual status, it is also true God had a plan for salvation from the foundations of the world and in His plan, Mary had a place. As people of faith, Mary's story has a deep and significant meaning for us. Grace is given without, and many times, in spite of spiritual condition. It was not Mary's state or condition but the willingness of her decision that drew the sovereign will of God. In this vein the early fathers found something so fascinating and deeply spiritual about the story of Mary they elevated her to a venerated status. As we look closer into the story of Mary we will see she is the template and prototype of the true mystical experience. Her experience is the key and summation of the entire Christian process. In her we find our spiritual likeness, our history, and our story. In the story of Mary the mystical life is foretold.

LUKE 1:35 And the angel answered and said unto her, The Holy Ghost shall come upon thee, and the power of the Highest shall overshadow thee: therefore also that holy thing which shall be born of thee shall be called the Son of God. 37 For with God nothing shall be impossible. 38 And Mary said, Behold the handmaid of the Lord; be it unto me according to thy word. And the angel departed from her. 41 And it came to pass, that, when Elisabeth heard the salutation of Mary, the babe leaped in her womb; and Elisabeth was filled with the Holy Ghost: 42 And she spake out with a loud voice, and said, Blessed art thou among women, and blessed is the fruit of thy womb. 43 And whence is this to me, that the mother of my Lord should come to me? 44 For, lo, as soon as the voice of thy salutation sounded in mine ears, the babe leaped in my womb for joy. 45 And blessed is she that believed: for there shall be a performance of those things, which were told her from the Lord. 46 And Mary said, My soul doth magnify the Lord, 47 And my spirit hath rejoiced in God my Saviour.

LUK 1:48 For he hath regarded the low estate of his handmaiden: for, behold, from henceforth all generations shall call me blessed. 49 For he that is mighty hath done to me great things; and holy is his name. 50 And his mercy is on them that fear him from generation to generation. 51 He hath shewed strength with his arm; he hath scattered the proud in the imagination of their hearts. 52 He hath put down the mighty from their seats, and exalted them of low degree.

In His grace, God chose Mary, a young woman with no obvious attributes that set her apart from hundreds of others. In her own words, she was someone who counted herself as a lowly maiden. In his power and mercy He came to her. His spirit was on her and in her and He communed with her within her heart and soul. God, being out of time and space, had a plan for creation before He created. This also includes the incarnation. Creation was created for Jesus and through Jesus. The plan for creation was completed in the mind of God before the act of creating. Therefore, Mary was in God's plan for the birth of Jesus before creation, but because of free will she had acquiescence. It was because of her free will and the obedience that followed from it she was blessed. We cannot know why Mary was chosen and set apart. God has always used men and women who seemed common and ordinary to do great things. So it was with the mother of God. Mary, by believing the child in her was indeed sent and fathered by the Holy Spirit of God and set in her virgin body for the redemption of man, became the first Christian.

" The Holy Ghost shall come upon thee, and the power of the Highest shall overshadow thee: therefore also that holy thing which shall be born of thee shall be called the Son of God." Luke 1:35

It was not through doctrine or church that they met but through a real and powerful personal communion. This is the essence of the mystical experience. God draws us and woos us to Him and in our desire to be with Him we are allowed an intimate communion with Him. In this spiritual state of togetherness with God, the Holy Spirit of God implants Christ in our spiritual wombs. Christ forms in us, grows in us, moves in us and through us until we give birth to Him through our hearts and souls and show Him to the world in our love and actions with spontaneous acts of love and serving. It is through a heart and mind that calls out to Him and declares, "Behold the handmaid of the Lord; be it unto me according to thy word." Only in this can we contain God's Spirit. Only in this will God hold us. By this alone comes the world's greatest experience. What we do not realize in our simplicity is each time Christ is birthed in us we are experiencing the mystical equivalent of the incarnation once again. Each time we nurture Him in us and show Him forth to others, we have become Mary and the great incarnation has come upon us.

ISA 9:6 For unto us a child is born, unto us a son is given: and the government shall be upon his shoulder: and his name shall be called Wonderful, Counsellor, The mighty God, The everlasting Father, The Prince of Peace. 7 Of the increase of his government and peace there shall be no end, upon the throne of David, and upon his kingdom, to order it, and to establish it with judgment and with justice from henceforth even for ever. The zeal of the LORD of hosts will perform this.

It is for this event that even if man had not fallen, still Christ would have come. He is the crown of mankind. He is the crowning of creation. He was destined from the foundation of creation to be the one and only avenue for the union of God and man. Such a union going far beyond any understanding communion could bring. Thus, we may commune with God but Christ lives in us, in a state that is distinct yet in union.

IN THIS LIFE

From a young age I thought the contemplative life would best suit those like me, but there was nowhere to go. Protestants do not have a place set aside for the contemplative. They are expected to find a way to live in the "real world". The church never addresses this path nor teaches us how to live it out in the harried world of today. Possibly they do not know. Certain lay groups have come into existence to fill the void left by the church itself. Groups like the Upper Room, the Emmaus Walk, and other Christian ministries and retreats give us insight into other ways of worship. They awaken a deeper desire for God, but they are a temporary change of venue. Most retreats last less than a week.

All of these give us insight into the heart of God. However, they cannot teach us to live toward this end since there is not time to establish a discipline or pattern for life in only a few days. They seek only to spark a hunger. To reach toward the heart of God one must first realize the intense emptiness within, even in the midst of this land of plenty. One must attempt to plumb the depths of their own heart and find it selfish, unworthy, and vile, even as others may admire or praise you. Lastly, vision of the true worth and presence of God must be sought. He should be sought without wavier but as humans we cannot be stable, steadfast, or pure. We must rely on His grace to draw us to Him.

The contemplative life in a modern world is one of walking introspection and self-observation. As we come to understand how truly sinful we are, we also come to understand the vastness of His grace and gift to us. As we watch our thoughts and actions closely and ask why we act and think as we do we will see all we are grows from a root of selfishness and pride.

What possible good could we do for God? None. He loves us in spite of what we are. This is grace.

The contemplative life in this rushed and demanding world is one of continual prayer and upward reaching to God. Beyond the basic doctrine discussed in this little work, and beyond the thoughts and understanding of man waits the embrace of God. Do not let your mind become muddled or confused in meaningless doctrine or debate. Do you know Jesus is the Son of God? Do you know He was born of a virgin, sinless, lived, and died for the sins of the world, including yours? Do you know you are forgiven through your faith in Christ? This begins our relationship with God. Now it is up to us to love Him and pursue Him as the beloved of our heart. It cannot be any more complicated than this. Even a child should be able to understand the Gospel, the good news. Jesus commanded us to permit the little children to come to him. Then He commanded us to have the heart of a child; simple, direct, open, and loving. He told us to simply have faith in Him.

There is wisdom in not relying on our own knowledge and abilities. There is wisdom in insecurity. We cannot assume we understand the heart and mind of God. We must continue to seek Him and seek His wisdom for us.

PRO 3:5 Trust in the LORD with all thine heart; and lean not unto thine own understanding. 6 In all thy ways acknowledge him, and he shall direct thy paths. 7 Be not wise in thine own eyes: fear the LORD, and depart from evil.

There are none more dangerous than people or denominations who believe they have the entire truth. There are none so proud and in error as those who believe they have the only way. If a church believes they are "The Way" they have supplanted even Christ.

JOH 14:6 Jesus saith unto him, I am the way, the truth, and the life: no man cometh unto the father, but by me. 7 If ye had known me, ye should have known my Father also: and from henceforth ye know him, and have seen him.

The contemplative man seeks God and not some "way". He seeks to know and love God more each day. It is not about some formula of baptism, names, titles, or membership. It is about seeking the face of God.

This contemplative life demands patience. We rely on the grace of God. Although we continually knock on the door of heaven with the urgings of our heart toward Him, it is up to God to open the door. We never know when we will knock and grace will open the door. We never know what God has in store for us when grace opens the door. It could be a calming breeze to our soul, a vision of hell, or God's overwhelming presence. To exemplify this I will tell you about a personal event.

Visions may be an expression of what the spirit can communicate in no other way. Certainly, there would be no need for visions and dreams if we were fully aware of those things of God. If we were fully His or could see Him or hear Him we would know those things which visions reveal to our dull hearts and minds. Visions are gifts for those who could not see any other way.

I once saw a vision, vivid as day. Walking in the woods, praying, and in spiritual pain, I came into a clearing. I looked up to see a wall of transparent blocks twelve feet high and twenty feel long. Through the wall I saw a mob of creatures, terrible and fierce, coming at me to destroy me. They looked to be an army of demons. Above the wall hovered an angel with a large pitcher in his hand. He began to pour a deep red liquid into the wall, filling it up as if it were hollow. The demons crashed into the wall, bouncing off, wincing in pain, unable to penetrate the wall, hitting it again and again to no avail. I looked at the angel, frightened and astonished. "The Blood of Christ is protecting you." He said. I knew what I was seeing was taking place in my life on a spiritual level I could not see. The burden of worry I had been carrying lifted from me and I fell to my knees and sobbed.

Wounded by love and stunned by grace, I was transfixed and unmoving, feeling the arms of God around my soul, I wanted nothing more than to stay.

We never know when we will be surprised by grace. Even if it never happens He is still God. We may never hear His voice or sense His presence, but He is still God. To know this is to live in Him. To recognize it is to have the manifest presence of God in our life.

In this life where we seek the love of God, we may meet Him along the way from time to time. When man meets God he is changed forever, but even if he does not meet God in a manifest way, man is still changed because God is slowly working in a personal way within our hearts right now. To be completely aware of His presence in our life will have the same effect as any manifestation because at that moment of realization He is manifest to you. The realization of God is the manifestation of God. Although it may not be in pillars of smoke and fire, we see Him in our lives, in our hearts, and in our world. Our souls exclaim:

PSA 8:1 O LORD, our Lord, how excellent is thy name in all the earth! ...

This is not to be found in the "religious" life. Liturgy, ceremony, repetition, prayers, yantra, mantra, movement, nor deprivation will bring us one step closer to Him. He is found in the searching. He is found in the desire to know Him. He is found in the depth of our love of Him.

(Those who would be partakers of eternal life) must further possess a vigilant and wakeful mind, distinguished by the knowledge of the truth, and richly endowed with the radiance of the vision of God; so as for them, rejoicing therein, to say *Thou, O Lord, will light my lamp: Thou, my God, wilt lighten my darkness* .   Cyril of Alexandria

... It is our duty, therefore, to draw near to the true light, even Christ, praising Him in psalms and saying, *Lighten mine eye, that I sleep not for death*... Let, therefore, our loins be girt, and our lamps burning, according to what has been spoken unto us.   Cyril of Alexandria

(The Son) Himself shed the divine and spiritual light on those whose heart was darkened; for which reason He said, *I am come a light into this world*). Cyril of Alexandria

Oh, union of unity, demanded of God by Jesus Christ for men and merited by him! How strong is this in a soul that is become lost in its God! After the consummation of this divine unity, the soul remains hid with Christ in God. This happy loss is not like those transient ones which ecstacy operates, which are rather an absorption than union because the soul afterwards finds itself again with all its own dispositions. Here she feels that prayer fulfilled -- John 17:21: "That they all may be one as thou Father art in me, and I in thee; that they also may be one in us."   Jeanne-Marie Bouvier de la Motte-Guyon

PSA 8:1...who hast set thy glory above the heavens.

PSA 18:46   The LORD liveth; and blessed be my rock; and let the God of my salvation be exalted.

PSA 34:3   O magnify the LORD with me, and let us exalt his name together.

PSA 34:8   O taste and see that the LORD is good: blessed is the man that trusteth in him.

PSA 40:1 I waited patiently for the LORD; and he inclined unto me, and heard my cry. 2 He brought me up also out of an horrible pit, out of the miry clay, and set my feet upon a rock, and established my goings. 3 And he hath put a new song in my mouth, even praise unto our God: many shall see it, and fear, and shall trust in the LORD.

ISA 40:31 But they that wait upon the LORD shall renew their strength; they shall mount up with wings as eagles; they shall run, and not be weary; and they shall walk, and not faint. 41:1 Keep silence before me, O islands; and let the people renew their strength:

Is this not the mystical life? Is this not the life we seek?

Christianity is NOT a religion; it is the proclamation of the end of religion. Religion is a human activity dedicated to the job of reconciling God to humanity and humanity to itself. The Gospel, however – the Good News of our Lord and Savior, Jesus Christ, is the astonishing announcement that God has done the whole work of reconciliation without a scrap of human assistance. It is the bizarre proclamation that religion is over – period. -- Robert F. Capon

SEEKING TRUTH BEYOND THE BOOK

Where is wisdom? Where is the path to God? How much has been discarded, covered, or destroyed by the church? Was it all in the name of power, greed, or control? Where is God in all of this?

We have discussed the making of canon. We have seen there were hundreds, if not thousands of books that were rejected. Many were rejected because they were not compatible with the doctrine of the emerging church power. Others seem to be spiritually sound yet were dismissed because they invited too much personal freedom of faith. Too much personal freedom of faith would lead to an erosion of the much-coveted control sought by the Emperor and the church hierarchy.

Knowing that books may have been set aside for such political reasons raises a heretical question. Should we look outside the Bible in our search for God? In a word, yes.

Truth is found in a pinch of clay, as well as in the pages of some books. But only some have this truth. Others are simply stories devised for entertainment or for the expansion of nonsensical ideas no more true that the fables of the Titans. How then do we discern the difference?

We are holy vessels of a holy God. We are filled with His presence and that presence communes with us moment by moment. Trust the Holy Spirit within you to guide you to truth. Use as a signpost those things you know to be perfect and good.

Truth "religion" is to love and seek God, love and have compassion for others, and to seek express God's love to a dark and hurting world.

Look now at a few lines of one book rejected. Quotes below are from The Gospel of Thomas, translated by Joseph Lumpkin and published by Fifth Estate.

Jesus said, If those who lead you say, "See, the Kingdom is in the sky," then the birds of the sky will precede you. If they say to you, "It is under the earth," then the fish of the sea will precede you. Rather, the Kingdom of God is inside of you, and it is outside of you.

Those who come to know themselves will find it; and when you come to know yourselves, you will understand that it is you who are the sons of the living Father. But if you will not know yourselves, you dwell in poverty and it is you who are that poverty.

Jesus said: Recognize what is in front of your face, and what has been hidden from you will be revealed to you. For there is nothing hidden which will not be revealed (become manifest), and nothing buried that will not be raised.

His Disciples asked Him, they said to him: How do you want us to fast, and how will we pray? And how will we be charitable (give alms), and what laws of diet will we maintain?

Jesus said: Do not lie, and do not practice what you hate, for everything is in the plain sight of Heaven. For there is nothing concealed that will not become manifest, and there is nothing covered that will not be exposed.

Jesus said: I have cast fire upon the world, and as you see, I guard it until it is ablaze.

Jesus said: I will give to you what eye has not seen, what ear has not heard, what hand has not touched, and what has not occurred to the mind of man.

His Disciples said: Show us the place where you are (your place), for it is necessary for us to seek it.

He said to them: Whoever has ears, let him hear! Within a man of light there is light, and he illumines the entire world. If he does not shine, he is darkness.

Jesus said: I stood in the midst of the world. In the flesh I appeared to them. I found them all drunk; I found none thirsty among them. My soul grieved for the sons of men, for they are blind in their hearts and do not see that they came into the world empty they are destined (determined) to leave the world empty. However, now they are drunk. When they have shaken off their wine, then they will repent (change their ways).

Jesus said: I-Am the Light who is over all things, I-Am the All. From me all came forth and to me all return (The All came from me and the All has come to me). Split wood, there am I. Lift up the stone and there you will find me.

Why was the above book, the Gospel of Thomas, banned? One reason may be that it gave a directive to the individual to seek the kingdom of God within oneself. In this simple statement there is no room left for clergy or church to intrude or control.

Although statements such as the one above may lead the reader to believe this author conceives the church to be evil by nature, this is not the case. Man himself has a propensity toward evil and the church can be no better than those in authority. Thus the church must constantly guard against all sins which befall men.

Seeking authority at the time the bible and doctrine were being set was an emperor who was attempting to use the church to focus his control over the empire and an emerging political church structure seeks to establish and spread its authority over the world of Christendom.

In short, the climate at the time may well have affected the books and doctrine selected out of the many available.

If we allow the spirit of God to judge what we hear or read, how can we go wrong?

God spoke to men in various ways and at sundry times. Protestants have chosen sixty-six books, written by around forty men. Were there no other spiritual leaders in the world? Of course there were.

His Disciples said to him: When will the Kingdom come? Jesus said: It will not come by expectation (because you watch or wait for it). They will not say: Look here! or: Look there! But the Kingdom of the Father is spread upon the earth, and people do not realize it.

CONCLUSION

ECC 12:10 *The preacher sought to find out acceptable words: and that which was written was upright, even words of truth. 11 The words of the wise are as goads, and as nails fastened by the masters of assemblies, which are given from one shepherd. 12 And further, by these, my son, be admonished: of making many books there is no end; and much study is a weariness of the flesh. 13 Let us hear the conclusion of the whole matter: Fear God, and keep his commandments: for this is the whole duty of man. 14 For God shall bring every work into judgment, with every secret thing, whether it be good, or whether it be evil.*

As I struggled to find a place to end this work it became obvious there was no ending. We may plumb the depths of the ocean, because they are deep but finite. We may look out to the stars -the distance is vast but can be measured. How then can we presume to define an ending for that one thing which we know to be infinite, immeasurable, and everlasting? What can be said except the journey is for a lifetime and forever beyond. Let us hear a conclusion. There is none but to Love God, Love others, do His will, seek after Him with all of your heart, and all will be good with your soul.

Christians must answer questions regarding the application of their faith. Why are the rates of crime, rape, and all such horrors higher most Christian nations? Why is it the less devout nations of Northern Europe have less over all crime than the more devout countries such as the North American countries? Do we dare blame it on the declining secular education in the Americas? That seems to be what the number show. What do we say to this when asked about the life-changing potential of God in our lives? Are we simply not able to understand or harness our faith? Do we not understand how to apply the concepts or words?

It is because we believe but we do not commune. We believe but we have not touched nor seen, because we have not stopped long enough to get out of our own way. We have mistaken church, Bible, doctrine, and laws for the one true God, and we have substituted knowledge of Him with knowing Him.

In espousing the following point I know I will incur the wrath of many. However, if we think about it carefully we will find it to be true. Church attendance, obedience to the law, knowledge of the Scriptures, prayer, if it is empty repetition, even worship, if it is empty of spirit, will not change the heart of man. Only by being in God's presence can we hope to get to know Him intimately and be changed by exposure to Him; as a child is changed and molded by the parent.

It would be easy for us to say that Christianity, or religion in general, does not work, but it would be premature to conclude such a thing before we throw away all of those things we have held so dear that have eclipsed the Lord himself, and honestly give our faith the one chance it deserves.

Most of our accepted doctrine is based on political maneuverings, man made opinions, and Bible verses that were taken out of context or added beyond the time of the apostles. All of these we must count as dung.

If scripture and doctrine were enough, we could have kept the law and could have been justified by the law.

Scripture, doctrine, and law were not enough. We must turn back to the first cause. It is not Bible nor doctrine, but God himself. If we wish to know Him better, we can do so, if we choose to extend our relationship to a state of intimacy. The act of knowing by experience is quite different than knowing by reading or by what we have been taught by others.

We may gain knowledge and even insight by seeking words of wisdom. Scripture is not empty. It is only a story told by one beggar to another about where food may be found. But a story about food will not fill the emptiness. Only eating will do that and no one can eat for you. You must find the food and eat it yourself.

Jesus came to set us free from the taskmaster of religion. Four hundred years later His teaching were hijacked by religious men.

A King and priests sat down to define Christendom. They defined it in order to label, box, and control its people. They selected books and creeds in order to restrict and regulate. But their definition should not restrict our journey.

They were no more than the least of us, and we are no less than the greatest of them. They were just men with a mission, to please the king and remain in authority. We should not be afraid to step beyond their shadow, their doctrine, or their books. This spiritual journey is an individual sojourn for each of us.

Let us seek God it the stillness of our souls and let us be still until we hear Him as loud as thunder over a calm lake.

Let us turn back to those few things Jesus himself instructed us to do. Let us rest in His words and not the words of preachers, priests or popes, for they will never be able to reach beyond their own interests.

Joseph Lumpkin

Here is the conclusion of the matter.

JOH 7:16 Jesus answered them, and said, My doctrine is not mine, but his that sent me. 17 If any man will do his will, he shall know of the doctrine, whether it be of God, or whether I speak of myself. 18 He that speaketh of himself seeketh his own glory: but he that seeketh his glory that sent him, the same is true, and no unrighteousness is in him.

Matthew 22:36-40

Master, which is the great commandment in the law? Jesus said to him, You shall love the Lord your God with all your heart, and with all your soul, and with all your mind. This is the first and great commandment. And the second is like unto it, You shall love your neighbour as yourself. On these two commandments hang all the law and the prophets.

You shall love the Lord your God with all your heart, and with all your soul, and with all your mind is the sum and fulfillment of the first 4 of the 10 commandments which define our responsibility to God.

You shall love your neighbour as yourself is the sum and fulfillment of the last 6 commandments which define our responsibility to each other.

On these two commandments hang all the law and the prophets. Jesus Christ hung on the cross to fulfill the law and the prophets and to teach us how to live. The rest of the Bible is commentary. To add one word to this would cause division and exclusion.

The love of God means unity and love. How do we measure our progress toward our communion with God and love of our neighbor? It is not by any self-imposed rule or by self-indulgent pharisaic standards. It is only this:

James 1:27 (New International Version)

27Religion that God our Father accepts as pure and faultless is this: to look after orphans and widows in their distress and to keep oneself from being polluted by the world.

Do you seek to know and love God?

Do you seek to help and care for others?

Do you take care not to get caught up in the world system of greed and power? (This includes the politics of nations and denominations.)

Most of all, can you be still and know He is God?

Can you wait upon the Lord? Even when it is not convenient to stop and be quiet?

If it is in our hearts to love and to do only these little things, we will do well, and I believe we will be changed.

Appendix "A"

Appendix "A" contains a partial list of predictions, starting with the earliest known apocalyptic utterance. It was written in a terse, informational style using many sentence fragments; so if you are an O.C.D. English teacher, turn back now. The rest of us will enjoy the laugh. This list is taken from several Internet sources, which, in turn, document their sources. For more information please see: www.lifepositive.com, www.2think.org, www.abhota.info, www.religioustolerance.org, and other sites.

2800 BC - According to Isaac Asimov's Book of Facts (1979), an Assyrian clay tablet dating to approximately 2800 BC was unearthed bearing the words "Our earth is degenerate in these latter days. There are signs that the world is quickly coming to an end. Bribery and corruption are common." This is one of the earliest examples of moral decay in society being interpreted as a sign of the soon-coming end of days.

634 BC - Apocalyptic thinking gripped Romans, who feared the city would be destroyed in the 120th year of its founding. There was a myth that 12 eagles had revealed to Romulus a mystical number representing the lifetime of Rome, and some early Romans hypothesized that each eagle represented 10 years. The Roman calendar was counted from the founding of Rome, 1 AUC (ab urbe condita) being 753 BC. Thus 120 AUC is 634 BC. (Thompson p.19)

389 BC – The first prophecy of Rome's destruction came and went. This caused some to figure that the mystical number revealed to Romulus represented the number of days in a year (the Great Year concept), so they expected Rome to be destroyed around 365 AUC (389 BC). (Thompson p.19)

1st Century -   Jesus said, "Verily I say unto you, there be some standing here, which shall not taste of death, till they see the Son of Man coming in his kingdom." (Matthew 16:28) Apostles waited for His return until their death. Paul preached about the soon return of Jesus.

70 A.D. - The Essenes, a sect of Jewish ascetics with apocalyptic beliefs, may have seen the Jewish revolt against the Romans in 66-70 as the final end-time battle. (Source: PBS Frontline special Apocalypse!)

2nd Century - The Montanists believed that Christ would come again within their lifetimes and establish a new Jerusalem at Pepuza, in the land of Phrygia. Montanism was perhaps the first bona fide Christian doomsday cult. It was founded around 156 A.D. by the prophet Montanus and two followers, Priscilla and Maximilla. Even though Jesus did not return, the cult lasted for several centuries. Tertullian was the most famous follower of this sect. He is quoted as saying, "I believe it just because it is unbelievable." (Gould p.43-44)

247 A.D. - Rome celebrated its thousandth anniversary this year. At the same time, the Roman government dramatically increased its persecution of Christians. Christians came to believe that this was the End Of Days. (Source: PBS Frontline special Apocalypse!)

365 A.D. - Hilary of Poitiers predicted the world would end in 365. (Source: Ontario Consultants on Religious Tolerance)

380 A.D. - The Donatists, a North African Christian sect headed by Tyconius, looked forward to the world ending in 380. (Source: American Atheists)

Late 4th Century - St. Martin of Tours (316-397) wrote, "There is no doubt that the Antichrist has already been born. Firmly established already in his early years, he will, after reaching maturity, achieve supreme power." (Abanes p.119)

500 A.D. - Roman theologian Sextus Julius Africanus (160-240) claimed that the End would occur 6000 years after the Creation. He assumed that there were 5531 years between the Creation and the Resurrection, and thus expected the Second Coming to take place no later than 500 A.D. (Kyle p.37, McIver #21)

500 A.D. - Hippolytus (died ca. 236), believing that Christ would return 6000 years after the Creation, anticipated the Parousia in 500 A.D. (Abanes p.283) Parousia is the return of Jesus to the earth.

500- A.D. The theologian Irenaeus, influenced by Hippolytus' writings, also saw 500 as the year of the Second Coming. (Abanes p.283, McIver #15)

793 A.D. - Apr 6, 793 - Spanish monk Beatus of Liébana prophesied the end of the world in the presence of a crowd of people, who became frightened, panicked, and fasted through the night until dawn. Hordonius, one of the fasters, was quoted as having remarked, "Let's eat and drink, so that if we die at least we'll be fed." This was described by Elipandus, bishop of Toledo. (Abanes p. 168-169, Weber p.50)

800 A.D. - Sextus Julius Africanus revised the date of Doomsday to 800 A.D. (Kyle p.37)

800 A.D. - Beatus of Liébana wrote in his Commentary on the Apocalypse, which he finished in 786, that there were only 14 years left until the end of the world. (Abanes p.168)

806 A.D. - Bishop Gregory of Tours calculated the End occurring between 799 and 806. (Weber p.48)

848 A.D. - The prophetess Thiota prophesied that the world would end this year. (Abanes p.337)

All dates shown here forward are A.D. unless otherwise noted.

970 - Mar 25, 970 – In Lotharingia, (a portion of the lands assigned to Emperor of the West, Lothair I,) theologians foresaw the end of the world on Friday, March 25, 970, when the Annunciation and Good Friday fell on the same day. They believed that it was on this day that Adam was created, Isaac was sacrificed, the Red Sea was parted, Jesus was conceived, and Jesus was crucified. Therefore, it followed that the end must occur on this day! (Source: Center for Millennial Studies)

992 - Bernard of Thuringia thought the end would come in 992. (Randi p.236)

995 – After the prophecy failed, seeing The Feast of the Annunciation and Good Friday also coincided in 992, some mystics conclude that the world

would end within 3 years of that date, repeating the 970 prophecies. (Weber p.50-51)

1000 – Whenever a couple of zeros appear at the end of the date there will be apocalyptic thoughts. There are many stories of paranoia around the year 1000. There are tales describing terror gripping Europe in the months before the date. There is disagreement about which stories are genuine since scholars claim ordinary people may not have even aware of what year it was. (See articles at "Center for Millennial Studies.") (Gould, Schwartz, Randi)

1033 - Jesus disappointed the Y-1-K crowd, so some irrepressible mystics re-thought the date, claiming there was a simple mistake. The return would occur at the thousandth anniversary of the Crucifixion, bringing the date to 1033. Burgundian monk Radulfus Glaber described a rash of millennial paranoia during the period from 1000-1033. (Kyle p.39, Abanes p.337, McIver #50)

1184 - Various Christian prophets foresaw the Antichrist coming in 1184. I do not know why. (Abanes p.338)

1186 – (Sep 23, 1186) - After calculating that a planetary alignment would occur in Libra on September 23, 1186 (Julian calendar), John of Toledo circulated a letter, known as the "Letter of Toledo", warning that the world was to going to be destroyed on this date, and that only a few people would survive. (Randi p.236)

1260 - Italian mystic Joachim of Fiore (1135-1202) determined that the Millennium would begin between 1200 and 1260. Where do these guys get their dates? (Kyle p.48)

1284 - Pope Innocent III expected the Second Coming to take place in 1284, 666 years after the rise of Islam. (Schwartz p.181)

1290 - The Joachites, who were followers of Joachim of Fiore, rescheduled the End of Time to 1290 when his 1260 prophecy failed. If at first you don't succeed, try, try again. (McIver #58)

1306 - In 1147 Gerard of Poehlde, believing that Christ's Millennium began when the emperor Constantine came to power, figured that Satan would become unbound at the end of the thousand-year period and destroy the Church. Since Constantine rose to power in 306, the end of the Millennium would be in 1306. (Source: Christian author Richard J. Foster)

1335 – The Joachites were still around, trying to figure things out. Their third prophecy of doomsday was 1335. Again, I have no idea why. (McIver #58) Joachites were very much preoccupied with the role of the Jews in prophecy and believed they had discovered the keys to understanding the timing of Bible prophecy.

1367 - Czech archdeacon, Militz of Kromeriz, claimed the Antichrist was alive and ready to march onto the stage of time. He would reveal himself between 1363 and 1367. The End would come between 1365 and 1367. Anti-psychotics were not invented yet. (McIver #67)

1370 - There is a thin line between visions and delusions. The proof is in the truth. Jean de Roquetaillade, a French ascetic foresaw the Millennium beginning in 1368 or 1370. The Antichrist was to come in the year 1366. (Weber p.55)

1378 - Arnold of Vilanova, a Joachite, wrote in his work "De Tempore Adventu Antichristi" that the Antichrist was to come in 1378. (McIver #62)

1420 - Feb 14, 1420 - Martinek Hausha, a Czech prophet, also known as Martin Huska was a member of the Taborite movement. He warned that the world would end in February 1420, February 14 at the latest. The Taborites rejected the corrupted church and insisted on biblical authority, not Papal authority. Even though Taborite theologians were versed in scholastic theology, they were among the first intellectuals to break free from centuries-old scholastic methods. (McIver #71, Shaw p.43)

1496 - The beginning of the Millennium, according to some 15th Century mystics. (Mann p. ix)

1504 - Italian artist Sandro Botticelli, a follower of Girolamo Savonarola, wrote a caption in Greek on his painting The Mystical Nativity: "I Sandro painted this picture at the end of the year 1500 in the troubles of Italy in the half time after the time according to the eleventh chapter of St. John in the second woe of the Apocalypse in the loosing of the devil for three and a half years. Then he will be chained in the 12th chapter and we shall see him trodden down as in this picture." He thought the Millennium would begin in three and a half years.. (Weber p.60)

1524 - Feb 1, 1524 - According to calculations of London astrologers made in the previous June, the end of the world would occur by a flood, (I thought God told us that would never happen again.), starting in London on February 1 (Julian). Around 20,000 people abandoned their homes, and a clergyman stockpiled food and water in a fortress he built. (Randi p.236-237)

1524 - Feb 20, 1524 -   Astrologer Johannes Stoeffler saw the conjunction on a different day. The planetary alignment in Pisces, a water sign, was seen as the end of the Millennium, and the coming of the end by world flood. (Randi p.236-237)

1525 -   Anabaptist Thomas Müntzer believed this date was the beginning of a new Millennium, and the "end of all ages." He led an unsuccessful peasants' revolt. The government disagreed with his prediction. He was arrested, tortured, and executed. (If he really thought it was the end of everything one wonders why a revolt would matter.) (Gould p.48)

1528 -   Stoeffler's first attempt to predict the end of the world in 1524 failed. He then recalculated Doomsday to 1528. (Randi p.238) (Actually, up until today, all predictions have failed. The proof is that you are reading this.)

1528 - May 27, 1528   - Reformer Hans Hut predicted the end would occur on Pentecost (May 27, Julian calendar). (Weber p.67, Shaw p.44)

1532 -   Frederick Nausea, a Viennese bishop, was certain that the world would end in 1532. He had heard reports of strange occurrences, including bloody crosses appearing in the sky alongside a comet. (I wonder if Mr. Nausea was sick when he got it wrong.) (Randi p. 238)

1533 -   Anabaptist prophet Melchior Hoffman's prediction for the year of Christ's Second Coming, to take place in Strasbourg. He claimed that 144,000 people would be saved, while the rest of the world would be consumed by fire. (Kyle p.59) (We should note that usually wherever the prophet resides would be where the end begins. If a prophet predicts the end of time, normally only his followers are destined to make it out alive.)

1533 - Oct 19, 1533 -   Mathematician Michael Stifel calculated that the Day of Judgement would begin at 8:00am on this day. (McIver #88)

1534 - Apr 5, 1534 -   Jan Matthys predicted that the Apocalypse would take place on Easter Day (April 5, Julian calendar.) He went on to say only the city of Münster would be spared. (Shaw p.45, Abanes p.338) (He must have lived near the city.)

1537 -   French astrologer Pierre Turrel announced four different possible dates for the end of the world, using four different calculation methods. The dates were 1537, 1544, 1801 and 1814. (Randi p. 239) He was playing the odds.

1544 -   Pierre Turrel's doomsday calculation #2. (Randi p. 239)

1555 - Around the year 1400, the French theologian Pierre d'Ailly wrote that 6845 years of human history had already passed. Using the "day as a thousand years" calculation. The "week of years theory places the 7th day or 7000 years at 1555. (McIver #72)

1556 - Jul 22, 1556 - A Swiss medical student, Felix Platter, writes about a rumor that on Magdalene's Day the world would end. (Weber p.68, p.249)

1583 - Apr 28, 1583   - Astrologer Richard Harvey predicts The Second Coming of Christ would take place at noon, on this day. A conjunction of Jupiter and Saturn would occur. Numerous astrologers in London had predicted the end. (Skinner p.27, Weber p.93) (A conjunction is when two planets align, according to how they appear in the sky. They must appear within a few degrees of one another.)

1584 - Cyprian Leowitz, an astrologer, predicted the end would occur in 1584. (Randi p.239, McIver #105)

1588 - The end of the world according to the sage Johann Müller (Also known as Regiomontanus – Latin for King's Mountain). He was a mathematician and astrologer. (Randi p. 239)

1600 - Martin Luther believed that the End would occur no later than 1600. (Weber p.66)

1603 - Dominican monk Tomasso Campanella believed that the sun would collide with the Earth. (Weber p.83)

1623 - Eustachius Poyssel, a numerologist used his occult art to calculate 1623 as the year of the end of the world. (McIver #125)

1624 - Feb 1, 1624 - The same astrologers who predicted the deluge of February 1, 1524 recalculated the date to February 1, 1624 after their first prophecy failed. (Randi p.236-237) This way they would not have to be alive to endure another embarrassment.

1648 - Using the Kabbalah, a type of Hebrew numerology, Sabbatai Zevi, a rabbi from Smyrna, Turkey, predicted the Messiah's coming would be in 1648. There would be signs and miracles. People may have been excited, that is until he revealed that the Messiah would be Zevi himself. (Randi p.239, Festinger)

1654 – The sighting of a nova in 1572 brought physician Helisaeus Roeslin of Alsace, to claim the world would end in 1654 in a firestorm. (Randi p.240)

1657 - A group calling themselves "The Fifth Monarchy Men," predicted the apocalyptic battle and the overthrow of the Antichrist would take place between 1655 and 1657. They were what we would call a fundamentalist group who attempted to take over Parliament. They wanted to make the country a theocracy. The problem with theocracy is that the ruling party gets to determine what God's laws are. (Kyle p.67)

1658 -   In his writings called, "The Book of Prophecies," Christopher Columbus claimed that the world was created in 5343BC, and would last 7000 years. Assuming no year zero, that means the end would come in 1658. Columbus was influenced by Pierre d'Ailly. (McIver #77)

1660 -   Joseph Mede claimed that the Antichrist appeared way back in 456, and the end would come in 1660. This meant there was a 1204-year spread from start to finish. (McIver #147)

1666 – Many times there are no reasonable explanation of the dates reached by the prophets. In this case we can see the reasoning, although it is somewhat dubious. The date is 1000 (millennium) + 666 (number of the Beast). The date seems right because it followed a period of war in England. Londoners feared that 1666 would be the end of the world. Their fears were heightened by The Great Fire of London in 1666. (Schwartz p.87, Kyle p.67-68)

1666 - Rabi Sabbatai Zevi recalculated the coming of the Messiah to 1666. He was arrested for inciting public fear, and given the choice of converting to Islam or execution. He wisely elected to convert. (Festinger)

1673 -   The prophecy of the group having failed the first time, Deacon William Aspinwall, a leader of the Fifth Monarchy movement, claimed the Millennium would begin by this year. (Abanes p.209, McIver #174)

1688 -   John Napier, the mathematician who discovered logarithms, calculated this as the year of doom. (Weber p.92)

1689 -   Pierre Jurieu, a Camisard prophet, predicted that Judgement Day would occur in 1689. The Camisards were Huguenots of the Languedoc region of southern France. (Kyle p.70)

1694 - Anglican rector John Mason calculated this year as the beginning of the Millennium. (Kyle p.72)

1694 - Drawing from theology and astrology, German prophet Johann Jacob Zimmerman determined that the world would end in the fall of 1694. Zimmerman gathered a group of pilgrims and made plans to go to America to welcome Jesus back to Earth. However, he died in February of that year, on the very day of departure. Johannes Kelpius took over leadership of the cult, which was known as Woman in the Wilderness. These were truly ladies in waiting. (Cohen p.19-20) (Kyle p.66)

1697 - The beginning of the Millennium, according to Anglican rector Thomas Beverly. (Kyle p.72, McIver #224)

1697 - The notorious witch hunter Cotton Mather of New England claimed the end of the world would be in 1697. After the prediction failed, he revised the date two more times. (Abanes p.338) (Does this mean he was "witchy – washy?")

1700 - John Napier was a physicist, astronomer, astrologer, mathematician, and the inventor of logarithms. This date is his second doomsday calculation, based on the Book of Daniel. (Weber p.92)

1700 - In his 1642 book, "The Personal Reign of Christ Upon Earth," a Fifth Monarchy Man, Henry Archer, set this as the date of the Second Coming. (McIver #158)

1705 - The Camisard group got busy predicting, and could not stop. 1705 was just the first of many predictions for the end of the world. (Kyle p.70)

1706 - The end, according to some Camisard prophets. Strike two!(Kyle p.70)

1708 - The end, according to some Camisard prophets. Strike three! (Kyle p.70)

1716 - Cotton Mather's end-of-the-world prediction #2. (Abanes p.338)

1719 - Apr 5, 1719 - The calculated return of a comet was to wipe out the Earth, according to Jacques Bernoulli, of the famous mathematical Bernoulli family. (Randi p.240-241)

1734 - Cardinal Nicolas of Cusa claimed doomsday was to come between 1700 and 1734. This was predicted in the 15th century. (Weber p.82, McIver #73)

1736 - Cotton Mather's end-of-the-world prediction #3. This guy never stops. He is the energizer bunny of doomsday prophets. (Abanes p.338) (Remember – this guy was the witch burner. If anyone else had missed like this he would have torched them.)

1736 - Oct 13, 1736 - William Whitson predicted that London would meet its doom by flood on this day, prompting many Londoners to gather in boats on the Thames. (Randi) (Remember the rainbow, guys... God's promise not to drown the world...?)

1757 - In a vision, angels supposedly informed mystic Emanuel Swedenborg that the world would end in 1757. Few took him seriously. (Randi p.241, Weber p.104) Must have been those Swedish meatballs.

1761 - Apr 5, 1761 - William Bell claimed the world would be destroyed by earthquake on this day. There had been an earthquake on February 8 and another on March 8. He figured those were warnings. Kind of the one-two-three of earthquakes. The paranoia of Londoners gave way to anger and he was tossed into Bedlam, the London insane asylum that gave us that wonderful word. However, being that it was London, they did the deed in a very civilized manner. (Randi p.241)

1763 - Feb 28, 1763 - Methodist George Bell foresaw the end of the world on this date. (Weber p.102)

1780 - May 19, 1780   Smoke from large-scale forest fires to the west darkened New England skies for several hours. Being the nervous group that they were, the New Englanders believed that Judgement Day had arrived. (Abanes p.217)

1789 -   Antichrist will reveal himself, according to 14th century Cardinal Pierre d'Ailly. (Weber p.59)

1790 -   The Second Coming of Christ, according to Irishman Francis Dobbs. (Schwartz p.181)

1792 -   The end of the world according to the Shakers. (Abanes p.338) The Shakers were originally located in England in 1747, in the home of Mother Ann Lee. The parent group was called the Quakers, which originated in the 17th century. Both groups believed that everybody could find God within him or herself, rather than through the organized church. Shakers tended to be more emotional in their worship. They are strict believers in celibacy, hence, their small numbers.

1794 -   Charles Wesley, brother of Methodist Church founder John Wesley, predicted Doomsday would be in 1794. (Source: Ontario Consultants on Religious Tolerance)

1795 -   English sailor Richard Brothers, calling himself "God's Almighty Nephew," predicted the Millennium would begin between 1793 and 1795. He expected the ten lost tribes of Israel would return. He also said God told him he would become king of England. He was shown the front door of the local insane asylum. (Kyle p.73, McIver #301)

1801 -   Pierre Turrel's doomsday calculation - Strike three! The first one targeted 1537. (Randi p. 239)

1805 -   Earthquake would wipe out the world in 1805, followed by an age of everlasting peace when God will be known by all. Presbyterian minister Christopher Love, was beheaded later. (Schwartz p.101)

1814   Pierre Turrel's doomsday calculation. Forth attempt... Please stop... just stop! The third attempt was in 1801. (Randi p. 239)

1814 - Dec 25, 1814 - This one is truly strange. A 64-year-old virgin prophet named Joanna Southcott claimed she would give birth to Jesus on Christmas Day. Witnesses claimed that she did appear pregnant. She died on Christmas Day. An autopsy proved that she was not pregnant. (Skinner p.109)

1820 - Oct 14, 1820 – Following on the heels of Southcott's death, a follower, John Turner, claimed the world would end. The prophecy failed and John Wroe took over leadership of the cult. (Randi p.241-242)

1836 -   John Wesley, the founder of the Methodist, foresaw the Millennium beginning in 1836. He said the sign would be that the Beast of Revelation would rise from the sea. (McIver #269)

1843 -   Harriet Livermore predicted Christ would return to the earth on this date. (McIver #699)

1843 - Apr 28, 1843 - Belief among William Miller's followers spawned gossip that the Second Coming would take place on this day. (Festinger p.16)

1843 - Dec 31, 1843 - Millerites expected Jesus to return at the end of 1843. (Festinger p.16)

1844 - Mar 21, 1844   - William Miller, leader of the Millerites, predicted Christ would return sometime between March 21, 1843 and March 21, 1844. He gathered a following of thousands of devotees. After the failed prophecy the cult experienced a crisis. They re-grouped and began reinterpreting the prophecy. This is more revisionist history of the church. (Gould p.49, Festinger p.16-17)

1844 - Oct 22, 1844   - Rev. Samuel S. Snow, an influential Millerite, predicted the Second Coming on this day. The date was soon accepted by Miller himself. On that day, the Millerites gathered on a hilltop to await the coming of Jesus. After the inevitable no-show, the event became known as the "Great Disappointment." It is said that Snow sold "ascension garments" to the waiting host and made a lot of cash on the deal. (Gould p.49, Festinger p.17)

Joseph Lumpkin

1845 - The remaining members of Miller's cult, now called the Second Adventists, and the forerunners of the Seventh Day Adventists, claimed this would be the Second Coming. (Kyle p.91)

1846 – Obviously, the first time failed, so this is another Second Coming according to the Second Adventists. (Kyle p.91)

1847 - Harriet Livermore's Parousia prediction #2. (McIver #699)

1847 - Aug 7, 1847 "Father" George Rapp, founder of a sect known as the Harmonists (aka the Rappites,) established a commune in Economy, Pennsylvania. He was convinced that Jesus would return before his death. His speech on his deathbed was moving - "If I did not know that the dear Lord meant I should present you all to him, I should think my last moment's come." Rapp died before making the introduction. (Cohen p.23, Thompson p.283, Encyclopedia Britannica) (Thus, the first Rapp group began and ended.

1849 - Yet another Second Coming according to the Second Adventists. (Kyle p.91)

1851 - AND, another Second Coming according to the Second Adventists. (Kyle p.91)

1856 - The Book of Revelation speaks of the King of the North invading Israel. The Crimean War in 1853-56 was seen by some as the Battle of Armageddon. Russia had planned to take control of Palestine from the Ottoman Empire. (McIver #437)

1862 - John Cumming of the Scottish National Church proclaimed the end of 6000 years since Creation. The world would end and the 1000 year reign of Jesus would begin. (Abanes p.283)

1863 - In 1823 Southcott, follower John Wroe, attempted and failed to walk on water. He then underwent a public circumcision. Many men may have been embarrassed. He then calculated that the Millennium would begin in 1863. (Skinner p.109)

1867 -   The Anglican minister Michael Paget Baxter was an obsessive - compulsive date setter. Writer and philosopher, Charles Taylor, of the 19th century documented Baxter's follies as he predicted the End of the world. (McIver #348)

1868 -   Michael Baxter claimed the Battle of Armageddon would take place this year. (Abanes p.338, McIver #349)

1869 – Baxter is back predicting another end. (McIver #350)

1870 - Jun 28, 1870 -   France would fall, Jerusalem would be the center of the world, followed by Christ's millennial reign on Earth. This according to Irvin Moore's book "The Final Destiny of Man." (McIver #746)

1872 – Remember Baxter?   He predicted another Armageddon in 1871-72 or thereabouts. (McIver #351)

1874 -   The end of the world according to the Jehovah's Witnesses. This is the first in a long, long, long list of failed doomsday prophecies by this group. (Gould p.50, Kyle p.93)

1876 - The Parousia according to the newly formed Seventh Day Adventists, a group founded by former Millerites. (Abanes p.339)

1878 -   You will lose count if you aren't careful. The end of the world according to the Jehovah's Witnesses. (Kyle p.93)

1880 -   Thomas Rawson Birks in his book First Elements of Sacred Prophecy determined that the end of the world would be in 1880 by employing the time-honored Great Week theory. (McIver #371)

1881 – Redundant! The end of the world according to the Jehovah's Witnesses. (Kyle p.93)

Joseph Lumpkin

1881 - The end of the world according to some pyramidologists, using the inch per year method. (Randi p.242)

1881 - 16th century prophetess Mother Shipton is said to have written the couplet:

The world to an end shall come

In eighteen hundred and eighty one.

In 1873, it was revealed that the couplet was a forgery by Charles Hindley, who published Mother Shipton's prophecies in 1862. People continued to buy and buy off on the book. (Schwartz p.122, Randi p.242-243)

1890 - Northern Paiute leader Wovoka predicted the Millennium. The prediction came from a trance he experienced during a solar eclipse in 1889. Wovoka was a practitioner of the Ghost Dance cult, a hybrid of apocalyptic Christianity and American Indian mysticism. (Gould p.56-57, p.69) As a note: Many spiritualists claim we all have American Indian guides in the spirit world. If one does the math it is immediately clear there aren't enough dead American Indians to go around.

1891 - In 1835 Joseph Smith, founder of Mormonism, foresaw the Second Coming taking place in 56 years' time, or about 1891. (Source: exmormon.org) As a side note, Smith also looked into a magic bag with stones in it to make his predictions. One such prediction was that the people of the moon were nice, conservative folk, who dressed in the Quaker fashion. (If someone these days were to stick his head into a bag and say things like this, he would be arrested for "huffing" glue.)

1895 - Reverend Robert Reid of Erie, Pennsylvania predicted and waited for The Millennium... and waited, and waited. (Weber p.176)

1896 – Baxter's back! Michael Baxter wrote a book entitled, "The End of This Age," in which he predicted the Rapture in 1896. According to Rev. Baxter, only 144,000 true Christians were to take the trip. (Thompson p.121) Recall that the rapture was not written about until the 1790's.

1899 -   Charles A.L. Totten predicted that 1899 was a possible date for the end of the world. (McIver #924) Every day is a possible date.

1900 - Father Pierre Lachèze foresaw Doomsday occurring in

1900, eight years after the Temple in Jerusalem was to be rebuilt. (Weber p.136)

1900 - Followers of Brazilian ascetic Antonio Conselheiro expected the end to come by the year 1900. (Thompson p.125-126)

1900 - Nov 13, 1900   Over 100 members of the Russian cult Brothers and Sisters of the Red Death committed suicide, expecting the world to end on this day. (Sources: Portuguese article)

1901 – The sect of Catholic Apostolic Church claimed that Jesus would return by the time the last of its 12 founding members died. The last member died in 1901. (Boyer p.87)

1901 – Baxter's back. Rev. Michael Baxter foresaw the end of the world in 1901 in his book "The End of This Age: About the End of This Century." (Thompson p.121)

1908 – March 12, 1908 - Once again, it's Michael Baxter. In his book, "Future Wonders of Prophecy," he wrote that the Rapture was to take place on March 12, 1903 between 2pm and 3pm, and Armageddon was to take place on this day, which is after the Tribulation. One could argue the need to catch away the church after leaving it through the tribulations. (McIver #353)

1908 - Oct 1908 - Pennsylvanian grocery store owner Lee T. Spangler claimed that the world would meet a fiery end during this month. Possibly he planned to smoke some ribs. (Abanes p.339)

Joseph Lumpkin

1910 -   One of the many manic times for the J.W.'s. The end of the world according to the Jehovah's Witnesses. (Kyle p.93) This, of course, was followed by a period of depression and a dose of Prozac.

1910 - May 18, 1910 - The arrival of Halley's Comet would have many believing that cyanide gas from the comet's tail would poison the Earth's atmosphere. Con artists took advantage of people's fears by selling "comet pills" to make people immune to the toxins. There is a sucker born every minute. (Weber p.196-198, Abanes p.339)

1911 -   19th century Scottish astronomer and pyramidologist Charles Piazzi Smyth measured the Great Pyramid of Giza and converted inches to years, concluding that the Second Coming would occur between 1892 and 1911. (Cohen p.94)

1914 - Oct 1, 1914 – Yet another amazing prediction by The Jehovah's Witnesses. They viewed World War I as the Battle of Armageddon. (Skinner p.102)

1915 - The beginning of the Millennium according to John Chilembwe, fundamentalist leader of a rebellion in Nyasaland (present-day Malawi). (Gould p.54-55, p.69) When the world didn't end he chose to force change.

1918 -   The end of the world according to the Jehovah's Witnesses. For the sake of your herbivorous lions, please stop! (Kyle p.93)

1918 - Dec 17, 1919   - According to meteorologist Albert Porta, a conjunction of six planets on this date would cause a magnetic current to "pierce the sun, cause great explosions of flaming gas, and eventually engulf the Earth." Panic erupted in many countries around the world because of this prediction, and some even committed suicide. A similar prediction surfaced again in the 1970's regarding a planetary alignment in 1982. This was known as the Jupiter effect. (Abanes p.60-61)

1925 - The end of the world according to the Jehovah's Witnesses. You must be kidding! (Kyle p.93)

1925 - Feb 13, 1925   Margaret Rowan claimed the angel Gabriel appeared to her in a vision and told her that the world would end at midnight on this date, which was Friday the 13th. (Abanes p.45)

1928 - Spring 1928 - J.B. Dimbleby calculated that the Millennium would begin in the spring of 1928. The true end of the world, he claimed, wouldn't take pace until around the year 3000. (McIver #495)

1934 – The final battle was to begin in 1934 according to Chicago preacher Nathan Cohen Beskin, as he stated in 1931. (Abanes p.280)

1935 - Sep 1935 - In 1931, Wilbur Glen Voliva announced, "the world is going to go 'puff' and disappear in September, 1935." (Abanes p.287) Well... ok then.

1936 - Herbert W. Armstrong, founder of the Worldwide Church of God, told members of his church that the Rapture would take place in 1936. Only his true followers would be saved. After the prophecy failed, he changed the date three more times. I suppose this was one of the things that would later lead his son, Ted, to separate from the church and start his own cult. Later, Ted would love his secretary more than the church or his wife. (Shaw p.99)

1938 -   Gus McKey wrote a pamphlet claiming the 6000th year since Creation would come between 1931 and 1938, signifying the end of the world. (Abanes p.283)

1941 - The end of the world according to the Jehovah's Witnesses. It just makes you angry after a while. (Shaw p.72)

1943 - Herbert W. Armstrong's second Rapture prediction. (Shaw p.99)

1945 - Sep 21, 1945 -   In 1938 a minister named Long had a vision of a mysterious hand writing the number 1945 and a voice saying the world would be destroyed at 5:33pm on September 21. His prophecy failed, and he never had his eyesight or hearing checked. (Source: Portuguese article)

Joseph Lumpkin

1947 - In 1889, John Ballou Newbrough (Known to himself as "America's Greatest Prophet") foresaw the destruction of all nations and the beginning of post-apocalyptic anarchy in 1947. I guess he wasn't such a great prophet after all. Newbrough was the founder of the Oahspe cult. (Randi p.243)

1952 - Billy Graham was speaking in 1950 when he announced, "We may have another year, maybe two years. Then I believe it is going to be over." (Source: Article by Hugo McCord)

1953 - Jan 9, 1953 – The end of the world, according to Agnes Carlson, the founder of a Canadian cult called the Sons of Light. (Source: Portuguese article)

1953 - Aug 1953 – In his book "The Great Pyramid, Its Divine Message," Pyramidologist, David Davidson, wrote that the Millennium would begin sometime during this month. (Source: article by John Baskette)

1954 - Dec 21, 1954 - Dorothy Martin (a.k.a. Marian Keech, aka Sister Thedra), leader of a cult called Brotherhood of the Seven Rays, also known as The Seekers claimed the world was to be destroyed by terrible flooding on this date. Martin claimed to channel an extra-terrestrial, who gave her knowledge of impending natural disasters. Her group was small, consisting of only a few firm believers. What made this case special was that the group allowed psychologists in to observe the group's reaction to the outcome. This case became the subject of Leon Festinger's book When Prophecy Fails, the classic, ground-breaking case study of cognitive dissonance and the effect that failed prophecy has on "true believers." (Festinger, Heard p.46-48, McIver #1949)

1957 - Apr 23, 1957 According to Jehovah Witness leader, Mihran Ask, a pastor from California, "Sometime between April 16 and 23, 1957, Armageddon will sweep the world! Millions of persons will perish in its flames and the land will be scorched." (Watchtower, Oct 15, 1958, p.613) Should we count this as a J.W. prophecy?

1958 - David A. Latimer, in his book "Opening of the Seven Seals and the Half Hour of Silence," predicted that the Second Coming would take place in 1956 or 1958, right after the Battle of Armageddon. (McIver #1501)

1959 - Apr 22, 1959   Victor Houteff, founder of the Davidians -- an offshoot of the Seventh Day Adventists -- prophesied that the End would be coming soon, but he never set a date. After his death, however, his widow Florence prophesied that the Rapture would take place on April 22, 1959. Hundreds of faithful gathered at Mount Carmel outside Waco to await the big moment, but it was not to be. (Thompson p.289) The cult continued fairly intact until 1981 when Vernon Howell joined the Branch Davidians. Howell heard from God and began to take over the cult. His authority and influence grew. Twenty-four-year-old Howell wedded fourteen-year-old Rachel Jones. Soon afterward Howell was forced out of Mt. Carmel with his wife. They moved to Waco, Texas. The group split and members of the group begin to live under Howell's leadership. Howell married thirteen-year-old Karen Doyle and twelve-year-old Michelle Jones (Rachel's little sister) as his third "wife." In spring of 1990 Vernon Howell changed his name to David Koresh. Koresh's temperament became increasingly volatile and irrational. He began preaching about a great war and the end of days. He claimed the government would attack. He had begun stockpiling weapons and provisions. In May-June 1992 the Bureau of Alcohol, Tobacco, and Firearms (ATF) launched its investigation of Koresh and the Davidians. Raids followed. Six Davidians died and four ATF agents were killed. Numerous individuals on both sides were injured. Raid turned to siege and between seventy-five and eighty-five Davidians died in the flames, including approximately twenty-five children. Nine members survived.

1960 - Pyramidologist Charles Piazzi Smyth (see the 1911 entry) claimed that the Millennium would begin no later than 1960. (Source: article by John Baskette)

1962 - Feb 4, 1962 - Psychic and astrologer, Jeane Dixon, calculated a planetary alignment on this day. It was going to destroy the world. The Antichrist was to be born the following day. (Abanes p.340) Jeane always had an eye toward the theatric. That's ok, until you start believing your own press.

1966 – Second miss by The Nation of Islam. They claimed that between 1965 and 1966, an apocalyptic battle would occur, resulting in the fall of the United States. (Kyle p.162) All of the "white devils" would be killed.

1967 -   The establishment of the Kingdom of Heaven, according to Rev. Sun Myung Moon. (Kyle p.148) Moon claimed to be the messiah.

Joseph Lumpkin

1967 - Jim Jones, of the People's Temple, had visions that a nuclear holocaust was to take place in 1967. (Weber p.214) "Can you say kool aid?"

1967 - Aug 20, 1967 - George Van Tassel, who claimed to have channeled an alien named Ashtar, proclaimed this time would be the beginning of the third woe of the Apocalypse, during which the southeastern US would be destroyed by a Soviet nuclear attack. (Alnor p.145) (And I thought that Ashtar was the other name for Chemosh, the Moabite god who demanded child sacrifice.)

1967 - Dec 25, 1967 - Danish cult leader Knud Weiking claimed that a being named Orthon was speaking to him, saying that there would be a nuclear war by Christmas 1967 that would disturb the Earth's orbit. His followers built a survival bunker in preparation for this catastrophe. Just as a note, if the earth's orbit is changed by only .5%, life as we know it would cease since temperatures would not support life. Bunkers would not work very well.

1969 - Aug 9, 1969 - Second Coming of Christ, according to George Williams, leader of the Morrisites, a 19th century branch of Mormonism. (Robbins p.77)

1969 - Nov 22, 1969 - The Day of Judgement, according to Robin McPherson, who supposedly channeled an alien named Ox-Ho. (Shaw p.154)

The 1960's must have brought out the lunatics. Everyone was channeling someone or some thing. Ever notice that no one channels Mr. Nobody?

1972 - Herbert W. Armstrong's Rapture prediction. (Shaw p.99) Armstrong pumped up his followers, telling them that only they know the truth and will go to heaven. Then he predicts the end so the flock would gather closer, be more devoted, and give more.

1973 - David Berg, also known as Moses David, leader of the Children of God, also known as the Family of Love, or just "The Family", predicted in his publication "The Endtime News" that the United States would be destroyed by the Comet Kohoutek in 1973. (McIver #2095)

1975 - The end of the world according to the Jehovah's Witnesses. (Kyle p.93) In this period of time I saw several J.W.'s that I knew run up huge credit card debt. When I asked about their reasoning I was informed they were not worried about paying it back since they would not be here. I also pointed out that in the event they would be correct, the debts they left would force those left to pay higher rates. That seemed to be our problem, not theirs. Bankruptcies followed for many J.W.s.

1975 - Herbert W. Armstrong's Rapture prediction number 4. (Shaw p.99) It is amazing that these guys have followers, barring those with memory problems.

1975 - The Rapture, so said preacher Charles Taylor. This begins a compulsive streak of predictions for Mr. Taylor. (Abanes p.99)

1976 - Charles Taylor's Rapture prediction number 2. (Abanes p.99)

1977 - John Wroe (the Southcottian who had himself publicly circumcised in 1823) set 1977 as the date of Armageddon. (Randi p.243)

1977 - William Branham predicted that the Rapture would take place no later than 1977. Just before this, Los Angeles was to fall into the sea after an earthquake, the Vatican would achieve dictatorial powers over the world, and all of Christianity would become unified. (Babinski p.277) All those buying surfside homes in Arizona were disappointed.

1977 - Pyramidologist Adam Rutherford expected that the Millennium would begin in 1977. (Source: article by John Baskette)

1978 -   In his book, "The Doomsday Globe," John Strong drew on scriptures, pyramidology, pole shift theory, young-earth creationism and other mysticism to conclude that Doomsday would come in 1978. (McIver #3237)

1980 - In his book, "Armageddon 198?", author, Stephen D. Swihart, predicted the End would occur sometime in the 1980s.

1980 - Charles Taylor's Rapture prediction number 3. (Abanes p.99)

1980 - Apr 1, 1980 - Radio preacher, Willie Day Smith, of Irving, Texas, claimed this would be the Second Coming. (Source: What About the Second Coming of Christ?)

1980 - Apr 29, 1980 - Leland Jensen, founder of the Bahá'ís "Under the Provisions of the Covenant", which is a small sect that mixes Bahá'í teachings with pyramidology and Bible prophecy, predicted that a nuclear holocaust would occur on this day, killing a third of the world's population. After the prophecy failed, Jensen rationalized that this date was merely the beginning of the Tribulation. (Robbins p.73)

1981 – Rev. Sun Myung Moon again announces the establishment of the Kingdom of Heaven. (Kyle p.148) I guess God didn't hear him the first time.

1981 - Charles Taylor's Rapture prediction number 4. (Abanes p.99)

1981 - Pastor Chuck Smith, founder of Calvary Chapel, wrote in his book "Future Survival," "I'm convinced that the Lord is coming for His Church before the end of 1981." Smith arrived at his calculation by adding 40 (one "Biblical generation") to 1948 (the year of Israel's statehood) and subtracting 7 for the Tribulation. (Abanes p.326) Way to go, Chuck!

1981 - June 28, 1981 - Rev. Bill Maupin, leader of a small Tuscon, AZ, sect named Lighthouse Gospel Tract Foundation, preached to his congregation, "rapture day was coming." Those who were saved would be "spirited aloft like helium balloons." Some 50 people gathered in a Millerite-like fashion. August 7, 1981. When his June 28 prediction failed, Bill Maupin claimed that doomsday would take place 40 days later. Maupin said that just as Noah's ark was gradually raised to safety over a period of 40 days, the same would happen to the world.

(Source: Philosophy and the Scientific Method by Ronald C. Pine and Interviews with former members.) Have you ever noticed that the more words in a church's title the more wacked they can be?

1982 - Charles Taylor's Rapture prediction number 5. (Abanes p.99) Number five? Number five! GEEEZ!

1982 - Using the Jupiter Effect to support his thesis, Canadian prophet Doug Clark, claimed there would be earthquakes and fires that would kill millions. First, Jesus was to return and rapture Christians away from the Tribulation (Abanes p.91)

1982 - Emil Gaverluk of the Southwest Radio Church suggested that the Jupiter Effect would pull Mars out of orbit and send it careening into the Earth. (Abanes p.100-101)

1982 - Mar 10, 1982 – The book, "The Jupiter Effect," by John Gribbin and Stephen Plagemann, stated that when the planets lined up, their combined gravitational forces were supposed to bring the end of the world. The book sold well and the theory inspired several apocalyptic prophecies. (Abanes p.62)

1982 - Jun 25, 1982 – One of the most persistent and greatest hoaxes of the twentieth century is that of Maitreya and his prophet, Benjamin Crème. Crème is a British artist and founder of Tara Center. Over the years he predicted Maitreya's arrival on the world scene several times. He finally set a date of April 25, 1982. Of course once a date is set humiliation is not far behind. Supposedly Maitreya rung him up to tell him it just wasn't time yet.

Some history will help here. The Prophecy of Maitreya, stating that gods, men, and other beings will worship him implies that he is a teacher and a type of messiah. A quote from a Buddhist text reads,

" (all) will lose their doubts, and the torrents of their cravings will be cut off: free from all misery they will manage to cross the ocean of becoming; and, as a result of Maitreya's teachings, they will lead a holy life. No longer will they regard anything as their own, they will have no possession, no gold or silver, no home, no relatives! But they will lead the holy life of chastity under

Maitreya's guidance. They will have torn the net of the passions, they will manage to enter into trances, and theirs will be an abundance of joy and happiness, for they will lead a holy life under Maitreya's guidance." (Trans. in Conze 1959:241)

Maitreya's coming is characterized by a number of physical events. The oceans are predicted to decrease in size, allowing Maitreya to cross them freely. Apparently this Messiah can't teleport or fly.

The event will also allow the unveiling of the "true" path of how to live. A new world will be built on these precepts. The coming ends a low point of human existence between the Gautama Buddah and Maitreya.

Crème's propaganda web page reads, "He has been expected for generations by all of the major religions. Christians know him as the Christ, and expect his imminent return. Jews await him as the Messiah; Hindus look for the coming of Krishna; Buddhists expect him as Maitreya Buddha; and Muslims anticipate the Imam Mahdi or Messiah."

Crème also took out an ad in the Los Angeles Times proclaiming "THE CHRIST IS NOW HERE", referring to the coming of Maitreya within 2 months. Crème supposedly received the messages from Maitreya through "channeling." (Grosso p.7, Oropeza p.155)

1982 - Fall 1982 - In the late '70s, Pat Robertson predicted the end of the world on a May, 1980 broadcast of the 700 Club. "I guarantee you by the end of 1982 there is going to be a judgment on the world," he said. (Boyer p.138)

1983 - Apocalyptic war between the U.S. and the Soviet Union, according to "The End Times News Digest." (Shaw p.182)

1983 - Charles Taylor's Rapture prediction number 6. (Abanes p.99)

1984 - Oct 2, 1984 - The end of the world according to the Jehovah's Witnesses. (Shermer p.203, Kyle p.91) You have got to love the unashamed, amazing chutzpah of these guys. The reasons they arrive at their dates show an amount of pure arrogance that is frightening. Since they believe that only 144,000 people will occupy heaven and since only members of their sect will make the cut, then when their membership reached 144,000 the rapture must occur. When that did not work, they reasoned that some were members but not true believers. Since money talks maybe the 144,000 will be made up of those who follow the rules and tithe. How ridiculous.

1985 - The end of the world according to Lester Sumrall in his book, "I Predict 1985." (Abanes p.99, 341)

1985 - Charles Taylor's Rapture prediction number 7. (Abanes p.99) It is time for a recap on Taylor. 1980 - Prophecy promoter Charles Taylor predicted the millennial reign of Christ to begin in 1995. He predicted the rapture would be in 1975, then in 1976, 1980, 1982, 1983, 1985, 1986, 1987, and, of course, 1989.

1985 - The Socialist National Aryan People's Party was convinced that Jesus would return in 1985. (Weber p.209) That's right, people. If you are white you can take the flight.

1985 - Mar 25, 1985 - The beginning of World War III, as prophesied by Vern Grimsley of the doomsday cult Family of God Foundation. This cult was a small offshoot of the Urantia Foundation, a loosely organized religious group that uses as its scripture a tedious 2000 page tome called the Urantia Book.

According to the on-line source, the Sceptic's Dictionary, "In short, the UB is over 2,000 pages of "revelations" from superhuman beings which "correct" the errors and omissions of the Bible. "Urantia" is the name these alleged superhumans gave to our planet. According to these supermortal beings, Earth is the 606th planet in Satania which is in Norlatiadek which is in Nebadon which is in Orvonton which revolves around Havona, all of which revolves around the center of infinity where God dwells. Others aren't so sure of the celestial origin of these writings. Matthew Block, for example, has identified hundreds of passages in the UB that are clearly based on human sources, but which are not given specific attribution. William Sadler, (the main author), admits on page 1343 that he used many human sources.

1987 - Charles Taylor's Rapture prediction number 8. (Abanes p.99) I thought about simply listing the prophecies from this guy in one line, but thought it better to place them in the time line simply for the humor.

1987 - Apr 29, 1987   Leland Jensen of the Bahá'ís "Under the Provisions of the Covenant" predicted that Halley's Comet would be pulled into Earth's orbit on April 29, 1986, and chunks of the comet would pelt the Earth for a year. The gravitational force of the comet would cause great earthquakes, and on April 29, 1987, the comet itself would crash into the Earth wreaking widespread destruction. When the prophecies failed, Jensen rationalized the failure as follows: "A spiritual stone hit the earth." (Robbins p.73, 78) What?

Joseph Lumpkin

1987   Charles Taylor's Rapture prediction number 9. (Abanes p.99) One must wonder what Taylor thinks when he reads lists like this one and sees his name over and over, and over, and over, and....

1987 - Aug 17, 1987   - Everyone must visualize whirled peas. This is the year of the "Harmonic Convergence," bringing world peace. New Age author José Argüelles claimed that Armageddon would take place unless 144,000 people gathered in certain places in the world in order to "resonate in harmony" on this day. (McIver #2023, Kyle p.156, Wojcik p.207)

1988 – The reports of our death have been greatly exaggerated. Hal Lindsey's bestseller, "The Late, Great Planet Earth," calls for the Rapture in 1988, reasoning that it was 40 years (one Biblical generation) after Israel gained statehood. (Abanes p.85)

1988 - Charles Taylor's Rapture prediction number ten. (Abanes p.99)

1988 - Canadian prophet Doug Clark suggested 1988 as the date of the Rapture, in his book "Final Shockwaves to Armageddon." (Abanes p.91)

1988 - David Webber and Noah Hutchings of the Southwest Radio Church suggested that the Rapture would take place "possibly in 1987 or 1988." (Abanes p.101)

1988 - TV prophet J.R. Church (got to love this name for a preacher) in his book, "Hidden Prophecies in the Psalms," used a theory that each of the Psalms referred to a year in the 20th century. This would mean that Psalm 1 represents the events in 1901, and so on. Why the twentieth century was so special can only be due to the fact Mr. Church was living in it. The Battle of Armageddon would take place in 1994. (Abanes p. 103)

1988 - Colin Deal wrote a book entitled, "Christ Returns by 1988: 101 Reasons Why." (Oropeza p.175) There is one reason why not. It is because no one knows the day.

1988 - Sep 13, 1988 - Edgar C. Whisenant lightened the wallets of many a believer with his best-selling book, "88 Reasons Why The Rapture Will Be In 1988." He predicted the Rapture between September 11 and 13 (Rosh Hashanah). After Whisenant's prediction failed, he insisted that the Rapture would take place at 10:55 am on September 15.

After that prediction failed, he released another book: "The Final Shout: Rapture Report 1989." When that prediction failed, Whisenant pushed the date of the Rapture forward to October 3. (Kyle p.121, Abanes p.93, 94) I think they were written around the same time.

1989 - Charles Taylor's Rapture prediction number 11. (Abanes p.99) Are you keeping track of these, because, if this guy lives long enough, sooner or later he will get it right. The problem with end of day's prophecies is if you do get it right, there will be no one left to know it.

1989 - In his 1968 book, "Guide to Survival," Salem Kirban used Bishop Ussher's calculations to predict that 1989 would be the year of the Rapture. (Abanes p.283)

1989 - In 1978, Oklahoma City's Southwest Radio Church published a pamphlet entitled God's Timetable for the 1980s in which were listed prophecies for each year of the 1980s, culminating with Christ's return and the establishment of his kingdom on Earth in 1989. With the exception of a couple of predictable astronomical events, none of the predictions came true.

1990 - Baptist preacher Peter Ruckman predicted that the Rapture would come round about the year 1990. (Source: article by Thomas Williamson)

1990 - The Jupiter Effect strikes again. Writer Kai Lok Chan, a Singaporean prophet, foresaw Jesus Christ returning sometime between 1986 and 1990. Armageddon (a war between the US and USSR) would take place between 1984 and 1988. He argued that the Jupiter Effect corroborated his claims. (McIver #2195)

1990 - Apr 23, 1990 - Elizabeth Clare Prophet, leader of the Church Universal and Triumphant, foresaw nuclear devastation and the end of most of the human race on this day, and convinced her followers to sell their property and move with her to a ranch in Montana. (Kyle p.156, Grosso p.7) In doing research, I have never heard such dribble as when I was instructed in her doctrine. According to E.C.P. Jesus is now a non-player. Michael has taken his place and is, of course, talking to her.

1991 - The Rapture, according to fundamentalist author Reginald Dunlop. (Shaw p.180)

1991 - Louis Farrakhan declared that the Gulf War would be the "War of Armageddon which is the final war." (Abanes p.307)

1991 - Mar 31, 1991 - An Australian cult looked forward to the Second Coming at 9:00 am on this day. They believed that Jesus would return through Sydney Harbour! (Source: Knowing the Day and the Hour)

1992 - Charles Taylor's Rapture prediction number 12. (Abanes p.99) Did I mention that he is the energizer bunny of Armageddon predictions?

1992 - Apr 26, 1992 - It was on April 26, 1989, Doug Clark announced on Trinity Broadcasting Network's show, " Praise the Lord," that World War III would begin within 3 years. (Abanes p.92) It was around this period of time I was employed at one of the TBN downlink transmitters as assistant engineer. Many times I received mail from little old ladies saying that they were giving their last few pennies on Earth to further the Kingdom of God. Pink hair dye, gaudy clothing, and jet fuel took most of it.

1992 - Apr 29, 1992 - When the LA riots broke out in response to the verdict of the Rodney King trial, members of the white-supremacist group Aryan Nations thought it was the final apocalyptic race war they had been waiting for. (20/20, NBC, Dec 12, 1999)

1992 - Sep 28, 1992 - Christian author Dorothy A. Miller in her book, "Watch & Be Ready! " predicted the "last trumpet" would sound on Rosh Hashanah, heralding the Second Coming. (McIver #2923)

1992 - "Rockin'" Rollen Stewart, a born-again Christian who made himself famous by holding up "John 3:16" signs at sporting events, thought the

Rapture would take place on this day. Stewart went insane, setting off stink bombs in churches and bookstores and writing apocalyptic letters in a mission to make people get right with God. He is now serving a life sentence for kidnapping. (Adams p.18-20)

1992 - Oct 28, 1992 – The Hyoo-Go or Rapture movement was spreading through South Korea like a plague. Lee Jang Rim, leader of the Korean doomsday cult Mission for the Coming Days (also known as the Tami Church), predicted that the Rapture would occur on this date. Lee was convicted of fraud after the prophecy failed. (Thompson p.227-228, McIver #2747)

1993 - David Berg of the Children of God claimed in "The Endtime News!" that the Second Coming would take place in 1993. The Tribulation was to start in 1989. (McIver #2095, Kyle p.145)

1993 - Nov 14, 1993 - This was Judgment Day, according to self-proclaimed messiah Maria Devi Khrystos (A.K.A. Marina Tsvigun), leader of the cult Great White Brotherhood. (Alnor p.93)

1993 - Dec 9, 1993 - The United nations recognized Israel on May 15, 1949. James T. Harmon added 51.57 years to the date and subtracted 7 to arrive at the date of the Rapture, approximately December 9, 1993. He also suggested 1996, 2012 and 2022 as alternative rapture dates. So, we still have a chance at this one. (Oropeza p.89)

1994 - R.M. Riley, in his book "1994: The Year of Destiny," wrote that 1994 would be the year of the Rapture. (McIver #3098)

1994 - Charles Taylor's Rapture prediction number 13. (Abanes p.99) YAWN!

1994 - Om Saleem, an Arab Christian, prophesied that the Rapture would take place in 1994, after this the Antichrist was to reveal himself. (Oropeza p.148)

Joseph Lumpkin

1994 - Dutch authors Aad Verbeek, Jan Westein and Pier Westein predicted the Second Coming in 1994 in their book, "Time for His Coming." (McIver #3348)

1994 - May 2, 1994 - Neal Chase of the Bahá'ís, "Under the Provisions of the Covenant," predicted that New York would be destroyed by a nuclear bomb on March 23, 1994, and the Battle of Armageddon would take place 40 days later. (Robbins p.79) It looks like everyone in the cult takes turns rolling dice to predict the end of time.

1994 - June 9, 1994 - Pastor John Hinkle claimed that God told him the Apocalypse would take place on this day. In a cataclysmic event, God was supposed to "rip the evil out of this world." When the prophecy failed, he claimed that it's only the beginning and it's taking place invisibly. (Oropeza p.167-168) I love invisible prophecies. I am wearing invisible pants right now.

1994 - Jul 25, 1994 - On July 19, 1993, Sister Marie Gabriel Paprocski announced to the world her prophecy that a comet would hit Jupiter on or before July 25, 1994, causing the "biggest cosmic explosion in the history of mankind" and bringing on the end of the world. Indeed, a comet did hit Jupiter on July 16, 1994. However, it is important to note that her announcement was made nearly two months after astronomer Brian Marsden discovered that Comet Shoemaker-Levy 9 would hit Jupiter. (Skinner p.116, Levy p.207)

1994 - Sep 23, 1994 - Reginald Dunlop claimed this was the last date encoded in the Great Pyramid of Giza, meaning that the world would not last beyond this date. (Oropeza p.128)

1994 - Sep 27, 1994   Harold Camping, head of Oakland's Family Radio and host of the station's Biblical discussion talk show, "Open Forum," predicted the end in his book, "1994?" (Camping p.526-7, p.531) I am assuming the question mark on the title begs an answer. No! No! He gave another prediction of Sep 29, 1994. And another for Oct 2, 1994. No, Harold. No! Sit... stay... (Abanes p.95)

1995 - Armageddon, according to Henry Kresyler, head of the doomsday group "Watchers in the Wilderness." (Shaw p.181)

1995 - Mar 31, 1995 - Harold Camping's doomsday prediction #4. He gave up setting dates afterwards. (Abanes p.95)

1996 - James T. Harmon's Rapture prediction number 2. (Oropeza p.89)

1996 - Nov 1996 - The Second Coming of Christ, as foreseen in doomsday author Salty Dok's book "Blessed Hope, 1996." (Oropeza p.48) Why is the blessed hope the destruction or escape from the world and seldom relates to our contribution to it?

1996 - Dec 13, 1996 - David Koresh predicted his own resurrection, according to the surviving Branch Davidian cult members. Koresh was a no-show. (Jordan p.113)

1996 - Dec 17, 1996- Psychic Sheldan Nidle predicted that the world would end on this date, with the arrival of millions of space ships. (Abanes p.341) According to Nidle's website, "Sheldan Nidle was born in New York City on Nov. 11, 1946, and grew up in Buffalo, New York. His first extraterrestrial and UFO experiences began shortly after his birth and were highlighted all through his childhood by various modes of contact phenomena, as well as accompanying manifestations - light-form communications, extraterrestrial visitations, and teaching/learning sessions on board spacecraft. During most of his life, he has enjoyed ongoing telepathic communications and direct 'core knowledge' inserts (etheric and physical implants). Sheldan has visually observed and physically experienced spacecraft throughout the years."

1997 - Mary Stewart Relfe claiming that God communicated with her in her dreams. She predicted the Second Coming in 1997, right after the battle of Armageddon. She continued, "America will burn" and be totally destroyed in 1993 or 1994. (Kyle p.120, Oropeza p.104)

1997 - Mar 23, 1997 - Richard Michael Schiller predicted that an asteroid trailing behind Comet Hale-Bopp would bring destruction to the Earth on this date. As the date drew near he claimed the world would be destroyed 9 months later when the Earth supposedly would pass through the comet's tail.

Joseph Lumpkin

1997 - Mar 26, 1997 - The infamous Heaven's Gate suicides occurred between March 24 and March 26, during a window of time predicted, a UFO trailing behind Comet Hale-Bopp would pick up their souls. Similarity between their prophecy and Schiller's one above are striking. The rumor of something following the comet started when amateur astronomer Chuck Shramek mistook a star for what he thought was a "Saturn-like object" following the comet. (Alnor p.13, 38)

1997 - Oct 1997 - The Rapture, according to Brother Kenneth Hagin.

1997 - Oct 23, 1997 - 6000th anniversary of Creation according to the calculations of 17th Century Irish Archbishop James Ussher. This date was a popular candidate for the end of the world. (Gould p.98)

1997 - Nov 27, 1997 - According to the Sacerdotal Knights of National Security, "A space alien captured at a UFO landing site in eastern Missouri cracked under interrogation by the CIA and admitted that an extraterrestrial army will attack Earth on November 27 with the express purpose of stripping our planet of every natural resource they can find a use for -- and making slaves of every man, woman and child in the world!" (Source: Ontario Consultants on Religious Tolerance)

1998 – According to Larry Wilson of "Wake Up America Seminars," the Second Coming would be around 1998. The Tribulation was supposed to start in 1994 or 1995, and during this period an asteroid was to hit the Earth. (Robbins p.220)

1998 - Centro, a religious cult in the Philippines, predicted that the end of the world would come in 1998. (Source: Ontario Consultants on Religious Tolerance)

1998 - The year of the Rapture, claimed Donald B. Orsden in his book, "The Holy Bible - The Final Testament": What is the Significance of 666?. "Take your super computers, you scientists, and feed the number 666 into them. The output will be the proof God gives that 1998 is the year Jesus will take the faithful with him...." (McIver #2986) During a period from 1999 and 2008 I worked as a system analyst on one of the fastest supercomputers in the U.S. The project was named, "Hypersonic Missile Technology." Out of the dozen or so rocket scientists there, none had the slightest idea of what he could possibly mean.

1998 - Henry R. Hall, author and nut case, predicts that the world will end in 1998 because, among other reasons, 666 + 666 + 666 = 1998. (McIver #2488)

1998 - Jan 8, 1998 – Thirty-one members of a splinter group of the Solar Temple cult headed by German psychologist Heide Fittkau-Garthe were convinced that the world would end at 8:00 pm on this day, but that the cult members' bodies would be picked up by a space ship. They were arrested by police on the Island of Tenerife, in the Canary Islands. The cultists were planning a mass suicide. (Hanna p.226 and FACTNet)

1998 - Mar 8, 1998 - All religions have their doomsday cults. One such cult is from Karnataka in southern India. They claimed that much of the world would be destroyed by earthquakes on this day, and the Indian subcontinent would break off and sink into the ocean. After the destruction, Lord Vishnu would appear on Earth. The leaders of the cult claimed that El Nino and the chaotic weather that accompanied it was a sign of the coming destruction.

1998 - Mar 31, 1998 - Hon-Ming Chen, leader of the Taiwanese cult God's Salvation Church, or Chen Tao - "The True Way" - claimed that God would come to Earth in a flying saucer at 10:00 am on this date. Moreover, God would have the same physical appearance as Chen himself. On March 25, God was to appear on Channel 18 on every TV set in the US. Chen chose to base his cult in Garland, Texas, because he thought it sounded like "God's Land." (Shermer p.204, McIver #2199)

1998 - May 31, 1998 - Author Marilyn J. Agee used convoluted Biblical calculations to predict the date of two separate Raptures. In her book "The End of the Age," she boldly proclaimed, "I expect Rapture I on Pentecost [May 31] in 1998 and Rapture II on the Feast of Trumpets [September 13] in 2007." (Agee)

When this failed she moved the date to Jun 7, 1998, then to Jun 14, 1998, then to Jun 21, 1998, and again on Sep 20, 1998, and May 22, 1999, and May 30, 1999, and June 20, 1999, and June 10, 2000, and Aug. 20, 2000 and May 28, 2001, and Nov 3, 2001, and Dec 19, 2001, and Jul 19, 2002, and Sep 13, 2007 (Oropeza p.89)

1998 - The Rapture, as per Tom Stewart's book 1998: Year of the Apocalypse. (McIver #3226)

1998 - Jun 6, 1998 - Eli Eshoh uses some numerical slight of hand to show that the Rapture was to take place in 1998. When nothing happened he claimed that it did indeed occur, but the number raptured was small enough not to be noticed. So… Eli was left behind?

1998 - Jul 5, 1998 - The Church of the SubGenius called themselves the only "One True Faith", (Don't they all?) designated this day X-Day. They expected the Xists from Planet X would arrive in flying saucers and destroy humanity on this day. Only ordained clergy who have paid their dues to the Church would be "ruptured" to safety! When that didn't come to pass, XX-Day was proclaimed to be July 5, 1999 and was declared the true end of the world. I can't wait until XXX-Day to see if they show up naked.

1998 - Sep 30, 1998 - Using Edgar Cayce's prophecies, Kirk Nelson predicted the return of Jesus on this date in his book "The Second Coming 1998."

1998 - Oct 10, 1998 - Monte Kim Miller, leader of the Denver charismatic cult "Concerned Christians", was convinced that the Apocalypse would occur on this date, with Denver the first city to be destroyed. The cult members mysteriously disappeared afterwards; but later resurfaced in Israel, where they were deported on suspicion of planning a terrorist attack at the end of 1999. Miller had also claimed he will die in the streets of Jerusalem in December 1999, to be resurrected three days later. (Sources: Watchman Fellowship, Ontario Consultants on Religious Tolerance)

1999 - Nov 1998 - The Second Coming and the beginning of the Tribulation, according to Ron Reese. He wrote that he had "overwhelming evidence" that this was true. (McIver #3081) He never showed anyone the evidence.

1999 - End of the world according to some Seventh Day Adventist literature. (Skinner p.105, Mann p.xiii) These mainline religions attempt to hide their mistakes from their followers. Most of their prophecies are never discussed with their believers.

1999 - End of the world according to the Jehovah's Witnesses. (Skinner p.102, Mann p.xiii) Speaking of hiding huge errors, the J.W.'s neglect to tell their followers that the church fathers were apocalyptic idiots.

1999 – It is astrologer Jeane Dixon again. She claimed the height of the Antichrist's power would be in 1999 when a terrible holocaust will occur, according to her book, "The Call to Glory." Dixon also claimed the Antichrist was born on Feb. 5,

1962. (Kyle p.153, Dixon p.168)

1999 - Edgar Cayce, The Sleeping Prophet, claimed a pole shift would cause natural disasters and World War III would begin. (Skinner p.127)

1999 - Linguist Charles Berlitz predicted the end of the world in his book, "Doomsday: 1999 A.D." (Kyle p.194)

1999 - Mar 25, 1999 - On September 25, 1997, Hal Lindsey predicted on his TV show, "International Intelligence Briefing," that Russia would invade Israel within 18 months. (Abanes p.286)

1999 - Apr 3, 1999 - The Rapture, according to H.J. Hoekstra. He believed we live on the inside of a hollow Earth. He used numerology to calculate the date of the Rapture.

1999 - May 8, 1999 - According to an astrological pamphlet circulating in India, the world was to meet its doom by a series of severe natural disasters on this date. This prediction caused many Indians to panic. (Source: BBC News)

1999 - Jun 30, 1999 - "Father" Charles L. Moore appeared on the Art Bell show November 26-27, 1998, claiming he knew the Third Secret of Fatima. According to Moore, the prophecy said that an asteroid would strike the Earth on June 30, bringing the End.

1999 - July 1999 - The month made famous by 16th century soothsayer Nostradamus, the month that people have wondered about for over four centuries, is now at long last a part of history. (Source: The Mask of Nostradamus by James Randi): The Quatrain reads,

"L'an mil neuf cens nonante neuf sept mois

Du ciel viendra un grand Roy deffraieur

Resusciter le grand Roy d'Angolmois

Avant apres Mars regner par bon heur."

The year 1999, seven months,

From the sky will come a great King of Terror:

To bring back to life the great King of the Mongols,

Before and after Mars to reign by good luck. (Quatrain X.72)

Between the time of Nostradamus and now the calendar changed. His seventh month, 13th day equates to August 13 of 1999. Both dates yielded nothing. According to Escape666.com, Nostradamus' King of Terror was to descend on Earth in September, heralding the beginning of the Tribulation and the Rapture. Escape666 said, regarding Nostradamus' infamous quatrain X.72: "now we know EXACTLY when he meant: SEPTEMBER 1999." However, as the end of September approached, they changed their date to October 12. They were embarrassed to try again.

1999 - Members of the Stella Maris Gnostic Church, a Colombian doomsday cult, went into Colombia's Sierra Nevada mountains over the weekend of July 3-4, 1999, weekend to be picked up by a UFO that would save them from the end of the world, which is to take place at the turn of the millennium. The cult members have disappeared. (Source: BBC News.)

1999 - Jul 5, 1999 – Remember X-day? Well, this is XX-day, according to the Church of the SubGenius. The Xists from Planet X and their saucers never came. Now all eyes are on XXX-day: July 5, 2000. Since it is XXX-day we assumed they will show up naked and have orgies.

1999 - Jul 7, 1999 - The Earth's axis was to shift a full 90 degrees at 7:00am GMT, resulting in a "water baptism" of the world, according to Eileen Lakes. (Get it? Baptism predicted by Lakes?) The site read,"

> 7:00 a.m., on Wednesday, July 7, 1999
>
> at the World Greenwich Mean Time
>
> The earth will turn right by 90 degrees very instantly." Very instantly seems a little redundant, so we reported her writing to the Department of Redundancy Department.

1999 - Jul 28, 1999 - A lunar eclipse would signify the end of the Church Age and the beginning of the Tribulation, according to Gerald Vano. (Source: The Doomsday List.)

1999 - Aug 1999 - A cult calling itself Universal and Human Energy, also known as SHY (Spirituality, Humanity, Yoga), predicted the end of the world in August. (Source: FACTNet)

1999 - Aug 6, 1999 - The Branch Davidians believed that David Koresh would return to Earth on this day, 2300 days (Daniel 8:14) after his death. (Source: Ontario Consultants on Religious Tolerance)

1999 - Aug 11, 1999 - During the week between August 11 and August 18 a series of astronomical events took place: the last total solar eclipse of the millennium (Aug 11), the Grand Cross planetary formation (Aug 18), the Perseid meteor shower (Aug 12), the returning path of NASA's plutonium-bearing Cassini space probe's orbit (Aug 17-18), and Comet Lee's visit to the inner solar system. Add to this the fact that some of these events are taking place before the end of July according to the Julian calendar (See Nostradamus' prediction), and you have a recipe for rampant apocalyptic paranoia. Many alarmists were convinced that the Cassini space probe would crash into the Earth on August 18. The nuclear fuel it carried would poison a third of the world's population with its plutonium, fulfilling the prophecy of Revelation 8:11 concerning a star named Wormwood -- supposedly a metaphor for radiation poisoning ("Chernobylnik" is the Ukrainian word for a purple-stemmed subspecies of the wormwood plant). But as expected, Cassini passed by the Earth without a hitch.

1999 - Aug 14, 1999 - Escape666.com originally proclaimed on their website that a doomsday comet would hit Earth between August 11-14. (McIver #3362).

1999 - Aug 18, 1999 - The end of the world, as foreseen by Charles Criswell King, also known as "The Amazing Criswell." In his 1968 bestseller "Criswell Predicts:" "The world as we know it will cease to exist...on August 18, 1999.... And if you and I meet each other on the street that fateful day...and we chat about what we will do on the morrow, we will open our mouths to speak and no words will come out, for we have no future." August 18 happens to be Criswell's birthday. (Abanes p.43)

1999 - Aug 24, 1999 - In 1996, Valerie James wrote in The European Magazine, "The configuration of planets which predicted the coming of Christ will once again appear on Aug 24, 1999." (Ontario Consultants on Religious Tolerance)

1999 - Sep 1999 - The End, according to televangelist Jack Van Impe. (Shaw p.131)

1999 - Sep 3, 1999 - Judgment Day was to be on September 2 or 3, according to the notorious Japanese doomsday cult Aum Shinrikyo. Only members of Aum were to survive. These were the same people who gassed public transportation with sarin gas.

1999 - Sep 9, 1999 - 9/9/99 was to be the date when all older computers were to reset or crash due to their clocks running out of bits. Y2K would bring modern civilization to its knees. (Source: SF Gate)

1999 - Sep 11, 1999 - Bonnie Gaunt used the Bible Codes to prove that Rosh Hashanah 5760 (September 11, 1999) is the date of the Rapture.

1999 - Michael Rood also jumped on the Rosh Hashanah bandwagon. He claimed that this day is the first day of the Hebrew calendar year 6001, and after it failed, he changed the date to April 5, 2000. In reality, this day was the first day of 5760, but Michael claimed that there was a mistake in the calendar.

1999 - Sep 23, 1999 - Author Stefan Paulus combines Nostradamus, the Bible and astrology to arrive at September 23 as the date that a doomsday comet will impact the Earth. (Paulus p.57)

1999 - The Korean "Hyoo-go" movement spawned the Tami Sect. Proponents predict the demise of this earth in October 1999. (Source: Korea Times)

1999 - Jack Van Impe, your typical televangelist, having missed his last prediction just one month ago, predicted the Rapture and the Second Coming for October 1999. (Wojcik p.212)

1999 - Nov 7, 1999 - Internet doomsday prophet, Richard Hoagland, claimed that an "inside source" called him anonymously and warned of three objects that will strike the earth on this day. The objects were supposedly seen during the August 11 eclipse.

1999 - Nov 29, 1999 - According to a vision he received in 1996, Dumitru Duduman claims that the destruction of America (i.e. Babylon) will occur around November 29, 1999.

1999 - Dec 21, 1999 - Sometime between November 23 and December 21, 1999, the War of Wars was to begin, claimed Nostradamus buff Henry C. Roberts. (Skeptical Inquirer, May/June 2000, p.6)

1999 - Dec 25, 1999 - The Second Coming of Christ, according to doomsday prophet Martin Hunter. (Oropeza p.57)

1999 - Dec 31, 1999 - Hon-Ming Chen's cult God's Salvation Church, now relocated to upstate New York, preached that a nuclear holocaust would destroy Europe and Asia sometime between October 1 and December 31, 1999. (Source: the Religious Movements Page)

2000 – It is true that each time the century mark rolls around people get edgy and make a lot of predictions. When it comes to those millennium markers people go a little crazy. The years 1000 and 2000 were favorites among prophets. Here as just a few of those predictions.

2000 - When his 1988 prediction failed, Hal Lindsey suggested the end might be in 2000, according to his recently published book, entitled "Planet Earth - 2000 A.D." (Lindsey p.306)

2000 - This is "The beginning of Christ's Millennium" according to some Mormon literature, such as the publication, "Watch and Be Ready: Preparing for the Second Coming of the Lord". The New Jerusalem will descend from the heavens in 2000, landing in Independence, Missouri. (McIver #3377, Skinner p.100) Like I said, the deed is always done where the prophet resides, because it is all about them.

2000 - 19th century mystic Madame Helena Petrova Blavatsky, the founder of Theosophy, foresaw the end of the world in 2000. (Shaw p.83)

2000 - In his book, "Observations upon the Prophecies of Daniel, and the Apocalypse of St. John", Sir Isaac Newton predicted that Christ's Millennium would begin in the year 2000 (Schwartz p.96)

2000 – Pop psychic, Ruth Montgomery predicted Earth's axis will shift and the Antichrist will reveal himself in 2000. (Kyle p.156, 195)

2000 - The establishment of the Kingdom of Heaven, according to Rev. Sun Myung Moon. (Kyle p.148)

2000 - The Second Coming, followed by a New Age, according to Edgar Cayce. (Hanna p.219)

2000 - The Second Coming, was forecasted in Ed Dobson's book, " The End: Why Jesus Could Return by A.D. 2000".

2000 - The end of the world according to Lester Sumrall in his book, "I Predict 2000". (Abanes p.99, 341)

2000 - The tribulation is to occur before the year 2000, said Gordon Lindsay, founder of the Christ for the Nations Ministry. (Abanes p.280)

2000 - According to a series of lectures given by Shoko Asahara, founder of Aum Shinrikyo (the group that set off poison gas in a subway), in 1992, 90% of the world's population would be annihilated by nuclear, biological and chemical weapons by the year 2000. (Thompson p.262)

2000 - One of the earliest predictions for the year 2000 was made by Petrus Olivi in 1297. He wrote that the Antichrist would come to power between 1300 and 1340, and the Last Judgment would take place around 2000. (Weber p.54)

2000 - According to American Indian spiritual leader Sun Bear, the end of the world would come in the year 2000 if the human race didn't shape up. (Abanes p.307)

2000 - 18th century fire-and-brimstone preacher Jonathan Edwards concluded that Christ's thousand-year reign would begin in 2000. (Weber p.171)

2000 - The world will be devastated by AIDS in the year 2000, according to Indian guru Bhagwan Shree Rajneesh. Afterwards, the world will be rebuilt by a peaceful matriarchal society. (Robbins p.164)

2000 - Religious fundamentalist and conspiracy theorist, Texe Marrs, stated that the last days could "wrap up by the year 2000." (Abanes p.311)

2000 – The Convulsionaries was one of the radical apocalyptic sects that emerged in early 18th century France. One of the members, Jacques-Joseph Duguet, anticipated the Parousia in 2000. (Kyle p.192)

2000 - Timothy Dwight (1752-1817), President of Yale University, foresaw the Millennium starting by 2000. (Kyle p.81)

Joseph Lumpkin

2000 - Martin Luther looked at 2000 as a possible end-time date, before finally settling on 1600. (Kyle p.192) Both were one of those "zero years."

2000 - Sukyo Mahikari, a Japanese cult, preaches that the world might be destroyed in a "baptism of fire" by 2000. (Source: ABC News)

2000 - A Vietnamese cult headed by Ca Van Lieng predicted an apocalyptic flood for 2000. But doomsday came much earlier for the cult members: he and his followers committed mass suicide in October 1993. (Source: Cult Observer archives)

2000 - End of Days will take place, say members of a Mormon-based cult near the Utah-Arizona border. Hundreds of members of the Fundamentalist Church of Jesus Christ of Latter-day Saints pulled their kids out of school in preparation for the Big Day. (Sep. 12, 2000 CNN article)

2000 - The Christian apocalyptic cult House of Prayer, headed by Brother David, expected Christ to descend onto the Mount of Olives in Jerusalem on this day. The Israeli government recently kicked them out of the country in a preemptive strike against their potential attempt to bring about the Apocalypse through terrorist acts such as blowing up the Dome of the Rock.

2000 - Bobby Bible, a 60-year-old fundamentalist, believed that Jesus would descend from Heaven at the stroke of midnight in Jerusalem and rapture his church.

2000 - A Philippine cult called Tunnels of Salvation taught that the world would end on January 1. The cult's guru, Cerferino Quinte, claimed that the world would be destroyed in an "all consuming rain of fire" on January 1. In order to survive the world's destruction, the cult members built an elaborate series of tunnels where he had stockpiled a year's worth of supplies for 700 people. (CESNUR)

2000 - UK native Ann Willem spent the New Year in Israel, expecting to be raptured by Jesus on New Year's Day. "It didn't happen the way it was supposed to," she said of the failure of the Rapture to take place. (USA Today p.5A, 1/3/00)

2000 - Jerry Falwell, a televangelist that some might mistake for a stand up comic is always a ray of sunshine and hope, which reminds me of Eeyore, foresaw God pouring out his judgment on the world on New Year's Day. According to Falwell, God "may be preparing to confound our language, to jam our communications, scatter our efforts, and judge us for our sin and rebellion against his lordship. We are hearing from many sources that January 1, 2000, will be a fateful day in the history of the world." (Christianity Today, Jan. 11, 1999)

2000 - Timothy LaHaye and Jerry Jenkins, authors of the bestselling Left Behind series of apocalyptic fiction, expected the Y2K bug to trigger global economic chaos, which the Antichrist would use to rise to power. (Source: Washington Post)

2000 - Jan 16, 2000 - Religious scholar Dr. Marion Derlette claimed the world is to end on January 16, according to an article in Weekly World News. This event is to occur after a series of natural and manmade catastrophes starting in 1997, and will be followed by an era of paradise on Earth. (This date is shown as January 6, 2000 in Richard Abanes' book "End-Time Visions." (Abanes p.43)

2000 - Feb 11, 2000 - On his broadcast on the morning of Feburary 7, 2000, televangelist Kenneth Copeland claimed that a group of scientists and scholars (he gave no specifics) studied the Bible in great detail and determined that Feb 11 would be the last day of the 6000th year since Creation, a date when the Apocalypse would presumably happen. Copeland did not imply he believed this to be accurate, though, but he went on to say that the Rapture will come soon. (Has anyone ever seen Copeland smile? So much for the joy of the Lord being our strength.)

2000 - Mar 2000 - The Rapture is to take place in March 2000, 3 1/2 years after Christ's Second Coming, according to Marvin Byers. (Oropeza p.29)

2000 - Apr 6, 2000 - The Second Coming of Christ according to James Harmston of the Mormon sect, "True and Living Church of Jesus Christ of Saints of The Last Days". (As opposed to the false death church?) (McIver #2496)

Joseph Lumpkin

2000 - Apr 2000 - The Whites, a family of ascetic doomsday cultists living near Jerusalem, expected the End to take place in March or April after the Ark of the Covenant was to reappear in a cave in the Old City in Jerusalem. They claimed that there was a mistake in the chronology of the Hebrew calendar and that the year 6001 will begin this Spring. In reality, Sep. 11, 1999 to Sep. 30, 2000 is the Hebrew year 5760. This means that the Hebrew year 6000 is 2240 A.D.

2000 - May 5, 2000 - According to archaeologist Richard W. Noone in his book, "5/5/2000 Ice: The Ultimate Disaster", a buildup of excess ice in Antarctica is causing the earth to become precariously unbalanced. All that's needed to upset this supposed imbalance and cause the pole shift, which would cause billions of tons of ice to go cascading across the continents. Where did this fool get his degree.

2000 - The Nuwaubians, also known as the Holy Tabernacle Ministries or Ancient Mystical Order of Melchizedek, claimed that the planetary lineup would cause a "star holocaust," pulling the planets toward the sun. (Alnor p.121)

2000 - May 9, 2000 - Toshio Hiji, having analyzed the quatrains of Nostradamus, announced that the Giant Deluge of Noah would inundate the Earth on May 9, 2000, and "all humans will be perished." (OK, that was a quote and his English stunk.) Prior to this, a third of the world's population was to be destroyed during an alien attack on October 3, 1999. But, what happens if the 1999 thing doesn't occur.

2000 - May 17, 2000 - "Dr." Rebecca S. Harrison claimed that Jesus would reappear on "EArth" (her capitalization) on May 17, to be followed by "A Mighty Battle" in June 2003.

2000 - Lakhota prophetess White Buffalo Calf Woman predicted that Jesus would return in a UFO this year.

2000 - Jun 2000 - A Ugandan cult calling itself the World Message Last Warning Church claims the End will come in June. Previously they had claimed the world would end in 1999. (Source: ABC News)

2000 - Jul 5, 2000 - XXX-day, according to the Church of the SubGenius. "THIS time the saucers will be XXX naked"!

2000 - Aug 20, 2000 - A man claiming the title of prophet and calling himself Ephraim claimed the 7-month Battle of Armageddon would begin on this day and the Rapture should have been March 20-22, 2000.

2000 - Sep 2000 - Jerry Grenough foresaw the end of the present age, and perhaps the Rapture, in September of 2000, using various passages from the Bible to divine this date. His prediction, of course, has been removed from his website, but it remains listed at the Doomsday List

2000 - Sep 17, 2000 - According to the measurements within the Great Pyramid of Giza, the Second Coming will occur on this date. (Abanes p.71)

2000 - Sep 19, 2000 - Somewhere between September 16 and 19, Phil Stone expects something he had dubbed the "Coastlands Disaster" to occur. He has derived his chronology from the Bible.

2000 - Sep 29, 2000 - According to the Jewish-based cult, "Love the Jew", whose website has disappeared without a trace, claimed the world would end on Rosh Hashanah, 2000. According to the cult, "America will be destroyed in one hour after the Rapture by an all out nuclear attack by Russia. Russia may also decide to destroy other countries as well at this time, such as South America, Mexico, Canada, notably the entire Western hemisphere will be a wasteland." A reference to the cult is available at The Doomsday List.

2000 - Oct 2000 - Elizabeth Joyce predicted nuclear war in October 2000 as a result of conflict in the Middle East. Her other failed prophecies, included one of the sun splitting in two. (Source: Doomsday has been cancelled!)

2000 - Oct 9, 2000 - Christian prophet Grant R. Jeffrey suggested this date as the "probable termination point for the last days. (Abanes p.341, McIver #2608)

2000 - Oct 14, 2000 - According to the House of Yahweh, the seven-year Tribulation began on September 13, 1993, when Yitzhak Rabin shook hands with Yasser Arafat at the White House. This means the end of the world is due on October 14, 2000. (Source: religioustolerance.org)

2000 - Nov 17, 2000 - The famous handshake between Arafat and Rabin on Sep 13, 1993 started the seven-year peace process, claims David Zavitz, and Armageddon will take place seven years later. David shows on this page why he thinks the Last Day will be on November 17, 2000.

2000 - Dec 31, 2000 - Joseph Kibweteere's doomsday prediction number two. On March 17, 2000, over 600 members of a Ugandan cult calling itself the "Movement for the Restoration of the Ten Commandments of God" sealed themselves into a church and were burned to death. It remains to be seen if it was a mass suicide, or a murder by their leader. Cult leader Joseph Kibweteere, who had previously claimed that the world would end on December 31, 1999, re-set his doomsday prediction to December 31, 2000 when his first prediction failed. (Source: CESNUR) I am convinced that the longer the name of the church or sect, the more insane the leader.

2001 - Mar 2001 - Dale Sumberèru claimed in his book "The Greatest Deception: An Impending Alien Invasion," claimed that March 22, 1997 was the beginning of the Tribulation, and the Second Coming will take place between July 2000 and March 2001. It seemed his book, "The Greatest Deception," was correctly named. (McIver #3239)

2001 - May 5, 2001 - Gabriel of Sedona, leader of the New Age doomsday cult "Aquarian Concepts Community", located in Sedona, Arizona, predicted the destruction of humanity between May 5, 2000 and May 5, 2001. Only people faithful to the cult will be saved from this destruction by UFOs. Beware of those UFO types.

2001 - Jul 2001 - Jamaican cult leader Brother Solomon and his Seventh-Day Adventist followers had staked out some space on the Mount of Olives in anticipation of witnessing the Second Coming, which he was convinced would occur sometime between mid-April 2000 and July 2001. Ganja will rot your brain.

2001 -Sep 11, 2001 - Not a single prophet, soothsayer, or fortuneteller saw what was coming. The World Trade Center was destroyed and the Pentagon attacked by madmen, causing thousands of deaths. This should prove beyond a doubt that the future is God's alone.

2001 - Sep 18, 2001   Charles Taylor, the daddy of all false doomsday prophets, takes another swipe at it. The rapture will be on Rosh Hashanah. (Oropeza p.57)

2001 - Dec 8, 2001 - The author of "The Ninth Wave" web site was convinced that the Church would be raptured on this date, and people will explain the disappearance as alien abductions.

2001 - Pyramidologist Georges Barbarin, subscribing to the concept of the Great Week, predicted that Christ's Millennium would begin in 2001. (Mann p.118)

2001 - According to the Unarius Academy of Science, aliens they called "space brothers" were to land near El Cajon, California, ushering in a new age. When it did not occur their explanation was, "The Space Brothers have not landed because we, the people of Earth, are not ready to accept advanced peoples from another planet." (Heard p.26-27) Well duh! Some people can't even deal with advanced people in their own neighborhood.

2001 - Gordon-Michael Scallion predicted major earth changes taking place between 1998 and 2001, culminating in a pole shift. (Heard p.26-27)

2001 - Nation of Islam numerologist Tynetta Muhammad figured that 2001 would be the year of the End. (Weber p.213) Every religion has its fools.

2002 - The end of the world, according to Church Universal and Triumphant leader Elizabeth Clare Prophet, following a 12-year period of devastation and nuclear war. (Kyle p.156) Clare never missed a beat. People are still buying her books and listening to her dribble.

2002 – According to the doomsday list, "Charles R. Weagle's now-defunct website, warning2002ad.com predicted a "nuclear judgement" on the world's industrialized nations in 2002.

2003 - May 5, 2003 - A UFO will pick up true believers on this date, according to the Nuwaubians, a Georgia cult headed by Dr. Malachi Z. York, who claims to be the incarnation of God and a native of the planet Rizq. (Like in, "believing this guy is taking a risk.) (Time Magazine, July 12, 1999)

2003 - May 13, 2003 - Nancy Lieder of ZetaTalk believes that the "end time" will take place on this day with the approach of a giant planet known as the "12th Planet". This planet supposedly orbits the sun once every 3600 years. The planet will cause...you guessed it! A pole shift!! Ms. Lieder gives some information about this on her Troubled Times site.

2003 - May 15, 2003 - A Japanese cult called Pana Wave, whose members dress in white, claimed that a mysterious 10th Planet would pass by Earth, causing its axis to tip. (Source: WWRN)

2003 - Nov 29, 2003 - The human race would all but wiped out by nuclear war between Oct 30 and Nov 29, 2003, according to Aum Shinrikyo. (Alnor p.98) These guys are like the crabby uncle you never liked, who always talked about killing people in the war. (Call a friend to see if they were right.)

2004   Major world events beginning in August 1999 will lead to full-scale war in the year 2000, followed by a rebirth from the ashes in 2004, according to Taoist prophet Ping Wu.

2005 - Oct 4, 2005 - The end of the world, according to John Zachary in his 1994 book "Mysterious Numbers of the Sealed Revelation." The Tribulation was to begin on August 28, 1998. I'm sorry. You got the wrong number. (McIver #3477)

2004 - Oct 17, 2004   Clay Cantrell took the dimensions of Noah's Ark and through some of his own unique mathematics arrived at this day as the date of the Rapture.

2005 – This actually marks the beginning of the end, since we are now waiting for the death of Pope Benedict for the prophecy to take place. In 1143, St. Malachy prophesied that there would only be 112 more popes left before the end of the world. Pope Benedict is the 111th, which means that the antichrist will be here in the early 21st century. According to Malachy, the last pope will be named Peter of Rome. (Skinner p.74-75)

2005 - Oct 18, 2005 - The beginning of Christ's Millennium, according to Tom Stewart in his book 1998: "Year of the Apocalypse." The Rapture was to take place on May 31, 1998, and the return of Jesus on October 13, 2005. (McIver #3226)

2006 - An atomic holocaust started by Syria was to take place between the years 2000 and 2006, according to Michael Drosnin's book, " The Bible Codes" (O'Shea p.178). Here's an excerpt from Drosnin's discredited book: "I checked 'World War' and 'atomic holocaust' against all three ways to write each Hebrew year for the next 120 years. Out of 360 possible matches for each of the two expressions, only two years matched both - 5760 and 5766, in the modern calendar the years 2000 and 2006. Rips, a supposed expert on Bible Code, later checked the statistics for the matches of 'World War' and 'atomic holocaust' with those two years and agreed that the results were 'exceptional.'"

2006 - The British cult, The Family, believed the end will come in 2006.

2007 - Apr 29, 2007 - In his 1990 book, "The New Millennium", Pat Robertson suggests this date as the day of Earth's destruction. (Abanes p.138)

2007 - Aug 2007 - Thomas Chase uses an incredible mishmash of Bible prophecy, numerology, Y2K, Bible codes, astrology, Cassini paranoia, Antichrist speculation, news events, New Age mysticism, the shapes of countries, Hale-Bopp comet timing, and more to show that Armageddon will happen around the year 2007, perhaps in August of that year.

2008 - Apr 6, 2008 - The beginning of Christ's millennial reign, according to Philip B. Brown.

2009 - According prophetess Lori Adaile Toye of the "I AM America Foundation," a series of Earth changes beginning in 1992 and ending in 2009 will cause much of the world to be submerged, and only 1/3 of America's population will survive. You can even order a map of the flooded USA from her website!

2010 - The final year according to the Hermetic Order of the Golden Dawn. (Shaw p.223)

2011 - Another possible date for Earth's entry into the Photon Belt. (See the May 5, 1997 entry)

2011 - Dec 31, 2011 - In an interesting parallel to the Harmonic Convergence concept, Solara Antara Amaa-ra, leader of the "11:11 Doorway" movement, claims that there's a "doorway of opportunity" lasting from January 11, 1992 to December 31, 2011 in which humanity is given the final chance to rid itself of evil and attain a higher level of consciousness, or doom will strike. (Wojcik p.206)

2012   James T. Harmon's Rapture prediction #3. (Oropeza p.89)

2012- Dec 21, 2012 - Terence McKenna combines Mayan chronology with a New Age pseudoscience called "Novelty Theory" to conclude that the collision of an asteroid or some "trans-dimensional object" with the Earth, or alien contact, or a solar explosion, or the transformation of the Milky Way into a quasar, or some other "ultranovel" event will occur on this day.

Dec 23, 2012   The world to end, according to the ancient Mayan calendar. (Abanes p.342)

2012 - NASA recently published a report detailing new magnetism on the Sun that will probably result in Major Solar Changes and destruction of satellite communications, GPS, Air Traffic, and Power Grids.

The report clearly states that a new Solar Cycle is possible resulting from a knot of magnetism that popped over the sun's eastern limb on Dec. 11th. 2007.

The report goes on to mention specific years which major Earthly impact will be seen. The exact quote which mentions these years states;

"Many forecasters believe Solar Cycle 24 will be big and intense. Peaking in 2011 or 2012, the cycle to come could have significant impacts on telecommunications, air traffic, power grids and GPS systems. (And don't forget the Northern Lights!) In this age of satellites and cell phones, the next solar cycle could make itself felt as never before."

Appendix "B"

Information on the Ending of the Book of Mark

Mark 16:9-20 has been called a later addition to the Gospel of Mark by most New Testament scholars in the past century. The main reason for doubting the authenticity of the ending is that it does not appear in some of the oldest existing witnesses. The writing styles suggest that it came from another hand. The Gospel is obviously incomplete without these verses, and so most scholars believe that the final leaf of the original manuscript was lost, and that the ending, which appears in English versions today (verses 9-20) was supplied during the second century. More than one scribe saw the book as incomplete and so supplied their versions of the ending. Scholars have pointed out that the witnesses which bring the verses into question are few, and that the verses are quoted by church Fathers very early, even in the second century. To represent this point of view we give below a long excerpt from F.H.A. Scrivener, together with its footnotes.

Scrivener was the undisputed expert in the 19th century of the existing Greek New Testament manuscripts, and on the KJV in its various editions. He did a thorough study of these ancient texts and published many of his findings. For example it was his opinion that some parts of the KJV follow only loosely the Greek text but very closely the Latin Vulgate.

"In some places the Authorised Version corresponds but loosely with any form of the Greek original, while it exactly follows the Latin Vulgate,"The Westminster Study Edition of the Holy Bible (Philadelphia: Westminster Press, 1948).

vv. 9-20. This section is a later addition; the original ending of Mark appears to have been lost. The best and oldest manuscripts of Mark end with ch. 16:8. Two endings were added very early. The shorter reads: "But they reported briefly to those with Peter all that had been commanded them. And afterward Jesus himself sent out through them from the East even to the West the sacred and incorruptible message of eternal salvation." The longer addition appears in English Bibles; its origin is uncertain; a medieval source ascribes it to an elder Ariston (Aristion), perhaps the man whom Papias (c. A.D. 135) calls a disciple of the Lord. It is drawn for the most part from Luke, chapter 24, and from John, chapter 20; there is a possibility that verse 15 may come from Matthew 28:18-20. It is believed that the original ending must have contained an account of the risen Christ's meeting with the disciples in Galilee (Chs. 14:28; 16:7).

Joseph Lumpkin

A Commentary on the Holy Bible, edited by J.R. Dummelow (New York: MacMillan, 1927), pages 732-33.

9-20. Conclusion of the Gospel. One uncial manuscript gives a second termination to the Gospel as follows: '*And they reported all the things that had been commanded them briefly (or immediately) to the companions of Peter. And after this Jesus himself also sent forth by them from the East even unto the West the holy and incorruptible preaching of eternal salvation.*'

Internal evidence points definitely to the conclusion that the last twelve verses are not by St. Mark. For, (1) the true conclusion certainly contained a Galilean appearance (Mark 16:7, cp. 14:28), and this does not. (2) The style is that of a bare catalogue of facts, and quite unlike St. Mark's usual wealth of graphic detail. (3) The section contains numerous words and expressions never used by St. Mark. (4) Mark 16:9 makes an abrupt fresh start, and is not continuous with the preceding narrative. (5) Mary Magdalene is spoken of (16:9) as if she had not been mentioned before, although she has just been eluded to twice (15:47, 16:1). (6) The section seems to represent a secondary tradition, which is dependent upon the conclusion of St. Matthew, and upon Luke 24:23f.

On the other hand, the section is no casual or unauthorised addition to the Gospel. From the second century onwards, in nearly all manuscripts, versions, and other authorities, it forms an integral part of the Gospel, and it can be shown to have existed, if not in the apostolic, at least in the sub-apostolic age. There is a certain amount of evidence against it (though very little can be shown to be independent of Eusebius the Church historian, 265-340 A.D.), but certainly not enough to justify its rejection, were it not that internal evidence clearly demonstrates that it cannot have proceeded from the hand of St. Mark. Bruce Metzger, A Textual Commentary on the Greek New Testament (Stuttgart, 1971), pages 122-126.16:9-20 The Ending(s) of Mark.

Four endings of the Gospel according to Mark are current in the manuscripts. (1) The last twelve verses of the commonly received text of Mark are absent from the two oldest Greek manuscripts, from the Old Latin codex Bobiensis, the Sinaitic Syriac manuscript, about one hundred Armenian manuscripts, and the two oldest Georgian manuscripts (written A.D. 897 and A.D. 913). Clement of Alexandria and Origen show no knowledge of the existence of these verses; furthermore Eusebius and Jerome attest that the passage was absent from almost all Greek copies of Mark known to them. The original form of the Eusebian sections (drawn up by Ammonius) makes no provision for numbering sections of the text after 16:8. Not a few manuscripts which contain the passage have scribal notes stating that older Greek copies lack it, and in other witnesses the passage is marked with asterisks or obeli, the conventional signs used by copyists to indicate a spurious addition to a document.

Several witnesses, including four uncial Greek manuscripts of the seventh, eighth, and ninth centuries as well as Old Latin, the margin of the Harelean Syriac, several Sahidic and Bohairic manuscripts, and not a few Ethiopic manuscripts, continue after verse 8 as follows (with trifling variations):

"But they reported briefly to Peter and those with him all that they had been told. And after this Jesus himself sent out by means of them, from east to west, the sacred and imperishable proclamation of eternal salvation."

All of these witnesses except this one also continue with verses 9-20.

The traditional ending of Mark, so familiar through the AV and other translations of the Textus Receptus, is present in the vast number of witnesses. The earliest patristic witnesses to part or all of the long ending are Irenaeus and the Diatessaron. It is not certain whether Justin Martyr was acquainted with the passage; in his Apology (i.45) he includes five words that occur, in a different sequence, in ver. 20.

In the fourth century the traditional ending also circulated, according to testimony preserved by Jerome, in an expanded form, preserved today in one Greek manuscript. Codex Washingtonianus includes the following after ver. 14:

"And they excused themselves, saying, 'This age of lawlessness and unbelief is under Satan, who does not allow the truth and power of God to prevail over the unclean things of the spirits [or, does not allow what lies under the unclean spirits to understand the truth and power of God]. Therefore reveal thy righteousness now — thus they spoke to Christ. And Christ replied to them, 'The term of years of Satan's power has been fulfilled, but other terrible things draw near. And for those who have sinned I was delivered over to death, that they may return to the truth and sin no more, in order that they may inherit the spiritual and incorruptible glory of righteousness which is in heaven.'"

How should the evidence of each of these endings be evaluated? It is obvious that the expanded form of the long ending has no claim to be original. Not only is the external evidence extremely limited, but the expansion contains several non-Markan words and as well as several that occur nowhere else in the New Testament. The whole expansion has about it an unmistakable apocryphal flavor. It probably is the work of a second or third century scribe who wished to soften the severe condemnation of the Eleven in 16.14.

The connection between ver. 8 and verses 9-20 is so awkward that it is difficult to believe that the evangelist intended the section to be a continuation of the Gospel. Thus, the subject of verse 8 is the women, whereas Jesus is the presumed subject in verse 9; in verse 9 Mary Magdalene is identified even though she has been mentioned only a few lines before (15.47 and 16.1); the other women of verses 1-8 are now forgotten.

In short, all these features indicate that the section was added by someone who knew a form of Mark that ended abruptly with ver. 8 and who wished to supply a more appropriate conclusion. In view of the inconsistencies between verses 1-8 and 9-20, it is unlikely that the long ending was composed ad hoc to fill up an obvious gap; it is more likely that the section was excerpted from another document, dating perhaps from the first half of the second century.

The internal evidence for the shorter ending is decidedly against its being genuine. Besides containing a high percentage of non-Markan words, its rhetorical tone differs totally from the simple style of Mark's Gospel.

Finally it should be observed that the external evidence for the shorter ending resolves itself into additional testimony supporting the omission of verses 9-20. No one who had available as the conclusion of the Second Gospel the twelve verses 9-20, so rich in interesting material, would have deliberately replaced them with four lines of a colorless and generalized summary. Therefore, the documentary evidence supporting (2) should be added to that supporting. Thus, on the basis of good external evidence and strong internal considerations it appears that the earliest ascertainable form of the Gospel of Mark ended with 16.8. At the same time, however out of deference to the evident antiquity of the longer ending and its importance in the textual tradition of the Gospel, the Committee decided to include verses 9-20 as part of the text, but to enclose them within double square brackets to indicate that they are the work of an author other than the evangelist.

Bruce Metzger, The Canon of the New Testament: its Origin, Development, and Significance (Oxford: Clarendon Press, 1987), pp. 269-270.

Today we know that the last twelve verses of the Gospel according to Mark (xvi. 9-20) are absent from the oldest Greek, Latin, Syriac, Coptic, and Armenian manuscripts, and that in other manuscripts asterisks or obeli mark the verses as doubtful or spurious. Eusebius and Jerome, well aware of such variation in the witnesses, discussed which form of text was to be preferred. It is noteworthy, however, that neither Father suggested that one form was canonical and the other was not. Furthermore, the perception that the canon was basically closed did not lead to a slavish fixing of the text of the canonical books. Thus, the category of 'canonical' appears to have been broad enough to include all variant readings (as well as variant renderings in early versions) that emerged during the course of the transmission of the New Testament documents while apostolic tradition was still a living entity, with an intermingling of written and oral forms of that tradition. Already in the second century, for example, the so-called long ending of Mark was known to Justin Martyr and to Tatian, who incorporated it into his Diatesseron. There seems to be good reason, therefore, to conclude that, though external and internal evidence is conclusive against the authenticity of the last twelve verses as coming from the same pen as the rest of the Gospel, the passage ought to be accepted as part of the canonical text of Mark."

This ends the quotes from Scrivener.

So, what is being said here? Bluntly stated, there is a mountain of evidence that points to the fact that none of the various endings to Mark are authentic. Yet, there is one ending that seems to have been accepted and that one we should keep, simply because it has been included for so long. I vehemently disagree. No error should be propagated simply because we are accustomed to it.

Let us re-examine the truth at every turn, and conform to the truth instead of twisting the truth around our preconceived ideas. Adding error in scripture to errors in reason only brings us back to where we have been, and where many still are.

Joseph Lumpkin

BIBLIOGRAPHY

The Bible. King James Version, unless otherwise noted.

Burghardt, Walter J., S.J. The Image of God in Man according to Cyril of Alexandria. Washington: Catholic University of America Press, 1957.

Cyril of Alexandria. Commentary on the Gospel of St. Luke. Trans. Robert Payne Smith. United States: Studion Publishers, 1983.

Cyril of Alexandria. Cyril of Alexandria: Select Letters. Trans. Lionel R. Wickham. Oxford: Oxford University Press, 1983.

Cyril of Alexandria. On the Unity of Christ. Trans. John Anthony McGuckin. Crestwood, NY: St. Vladimir's Seminary Press, 1995.

The sayings of the Desert Fathers : the alphabetical collection. Trans. Benedicta Ward, SLG. Kalamazoo, Michigan: Cistercian Publications Inc., 1984, 1975.

Gregory of Nazianzus. Orations. Trans. under the editorial supervision of Philip Schaff and Henry Wace.

International Consultation on English Texts (ICET) and the English Language Liturgical Consultation (ELLC)

John Climacus. The Ladder of Divine Ascent. Trans. Colm Luibheid and Norman Russell. Mahwah, New Jersey: Paulist Press, 1982.

The Lenten Triodion, liturgical prayers recited by the Eastern Orthodox Church during the season of Lent. The nten Triodion. Trans. The Community of the Holy Myrrbearers. The Lenten Triodion. Trans. Mother Mary and Archimandrite Kallistos Ware. London: Faber and Faber, 1977.

St. Nikodimos of the Holy Mountain and St. Makarios of Corinth. The Philokalia, The Complete Text. Trans. G.E.H. Palmer; Philip Sherrard; and Kallistos Ware. London: Faber and Faber Limited, (Vol. 1) 1979, (Vol. 2) 1981

Symeon the New Theologian. Symeon the New Theologian: The Discourses. Trans. C.J. de Catanzaro. Ramsey, N.J.: Paulist Press, 1980. Symeon the New Theologian. On the Mystical Life: The Ethical Discourses. Trans. Alexander Golitzin. Crestwood, NY: St. Vladimir's Seminary Press, 1996.

Angela of Foligno. Angela of Foligno: Complete Works. Mahwah, New Jersey: Paulist Press, 1993.

Anonymous. The Cloud of Unknowing and Other Works. Trans. Clifton Wolters. New York: Penguin Books USA, Inc., 1961, 1978.

Catherine of Siena. Catherine of Siena: The Dialogue. Trans. Suzanne Noffke, O.P. Mahwah, New Jersey: Paulist Press, 1980.

St. John of the Cross, a Spanish Mystic, who lived from 1542 to 1591. John of the Cross. Ascent of Mount Carmel. Trans. E. Allison Peers.

Julian of Norwich, an English mystic who lived from 1342 to 1413. Julian of Norwich. Revelations of Divine Love. Ed. Grace Warrack

Brother Lawrence of the Resurrection. The Practice of the Presence of God. Mount Vernon, NY: Peter Pauper Press, Inc., 1963.

Bonaventure by Ewert Cousins Mahwah, New Jersey: Paulist Press, 1978

Thomas Merton. Thoughts in solitude. Boston: Shambhala Publications, Inc., 1956, 1958.

Nicholas of Cusa. Nicholas of Cusa: Selected Spiritual Writings. Trans. Hugh Lawrence Bond. Mahwah, New Jersey: Paulist Press, 1997.

Teresa of Avila. Interior Castle. Trans. E. Allison Peers. New York: Bantam Doubleday Dell Publishing Group, Inc., 1990.

Teachings of the Christian Mystics by Andrew Harvey; Shambala Boston and London

Thomas à Kempis. The Imitation of Christ. Trans. Richard Whitford, moderenized by Harold C. Gardiner. New York: Doubleday, 1955.

Jacob Boehme. The Supersensual Life. Trans. William Law.

A. W. Tozer. The Pursuit of God. Wheaton, Ill.: Tyndale House, 1982.

Meister Eckhart. Meister Eckhart: Selected Writings. Trans. Oliver Davies. New York: Penguin Books USA, Inc., 1994.

Jeanne-Marie Bouvier de la Motte-Guyon. Autobiography of Madame Guyon.

Marguerite Porete. Marguerite Porete: The Mirror of Simple Souls. Trans. Ellen L. Babinsky. Mahwah, New Jersey: Paulist Press, 1993.

Mysticism in World Religions   by Deb Platt

Wikipedia, the free encyclopedia.

W.R. Lumpkin A Southern Baptist pastor of more than 25 years.

The Gospel of Thomas, by Joseph Lumpkin, published by Fifth Estate

Joseph Lumpkin

Are you Really That Stupid, by Joshua Christian, published by Fifth Estate

Dark Night of the Soul, by Joseph Lumpkin, published by Fifth Estate

Mystical Christianity, by Joseph Lumpkin, published by Fifth Estate

Notes

Notes

Notes

Joseph Lumpkin

Notes

Notes